VARIORUM COLLECTED STUDIES SERIES

The Practice of Medieval Music

Thomas Forrest Kelly

Thomas Forrest Kelly

The Practice of Medieval Music

Studies in Chant and Performance

ASHGATE
VARIORUM

ML
3082
K29
2010

Published in the Variorum Collected Studies Series by

Ashgate Publishing Limited
Wey Court East
Union Road
Farnham, Surrey
GU9 7PT
England

Ashgate Publishing Company
Suite 420
101 Cherry Street
Burlington, VT 05401–4405
USA

Ashgate website: http://www.ashgate.com

ISBN 978–1–4094–0527–6

British Library Cataloguing in Publication Data

Kelly, Thomas Forrest.
   The practice of medieval music : studies in chant and performance.
   – (Variorum collected studies series ; CS954)
   1. Gregorian chants – History and criticism.
   2. Performance practice (Music) – History – To 1500.
   3. Music – 500–1400.
   I. Title II. Series
   782.3'222'00902–dc22

   ISBN 978–1–4094–0527–6

Library of Congress Control Number: 2010921445

VARIORUM COLLECTED STUDIES SERIES CS954

CONTENTS

CONTENTS

This volume contains xii + 358 pages

INTRODUCTION

The studies in this volume, published over a number of years in a variety of places, are assembled here in order to give the reader a view of some key areas of medieval music, and together to form a synoptic panorama of several interlocking areas of research.

The center of it all is the music expressed in the medieval liturgy. It is the body of music that is most ancient, most complete, and most widespread, of all the music that survives from the Western Middle Ages.

Two studies deal with the liturgy of the city of Rome and its environs, and with the connection of Rome with other liturgies and musics. The so-called "Old-Roman" chant, that musical dialect found only in a small number of Roman manuscripts from the 11th to the 13th century, is considered in relation to the Gregorian chant in Chapter I. I had the good fortune to discover the earliest surviving source of Old-Roman office music, and a study of the liturgy of that source and its music leads to interesting conclusions about the growth of the Roman liturgy, and about its relation to the standard Gregorian chant. Chapter II is another longitudinal study of the liturgy of the city of Rome considering only one small detail: the blessing of the paschal candle on the vigil of Easter. The sources of information are many, and allow us to trace the gradual adoption of this originally non-Roman practice, and its gradual acceptance, first in the suburbican churches, then the city itself, and finally the papal liturgy.

Six chapters are concerned with embellishments to the music of the liturgy. As the official liturgical chant becomes fixed and is considered immutable, the creative musical and poetic spirits of the later middle ages chose to embellish the chants with interpretive additions. Adding text and music to a chant, as an introduction or a series of interpolations in the course of the chant, produced a sort of musical and theological framework in which to understand the chant itself. (In some ways this is rather like the antiphons sung before and after psalms in the daily office.)

These musical and textual additions are called by a variety of names, but most often, in the middle ages and now, they are called *tropes*. There is a large repertory of these interpolative compositions, and they have been widely studied, and most of their texts (but not their music) published in the Stockholm series *Corpus Troporum*.

Chapter III is concerned with one kind of trope, a specific moment in the liturgy when the celebrant of the Mass approaches the altar to sing the opening words of the *Gloria in excelsis*. This moment engendered its own little ceremony, with a sung invitation to the celebrant, and sometimes a reference to the specific feast-day on which it was sung. A wide variety of these introductory tropes is found in medieval manuscripts, and this chapter seeks to understand their distribution and their meaning.

Five further chapters are concerned with the art of the prosula. This is a relatively little-studied phenomenon that allows us a view on medieval piety and poetry, and permits also a fuller understanding of the performance of medieval music, and of the meaning of the signs used in its writing. A prosula, defined simply, is a text added, one syllable per note, to a long series of notes originally intended for a single syllable in a liturgical chant. These long melodies, called *melismas*, can be found in a variety of liturgical genres, and the addition of prosulae to the melismas are sometimes done with amazing artistry; in the best cases, the prosula successfully integrates itself into the interrupted text; it forms its words according to the musical groupings of the melisma's neumes; it uses the assonance of the melisma's vowel; and it comments on the base liturgical text. Doing all this in the context of a pre-existent musical form is a virtuoso feat. Chapters IV–VIII deal with specific aspects of the prosula; their use in the music of the office; the nature of their performance; the prosulae of the famous *neuma triplex*; and a remarkable late-medieval survival related to the prosula.

A group of studies concerns itself with medieval scrolls. For certain purposes the rotulus continued to be employed as a format for writing for many centuries after the near-universal adoption of the codex. The reasons for the use of scrolls are several: indeterminate length (mortuary rolls, legal records); portability (actors' "roles," processional music); shape (genealogies, route maps); archaizing quality (diplomas, many liturgical rolls). My interest in rolls came about through my extensive study of the illustrated Exultet rolls of southern Italy (*The Exultet in Southern Italy*, Oxford 1996), and some interesting case studies are gathered here. In one case, Chapter IX, the various ways of writing – and altering – a repetitive melody on the Exultet rolls gives a view onto medieval ornamentation and improvisation. Two other studies (Chapters X and XI) consider the use of liturgical rolls at the Cathedral of Benevento and in the Ambrosian liturgy of Milan.

Two final chapters deal with aspects of later medieval music. Chapter XII explores the medieval concept of the composer by attempting a list of medieval composers of liturgical chant, and assembling the texts that ascribe music to composers; not surprisingly, most of those named are not what we would call composers, but authorities (St Gregory, St Ambrose), poets (Prudentius, Venantius Fortunatus), and only occasionally persons who are skilled in music (Hermannus Contractus). But the study tells us a great deal about how medieval thinkers and writers conceived of the creation of music.

Chapter XIII reports on an attempt at polyphonic composition in the margin of a manuscript of Montecassino. It hints at the largely unwritten practices of which we can have only the rarest of glimpses.

Taken together, these studies, I hope, can suggest to the reader the richness of the medieval musical landscape, the artistry of medieval musicians, and the challenges that lie ahead for scholarship intended to bring us closer to a medieval understanding of the place of music in the world.

THOMAS FORREST KELLY

Cambridge, Massachusetts
December 2009

PUBLISHER'S NOTE

The articles in this volume, as in all others in the Variorum Collected Studies Series, have not been given a new, continuous pagination. In order to avoid confusion, and to facilitate their use where these same studies have been referred to elsewhere, the original pagination has been maintained wherever possible.

Each article has been given a Roman number in order of appearance, as listed in the Contents. This number is repeated on each page and is quoted in the index entries.

ACKNOWLEDGEMENTS

Grateful acknowledgement is made to the following individuals, institutions and publishers for their kind permission to reproduce the articles included in this volume: Cambridge University Press (for Chapter I); Dom Daniel Saulnier, Abbaye Saint-Pierre de Solesmes (II); the American Musicological Society, Inc. (III, IV, V); Georg Olms Verlag AG, Hildesheim (VI, X); the International Musicological Society, Feldmeilen (VII); Harvard University Department of Music, Cambridge, Massachusetts (IX); Yale University Library, New Haven, Connecticut (XI); the Fondazione Levi, Venice (XII); and Constanza A. Olschki, Florence (XIII).

For permission to reproduce images included in the volume, I would like to thank l'Archivio Storico Notarile di Sutri (for figs 1 and 2 in Chapter I); the Bibliothèque nationale de France (plate 17.2 in Chapter VIII); the American Institute of Musicology (*Speculum Musicae*) (plate 17.3 in Chapter VIII); Archivio storico di Montecassino (plate 2 in Chapter IX and plates 1a and 1b in Chapter XIII); the Biblioteca Capitolare dell'arcidiocesi di Bari-Bitonto (plates 1, 4 and 5 in Chapter IX); Archivio del Museo del Duomo, Salerno (plate 6 in Chapter IX); the Biblioteca Diocesana di Troia (fig. 3 in Chapter IX); and the Biblioteca Capitolare, Benevento (figs 1–8 in Chapter X).

I

OLD-ROMAN CHANT AND THE RESPONSORIES OF NOAH: NEW EVIDENCE FROM SUTRI

Among the manuscript fragments in the Archivio comunale of Sutri (Province of Viterbo), Italy, are four consecutive folios of an Old-Roman antiphoner of the later eleventh century. The two bifolios are now identified as fragments 141 (Frammenti teologici 40) and 141bis (Frammenti teologici 41). These fragments, which preserve music for the feasts of Sexagesima, Quinquagesima and Ash Wednesday, are remnants of what appears to be the oldest witness of Old-Roman music for the office. When added to the two surviving antiphoners (London, British Library, Add. MS 29988, of the twelfth century, and Vatican City, Biblioteca Apostolica Vaticana, MS San Pietro B 79, of the end of the twelfth century)[1] and two recently discovered fragments (in Frosinone and Bologna),[2] the Sutri fragments bring to five the number of Old-Roman antiphoners of which at least some evidence survives. It begins to appear that manuscripts of this music were once not so rare. The Sutri fragments show some unusual liturgical characteristics that provide new information on the Roman liturgy; I will discuss these aspects shortly.

A collection of manuscript fragments detached from notarial protocols is kept at Sutri in a wooden box in the Archivio. The fragments were removed in the early years of the twentieth century after a visit to the archive in the summer of 1904 by Ernesto Monaci, who noticed many manuscript fragments used as bindings.

---

[1] Facsimile edition ed. B. G. Baroffio and S. J. Kim: *Biblioteca Apostolica Vaticana Archivio S. Pietro B 79*, 2 vols. (Rome, 1995).

[2] Frosinone, Archivio di Stato, Collezione delle pergamene 82 (99): see G. Baroffio, 'Un nuovo testimone della tradizione musicale romana', *Rivista Storica del Lazio*, 4 (1996), 23–8; Bologna, Museo Internazionale e Biblioteca della Musica Q. 3, frammento 19; see Baroffio, 'L'antifonario romano-antico: Una reliquia del IV testimone', *Rivista Internazionale di Musica Sacra*, 27 (2002), pp. 145–8.

I

Under the direction of the archivist, Francesco Cialli, 159 fragments were detached from their volumes and restored at the laboratory of the Biblioteca Vallicelliana in Rome. Each piece was assigned a number in a single series, and a second number referring to the volume of protocols from which it was detached. The fragments were divided into four categories: notarial, liturgical and patristic, juridical, and literary, and for each category a special binder was prepared, in which the fragments are now stored in their box.[3]

After their return to Sutri, the juridical and notarial fragments were described in the scholarly literature,[4] and a few facsimiles published in the *Archivio Paleografico Italiano*.[5] No report was made at the time on the liturgical fragments. More recently, a pamphlet published at the behest of the Comune di Sutri and the Province of Viterbo takes notice of these fragments.[6] Two colour photographs (very small and almost illegible) reproduce one side of each of the fragments reported here.[7]

In that booklet Paola Supino Martini, after discussing fragments of a homiliary, describes our fragments as follows: 'The other liturgical fragment (numbers 40, 41) – for which there really does not seem to be a notarial provenance[8] – is composed of two mutilated bifolios, belonging to a single elegant *Graduale* of the end of the eleventh century, of fine parchment, written in calligraphic romanesca minuscule, with typical initials decorated with interlaces, outlined in red and touched with green (tavole V–VI); a precious book, then, very similar to the *Graduale* of S. Cecilia in Trastevere of 1071 (Cologny-Genève, Bodmer 74), and to the more or less contemporaneous one, perhaps of Lateran origin, now Vat. lat.

---

[3]   Monaci's visit and the subsequent restoration are described in E. Monaci, 'Frammenti di antiche pergamene a Sutri', *Rendiconti dell Regia Accademia dei Lincei, Classe di Scienze Morali, Storiche e Filologiche*, ser. 5, vol. 16 (1907), pp. 403–4.

[4]   A. Finocchiaro-Sartorio, 'Frammenti giuridici di antiche pergamene rinvenute a Sutri', *ibid.*, pp. 405–55; V. Federici, 'I frammenti notarili dell'Archivio di Sutri', *Archivio della Società Romana di Storia Patria*, 30 (1907), pp. 463–71. Federici also published, from a fragment at Sutri, an account of a miracle of 1399 in 'Il miracolo del crocifisso della compagnia dei Bianchi a Sutri', in *Scritti di storia, di filologia e d'arte*, nozze Fedele–De Fabritiis (Naples, 1908), pp. 106–18.

[5]   Vol. 8 (Rome, n.d.), fasc. 28.

[6]   L. Miglio and P. Supino Martini, *Frammenti: Storie di codici e notai nell'Archivio comunale di Sutri* (Rome, [1997]).

[7]   Tavola V shows what we will call folios A^v and D^r, from fragment 141; Tavola VI shows folios C^v and B^r from fragment 141bis.

[8]   In fact there is a notarial provenance: see below.

Old-Roman Chant and the Responsories of Noah

5319.'⁹ (See Figures 1 and 2.) The Archivista of the Archivio Municipale, Dr Carlo Tedeschi of the University Ca' Foscari, Venice, has generously given his time and expertise, and I acknowledge his help with gratitude.

DESCRIPTION

The two bifolios have paper labels attached to each, numbered 40 and 41 (these are the last two numbers assigned to the liturgical and theological fragments); the stamped number 141 appears on each bifolio beside the paper label, and a pencilled 'bis' appears beside the stamped 141 on fragment 41. The numbers 141 and 141bis refer to a list in the hand of Francesco Cialli, kept inside the box in two copies (one of them signed and dated 2 October 1905), referring to the notarial protocols from which each fragment was detached. The fragments also bear blue pencil indications '141' and '1' on one, '141' and '2' on the other; fragment 141 also bears a pencil signature 'F. Cialli'. The fragments will be referred to here as 141 and 141bis.

The two bifolios were detached from a notarial protocol assembled by the notary Stefano Marcoli between 1389 and 1392, and served as its outer binding.¹⁰ Marcoli, 'notarius publicus et iudex ordinarius', was a native of Civita Castellana (as he indicates in most of his documents), and was active in Sutri from 1371 to 1410, to judge from the dates of his surviving notarial acts.

The bifolios were sewn together (corresponding holes in the two bifolios (folios C and D) show where they were overlapped) and

---

⁹ 'L'altro frammento liturgico (nrr. 40, 41) – per il quale non sembra in realtà evincersi una provenienza notarile – è costituito da due bifolii mutili, appartenuti ad uno stesso elegante *Graduale* della fine del secolo XI, di ottima pergamena, vergato in calligrafica minuscola romanesca, con tipiche iniziali decorate ad intrecci, delineate in rosso e toccate di verde (tavv. V–VI): un libro pregiato, dunque, molto vicino al *Graduale* di S. Cecilia in Trastevere, del 1071, (Cologny-Genève, Bodmer 74), e a quello più o meno coevo, forse di origine lateranense, oggi Vat. lat. 5319.' Miglio and Supino Martini, *Frammenti*, p. 8. Supino Martini also mentions the fragments, but more briefly, in her *Roma e l'area grafica romanesca (secoli X–XII)* (Alessandria, 1987), p. 233, n. 8 ('I nrr. 40 e 41, due bifoli variamente mutili, da un coevo [i.e., end of the eleventh century], elegante *Antifonario*, vergato in calligrafica romanesca, con tipiche iniziali ornate, delineate in rosse e toccate di verde.'

¹⁰ The volume from which they were removed has a binding, evidently applied during the restoration at the Biblioteca Vallicelliana, labelled 'Stefano Marcoli An. 1389–90'. The latter date has been altered in pencil to read '92'.

I

Figure 1   Sutri, Archivio comunale frammento 141bis (Frammenti teologici 40),
showing folios C^v and B^r

wrapped around Marcoli's volume late in the year 1392.[11] The
vertical dimensions of the notarial volume match exactly those of
the trimmed fragments; wear and water stains on the outer edges of
the fragments correspond with the state of Marcoli's volume.[12] At
some point between the detaching of the leaves from the original

[11] The volume is made of a series of fascicles, each of which begins with a new document.
Evidently the volume was assembled only after a suitable number of fascicles had accumulated.
(If the volume had been assembled first, the documents would surely continue from the end
of one fascicle to the beginning of the next.) The last document in the last fascicle is dated
7 September 1392.

[12] Many manuscript fragments at Sutri have been detached from Marcoli's volumes, and others
remain in place. There are, however, no further fragments in the Archivio at Sutri of the
manuscript discussed here.

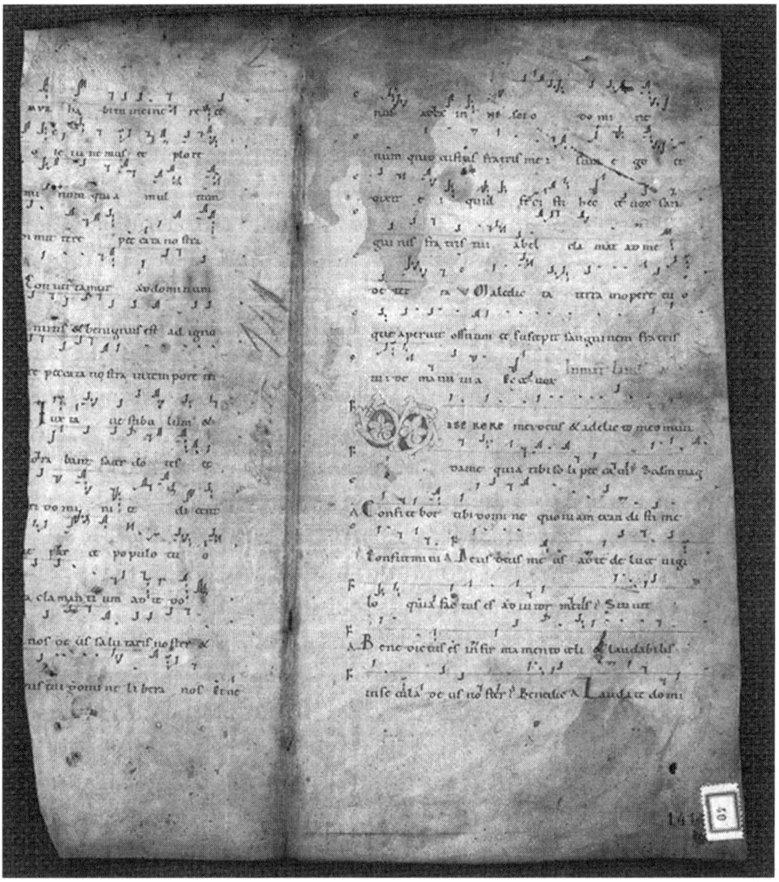

Old-Roman Chant and the Responsories of Noah

Figure 2   Sutri, Archivio comunale frammento 141 (Frammenti teologici 41), showing folios D^v and A^r

manuscript and their use as binding material, a fourteenth-century hand (not that of Marcoli) evidently read the pages and wrote some relevant text (some of it goes across an opening that would not have been available had the leaf still been bound in the original manuscript).[13]

---

[13] Across the flesh side of fragment 141bis, the following texts are written near the beginning of the responsory *Temptavit Deus Abraham*: 'Deus Abraham/Deus Jacob/Deus Ysaac'; 'Deus Abraham'; 'Ysaac autem genuit Iacob'; 'Domine Deus noster quam admirabile est nomen tuum in universa terra'.

These leaves are from a very handsome manuscript. The parchment, now yellowish and worn at the edges, is thin and of excellent quality. The writing area of a page is 13.2 × 22.5 cm (measured on fol. Aʸ); the full size of the manuscript can only be estimated from the present reduced margins, but if the outer margin was at least as wide as the upper margin, the manuscript had dimensions not smaller than 17.7 × 30.6 cm. Double bounding lines define inner and outer margins, and series of drypoint lines spaced 4 mm apart are used in groups of four (one for text, three for music) to provide for fourteen long lines of music and text per page.

The text, in a calligraphic romanesca minuscule, is written in a dark brown ink; slightly darker ink is used for the musical notation; an orange-red ink is used for rubrics, initial letters, and the F-line of the musical notation. The smallest initial letters, of antiphons and responsory verses, are black touched with orange or with orange and yellow. The smallest coloured initials, used for the opening letters of responsories and for rubrical letters (R., a., v., p.) are in orange ink, sometimes touched with green and yellow. Larger initials, which may occupy one, two, or three lines, are made of an interlace pattern with foliage decoration outlined in red ink, the spaces outside the letters being filled with green and yellow ink. Such letters are frequently to be found in central Italian manuscripts of this period, including the two suriviving Old-Roman graduals.[14] The musical notation, very carefully written, uses the three drypoint lines above the text to align the music. C- or F-clefs are found at the beginning of each line, and where appropriate a red line is drawn to show the pitch F. No yellow line is used.

The two bifolios are evidently the two innermost leaves of a quire. The hair side of fragment 141bis provides the two innermost pages, and the flesh side of fragment 141 wraps around the flesh side of 141bis to provide the next innermost bifolium. We shall refer to the contents of the leaves as folios A, B, C and D, where folios B and C are fragment 141bis, A and D are fragment 141.

How such fragments came into the hands of a notary of Sutri in the fourteenth century can only be a matter for speculation. All surviving books of Old-Roman chant, so far as we can tell, seem to

[14] See above, n. 9.

be for urban use, and it seems unlikely that these fragments represent the liturgy of Sutri. But there were occasions, when the manuscript was new, on which a pope found himself at Sutri and might well have required the presence of singers and manuscripts. A practice of papal visits resulted in two synods at Sutri in the eleventh century (in 1046 and 1059, too early for the passing on of this manuscript), during a time of considerable papal disarray; in 1120 the antipope Gregory VIII was besieged at Sutri by Calixtus II. Whether some papal occasion brought a book of Roman chant to Sutri cannot now be known; but there was such a book there in the fourteenth century, of which only these fragments seem to have survived.

CONTENTS

The contents of the Sutri fragments are particularly interesting in that they may preserve a state of the pre-Lenten season representing an earlier layer than that of the other Roman or Frankish musical witnesses to these feasts. The eight pages of the Sutri fragments provide liturgical material for the office from Sexagesima to Ash Wednesday. The contents are summarised in Table 1. The material in the Sutri fragment matches that of the Roman antiphoner San Pietro B 79 closely (the other Roman antiphoner, British Library Add. 29988, very unfortunately has a large lacuna covering all of this section of the year). The only variants, and they are few, are matters of very small detail. The Sutri fragments are closer in melodic tradition to B 79 than they are to the London antiphoner, to judge from the nature of the variants between B 79 and London in other portions of the year.

There is almost no music in the Sutri fragments not already known from B 79; there is an additional Gospel-antiphon, at no. 14, for weekdays of Sexagesima,[15] and an extra Gospel-antiphon (at no. 35) for Quinquagesima;[16] Sutri has an invitatory (at no. 19) for Quinquagesima which is found in B 79 for Sexagesima. There are also three *versus ad repetendum* (at nos. 13, 14 and 37) which give

---

[15] The antiphon in this form is not known in the Frankish, or so-called Gregorian, chant (hereafter GREG): it seems to be an adaptation of the antiphon at no. 13, abbreviating it and changing its mode – an interesting phenomenon in itself.

[16] A similar antiphon is in GREG: CAO 2716; full reference to CAO in App. 2.

Table 1   *Contents of the Sutri fragments compared with San Pietro B 79*
Italic indicates where the two sources diverge.

Sutri Fragments	BAV San Pietro 79
[Dominica in sexagesima]	**Dominica in septuagesima**
1 R. Ubi est abel	R. Ubi est abel
v. Maledicta terra	v. Maledicta terra . . .
	Dominica in sexagesima Stat ad scm Paulum
	. . .
2	R. Quadraginta dies
	v. Noe vero
3	R. Ponam arcum
	v. Cumque obduxero
4	R. Hedificavit Noe
	v. Ecce ego statuam
5	[+4 resp. from Sunday office, 1 of Peter]
In mat. laud. a.	**in laudibus a.**
6 a. Miserere mei deus et a delicto	a. Miserere mei deus et a delicto
ps. Secundum magnam	ps. Miserere mei deus
7 a. Confitebor tibi domine quoniam exaudisti	a. Confitebor tibi domine quoniam exaudisti
ps. Confitemini	ps. Confitemini
8 a. Deus deus meus ad te de luce	a. Deus deus meus ad te de luce
ps. Sitivit	ps. Deus deus meus
9 a. Benedictus es in firmamento	a. Benedictus es in firmamento
ps. Benedic<ite>	ps. Benedicite
10 a. Laudate dominum de celis	a. Laudate dominum de celis
ps. Laudate eum	ps. Laudate
in evangelio a.	**in evangelio a.**
11 a. Qui verbum dei retinet	a. Qui verbum dei retinet
v. Aliut centcsimum	ps. Benedictus
12	*a. Tu es pastor ovium*
	* v. Solve iubente R. Qui facis ut*
13 a. Semen cecidit . . . in patientia.	a. Semen cecidit . . . in patientia.
v. Aliut centtesimum	v. Aliut centtesimum
14 *a. Semen cecidit in terram . . . fructum.*	
v. Aliut centesi<mum>	
15 a. Hiesus hec dicens clamabat	a. Hiesus hec dicens clamabat
16 a. Si vere fratres divites esse	a. Si vere fratres divites esse
17 a. Si culmen veri honoris	a. Si culmen veri honoris
18 a. Vobis datum est nosse	a. Vobis datum est nosse
Dominica in quinquagesima	**Dominica in quinquagesima. Statio in basilica beati Petri principis apostolorum.**
19 inv. Regem magnum dominum	inv. Dominum qui fecit nos
20 R. Temptavit deus abraham	R. Locutus est dominus ad abraham
v. Immola deo sacrificium	v. Benedicens benedicam

Old-Roman Chant and the Responsories of Noah

Table 1   *Continued*

	Sutri Fragments	BAV San Pietro 79
21	R. Locutus est dominus ad abraham v. Benedicens benedicam	R. Temptavit deus abraham v. Immola deo sacrificium
22	R. Deus domini mei habraham dirige v. Deus qui perduxisti me	R. Deus domini mei habraham dirige v. Deus qui perduxisti me
23	R. Veni hodie ad fontem aque v. Igitur puella cui dixero	R. Veni hodie ad fontem aque v. Igitur puella cui dixero
24	R. *Tolle arma tua pharetra* *v. Cumque venatu*	R. Deus qui sedes*
25	R. *Ecce odor filii mei* *v. Qui maledixerit tibi*	R. Notas michi fecisti*
26	R. *Det tibi deus de rore* *v. Et incurventur ante te*	
27	R. Cecus sedebat secus v. Et qui preibant	R. Cecus sedebat secus v. Et qui preibant
28		R. *Petre [amas me]**
	In laudibus ant.	**In laudibus**
29	a. Secundum multitudinem miserationum ps. Miserere	a. Secundum multitudinem miserationum ps. Miserere
30	a. Deus meus es tu et confitebor tibi ps. Confitemini	a. Deus meus es tu et confitebor tibi ps. Confitemini
31	a. Ad te de luce vigilo	a. Ad te de luce vigilo ps. Deus deus meus
32	a. Ymnum dicite et superexaltate eum ps. Omnia opera	a. Ymnum dicite et superexaltate eum ps. Benedicite
33	a. Omnes angeli eius ps. Laudate.	a. Omnes angeli eius ps. Laudate evo dns reg.
	In evangelio	**In evangelio**
34	a. Transeunte domino clamabat. ps. Ben[?]	a. Transeunte domino clamabat. ps. Benedictus
35	a. *Et qui preibant increpabant*	
36	a. Cecus magis ac magis clamabat ps. Eu[ouae]	a. Cecus magis ac magis clamabat
37	a. Miserere mei fili david	a. Miserere mei fili david
38	v. Et confestim vidit *a. Cecus sedebat secus viam.*	
39	a. Omnis plebs ut uidit	a. Omnis plebs ut vidit ps. Magnificat
	Feria IIII caput ieiunii Statio [ad s. Savinam?]	**Feria IIII caput ieiunii. Collecta ad s. Anastasiam. Statio ad s. Savinam.**
40	R. Immutemur habitu in cinere v. Convertamur ad dominum	R. Immutemur habitu in cinere v. Convertamur ad dominum
41	R. Juxta vestibulum et altare v. Adiuva nos deus salutaris noster ///	R. Juxta vestibulum et altare v. Adiuva nos deus salutaris noster . . .

I

Table 1   *Continued*

Table 1   *Continued*

Sutri Fragments	BAV San Pietro 79
	Dominica prima in quadragesima.
	Statio ad s. Io. Lateran.
	. . .
42	R. Tolle arma tua
	v. Cumque venatu
43	R. Ecce odor Filii mei
	v. Qui maledixerit
44	R. Det tibi deus
	v. Et incurbentur
45	R. Ecce nunc tempus
	v. In omnibus
46	R. **E**mendemus
	v. Peccavimus
47	R. In ieiunio
	v. Inter vestibulum
48	R. Paradisi portas
	v. Ecce nunc
49	R. Petre amas*
50	R. Tribularer si nescirem
	v. Et Petrum
51	R. Abscondite elimosinam
	v. Honora dominum
52	R. In te domine sperent
	v. Invoca

*incipit only

valuable information on Roman psalmody, since they include the mediation of the psalm-tone. But essentially the music is already known from surviving manuscripts.[17]

Particularly interesting is what is not present in the Sutri fragments. What is missing is a series of responsories drawn from the story of Noah; such a series normally comes between the story of Adam (the last responsory of which is normally *Ubi est Abel*, here in position number 1) and the story of Abraham, which begins here at position 20.

---

[17] I do not see evidence of the division of antiphons into two halves by the use of a majuscule or oversized letter, as observed in B79 by Edward Nowacki; see his 'The Performance of Office Antiphons in Twelfth-Century Rome', *Cantus Planus: Papers Read at the Third Meeting, Tihany, Hungary, 19–24 September 1988* (Budapest, 1990), pp. 79–92; on the versus ad repetendum, see especially p. 86.

Old-Roman Chant and the Responsories of Noah

Series of responsories drawn from Genesis and Exodus are found in all surviving antiphoners during this season of the year. These series reflect the systematic reading of the first books of the Old Testament, beginning with Genesis. The responsories are arranged in 'Historiae'–the histories of Adam, Noah, Abraham, Jacob, Joseph and Moses. The fact is that there is no surviving antiphoner, to my knowledge, Roman or Frankish, that lacks responsories of Noah between those of Adam and those of Abraham. Now there is the Sutri fragment, in which there is no history of Noah. This might seem to be an error, but a close examination of the complex situation of pre-Lent shows that this is a key witness in the development of the liturgy, and may have some bearing on the relationship of Old-Roman and Gregorian chant.

Historiae and responsories

The extension of the preparation for Easter by the addition of Quinquagesima, Sexagesima, and finally Septuagesima, was a series of progressive additions to the Lenten Sundays in the sixth and seventh centuries. Resisted in Gaul,[18] the creation of pre-Lent is a Roman phenomenon. Quinquagesima is attested by the beginning of the sixth century.[19] The date of the introduction of Sexagesima is problematic;[20] Septuagesima may have existed at the time of

---

[18] G. Morin, 'Un lectionnaire mérovingien avec fragments du texte occidental des Actes', *Revue Bénédictine*, 25 (1908), pp. 162–6, at 162–3; J. Froger, 'Les anticipations du jeûne quadragési-mal', *Mélanges de Sciences Réligieuses*, 3 (1946), pp. 207–34, at 214–15; C. Callewaert, 'Notes sur le carême primitif gallican', *Ephemerides Liturgicae*, 41 (1927), pp. 58–67, 225–36, repr. in Callewaert, *Sacris erudiri: Fragmenta liturgica collecta a monachis Sancti Petri Aldenburge in Steenbrugge ne pereant* (The Hague, 1962), pp. 529–47, at 533; C. Vogel, *Medieval Liturgy: An Introduction to the Sources*, rev. and trans. W. G. Story and N. K. Rasmussen, with the assistance of J. K. Brooks-Leonard (Washington, DC, 1986), p. 310.

[19] Unknown to Leo the Great (440–61), it is mentioned in the notice of Pope Telesphorus in the *Liber pontificalis* and by Pope Vigilius: Froger, 'Les anticipations', pp. 215–16; A. Chavasse, 'Le carême romain et les scrutins prébaptismaux avant le IXe siècle', *Recherches de Science Réligieuse*, 35 (1948), pp. 325–81; id., 'Temps de préparation à la Pâque d'après quelques livres liturgiques romains', *Recherches de Science Réligieuse*, 37 (1950), pp. 125–45, at 130; Vogel, *Medieval Liturgy*, p. 310; P. Bernard, *Du chant romain au chant grégorien: (IVe–XIIIe siècle)* (Paris, 1996), pp. 194–6.

[20] Some have thought that it dates from Gregory the Great; at any rate it was not known to Pope Vigilius in 538 (Froger, 'Les anticipations', p. 233, n. 1; Chavasse, 'Temps de préparation', p. 130); it was condemned by the Council of Orléans in 541, but it is attested in the *Regula magistri* (c. 530–40): Vogel, *Medieval Liturgy*, pp. 310–11.

I

Gregory the Great,[21] but more likely came into existence around 650.[22]

The reading of the Bible, beginning with Genesis, in Lent is witnessed from the seventh century. Or rather, the Heptateuch (Genesis plus Joshua and Judges, perhaps also Ruth) is begun at some point in the spring, beginning at different times according to the sources:

• According to Andrieu's Ordo Romanus XIV (perhaps from St Peter's in the seventh century, but adapted for Frankish use), the reading of the Heptateuch begins in springtime ('tempore veris'), a week before Lent, and ends a week before Easter, thus for six weeks beginning at Quinquagesima.[23] This ordo begins the annual list with this series, suggesting that the beginning of the Frankish year, rather than the placement of Lent, is what triggers the cycle.

• A newly discovered Ordo, named 'Ordo Romanus XXX' by Peter Jeffery, and originating in England in the eighth century, in a cycle beginning with Easter, begins the readings of the Heptateuch at Sexagesima: 'In sexagissima enim usque in ebdomadam maiorem ante pascha legitur eptaticum.'[24]

• Ordo XIIIA, from the first half of the eighth century, moves the series earlier, describing the reading of the Heptateuch, and the

[21] It is mentioned in a homily, although Chavasse argued that the homily was not for Septuagesima but for the feast of St Lawrence (A. Chavasse, 'L'évangéliare romain de 645: Un receuil. Sa composition (façons et matériaux)', Revue Bénédictine, 92 (1982), pp. 33–75, at 48), but this has been refuted (L. J. Crampton, 'St. Gregory's Homily XIX and the Institution of Septuagesima', in Papers Presented to the Fifth International Conference on Patristic Studies, ed. F. L. Cross, 2 vols. (Studia Patristica, 10–11; Berlin, 1970–2), i, pp. 333–6; see also J. W. McKinnon, 'Antoine Chavasse and the Dating of Early Chant', Plainsong and Medieval Music, 1 (1992), pp. 123–47, at 127).

[22] Chavasse, 'Temps de préparation', pp. 144–5; id., 'Les plus anciens types du lectionnaire et de l'antiphonaire romains de la messe: Rapports et date', Revue Bénédictine, 62 (1952), pp. 3–94, at 48, n. 1; p. 55, n. 1; Bernard, Du chant romain, pp. 200–1; Vogel, Medieval Liturgy, pp. 310–11. See the very helpful tables in Vogel, pp. 404–5.

[23] M. Andrieu, Les Ordines Romani du haut moyen âge, 5 vols. (Spicilegium Sacrum Lovaniense. Études et documents, 11, 23, 24, 28, 29; Louvain 1931, 1948, 1951, 1956, 1961), iii, p. 39; the earliest source is from the tenth century, but the text may have originated at St Peter's in the second half of the seventh (Andrieu, iii, p. 35).

[24] The text, presented by Professor Jeffery at the annual meeting of the American Musicological Society in Houston on 15 November 2003, is found in Sankt Paul in Kärnten, MS 2/1, fol. 1ᵛ.

annual cycle, as beginning at Septuagesima, the Heptateuch concluding two weeks before Easter.[25]

What is probably originally a seasonal practice[26] becomes a Lenten one, and is moved progressively earlier as a result of the creation of the Sundays of pre-Lent.

Responsories of Noah

We can now observe this same shift in the Old-Roman manuscripts. In the Sutri fragment, to judge from the surviving responsory of Adam, *Ubi est Abel*, the biblical readings begin on Sexagesima (which is not unusual), and there is no historia of Noah, which is unique among surviving antiphoners. In the only other Roman antiphoner we can compare – that is, San Pietro B 79, written a century later – the readings begin a week earlier, at Septuagesima, creating a space that will need to be filled somehow. In B 79 the gap is at Sexagesima, and it is filled by adding three responsories of Noah (at numbers 2, 3 and 4 in Table 1), the remaining responsories for that Sunday being drawn from the regular Sunday office. There are actually three more responsories of Noah in a sort of appendix near the end of the manuscript (fol. 190ʳ⁻ᵛ). The presence of Noah in B 79 looks to be an incomplete attempt to fill a newly created void.

Septuagesima for a long time, and in many traditions, was the day after which the singing of the word *Alleluia* was suspended for the Lenten season, not to be heard again until the vigil of Easter. In many places *Alleluia* was sung as the text for all the antiphons and responsories at all the offices, and indeed there is a great deal of medieval poetry and ceremonial connected with the so-called 'farewell to the Alleluia'.[27] It seems safe to assume that an

[25] Andrieu, *Les Ordines*, ii, p. 481; on the date, ii, p. 478.

[26] These documents are descriptions of biblical readings throughout the year, beginning, as Ordo XIV, 'tempore veris', and perhaps corresponding with the beginning of the Frankish year on 1 March, independent of the shifting of Easter and the increasing length of the penitential season. Another example of the adjustment of a calendrical phenomenon to the moveable Easter cycle is the fixing of the March Ember Days in the first week of Lent regardless of the actual date. See G. Morin, 'L'origine des Quatre Temps', *Revue Bénédictine*, 14 (1897), pp. 337–46, at 342–3; L. Brou, 'Une ancienne station romaine à Saint-Pierre pour le dimanche précédant les Quatre-Temps', *Ephemerides Liturgicae*, 60 (1946), pp. 143–150, at 144, n. 3; A. Chavasse, 'Les messes quadragésimales du sacramentaire gélasien', *Ephemerides Liturgicae*, 63 (1949), pp. 257–5, at 260–6; Bernard, *Du chant romain*, pp. 190–1.

[27] See M. Robert, 'Les adieux à l'Alléluia', *Études Grégoriennes*, 7 (1967), pp. 41–51.

I

antiphoner that provides *Alleluia* at Septuagesima begins the reading of the Heptateuch on the following week, and contrariwise, it seems likely that the Sutri antiphoner, which begins with Adam at Sexagesima, provided *Alleluia* as the text for antiphons and responsories on Septuagesima.

We know that Septuagesima was celebrated with *Alleluia* at the time of Amalarius of Metz in the ninth century,[28] and the same is true in the Frankish tradition from the time of our earliest antiphoners later in the same century (these are summarised in Table 2, Group 2; for the sources, see App. 2). But these practices were abandoned or abolished in many places. We are told that Pope Alexander II, who died in 1073 – a date that may fall between the making of the Sutri manuscript and that of St Peter's – ordered the readings of Genesis to begin on Septuagesima, replacing the Alleluias on that day.[29] And Alexander's successor, the great Gregory VII, ordered that Sexagesima should have its own responsories, the history of Noah.[30] To judge only from surviving Roman sources, it would appear that the responsories of Noah, found only in B 79, were created in the twelfth century as a response to a new papal decree. But there is another Roman source, no longer available to us but of critical importance in this matter: namely the Roman antiphoners consulted by Amalarius of Metz and described in his *Liber de ordine antiphonarii*. Amalar consulted Roman antiphoners about 832 at Corbie,[31] and he says that they do have responsories of Noah, but that these are found joined to the old responsories of Quadragesima: 'Responsorios de Noe . . . inveni

---

[28] Amalarius, *Liber de ordine antiphonarii*, ch. 30, ed. J. M. Hanssens, in *Amalarii Episcopi Opera Liturgica Omnia*, ed. J. M. Hanssens, 3 vols. (Studi e testi, 138–40; Vatican City 1948–50), iii, pp. 65–7.

[29] Reported by Bernold of Constance in his *Micrologus de ecclesiasticis observationibus*: 'In Septuagesima Heptateuchum incipiunt. Unde et Alexander papa secundus constituit ut responsoria de eadem historia in eadem Dominica incipiantur, quae et in sequenti Dominica repetantur. *Alleluia* etiam in Sabbato ad vesperam jussit dimitti ante Septuagesimam'; J.-P. Migne, *Patrologiae cursus completus. Series latina*, 221 vols. (Paris, 1878–90), cli, col. 1012, cited from the Patrologia Latina database (Chadwick-Healey Inc., 1995).

[30] According to Radulph de Rivo, who read about it at the Lateran: 'Gregorius autem septimus, ut legi Romae apud Lateranum, instituit, ut dicta dominica Sexagesimae sua historia propria de Noe decoraretur, et dominica Quinquagesimae historiam de Abraham occuparet'; P. C. Mohlberg, *Radulph de Rivo: Der Letzte Vertreter der altrömischen Liturgie*, 2 vols. (Münster in Westf., 1915), ii, p. 101.

[31] In his *Prologus antiphonarii* Amalar describes his visit to Corbie and his examination of the Roman antiphoners, various aspects of which are reported elsewhere in his works, especially in the *Liber de ordine antiphonarii*. See Hanssens, *Amalarii episcopi*, i, pp. 361–3.

Old-Roman Chant and the Responsories of Noah

coniunctos in romanis antiphonariis cum antiquis responsoriis de quadragesima.' (Amalar's comments are excerpted in Appendix 1.)

Amalar proposed, for his new antiphoner, to move the responsories of Noah to their proper textual place, preceding the responsories of Abraham at Quinquagesima; and that is where they are found in all the early manuscripts of the Frankish tradition, beginning with the antiphoner of Compiègne written some fifty years later (see Table 2; Compiègne appears as the siglum C among the CAO secular manuscripts). In the earliest surviving sources – Group 2, from as early as the ninth century – the readings begin at Sexagesima, and the histories of Noah and Abraham are found together at Quinquagesima. In other sources – those in Group 3, none of them dating before the end of the tenth century – the readings are advanced to begin at Septuagesima,[32] and the history of Adam also moves to Septuagesima. In this latter case, however, the remaining histories are not spread out to fill the gap: there is either nothing at all provided for Sexagesima, or an indication that the responsories of Septuagesima are to be repeated. So the responsories of Noah were not created to fill a gap when the readings were advanced to Septuagesima: Noah was there before the gap was created, sharing a Sunday with Abraham, possibly as a result of Amalar's meddling with the Roman antiphoner.[33]

In Group 4 we see that Noah has Sexagesima to himself only from the twelfth century; the history of Noah – sometimes with an enriched series of responsories – is found alone at Sexagesima in this period only in some Italian manuscripts, perhaps under the influence of Gregory VII; later, the historia will be expanded in a variety of ways.[34]

The Sutri fragments confirm one of Amalar's statements: that responsories of Noah were not found at Quinquagesima in Roman antiphoners; what they do not tell us, because they are too fragmentary, is whether responsories of Noah are to be found at the

---

[32] The Mont-Renaud manuscript, dating from the tenth century, shows that at least one Frankish monastic environment began the readings on Septuagesima, as in Andrieu's Ordo XIIIA, well before the decree of Alexander II.

[33] A study of the historiae of pre-Lent, based on a larger number of manuscripts, and including references to responsories not mentioned in Table 3, was presented by László Dobszay at the Cantus Planus conference in Lillafüred, Hungary in August 2004; a printed study is forthcoming.

[34] See the forthcoming study by László Dobszay mentioned in the previous note.

I

Table 2   *Historiae of Pre-Lent in antiphoners of the office*

	Cursus, date Sec=Secular Mon=Monastic	Septuagesima	Sexagesima	Quinquagesima
GROUP 1: Historiae begin at Sexagesima, no Noah				
ROM				
Sutri	**Sec, s. xi**[ex]	**[Alleluia?]**	**Adam**	**Abraham, Jacob**
GREG				
(no witness)				
GROUP 2: Historiae begin at Sexagesima, Noah and Abraham share Quinquagesima				
ROM				
(no witness)				
GREG				
CAO secular				
CGBEMV	Sec, s. ix and later	Alleluia	Adam	Noah, Abraham
Albi 44	Sec, s. ix[4/4]	Alleluia	Adam	Noah, Abraham
Chiavenna	Sec, s. xi	Alleluia	Adam	Noah, Abraham
Utrecht 406	Sec, s. xii	Alleluia	Adam	Noah, Abraham**
Florence Arc.	Sec, s. xii	Alleluia	Adam	Noah, Abraham
Metz 461	Sec, s. xiii	Alleluia	Adam	Noah, Abraham
CAO monastic				
H	Mon, *c.* 1000	Si obl. *cum rel.*	Adam	Noah, Abraham
DFS	Mon, s. xii, s. xii, s. xi	Alleluia	Adam	Noah, Abraham
Paris lat. 1085	Mon, s. x[4/4]	Alleluia	Adam	Noah, Abraham
Toledo 44.1	Mon (?), s. xi[2/4]	Alleluia	Adam	Noah, Abraham
Metz 83	Mon, s. xiii	Alleluia	Adam	Noah, Abraham
GROUP 3: Historiae begin at Septuagesima, gap or repetition at Sexagesima				
ROM				
(no witness)				
GREG				
Mont-Renaud	Mon, s. x	Adam	none	Noah, Abraham
Rome, Vall. C 5	Mon, s. xii/xiii	Adam	Adam*	Noah, Abraham
Valen. 114	Mon, s. xii	Adam	Adam*	Noah, Abraham
CAO R	Mon, s. xiii	Adam	none	Noah, Abraham
Arras 465	Mon, s. xiv	Adam	none	Noah, Abraham
Paris 12044	Mon, s. xii	Adam	Adam*	Noah, Abraham
Tol 44.2	Sec, s. xi[ex]	Adam	Adam*	Noah, Abraham
Aachen G 20	Sec, s. xii?	Adam	none	Noah, Abraham
GROUP 4: Historiae begin at Septuagesima, Noah fills Sexagesima				
ROM				
B 79	**Sec, s. xii**	**Adam**	**Noah**[a]	**Abraham**
Liber politicus	**Sec, s. xii**	**Adam**	**Noah**	**Abraham**
Bernhard	**Sec, s. xii**	**Adam**	**Noah**	**Abraham**

106

Old-Roman Chant and the Responsories of Noah

Table 2 *Continued*

	Cursus, date Sec = Secular Mon = Monastic	Septuagesima	Sexagesima	Quinquagesima
GREG				
Piacenza 65	Sec, s. xii	Adam	Noah	Abraham
Lucca 602	Sec, s. xii/xiii	Adam	Noah	Abraham
CAO L (Ben 21)	Mon, s. xii/xiii	Adam	Noah	Abraham
Lucca 601	Mon, s. xii	Adam	Noah	Abraham
MC ordo	Mon, s. xii^{in}	Adam	Noah	Abraham
Lucca 603	Mon, s. xii	Adam	Noah	Abraham
Florence, C. s. 56	Mon, s. xii^{ex}	Adam	Noah***	Abraham***

[a]Note presence of three additional Noah responsories in appendix.
*Repetition of responsories of Septuagesima indicated by rubric.
**Mislabelled as Quadragesima.
***Six responsories of Noah, six from elsewhere; seven responsories of Abraham, five from elsewhere.

beginning of Lent as in the Roman antiphoners that Amalar saw. But the curious situation of B 79 suggests that Amalar should be believed in this also. The responsories provided in B 79 for the first Sunday of Lent are shown in Table 1, at positions 42 to 52. There are the first three responsories of Jacob, beginning *Tolle arma tua*, followed by a complete set of penitential responsories beginning with a very large initial letter. (There is also one responsory of St Peter, perfectly standard in this Vatican manuscript.)

Those curiously placed Jacob responsories have been brought here, I suggest, to replace three responsories of Noah which stood in this position in B 79's model, but which have been moved to an earlier place in this manuscript, to positions 2, 3 and 4, in response to Gregory VII's wishes. These three responsories beginning with *Tolle arma tua*, which normally begin the series of Jacob on the second Sunday of Lent, have been advanced in both these Roman manuscripts: in B 79, they move forward to the first Sunday of Lent, to fill the gap once occupied, according to Amalar, by Noah. In Sutri, the Noah responsories probably occupied the same place at the beginning of Lent as in the ninth-century books that Amalar saw; perhaps the pages that can confirm this will turn up one day. In the pages that survive at Sutri, the same *Tolle arma tua* series, in positions 24, 25 and 26, has been advanced to fill a space where there are no proper responsories; if I am right, they also come out of historical order, before the responsories of Noah, which cannot be moved from Quadragesima.

The Noah responsories are placed out of narrative order in the Roman antiphoners, as Amalar notes, because of the parallel between the forty days of Lent and the forty days of rain. The first of the Noah responsories as Amalar saw them, and the only one he names, begins with words which announce the forty days of Lent, and the forty days of rain: *Quadraginta dies et noctes.*

BORROWING ADDITIONAL RESPONSORIES

At Rome, it was not until the turn of the twelfth century that the Alleluias of Septuagesima were suppressed, that the responsories of Adam were moved forward to Septuagesima, and that the responsories of Noah were detached from Lent and moved to Sexagesima. It appears, then, that the three responsories of Noah, now in positions 2, 3 and 4 in B 79, are the Roman responsories which stood at the first Sunday of Lent when Amalar saw them in the ninth century.

Three seemed not very many, apparently, and by the time the end of B 79 was reached, 122 folios later, three more responsories of Noah were added to the book, written in a section of the manuscript that includes additional materials out of liturgical order. Where did those three additional responsories come from? Despite their Roman aspect, it seems clear that they were borrowed from the Franks.

Table 3 gives at the top a list of responsories of Noah in the Frankish tradition, with their incipits arranged in biblical order. Below this is a table where the presence and ordering of these responsories in various manuscripts is indicated horizontally by using the numbers and letters assigned to each incipit. Note group C, headed by the ninth-century antiphoner of Compiègne. All these manuscripts have the same six responsories of Noah, though not always in the same order (and Monza has one difference); these are the same six texts found in the antiphoner of St Peter's. Groups A and B have sets of four or five responsories, all of them subsets of the six texts in group C, and all including the three responsories (4, 10, 7), in bold numbers, that are the three responsories in the main body

Old-Roman Chant and the Responsories of Noah

Table 3   *Responsories of Noah in manuscripts of the Frankish tradition*

Responsoria de Noe (texts in biblical order)
1 Dixit Dominus ad Noe finis Genesis 6: 13
2 Noe vir iustus 7: 8
3 In articulo diei illius 7: 13
4 Quadraginta dies 7: 15
5 Recordatus Dominus Noe 8: 1
6 Locutus est Dominus ad Noe 8: 15
7 Aedificavit Noe 8: 20, 9: 7
8 Benedixit Deus Noe 9: 1
9 Ecce ego statuam 9: 9
10 Ponam arcum 9: 13
11 Per memetipsum 9: 15

Other responsory texts, not from Noah
A Deus qui sedes super
B Factus est sermo domini ad Abraham 15: 1
C Obsecro domine ne irasceris 18: 32
G (Responsory text from Gospel)

[San Pietro B 79]		4		10	7			1* 2* 11*
A. 4 responsories								
Hartker		4		10	11 7			
Silos		4		10	11 7			
Mont-Renaud		4 7		10	11			
Albi 44		4 7		10	11			
B. 5 responsories								
Toledo 44.2		4		10	11 7			2
Rome, Vall C 5	2 1	4 7		10				
C. 6 responsories								
Compiègne		4	1 2	10	11 7			
Paris 1085	1 2	4 7		10	11			
Florence, Arc.	1 2	4 7		10	11			
Florence C.s. 56		4	1	10 2	11 7			
Chiavenna		4	1 2	10	11 7			
Paris Lat. 12044		4	1	10	11 7			
Monza		4	1	10	11 7 6			
Toledo 44.1	2 1	4 7		10	11			
D. 6 responsories	1	4		B 10	11 7	C		2
with additions								
Verona								
Lucca 601	2 A 1	4 7		10	11			
Aachen	1 2	4		10	11 7	9		
E. Sexagesima filled in,								
in roughly biblical order								
L (Ben 21)	1 2	4	3 5 6			7 8 G 9	10 11	
MC ordo	1 2	4	3 5 6			7 8 9	10 11	G
Piacenza 65	1 2	4	3 6	10	11 7	9		5 8

*in appendix, fol. 190ʳ

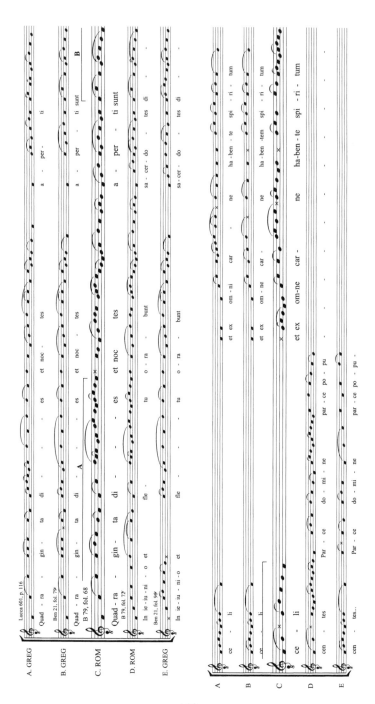

110

Old-Roman Chant and the Responsories of Noah

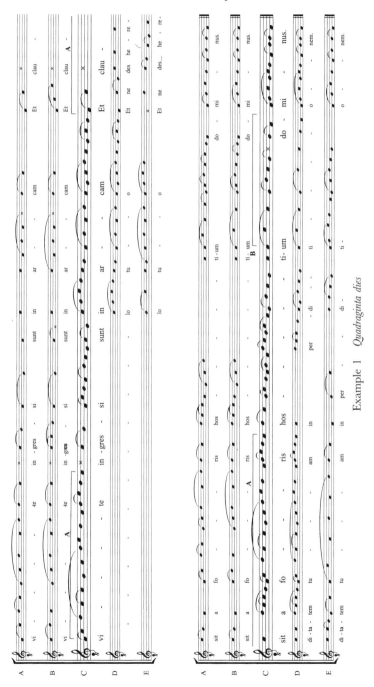

Example 1 *Quadraginta dies*

of B 79, and that I suggest are the Roman responsories seen by Amalar.

It seems an impossible coincidence that the six responsories of Noah in San Pietro B 79 should be those most widely known for more than two centuries in the Frankish tradition. A Frankish source like those in group C must have provided material for three more responsories of Noah (numbers 1, 2 and 11) in twelfth-century Rome, which are included in a later portion of San Pietro B 79.

What about their music? In broadest terms, two of the three responsories of Noah in the main part of the Roman manuscript are very much part of their repertory: they are filled with melodic turns of phrase that are typical of responsories in their mode, and they cannot be distinguished from other Roman responsories in their genre.[35] As to their relationship with the corresponding Frankish responsories, there is the sort of similarity that is often observed when the Roman and Frankish chants are compared: a general conformity of shape and structure between corresponding melodies, despite a very different melodic aspect in the two tradition. Example 1 shows *Quadraginta dies* in its relation to the Roman responsory with which it is most closely related, and to the corresponding Frankish responsories. The second responsory, *Ponam arcum*, is likewise an integral part of its repertory, more closely related, through shared music, to other Roman responsories than the corresponding Frankish responsory is integrated into its repertory. (The third responsory, *Edificavit Noe*, is unusual in both its Roman and Frankish forms, and deserves a separate study.)

The three responsories added at the end of San Pietro B 79 do not constitute a stylistically consistent group. *Noe vir iustus*, Example 2, is not made in the usual way by selecting from a fund of common musical material in order to reflect the shape of a particular text in a well-understood context. It has more the nature of a contrafact,

---

[35] There is no systematic study of the Old-Roman responsories; preliminary investigation suggests that they are similar in many ways to the musical structures found in Frankish chant: a series of eight formulaic verse-tones, one for each mode; a set of musical formulae drawn upon to make the responds; the presence, in each mode or maneria, of a substantial number of responds that do not draw upon the central fund of formulae. See L. Dobszay et al., 'G-mode Responsories in Old Roman Chant', *Cantus Planus: Papers Read at the 9th Meeting Esztergom and Visegrád, 1998* (Budapest, 2001), pp. 339–85; classic studies of responsories in Frankish chant are W. H. Frere's introduction to *Antiphonale Sarisburiense: A Reproduction in Facsimile from Early Manuscripts* (London, 1901–25, repr. Farnborough, Hants., 1966) and W. Apel, *Gregorian Chant* (Bloomington, Ind., 1958), pp. 330–4.

Old-Roman Chant and the Responsories of Noah

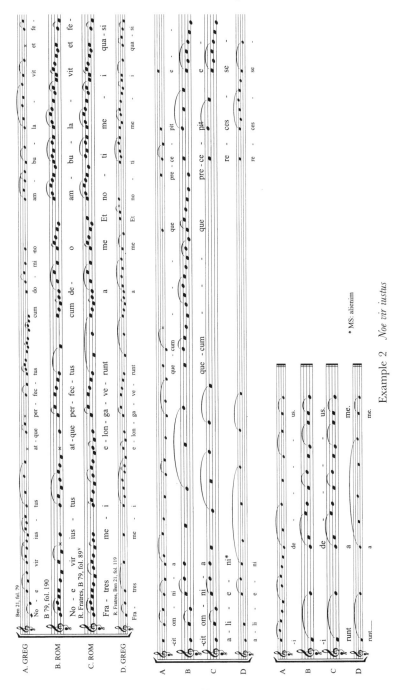

Example 2 *Noe vir iustus*

applying a chosen text to a melody originally designed for another text. The Roman melody, line B, is an adaptation of this text to the music of a single Roman responsory, *Fratres mei*, line C; the Frankish melody, line A, can be seen to be unrelated to the Roman, and unrelated also to the Frankish version of *Fratres mei*, line D. If the Roman responsory had borrowed the melody along with the text, it is difficult to see how the two Roman responsories here could be so closely related while their Frankish counterparts are so dissimilar.

The responsory *Dixit dominus ad Noe* is a similar adaptation of a Frankish text: it is a well-made adaptation of the text to musical phrases of G-mode responsories.[36] A Frankish melody, appearing sometimes in mode 6 and sometimes in mode 8,[37] is only vaguely related to the Roman melody; and the responsories *Hic est dies*, *Congregate*, *Centum quadraginta*, whose Roman melodies match many passages of *Dixit dominus ad Noe*, do not correspond in the same way in their Frankish versions.

The last of the six Roman responsories, *Per memetipsum iuravi*, Example 3, is an adaptation not only of a Frankish text but also of its melody. The Roman melody, even if it looks and feels Roman, has no real relationship to other melodies or turns of phrase in this mode: it is based on a Frankish melody, but without an awareness of that melody's relationship to its repertory, and with no regard to the received melody's internal structure. Note in Example 3 that the Frankish melody uses four times the same or similar cadence on C (marked with the letter A) while the Roman melody does not observe this pattern, either by using a recurring formula or by cadencing on the same note. This is perhaps a late and garbled adaptation; the very writing of the responsory in the manuscript suggests irregularity and hesitation. The scribe of B 79 is perhaps ashamed to be writing such a piece.

---

[36] I had at first thought that the Roman responsory was a contrafact, derived from two Roman responsories, the first half of *Hic est dies preclarus* (B 79, fol. 40) and the second part of *Congregate sunt* (fol. 162ʳ; *Centum quadraginta*, fol. 53ᵛ, also shares much of this second portion); while this remains a possibility, Ellen Exner of Harvard University has demonstrated that *Dixit dominus ad Noe* is a well-made G-mode responsory, in an unpublished seminar paper comparing many responsories and their formulae.

[37] Readily consultable versions from manuscripts reproduced in the *Paléographie musicale* are Benevento, Biblioteca capitolare 21, fol. 79 (mode 6), and Lucca, Biblioteca capitolare 601, p. 116 (mode 8).

Old-Roman Chant and the Responsories of Noah

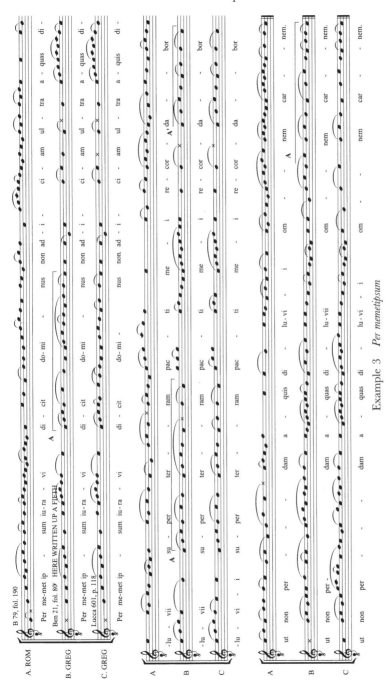

Example 3 *Per memetipsum*

I

The responsories of Noah at the end of B 79 are therefore probably adaptations from Frankish sources; if they were melodically identical with those in the Frankish manuscripts, the borrowing would be obvious. (Such direct borrowing does exist for the canticles of the Easter Vigil in the Roman manuscripts.) But this case is more complicated, and more interesting, because these additional Noah responsories look entirely Roman in Rome; we might not think to take a closer look if we did not have the Sutri fragment. But if we know that three of these responsories were borrowed, at a late date, from the Frankish tradition, we have a rare opportunity to be certain about the direction of transmission in cases where Roman and Frankish melodies are similar but far from identical.

There has been revived interest recently in the melody of Roman chant, for its own sake and for what it can tell us of the pre-history of the Roman and the Frankish dialects. Recent contributions by Kenneth Levy, John Boe, Alejandro Planchart, Andreas Pfisterer, Emma Hornby and others have sought to establish chronological relationships between like pieces in the two repertories.[38] This fragment from Sutri, small as it is, nevertheless has its own contribution to make to that continuing investigation.

APPENDIX 1

Excerpts from Amalarius, *Liber de ordine antiphonarii* on the placement of the responsories of Noah

[XXXIII. De quinquagesima] Responsorios de Noe, qui in isto ordine habent locum, inveni coniunctos in romanis antiphonariis cum antiquis responsoriis de quadragesima. De qua coniunctione non est mihi aliquid dicendum, praesertim cum in ipso sequar modernos in nostra ecclesia, qui

---

[38] K. Levy, 'A New Look at Old Roman Chant', *Early Music History*, 19 (2000), pp. 81–104; id., 'A New Look at Old Roman Chant II', *ibid.*, 20 (2001), pp. 173–197; id., 'Gregorian Chant and the Romans', *Journal of the American Musicological Society*, 56 (2003), pp. 5–41; J. Boe, 'The Roman *Missa sponsalicia*', *Plainsong and Medieval Music*, 11 (2002), pp. 127–66; id., '*Deus Israel* and Roman Introits', *ibid.*, 14 (2005), pp. 125–76; A. Pfisterer, *Cantilena Romana: Untersuchungen zur Überlieferung des gregorianischen Chorals* (Beiträge zur Geschichte der Kirchenmusik, 11; Paderborn, 2002); A. E. Planchart, 'The Opening Chant at Easter in the Latin West', in T. Gialdroni (ed.), '*Et facciam dolçi canti*: Studi in onore di Agostino Ziino in occasione del suo 65° compleanno* (Lucca, 2004), pp. 61–96; E. Hornby, 'The Transmission of Western Chant in the 8th and 9th Centuries: Evaluating Kenneth Levy's Reading of the Evidence', *Journal of Musicology*, 21 (2004), pp. 418–57.

I

Old-Roman Chant and the Responsories of Noah

cum responsoriis de quinquagesima ante Abraham posuerunt eos. Iuxta contextum scilicet historiae, ordo est ut inter responsorios de Adam et Abraham inserti sint de Noe.[39]

> The responsories of Noah, which have their place in this ordo, I found in the Roman antiphoners joined with the ancient responsories of Quadragesima. I have no comment on that situation, although in this ordo I follow the modern ones in our church, who placed them with the responsories of Quinquagesima before Abraham. That is to say, according to the context of the *historia*, the [proper] ordo should be that the responsories of Noah are inserted between those of Adam and Abraham.

Quomodo conveniens sit numeri sacramentum quadraginta dierum et noctium quibus caeli aperti sunt, cum ebdomada praesenti, occasionem intellegendi ponam ex dictis sancti Agustini . . . De quo mysterio ex dictis sancti Agustini habemus scriptum in Libello officiali . . .

> Let me take this occasion to understand how we are to understand the mystery of the number of forty days and nights during which the skies were opened matches with the present week from the sayings of Saint Augustine . . . of which . . . we wrote in the *Liber officialis*.

A praesenti feria quarta [he has just mentioned 'feria quarta quae vocatur caput ieiunii'] sunt quadraginta sex dies usque ad publicum baptismum. Quamvis ordo non teneat, ut in eadem feria quarta primo cantetur responsorius 'Quadraginta dies et noctes', tamen iuxta ordinem historiae primus cantatur in ea dominica nocte cui subditur in sua ebdomada feria quarta caput ieiunii.

> From this [Ash] Wednesday there are forty-six days until the public baptism. Although the ordo does not prescribe that the responsory *Quadraginta dies et noctes* should be sung first on that day, all the same according to the order of the *historia* it is sung first on that Sunday night whose week includes Ash Wednesday.

Et iuxta ordinem historiae et iuxta sacramentum quod cuditur de ratiocinatione quadragesimi numeri, congruum locum habent responsorii de Noe in quinquagesima ante Abraham. Responsorios de Abraham, ut priores, ordinavi iuxta ordinem historiae, et in novissimo posui duo de evangeliis quae in eadem ebdomada leguntur.

> And according to the order of the *historia*, and according to the mystery that has been forged from the reasoning of the number 40, the responsories of Noah have their proper place in Quinquagesima before Abraham. The responsories of Abraham, like the earlier ones, I have ordered according to the order of the *historia*, and at the end I have placed two [responsories] of the gospels which are read in that week.

[39] *Amalarii Episcopi Opera liturgica omnia*, ed. J. M. Hanssens, 3 vols. (Studi e testi, 138–40; Vatican City, 1948–50), iii, pp. 70–1. Translations are my own, with thanks to Jan Ziolkowski.

117

APPENDIX 2

Sources cited

Aachen	Aachen, Domarchiv, MS 20. Antiphoner, s. xiii, secular, Aachen, 'antiphonale Franconis'
Albi 44	Albi, Bibliothèque municipale, MS 44. Gradual/antiphoner, s. ix^{ex}, secular, Albi
Arras 465	Arras, Bibliothèque municipale, MS 465. Breviary, s. xiv, monastic, St-Vaast, Arras
B 79	Vatican City, Biblioteca Apostolica Vaticana, Archivio di San Pietro, MS B 79. Antiphoner, s. xii, secular, St Peter's, Rome. Facs. edn ed. B. G. Baroffio and S. J. Kim, *Biblioteca Apostolica Vaticana Archivio S. Pietro B 79*, 2 vols. (Rome, 1995)
Ben 21	Benevento, Biblioteca capitolare, MS 21. Antiphoner, monastic, s. xii, Benevento(?). Facs. edn, Paléographie musicale, 22 (Solesmes, 2001)
Bernhard	Cardinal Bernard, prior of the Lateran, 'ordo officiorum ecclesiae lateranensis', s. xii^{ex}, ed. Ludwig Fischer, *Bernhardi cardinalis et lateranensis ecclesiae prioris Ordo officiorum* (Historische Forschungen und Quellen, 2–3; Munich and Freising, 1916)
CAO	*Corpus antiphonalium officii*, ed. R.-J. Hesbert, 6 vols. (Rome, 1963–79). Indexes and textual editions of 12 manuscripts
CAO secular:	C: Paris, Bibliothèque nationale de France, MS lat. 17436. Gradual-antiphoner (secular), 868–80, Compiègne
	G: Durham, Cathedral Chapter Library, MS B. iii. 11. Antiphoner, s. xi, secular, northern France (incomplete). Facs. edn, *Pars antiphonarii: A Reproduction in Facsimile of a Manuscript of the Eleventh Century in the Chapter Library at Durham (Ms. B.iii. II)* (London, 1923)
	B: Bamberg, Staatsbibliothek, MS Lit. 23. Antiphoner, s. xii^{ex}
	E: Ivrea, Biblioteca capitolare, MS 106. Antiphoner, s. xi, secular, Ivrea
	M: Monza, Biblioteca capitolare, MS 12/75. Gradual/antiphoner, s. xi^{in}, secular
	V: Verona, Biblioteca capitolare, MS XCVIII. Antiphoner, s. xi, Verona
CAO monastic:	H: St. Gallen, Stiftsbibliothek, MS 390–91. Antiphoner ('Hartker'), c. 1000, monastic, St. Gallen. Facs. edn, Paléographie musicale, ser. 2, vol. 1 (rev. edn., Solesmes, 1992)
	D: Paris, Bibliothèque nationale de France, MS lat. 17296. Antiphoner, s. xii, monastic, St-Denis
	F: Paris, Bibliothèque nationale de France, MS lat. 12584. Antiphoner (in a composite volume), s. xii, monastic, St-Maur de Glanfeuil, later at St-Maur-des-Fossés
	S: London, British Library, Add. MS 30850. Antiphoner, s. xi, monastic, Silos
CAO L	=Ben 21

Old-Roman Chant and the Responsories of Noah

CAO R	Zürich, Zentralbibliothek, MS Rh. 28. Antiphoner (in a composite volume), s. xiii, monastic, Rheinau
Chiavenna	Chiavenna, Biblioteca capitolare S. Lorenzo, MS s.n. Antiphoner, s. xi, secular, Chiavenna
Compiègne	= *CAO* secular C
Florence Arc.	Florence, Arcivescovado, Biblioteca, MS s.n. Antiphoner, s. xii, secular, Florence
Florence, C. s. 560	Florence, Biblioteca Medicea Laurenziana, Conv. Sopp. 560. Antiphoner, s. xii^{ex}, monastic, Vallombrosa
Hartker	= *CAO* monastic H
Liber pol.	Benedict, canon of St Peter's, 'Liber politicus', *c.* 1140–3, ed. in vol. 2 of Paul Fabre and Louis Marie Olivier Duchesne, *Le Liber Censuum de l'église romaine*, 3 vols (the third, of indexes, by Duchesne with Pierre Fabre and G. Mollat) (Bibliothèque des écoles françaises d'Athènes et de Rome, 2nd ser., vol. 6; Paris, 1905 (vols. 1–2), 1952 (vol. 3))
Lucca 601	Lucca, Biblioteca capitolare, MS 601. Antiphoner, s. xii, secular (Camaldolese), St Peter's, Pozzeveri. Facs. edn, Paléographie musicale, 9 (Solesmes, 1906, repr. Berne, 1974)
Lucca 602	Lucca, Biblioteca capitolare, MS 602. Antiphoner, s. xii/xiii, Lucca
Lucca 603	Lucca, Biblioteca capitolare, MS 603. Antiphoner, s. xii, S. Maria Pontetetto
MC ordo	The ordinal of Montecassino, s. xi^{ex}, surviving in various versions in 8 MSS dating from the late 11th to the 13th century; five are from the orbit of Montecassino (Montecassino, Archivio della Badia, MSS 198 and 562; Paris, Bibliothèque Mazarine, MS 364; Vatican City, Biblioteca Apostolica Vaticana, MS Urb. lat. 585; Los Angeles, J. Paul Getty Museum, MS 83.ML.97 (Ludwig IX.1, *olim* Montecassino 199), three adapted for use at Benevento (Naples, Biblioteca nazionale, MS VI E 43; Vatican, MS Vat. Lat. 4928; Benevento, Biblioteca capitolare, MS 66). Edition forthcoming in *Spicilegium friburgense*
Metz 83	Metz, Bibliothèque municipale, MS 83 (destroyed). Antiphoner, s. xiii^{in}, monastic, St-Arnould, Metz
Metz 461	Metz, Bibliothèque municipale, MS 461 (destroyed). Breviary, s. xiii^{ex}, Metz cathedral
Mont-Renaud	Private collection, 'MS du Mont-Renaud', gradual/antiphoner, s. x, monastic, northern France, prob. written at Corbie, used at St-Eloy, Noyon. Facs. edn, Paléographie musicale, 16 (Solesmes, 1989)
Monza	Monza, Biblioteca capitolare, MS 15/79. Antiphoner, s. xii, secular, S. Mayeul, Pavia
Paris 1085	Paris, Bibliothèque nationale de France, MS lat. 1085. Antiphoner (abbreviated), s. x$^{3/4}$, monastic, St-Martial, Limoges
Paris 12044	Paris, Bibliothèque nationale de France, MS lat. 12044. Antiphoner, s. xii^{in}, monastic, St-Maur-des-Fossés

I

Piacenza 65	Piacenza, Basilica di S. Antonino, Biblioteca e Archivio Capitolari, MS 65. Antiphoner (in a composite volume), s. xii, secular, Piacenza Cathedral. Facs. edn, *Liber magistri: Piacenza Biblioteca capitolare C. 65* (Piacenza, 1997)
Rome, Vall. C 5	Rome, Biblioteca Vallicelliana, MS C 5. Antiphoner, s. xi/xii, monastic, San Sisto vecchio, Rome
Silos	= *CAO* monastic S
Toledo 44.1	Toledo, Biblioteca capitular, MS 44.1. Antiphoner, s. xi/xii, elements of secular and monastic cursus; from Auch?
Toledo 44.2	Toledo, Biblioteca capitular, MS 44.2. Antiphoner, s. xi^{ex}, secular, made for Toledo Cathedral (at Moissac?)
Utrecht 406	Utrecht, Bibliotheek der Rijksuniversiteit, MS 406 (3.J.7). Antiphoner, s. xii, secular, St Mary's Church, Utrecht. Facs. edn, *Utrecht, Bibliotheek der Rijksuniversiteit, MS 406 (3.J.7)* (Ottawa, 1997)
Valen. 114	Valenciennes, Bibliothèque municipale, MS 114. Antiphoner, s. xii, monastic, St-Amand
Verona	= *CAO* secular V

II

CANDLE, TEXT, CEREMONY: THE EXULTET AT ROME

In the late thirteenth century Cardinal Stefaneschi's handsomely illustrated Exultet of St. Peter's, now Vatican Library, San Pietro B 78[1], gives us a clear view of what has become a highly dramatic moment in the liturgy of the Easter vigil: the blessing of the paschal candle. The deacon is assisted in the ambo by the subdeacon and two acolytes. A triple candlestick, resembling a pitchfork, brings the new fire to the ambo; the paschal candle is lit from it during the singing, and later still an assistant below lights lamps. We are given what appears to be a view of the pulpit and paschal candle of St. Peter's. This ritual, which accompanied the singing of *Exultet iam angelica turba celorum* to a beautiful melody, is the same practice as that which entered the Missal of Pius V, and for centuries remained the standard ceremonial of the Roman Catholic Church.

But there was a time when the Roman church did not use the Exultet; when the pope used no paschal candle. How did it happen that a practice foreign to papal ceremony came to be represented as the practice of the Roman church and as a model to be adopted universally?

The history is a complicated one, because the various elements of this ceremony did not arrive all at once, nor were they adopted at Rome in the same way in every church of the city. The church at Rome itself evidently had no ceremony whatever using a paschal candle until after the practice was well established practically everywhere else.

The story has several parts: first, the increasing use of a paschal candle in the city, even though it was for a long time not used in papal rites; second, the gradual adoption of a foreign text, the Exultet, in favor of the local text for blessing the candle; and third, the addition of further elements to the ceremonial, such as the procession with a triple *Lumen Christi* and the singing of the Exultet from an ambo next to a very large candlestick; all these only gradually came together to create the impressive ceremonial in Cardinal Stefaneschi's volume.

---

1. On the manuscript see Marc DYKMANS, *Le cérémonial papal de la fin du moyen âge à la renaissance*, 4 vols., Bibliothèque de l'Institut historique belge de Rome, 24-27 (Brussels, Rome: Institut historique belge de Rome), 2: 93-94.

It is always problematical to discover information about the liturgical practices of the city of Rome itself, for although almost all books of the "Roman" liturgy intend in some sense to represent a universal practice, more often than not they represent some aspects of the Roman liturgy as their scribes perceive it, but also a good measure of their local practice; this is what makes the study of manuscripts and of liturgy interesting, of course, but it makes for special problems with regard to the city of Rome. Here we will try to gather the evidence that survives from Roman books themselves—books made for and used in the city of Rome—along with other material that has some bearing on the problem in an attempt to sketch the history of a single but important moment in the liturgical year of the Roman church. Such a study may contribute something to an understanding of the problems involved in research on Rome, and to a larger picture of the liturgical and ceremonial life of the city itself, as distinct from the Roman liturgy in the larger sense.

THE CANDLE

The papal liturgy of Rome, as seen in documents reflecting the rites of the pope's own cathedral chuch, the Lateran basilica, includes no candle and no blessing. The early sacramentaries representing Roman papal use make no mention of the candle: these include the Verona collection of masses, also known as the "Leonine" sacramentary of the early seventh century, a copy of Roman presbyteral masses adapted for papal use[2]; the seventh-century papal book adapted for use by priests at St. Peter's, and copied in the mid-ninth century, now Padua D 47[3]; the late seventh-century Trent sacramentary, a

---

2. Verona, Bibl. capitolare MS 85; ed. Leo Cunibert MOHLBERG, Leo EIZENHÖFER, and Petrus SIFFRIN *Sacramentarium Veronense*. Rerum ecclesiarum documenta, Series maior, Fontes 1 (Rome: Herder, 1956).

3. Ed. Cunibert MOHLBERG, *Die älteste erreichbare Gestalt des Liber sacramentorum anni circuli der römischen Kirche (Cod. Pad. D 47, fol. 11r-100r)*, Liturgiewissenchaftliche Quellen und Forschungen, 11-12 (Münster in Westfalen: Aschendorff, 1927); the manuscript is included as a witness in Jean DESHUSSES, *Le sacramentaire grégorien: Ses principales formes d'après les plus anciens manuscrits*, 3 vols, Spicilegium friburgense, 16, 24, 28 (Fribourg/S.: Presses Universitaires, 1971 (2d ed. 1979), 1979, 1982).

papal sacramentary modified for the use of Salzburg[4]; and the early ninth-century sacramentary of Hadrian (of which a copy survives as Cambrai 164)[5].

In addition to the negative testimony of the sacramentaries themselves, further information from *ordines romani* and other ceremonial books provide details of the papal liturgy of Holy Saturday at the Lateran basilica. It seems clear that a special candle-blessing played no part in the ceremonies witnessed by Charlemagne when he attended the Easter vigil at the Lateran in 774, since the eighth-century *ordines romani* describing papal rites continue to include no mention of the Exultet or of a candle.

A Frankish observer at the Lateran in the first half of the eighth century recorded the fact that there is no paschal candle there. His description, brief as it is, is the first in a series of *ordines romani* which describe the rites of Rome (the *ordines romani* are numbered here following the edition of Michel Andrieu; this is ordo 23)[6].

> On Holy Saturday, about the seventh hour, the clergy enter the church, but not the holy father. And the deacons together with the subdeacons in chasubles go into the sacristy, and two regional [notaries] each light *faculas* from that light which had been reserved since Good Friday, and they come to the altar. The deacons stand at the throne and the bishops sit in the choir. And the lector goes up into the ambo, and reads the Greek lesson... (See Appendix, Text A)

This description of the Lateran ceremony does mention light, and new fire: two regional notaries each light small torches (*faculas*) from the new fire which had been lit on Good Friday, and they come and stand at the altar; cardinal deacons stand around the papal seat; cardinal bishops sit in the choir; the pope has not yet appeared; and the lessons begin, using both Greek and Latin, along with prayers and tracts. After the lessons, litanies conduct the procession to the baptistry, where the pope blesses the water, using the same torches that the *regionarii* have brought with them. Nowhere

---

4. Ed. Ferdinando DELL'ORO et al., eds, *Fontes liturgici: Libri sacramentorum*. Monumenta liturgica ecclesiae Tridentinae saeculo XIII antiquiora, 2/a (Trento: Società Studi Trentini di Scienze Storiche, 1985), 1-416.

5. Ed. DESHUSSES, *Le sacramentaire grégorien*.

6. Michel ANDRIEU, *Les Ordines Romani du haut moyen âge*, 5 vols, Spicilegium Sacrum Lovaniense. Études et documents, 11, 23, 24, 28, 29 (Louvain: Spicilegium Sacrum Lovaniense, 1931, 1948, 1951, 1956, 1961).

is there mention of a paschal candle, or of its blessing with any text whatever.

Ordo 24, of the second half of the century, reflects the use of the Lateran, but adapts the papal liturgy where necessary for the use of a bishop in his cathedral. The reader is cautioned that there is no prayer before the first lesson: the use of such a prayer is the practice of the titular churches as reflected in the Gelasian sacramentary, which the compiler evidently knows, but it is not used at the Lateran. There is no mention of a paschal candle.

> On Holy Saturday, all come into the church, and then there are lit two candles, which are held by two notaries, one at the right corner of the altar and the other at the left. And the lector goes up into the ambo. He does not say *Lectio libri Genesis*, but begins *In principio*, plainly; and likewise for all the lessons. And before *In principio* no collect is said. (Text B)

Ordo romanus 30B, of the late eighth century, derives from a Roman source; this is evident from the mention of the Constantinian basilica, and from the absence of priests; there is, however, a priest who says the collects: this is an adaptation, but one which keeps very close to the Roman model. The compiler had ordo 30A at hand (see Text F), but he deliberately omitted the blessing of the candle, based on his knowledge of Rome or of Roman documents.

> The order in which Holy Saturday is to be celebrated. In the middle of the night one must get up and, as we have said, extinguish the lamps, except that one lamp is lit in order to read.
>
> Afterwards, in the day, at the eighth hour, all the clergy and people proceed to the church, and the archdeacon goes into the sacristy with the other deacons and changes his clothes for those of the holy day. And they proceed from the sacristy, and two lit torches (*faculae*) are carried before them by subdeacons, and the deacons come before the altar, and kiss it, and go to the pontiff's throne, and the deacons stand behind the altar, holding the torches until the lessons have been completed... (Text C).

But the papal rite is not the only liturgy of Holy Saturday; there is a double celebration of the paschal vigil in Rome in the seventh and eighth centuries, the pope celebrating at the Lateran, and all the cardinal priests celebrating in their respective titular churches. Reports of Roman ceremonies, therefore, must be examined to see whether they report the papal or the stational liturgy (or indeed the liturgy of the city at all), for even though the pope's liturgy makes no use of the paschal candle until the tenth century or later, the practice was adopted from the outside towards the center: that is, it was first used in outlying churches of the *parrochia* in the sixth century, adopted later in the titular churches during the seventh, and only much later accepted at the Lateran. To see this clearly, though, we must proceed in re-verse order, looking first at the titular churches.

On Holy Saturday, each cardinal priest celebrates in his own church, his *titulus*, which explains the absence of the cardinal priests among the cardi-nal deacons and bishops at the Lateran. Ordo 30B, of the late eighth century, makes this clear:

> On that night, all the cardinal priests do not stand there [at the Lateran
> with the pope], but each says mass at his own titulus, and he has permission
> to sit in the seat and to say the *Gloria in excelsis deo*.[7]

The Gelasian sacramentary represents this titular liturgy, and gives us a view of the practice of the titular churches of early seventh-century Rome; and it is here that we have our oldest evidence of the paschal candle.[8] The service in the titular churches begins at the eighth hour, thus in midafter-noon, later than the papal service at the Lateran, doubtless to accomodate the bringing of the *Sancta* or *fermentum*—consecrated bread from the pope's mass—to each of the titular churches; only after the arrival of the fermen-tum, and its placement in the chalice, can the priest continue with the con-secration.

The service in the titular churches begins with a litany in procession, and proceeds with the blessing of the paschal candle. The archdeacon blesses the candle, apparently in front of the altar, with the prayer *Deus mundi condi-tor*. This prayer, taken up in some later sacramentaries, may have originated at Rome.[9] There is no evidence of any particular musical intonation.

7. "Ipsa nocte, omnes presbiteri cardinales non ibi stant sed unusquisque per tit-ulum suum facit missa et habet licentiam sedere in sede et dicere Gloria in excelsis Deo." M. ANDRIEU, *Les Ordines*, 3: 474.

8. A discussion of the ceremonies described in the Gelasian ordo, along with a demonstration of its intention for titular churches, is in Antoine CHAVASSE, *Le sacra-mentaire gélasien (Vaticanus Reginensis 316). Sacramentaire presbytéral en usage dans les titres romains au VIIe siècle*, Bibliothèque de théologie, série 4, Histoire de la théologie,1 (Tournai: Desclée, 1958); a discussion of the opening of the vigil includ-ing the blessing of the candle is on pp. 101-107.

9. On the Roman origin of *Deus mundi conditor*, see A. CHAVASSE, *Le sacramentaire gélasien*, 102-06; Jordi PINELL, "La benedicció del ciri pasqual i els seus textos", in *Liturgica 2. Cardinali I. A. Schuster in memoriam*. Scripta et documenta, 10 (Montser-rat: Abbatia Montserrat, 1958), 1-119 at 9-10, 51-2, 67-9, 80-1. An interesting visual argument for the Italian origin of the prayer is made in Theodor KLAUSER, "Eine rät-selhafte Exultetillustration aus Gaeta", *Corolla Ludwig Curtius* (Stuttgart, 1937), 168-76, repr. in Theodor KLAUSER: *Gesammelte Arbeiten zur liturgiegeschichtlichen*

First then, about the eighth hour, they proceed to the church and enter the sacristy and vest themselves as is customary. And the clergy begin the litany, and the priest proceeds from the sacristy with the sacred ministers. They come before the altar and and stand with head bowed until they say *Agnus Dei* [i.e., the end of the litany].... Then the priest, arising from prayer, goes behind the altar and sits in his seat. Then the archdeacon comes before the altar, taking fire from that reserved on Good Friday, makes a cross on the candle and lights it, and he performs the blessing of the candle, *Deus mundi conditor*.... After this the priest rising from his seat says the prayers of the Paschal vigil, as they are found in the sacramentary. (Text E)

The chief features to note here, distinct from the rite at the Lateran, are (1) beginning with a litany; (2) blessing the candle (with *Deus mundi conditor*, not *Exultet*); and (3) the presence of a collect before the first lesson (evident in the sacramentary from the arrangement that follows. See also below). The eighth-century ordo romanus 30A (Text F) repeats this form almost exactly.

But things were not always so in these churches. The description of Holy Saturday in the Gelasian sacramentary is made of an older and a newer layer, as Antoine Chavasse has demonstrated: these have been cobbled together leaving the joints exposed, and allowing us to see that the paschal candle is part of the recent layer: the texts from the older layer make no mention of the candle;[10] it may be that an older practice using a candle is superseded: but more likely, I think, is that the use of a paschal candle was a relatively recent phenomenon at the time the sacramentary was assembled: probably at the beginning of the seventh century there was no paschal candle in the titular churches.

Indirect evidence from ordo romanus 24 (Text B), compiled in the second half of the eighth century, but evidently representing an earlier state of the Roman liturgy, supports this hypothesis; its information suggests that the sources consulted in making the ordo did not prescribe the paschal candle in the titular churches. Ordo 24 (Text B) is not directly concerned with the titular churches: it adapts the papal liturgy for the use of a bishop in his

---

Kirchengeschichte und christlichen Archäologie, ed. Ernst Dassmann, Jahrbuch für Antike und Christentum, Ergänzungsband 3, 1974 (Münster in Wesfalen: Aschendorff, 1974), 255-63 and Tafel 1a. Hermanus A. P. Schmidt, however (*Hebdomada sancta* 2 vols. [Rome: Herder, 1956, 1957], 2: 638), sees the matter differently: *Deus mundi* comes from northern Italy or southern Gaul, whence it was added at a later stage to the Gelasian sacramentaries. For the text, see note 25 below.

10. A. Chavasse, *Le sacramentaire gélasien*, 96-97.

cathedral, and thus it reflects the use of the Lateran, making adaptations where necessary. The user is cautioned, however, that there is no prayer before the first lesson: this is the practice of the titular churces, which the compiler evidently knows, but it is not used at the Lateran. The blessing of a candle is omitted here: it was not practiced at the Lateran. But if candles were regularly blessed at the titular churches, would not the compiler have given the same sort of warning that he does for the prayer before the first lesson? He is not concerned to warn the user, no doubt because in his sources the candle was not blessed in the titular churches either.

A still earlier state is represented by ordo romanus 26 (Text G), made in the third quarter of the eighth century for a church of suburban Rome. A distinction is made in the description of the rites of Holy Saturday between the practices in cities elsewhere (*in forenses civitatibus*), where the candle is blessed with *Deus mundi conditor*, and the "catholic church within the city of Rome" (*catholica ecclesia infra civitatem romanam*), where the candle is not thus blessed. The ordo goes on to describe the practice of the Lateran, which is, on Holy Saturday as at all times the center (ecclesia catholica?) of the unified liturgical practice of the entire city.

> On that day, then, at the ninth hour, fire is struck from stone in a place outside the basilica; if there should be an oratory, it is struck at the doorway; otherwise, in a place chosen beforehand, so that from the fire a candle may be lit. This candle should be placed in a candlestick and carried into the church by the *mansionarius*, in the presence of the congregation or the people. And from that fire, in the church or in the place where it is lit, one lamp is kept until Holy Saturday to light the candle which is to be blessed on that day, according to the form contained in the sacramentary.[11]

> And this order for blessing the candle is used in foreign cities; but in the catholic church within the city of Rome it is not so blessed. But early in the morning of Holy Saturday at the Lateran the archdeacon comes into the church and places wax in a large clean vessel and mixes it with oil and blesses the wax and from it he forms the likeness of lambs, and he keeps them in a clean place.

11. The striking of new fire here is described on Maundy Thursday, and the mansionarius' candle will be used to light the lamps before the altar that are progressively extinguished during the office of lauds; the ceremony is repeated for Good Friday and Holy Saturday. From the same fire on Maundy Thursday is reserved a lamp which will light the paschal candle. Later in the ordo, however, it is indicated that new fire is struck also on Good Friday and Holy Saturday. On the complexities of the various rites of the new fire, see M. ANDRIEU, *Les ordines*, 3: 313-21; Bernard CAPELLE, "La procession du Lumen Christi au samedi-saint", *Revue bénédictine* 44 (1932), 105-118.

On the octave of Easter these lambs are given to the people by the archdeacon after the communion of the mass, and with them in their houses they light them to burn incense, in case of any necessity of tribulation that may befall them. And in foreign cities they do likewise with the candle. (Text G)

The author of ordo 26 is not centrally concerned with Holy Saturday: he is assembing material about the striking of new fire on Maundy Thursday and the two following days; he describes the uses of this fire on Holy Saturday, and his ordo relates two practices which do not correspond to his own: practices of other related places. On the one hand, in dioceses outside the city,[12] *hic agitur*; on the other, in the Lateran, other practices are described. His practice, then, is neither of these: it is not the Lateran and its associated churches—the tituli—and it is not the non-Roman dioceses. It is an area between the two: the other churches of the diocese Rome, the churches of the *parrochia*, where, according to the sixth-century version of the *Liber pontificalis*, the right to bless the candle was conceded by Pope Zosimus (Text D).

Whether the candle was actually used at the time of Pope Zosimus (417-18) is called into question by the fact that wax (*cera*) and not a candle (*cereus*) is mentioned in the earlier recensions of the *Liber pontificalis*; but the sixth-century revised text names the candle and demonstrates its use by that time in the *parrocchia* (that is, the churches within the diocese, but not in the city, of Rome).[13] The Gelasian sacramentary shows the practice of the paschal candle entering the titular churches in the seventh century; it had not been practiced there before, if we can trust the absence of the candle from the lower layer of the Gelasian. As for the adoption of the paschal candle at the Lateran, we shall see that it comes some three centuries later.

12. The distinction between *forenses* and *suburbanis* is not always clear. At the crucial point where Ordo 26 notes that this order of blessing the candle is used in *forensibus civitatibus*, two manuscripts have the reading *suburbanis civitatibus*. See M. ANDRIEU, *Les ordines*, 3: 326.

13. On this use of the term *parrochia* see A. CHAVASSE, *Le sacramentaire gélasien*, 102-03. On *cera* and *cereus* in this context see M. ANDRIEU, *Les ordines*, 3: 321n3.

THE TEXT

Even though we can establish the gradual adoption of the paschal candle in the rites of Holy Saturday in Rome, beginning with the fringes of the city and moving inward, we have not determined what text was used in these early stages. In the Gelasian sacramentary, for the titular churches in the seventh century, the text is *Deus mundi conditor*. How then does the Exultet come to replace the *Deus mundi conditor* in the churches of Rome itself? The process is again one of importation, and to see it we must examine first the early stages of the *benedictio cerei*, and then the process by which the Exultet enters the Frankish liturgical books, before returning to our central question of the Exultet in Rome itself.

In the earliest documented usage of the easter candle, its blessing was expected to be provided anew each year. A letter probably written by St. Jerome tells us much about the early practice of the Easter candle;[14] Writing in 384, Jerome replied to Praesidius of Piacenza, who had requested from Jerome a *praeconium paschale* for his own use. Praesidius was evidently expected to produce a prayer every Easter; the text of the prayer was not fixed, and he was seeking the doctor's literary help.

---

14. The letter is attributed to Jerome by Germain MORIN in "Un écrit méconnu de Saint Jérôme", *Revue Bénédictine* 8 (1891), 20-27; and despite doubts going back as far as Erasmus, and voiced anew by L. Duchesne (Louis Marie Olivier DUCHESNE, *Le liber pontificalis*, 2d ed., 3 vols, the third ed. Cyrille Vogel [Paris: E. de Boccard, 1955-7], 3: 84), Morin continued to champion Jerome's authorship: see his *Études, textes, découvertes*, Anecdota maredsolana, 2d series, 1 (Paris: A. Picard, 1913) 21-22, and "La lettre de Saint Jérôme sur le cierge pascal. Réponse à quelques difficultés de M. l'abbé L. Duchesne", *Revue bénédictine* 9 (1892), 392-7; on the history of the attribution of the letter, see Henri LECLERCQ, "Pâques. VII. Le *praeconium paschale*", *Dictionnaire d'archéologie chrétienne et de liturgie*, vol. 13.2, cols. 1569-70. The letter itself is printed, among other places, in SCHMIDT, *Hebdomada sancta*, 2: 629-33; Germain MORIN, "Pour l'authenticité de la lettre de S. Jérôme à Présidius", *Bulletin d'ancienne littérature et d'archéologie chrétiennes* 3 (1913), 52-58, at 54-8; Jacques-Paul MIGNE, *Patrologiae cursus completus. Series latina*, 221 vols. (Paris, 1878-1890) (=PL) 30, cols. 188-94.

But Jerome did not help, and did not approve. Such prayers, says Jerome, far from relying on scriptural authority, borrow from pagan authors and adopt their rhetorical style: he particularly dislikes the praise of the bees, whose language is borrowed from Vergil. Jerome says that the *praeconium paschale* is a difficult matter, and that no one has done it well so far. He refuses Praesidius' request for a written praeconium but agrees to help him orally, albeit off the record.

The early history of the blessing of the paschal candle confirms what we learn from Jerome: it is a widespread practice, the blessing itself varying with the place and the celebrant. Only at a later stage does a text become fixed. We have texts or other evidence from fourth- or fifth-century Spain,[15] fifth- and sixth-century north Africa,[16] early sixth-century Pavia,[17] early sev-

15. A hymn (4th-5th century) of Prudentius, *Inventor rutili*, is clearly inspired by the Easter vigil, though probably intended for use at vespers on ordinary occasions; see Adolph FRANZ, *Die kirchlichen Benediktionen im Mittelalter*, 2 vols (Freiburg im Breisgau: Herder, 1909), 531; PINELL, "La benediccó", 4n3; the text is printed in Johann BERGMAN, *Aurelii Prudentii Clementis carmina*, Corpus scriptorum ecclesiasticorum latinorum, 61 (Vienna and Leipzig: Hoelder-Pilcher-Tempsky, 1926), 25-31; also in PL 59, cols. 813-831.

16. St. AUGUSTINE (354-430) quotes, in *De Civitate Dei* (413-426) a passage from his own *laus cerei*, "quod in laude quadam Cerei breviter versibus dixi:" and there follow three hexameters; the text is widely reproduced; Aurelius AUGUSTINUS, *De civitate dei*, ed. Emanuel Hoffmann, 2 vols, Corpus scriptorum ecclesiasticorum latinorum, 40.V.1-2 (Prague-Vienna-Leipzig: Tempsky, Freytag, 1899-1900), 2: 108; SCHMIDT, *Hebdomada Sancta*, 2: 627; PINELL, "La benediccò", 100. A text, preserved as a sermon attibuted to St. Augustine, is likely, as Patrick Verbraken has argued, to be a north African blessing of the paschal candle from around the time of bishop Fulgentius of Ruspe (d. 533). VERBRAKEN,"Une 'laus cerei' africaine", *Revue bénédictine* 70 (1960), 301-306; the text is printed there, 303-6; also in PL 46, cols. 817-21.

17. Ennodius, who was bishop of Pavia at his death in 521, has left two lengthy formulas for blessing the candle; his texts are printed in SCHMIDT, *Hebdomada sancta*, 2: 633-7; PINELL, "La benediccò", 92-95, both based on Guilelmus [Wilhelm] HARTEL, *Magni Felicis Ennodii opera omnia*, Corpus scriptorum ecclesiasticorum, 6 (Vienna: Carl Gerold's Sohn, 1882): 415-22; also edited in Fredericus [Friedrich] VOGEL, *Magni Felicis Ennodi opera*, Monumenta Germaniae Historica (=MGH), Auctores antiquissimi, 7 (Berlin: Weidmann, 1885): 18-20, 109-110.

II

enth-century Ravenna,[18] seventh-century Spain,[19] seventh-century Bobbio,[20] ninth-century Lyon,[21] and evidence of a text from Montecassino now lost.[22] In addition to these, a particular text, which begins *Exultet iam angelica turba celorum*, serves as the introductory portion of three versions of the

18. In a letter of 601, Pope Gregory the Great encourages the ailing Bishop Marinianus to avoid the exertions of the approaching Easter season, which for him would include the "prayers which are to be said over the candle in the church of Ravenna". "A vigiliis quoque temperandum est; sed et preces illae quae super cereum in Ravennati civitate dici solent vel expositiones evangelii, quae circa paschalem sollemnitatem a sacerdotibus fiunt, per alium dicantur": *MGH, Epistolarum tomus II: Gregorii papae registrum epistolarum Tomus II*, ed. Ludwig M. HARTMANN (Berlin: Weidmann, 1893-9), 282-3.

19. A blessing (*contestata*) from a seventh-century Escorial manuscript (*Quam mirabilis sit ecclesiae catholicae pulcritudo*) is edited in PINELL, "La benediccìò", 97-100; Giovanni MERCATI, *I. Un frammento delle ipotiposi... II. Paralipomena ambrosiana con alcuni appunti sulle benedizioni del cereo pasquale*, Studi e testi, 12 (Rome: Tipografia vaticana, 1904): 40-3.

20. A hymn *Ignis creator igneus*, found in the seventh-century Antiphonary of Bangor (Milan, Bibl. Ambrosiana, MS C.5.inf, there labeled *hymnus quando coeria* [usually printed as *cereum*] *benedicitur*) and in a tenth-century Bobbio manuscript (Turin, Bib. naz. MS G. v. 38, there labeled as *Ymnus in Sabato sancto ad cereum benedicere*), is a blessing of the paschal candle influenced in its language by the Gelasian *Deus mundi conditor*, and likely composed at Bobbio, where the Gelasian blessing was surely in circulation by the early seventh century. CHAVASSE, *Le sacramentaire gélasien*, pp. 687-9; for a discussion of the hymn and its sources see Michael CURRAN, *The Antiphonary of Bangor and the Early Irish Monastic Liturgy* (N.P. [Dublin?]: Irish Academic Press, 1984), 59-65 and notes, 216-19.

21. A *carmen de cereo paschale* of Drepanius (Florus of Lyons) is modelled on older texts. DREVES (in *Analecta hymnica medii aevi*, ed. Guido Marie DREVES, Clemens BLUME, and Henry Marriott BANNISTER, 55 vols [Leipzig: O. R. Reisland, 1886-1922], 50: 210), suggests that Drepanius is the mid-ninth century Florus, a deacon of the church of Lyons; the hymn is printed in *Analecta hymnica* 50: 217-8, PL 61, cols 1087-8.

22. Guillaume Durand, Bishop of Mende, refers to a composition by a certain Peter, a deacon of Montecassino, no longer in use. "...sed beatus Amb. benedictionem dictavit; quanquam Augu. et Petrus diaconus Cassinensis monachus, alias benedictiones dictaverunt, quae in usu non sunt." DURANDUS, *Rationale divinorum officiorum* (Venice: Gratiosus Perchianus, 1568), 232 (bk. 8, ch. 80).

II

18

blessing of the paschal candle: in southern Italy,[23] at Milan,[24] and in the Gallican churches, from where it will be adopted at Rome.

But the text first used at Rome, so far as we can tell (we have no record of how Jerome came to detest the practice of his day), is not the Exultet, but the prayer *Deus mundi conditor*[25]; this is a long rhetorical composition, using the themes which are found throughout such texts: praise to the creator of light, an offering of the candle, praise of the light by use of examples from biblical history, praise of the candle and of the bees, and the chastity of the bees made analogous to the chastity of the mother of the savior, of him who rises from death on this night. The prayer is followed by the blessing of the lit candle, *Veniat ergo, omnipotens deus, super hunc incensum.* The *Deus mundi conditor* appears in the Gelasian sacramentary (Text E), and is specified in ordo 30A (Text F); it is the earliest surviving text from Rome, and may have originated there.[26]

The Exultet, in the version that will ultimately be adopted at Rome, appears first not in Roman books but in the "Gallican" sacramentaries of the

23. On the special text and melody of the Exultet in southern Italy see *Paléographie musicale* (=PM), vol. 14: *Le codex 10 673 de la Bibliothèque vaticane, fonds latin (xf siècle. Graduel bénéventain* (Tournai: Desclée, 1931; repr. Bern: Lang, 1971), 375-422, and Thomas Forrest KELLY, *The Exultet in Southern Italy* (New York: Oxford University Press, 1996).

24. The text of the Milanese Exultet is printed in PINELL, "La benediccio", 90-2, from Marco MAGISTRETTI, *Manuale ambrosianum ex codice saec. XI olim in usum canonicae vallis travaliae*, 2 vols., Monumenta veteris liturgiae ambrosianae, 2-3 (Milano: Hoepli, 1904-1905), 2: 199-202; in SCHMIDT, *Hebdomada sancta*, 2: 645-7, from Pamelius' 1571 edition; in Otto HEIMING, *Corpus ambrosiano-liturgicum I. Das Sacramentarium triplex. Die Handschrift C 43 der Zentralbibliothek Zürich*, Liturgiewissenschaftliche Quellen und Forschungen, 49 (Münster Westfalen: Aschendorff, 1968) , 110-12; and in Paul CAGIN, ed. [anonymously] *Codex sacramentorum bergomensis*, Auctuarium solesmense, Series liturgica, Tomus 1 (Solesmes, St. Pierre, 1900), 65, from the tenth-century sacramentary of Bergamo.

25. The text is printed in Leo Cunibert MOHLBERG, Leo EIZENHÖFER, and Petrus SIFFRIN, ed., *Liber sacramentorum romanae aeclesiae ordinis anni circuli (Cod. Vat. Reg. lat. 316/Paris Bibl. Nat. 7193, 41/56)*, Rerum æcclesiasticarum documenta, Series maior, Fontes 4 (Roma: Herder, 1960), 68-70; PINELL, "La benediccio", 85-86.

26. See above, note 9.

THE EXULTET AT ROME

eighth century,[27] none of them from Rome; the text of the Exultet, however, was in use probably since at least the sixth century.[28] At a later stage, the two blessings, Gelasian and Gallican, *Deus mundi conditor* and *Exultet*, are combined in various ways in the so-called mixed Gelasian sacramentaries of the eighth century. Three of these, the St. Gall, Rheinau, and Prague sacramentaries, continue the Gallican practice of the Exultet;[29] others (Gellone, Angoulême, Phillipps) combine the two practices, giving first the *Deus mundi conditor*, and then the Exultet (Phillipps reverses this order).[30] These books, designed for circulation in the north, will affect

27. The three pure Gallican sacramentaries are (1) the "Missale Gallicanum Vetus", early eighth century (Vatican, Biblioteca Apostolica Vaticana, MS Pal. lat. 493; ed. Leo Cunibert MOHLBERG, Leo EIZENHÖFER, and Petrus SIFFRIN *Missale Gallicanum Vetus (Vat. Palat. lat. 493)*, Rerum ecclesiasticarum documenta, Series maior, Fontes 3 (Roma: Herder, 1958); the Exultet, nos. 132-135, pp. 35-37); (2) the "Bobbio missal", eighth century (Paris, Bib. nat. MS lat. 13246, ed. Elias Avery LOWE, *The Bobbio Missal. A Gallican Mass-Book (MS. Paris Lat. 13246)*, 3 vols, Henry Bradshaw Society, 53, 58, 61 (with André WILMART and Henry A. WILSON) (London: Harrison, 1917, 1920, 1924); the Exultet, no. 227, pp. 69-70); (3) the "Missale Gothicum", Autun, 8th century (Vatican, Biblioteca Apostolica Vaticana, MS Reg. lat. 317, ed. Leo Cunibert MOHLBERG, *Missale Gothicum. (Vat. Reg. lat. 317)*, Rerum ecclesiasticarum documenta, Series maior, Fontes 5 (Roma: Herder, 1961); the Exultet, no. 225, pp. 59-61).

28. The Exultet is quoted in two Gelasian masses, for Friday in Easter Week and for Holy Saturday; if these passages quote the Exultet, and not the other way around, then the Exultet must have been fixed at least by 585, when the second Council of Mâcon prescribed attendance at masses of Easter Week: these masses must have been composed, including their quotations of the Exultet, at least by then. Michel HUGLO, "L'auteur de l' '*Exultet*' pascal", *Vigiliae christianae* 7 (1953), 79-88 at 83; note that Klaus GAMBER ("Älteste Eucharistiegebete der lateinischen Osterliturgie", in Balth. FISCHER and J. WAGNER, eds., *Paschatis sollemnia* [Freiburg, Basel, Vienna, 1960], 159-178) feels that the borrowing may have been in the other direction.

29. Unless of course they represent a subsequent purification of the double transmission of the other eighth-century Gelasians.

30. The St. Gall sacramentary, St. Gall, eighth century (Sankt Gallen, Stiftsbibliothek, MS 348), ed. Leo Kunibert MOHLBERG, *Das fränkische Sacramentarium Gelasianum in alamannischer Überlieferung (Codex Sangall. No. 348)*, Liturgiewissenschaftliche Quellen und Forschungen 1-2 (Münster Westfalen: Aschendorff, 1918, 3d ed. St. Galler Sakramentar-Forschungen 1, 1971): the Exultet, nos. 538-9, pp. 81-3); the Rheinau sacramentary, 8th/9th century, Chur (Zürich, Zentralbibliothek, MS Rh 30; ed. Anton HÄNGGI and Alfons SCHÖNHERR, *Sacramentarium rheinaugiense. Handschrift Rh 30 der Zentral bibliothek Zürich*, Spicilegium friburgense, 15 (Freiburg Schweiz: Universitätsverlag, 1970): the Exultet, nos. 424-5, pp. 130-132); the Prague Sacramentary, late 8th century, Regensburg (Prague, Knihovna Metropolitni Kapi-

the rites of Holy Saturday in Rome by adding or substituting the *Exultet*, which will soon make its way to the city.

When the Roman liturgy was sent north to King Pipin by Pope Hadrian I, the papal liturgy contained in the so-called Gregorian sacramentary of Hadrian naturally made no reference to the blessing of a candle[31]; when Benedict of Aniane added material to the Hadrianum to bring it into line with the prevailing Frankish practice of the early ninth century, he began the supplement with additions for the rites of Holy Saturday, and included from the eighth-century Gelasians both the *Deus mundi conditor* and the *Exultet*. The two blessings are also presented as alternatives in a few early fragmentary sources[32], and in the Roman-German Pontifical, a compilation of the

toly, MS O. 83, ed. Alban DOLD and Leo EIZENHÖFER, *Das prager Sacramentar [Cod. O. 83 (fol. 1-12) der Bibliothek des Metropolitakapitels]*, 2 vols, Texte und Arbeiten, I. Abteilung, 38/42 (Beuron: Beuroner Kunstverlag, 1944,1949); the Exultet no. 95, vol.2, pp. 55*-57*); the sacramentary of Gellone, 8th century (Paris, Bib. nat. MS lat. 12048, ed. Antoine DUMAS and Jean DESHUSSES, *Liber sacramentorum Gellonensis*, 2 vols, Corpus christianorum Series latina, 159-159A (Turnhout: Brepols, 1981): the Exultet, nos. 677-8, pp. 93-5); the sacramentary of Angoulême, 8th century (Paris, Bib. nat. MS lat. 816; ed. Patrick SAINT-ROCH, *Liber sacramentorum Engolismensis (Manuscrit B. N. Lat. 816. Le Sacramentaire Gélasien d'Angoulême)*,Corpus Christianorum, Series latina, 159C (Turnhout: Brepols, 1987): the Exultet, nos. 733-4, pp. 108-110); the "Phillipps" sacramentary, 8th century (Berlin, Staatsbibliothek, MS Phillipps 1667; ed. Odilo HEIMING, *Liber sacramentorum Augustodunensis*, Corpus christianorum Series latina, 159B (Turnhout: Brepols, 1984): the Exultet, nos. 520-1, pp. 61-3).

31. The many witnesses are edited in DESHUSSES, *Le sacramentaire*, vol. 1; the Exultet is also lacking in many mixed Gregorian sacramentaries, such as Paris, Bibl. nat. MS lat. 12051, of the second half of the 9th century; see Klaus GAMBER, *Codices liturgici latini antiquiores* (=CLLA), Spicilegii Friburgensis Subsidia 1, 2 vols. in 3 parts (Freiburg Schweiz: Universitätsverlag, vols. 1,1 and 1,2, 2d ed. 1968; vol. 1A [Supplementum], 1988), 255, and no. 901, pp. 409-10.

32. The *Deus mundi conditor* precedes the Exultet in a fragment of a Gelasian sacramentary of the 8th/9th century from southeast Germany: Vienna, Österreichische Nationalbibliothek, Cod. Ser. n. 13706 (see Klaus GAMBER, "Eine ältere Schwesterhandschrift des Tassilo-Sakramentars in Prag", *Revue bénédictine* 80 [1970], 156-162 at 160-61); and in a fragmentary leaf from about 800 (Munich, Bayerisches Staatsbibliothek MS Clm 29163d) the *Deus mundi conditor* is followed by the rubric *item benedictio cerei* and then the second portion of the Exultet, from the preface onward: see GAMBER, CLLA, no. 633, pp. 310-11, and GAMBER, "Eine ältere Schwesterhandschrift", 59-60).

early tenth century made in Mainz for use by Frankish bishops.[33] Gradually, however, the Exultet gains the upper hand in these Frankish sources,[34] and the tradition of *Deus mundi conditor* is lost to sight.[35]

It is no easy matter to establish the moment of the arrival of the Exultet in Rome itself, and its adoption in at least some of the churches of the city. Our earliest records are not strictly Roman, since they are Frankish *ordines romani*, which report on the practices of city but adapt them in varying degrees for the needs of a local congregation.

The earliest clear reference to the Exultet in Rome comes in the early ninth century, in ordo romanus 25 (text P):

> On the same day, Holy Saturday, at the eighth hour, all the priests of the city and the suburbs come together and all the clergy and people in the designated church. And this is the order for blessing the candle by deacons in suburban churches, as contained in the sacramentary, with these words: *Exultet iam angelica turba caelorum*, up to: *implere praecipiat. Per.* Then *Sursum corda.* Resp: *Habemus ad dominum. Gratias agamus domino Deo nostro.* Resp.: *Dignum et iustum est. V. D. vere quia dignum et iustum est ut invisibilem Deum patrem omnipitentem filiumque unigenitum,* up to: *in his paschalibus gaudiis conservare digneris. Per.*

This ordo appears as an interpolation in the MS Wolfenbüttel 4175.[36] Borrowing from ordo 24 and, later, from ordo 26 (which speaks of the candle in *forensibus civitatibus*), the scribe makes it appear that the Exultet is used at Rome; however, in fact he has added it in here himself, and is perhaps only grafting Frankish practice onto a Roman model.

33. See Cyrille VOGEL and Reinhard ELZE, *Le pontifical romano-germanique du dixième siècle*, 3 vols, Studi e testi, 226-7, 229 (Vatican City: Biblioteca Apostolica Vaticana, 1963, 1972) 2: 95-9.

34. Sometimes the received Roman liturgy is supplemented using only the Exultet and not the double tradition of Benedict of Aniane; a sacramentary of Salzburg of the early ninth century, which is otherwise identical to the Gregorian sacramentary of Padua, inserts the Exultet before the prayers for the lessons of the Holy Saturday vigil. The sacramentary (Deshusses' siglum Z5) survives as fragments in Salzburg, Munich, and Vienna. See DESHUSSES, *Le sacramentaire grégorien*, 1: 715.

35. The *Deus mundi conditor* has however a little more history. The final portion of the prayer, which begins *Veniat ergo super hunc incensum*, gradually got separated and, through a misunderstanding of the word *incensum* (which originally referred to the lit candle), survived as a blessing of incense or of the grains of incense inserted into the paschal candle. See KELLY, *The Exultet*, 61n81, and the discussion below.

36. Andrieu attributes it to the same monk of Wissemburg who adapted other material to Frankish use (ANDRIEU, *Les ordines*, 3: 301).

A similar case is ordo 31 (Text Q), of the late ninth or early tenth century, which also names the Exultet:

> Of the order for blessing the candle. At the eighth hour the priests and levites enter the sacristy and put on the vestments in which they are to celebrate the vigil.
>
> And having lit the candle which is to be blessed from the new fire, the pontifex with the sacred ministers proceeds into the church in silence, and that same candle is carried before him and placed in a candelabrum before the altar. The pontifex prays, and as he rises he kisses the altar and goes to his seat.
>
> Then the archdeacon, dressed in a dalmatic, having asked for a blessing, says: *Exultet iam angelica turba celorum*, to the end. Then *Dominus vobiscum*. And then resp.: *Et cum spiritu tuo*. He says: *Sursum corda*. Resp.: *Habemus ad dominum*. He says: *Gratias agamus domino Deo nostro*. Resp.: *Dignum et iustum est*. And he performs the consecration of the candle, singing as for the canon.
>
> After which two candles, each the height of a man, are lit from that same candle, and they are held by two notaries, one at the right corner of the altar and the other at the left, and from that fire are all the lights lit, they all having been extinguished beforehand.
>
> Then the lector goes up into the ambo and does not say *Lectio libri Genesis*, but begins plainly, *In principio creavit Deus celum et terram*, and likewise for the other lections. And before *In principio* no prayer is said.[37]

But these sources are Frankish, and may represent the amalgamation of Roman practice with Frankish. What are the sources from Rome itself which present us with the text of the Exultet? They are not early, and they provide a variety of textual forms, adding text received from the north to an indigenous Italian, but certainly not papal, and possibly not originally Roman, tradition. Before examining them we should review some details of the textual tradition of the Exultet itself.

---

37. ANDRIEU, *Les ordines*, 3: 500. Ordo 28 (Text M), about a century earlier, uses almost exactly this same language, but without naming the Exultet. The deacon begins with *Dominus vobiscum* answered by *Et cum spiritu tuo*, after which he pronounces an *oratio* (*Deus mundi conditor*?), then the priests sit, but the deacons remain standing, for a continuation beginning *Sursum corda*. We cannot be sure that the Exultet and its preface-tone continuation are intended. The text is edited in ANDRIEU, *Les ordines*, 3: 403-4. Note also that Ordo 32, in the version of Cambridge, Corpus Christi College MS 192 (mid of the 10 c., Text O), uses the same language, but specifies the Exultet, calling it an *oratio*, but not mentioning the *Dominus vobiscum* that precedes the *oratio* in ordo 28; ANDRIEU, *Les ordines*, 3: 521-23.

II

The earliest texts of the Exultet, we have said, are in the Gallican sacramentaries and the eighth-century Gelasian sacramentaries, Frankish books
representing the practices of the eighth century.[38] Fairly early on, certain alterations were practiced on the original text, for theological reasons or esthetic ones. Particularly noteworthy in this respect is the omission of a reference to the necessity and felicity of Adam's sin ("O certe necessarium Adae
peccatum, quod Christi morte deletum est; O felix culpa quae talem ac tantum meruit habere redemptorem"); this passage is absent in manuscripts
from as early as the ninth century, probably under the influence of the
Roman-German Pontifical, which omits it,[39] as do the witnesses of Andrieu's
ordo romanus 50.[40] It is missing in many German manuscripts, and some
French ones, though it is normally present in Italy.[41] Likewise the extensive
praise of the bees, long considered to be of questionable taste by such authorities as Saint Jerome,[42] is removed from the version of the Exultet transmitted to Rome in the Roman-German Pontifical.

38. There is evidence, however, that the text of the Exultet dates back at least to
the sixth century; see above, note 28.

39. VOGEL and ELZE, Le *pontifical*, 2: 98.

40. ANDRIEU, *Les ordines*, 5: 269-70. These include the eleventh-century south Italian manuscripts Montecassino 451 and Vallicelliana D 5.

41. In German sources, the passage is present in the Rheinau and St. Gall sacramentaries, and in St. Gall MS 251; but it is already absent in the supplement to the
Hadrianum as presented in Cologne 88 and 137 (9/10 century; DESHUSSES, *Le sacramentaire*, siglum V), in later manuscripts of St. Gall (338, 339, 341, 342) as well as the
many German sources of the Romano-Germanic Pontifical. The passage is also lacking in the Bobbio missal, which however had other unusual abridgements as well. Ul-
rich of Cluny reports that Abbot Hugo (d. 1109) had it removed from books at the
abbey (in which it presumably was present until that time): "In cuius (sc. the Exultet) quodam loco cum aliquando non bene haberetur *O felix culpa, et quod peccatum
Adae necessarium esset*, ante hos annos domnus abbas optime fecit, quod fecit abradi
et ne amplius legeretur interdixit." (PL 149, col. 663). On French manuscripts, see
FRANZ, *Die kirchlichen*, 1: 540-1.

42. It may be this attribution to St. Augustine, or the fact that St. Augustine was
known to have composed a *laus cerei*, that gave impetus to a medieval tradition that
asserts St. Augustine's authorship of the Exultet in a version which, revised by St.
Jerome (who saw to the removal of the pagan Virgilian bees), is now sung throughout the church. It is thus presented in the so-called pontifical of Poitiers: "Usum
benedicendi cereum a b. Augustino repertum tradit ecclesia. Qui benedictionem illius perficiens a sancto Hieronymo reprehensus est, cur Virgilica verba inseruerit;
sed sicut ab eodem beato Hieronymo emendata tunc fuit, ita nunc per ecclesias canitur;" cited in FRANZ, *Die kirchlichen*, 533-4: on the pontifical, see above, note 35.

But the Exultet without the Frankish omissions was already a feature of the Roman landscape from the earliest surviving documents, though the sources date only from the eleventh century. The earliest securely Roman Exultet is that of San Lorenzo in Damaso of the early eleventh century (Rome, Bibl. Vallicelliana E 5), and it provides a full text; the complete text is found also in the twelfth-century sacramentary Vatican, San Pietro F 15 (which however may not be from the city itself).

Thus the alteration of either of the two passages just mentioned in a manuscript of Roman provenance indicates that its Exultet was adopted or altered or adapted under Frankish influence rather than continuing the long local tradition of suburban churches.

Even when the Frankish omissions begin to be made, the various ways in which some surviving manuscripts choose to alter the praise of the bees, and the fact that they often retain the passage about Adam's sin, makes clear that a local version of the text which contained these passage was in circulation well before the arrival of the Frankish pontifical. The various abbreviations practiced in the praise of the bees in Roman and central Italian manuscripts is shown in Table 1, and they demonstrate that there was no uniform Roman tradition in this matter.

The earliest Roman copy of the Roman-German Pontifical is Rome, Biblioteca Alessandrina 173; it is an eleventh-century copy based on a German model.[43] The Exultet transmitted in this pontifical represents a tradition that will ultimately prevail; its text is found in other Roman manuscripts from the twelfth century onward: in Vatican, San Pietro F 14 (early twelfth century); San Pietro F 12 (twelfth century); in the thirteenth-century sacramentaries Vatican, Santa Maria Maggiore 40, in San Pietro B 78 (s13); and in many later manuscripts.

But there are other versions in Rome as well. An Exultet which omits only a portion of the praise of the bees, and which retains the passage about

---

43. The text is edited in ANDRIEU, *Les ordines*, 5: 268-71, as MS A. Ordo 50 was taken verbatim into the pontifical. The text in Alessandrina 173 is not, despite Capelle's assertion (Bernard CAPELLE, "L'*Exultet* pascal œuvre de saint Ambroise", in *Miscellanea Giovanni Mercati* 1, Studi e testi 121 [Vatican City: Biblioteca Apostolica Vaticana, 1946], 219-246), a re-expansion of the the text of the Roman-German pontifical (=PRG). The PRG text reached central Italy early and was adopted into other books, as is evident in the missal Vat. lat. 4770, of the late tenth or early eleventh century.

Adam's sin—a text which could not have been produced from the PRG—is in Florence, Bibl. Riccardiana 299 (late 11th century); and a longer omission than that of the PRG is in Vat. lat. 12989 (from the Lateran, c1200), and Bibl. Angelica 1606 (an eighteenth-century copy of a lost thirteenth-century sacramentary).[44]

[Table 1: see the next page]

Other surviving sources from the eleventh and twelfth centuries make it clear that the Exultet was in regular use in the churches of Rome. The monastic sacramentary Vatican, San Pietro F 12, of the late eleventh century, provides an Exultet which omits the praise of the bees but includes the references to Adam's sin.[45] From the early twelfth century, the sacramentary Vatican, San Pietro F 14, from San Salvatore in Primicerio (S. Trifone), also provides the Exultet but without giving ceremonial rubrics.[46] At St. Peter's, the sacramentary Vatican, San Pietro F 18, from the late twelfth or early thirteenth century,[47] prescribes the Exultet but omits its text. From the first half of the thirteenth century comes Santa Maria Maggiore 40, from the monastery of Saints Andrew and Bartholomew, which provides a full text and rubrics.[48] The Roman pontifical of the twelfth century also includes the ceremonies of Holy Saturday, including the Exultet, but the earliest of these pontificals that may have been made in Rome date from the fourteenth century,[49] and hence are of little use to us in stuying the earlier history of the city itself.

44. These last omit also the "O certe necessarium". The variety of cuts operated in the praise of the bees is illustrated for south Italian manuscripts in KELLY, *The Exultet*, 65-9.

45. See Paola SUPINO MARTINI, *Roma e l'area grafica romanesca (secoli X-XII)* (Alessandria: Edizioni dell'Orso 1987), 82-3.

46. SUPINO MARTINI, *Roma*, 82 and n98; on the localization, see also Pierre JOUNEL, *Le culte des saints dans les basiliques du Latran et du Vatican au douzième siècle*, Collection de l'École française de Rome, 26 ([Rome], École française de Rome, 1977), 36-7.

47. See Pierre SALMON, *Les manuscrits liturgiques latins de la Bibliothèque Vaticane*, 5 vols, Studi e testi, 251, 253, 260, 267, 270 (Vatican City: Biblioteca Apostolica Vaticana, 1968, 1969, 1970, 1971, 1972), 2: 78.

48. Rubrics transcribed below as text Z.

49. Sources possibly from Rome include San Pietro H 54 (s. 14), Vat. lat. 1153 (s. 14), Vat. lat. 1155 (s. 14), Vat. lat. 4745 (s. 14ex); see the descriptions of manuscripts in ANDRIEU, *Le pontifical*, vol. 2. The twelfth-century pontifical Vat. Ottob. lat. 270 lacks the ordo for Holy Saturday.

Table 1: Omissions of the praise of the bees in Roman and central Italian manuscripts of the Exultet.

The brackets below show the text omitted in the manuscripts indicated.

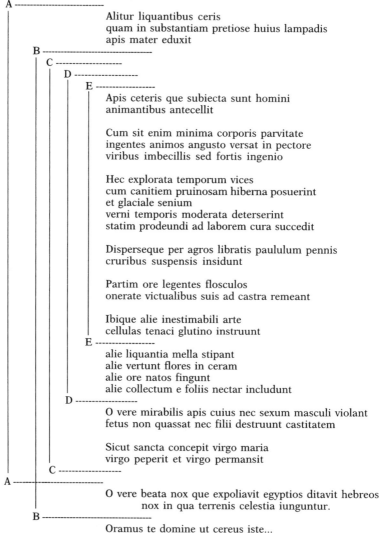

Sed iam columne huius preconia novimus
quam in honore dei rutilans ignis accendit

Qui licet sit divisus in partes
mutuati tamen luminis detrimenta non novit

A ─────────────────────────

Alitur liquantibus ceris
quam in substantiam pretiose huius lampadis
apis mater eduxit

B ─────────────────────────

C ──────────────────

D ──────────────────

E ──────────────────

Apis ceteris que subiecta sunt homini
animantibus antecellit

Cum sit enim minima corporis parvitate
ingentes animos angusto versat in pectore
viribus imbecillis sed fortis ingenio

Hec explorata temporum vices
cum canitiem pruinosam hiberna posuerint
et glaciale senium
verni temporis moderata deterserint
statim prodeundi ad laborem cura succedit

Disperseque per agros libratis paululum pennis
cruribus suspensis insidunt

Partim ore legentes flosculos
onerate victualibus suis ad castra remeant

Ibique alie inestimabili arte
cellulas tenaci glutino instruunt

E ──────────────────

alie liquantia mella stipant
alie vertunt flores in ceram
alie ore natos fingunt
alie collectum e foliis nectar includunt

D ──────────────────

O vere mirabilis apis cuius nec sexum masculi violant
fetus non quassat nec filii destruunt castitatem

Sicut sancta concepit virgo maria
virgo peperit et virgo permansit

C ──────────────────

A ─────────────────────────

O vere beata nox que expoliavit egyptios ditavit hebreos
nox in qua terrenis celestia iunguntur.

B ─────────────────────────

Oramus te domine ut cereus iste...

A: alitur--permansit
Vatican City, Biblioteca Apostolica Vaticana Vat. lat. 12989
    Sacramentary, ca. 1200, Lateran
Rome, Biblioteca Angelica 1606
    Sacramentary, 13 c., Santa Maria ad Martyres. (18 c. copy)

B: exudit...iunguntur
Rome, Biblioteca Vallicelliana B 43; Sacramentary, 12 c.?

C: exudit...permansit
Vatican City, Biblioteca Apostolica Vaticana Vat. lat. 4770, Missal, central Italy, 10 c.
Vatican City, Biblioteca Apostolica Vaticana Archivio di San Pietro F 12
    Evangelary, Sacramentary, late 11 c., St. Peter's
Rome, Biblioteca Vallicelliana B 8, Sacramentary, Norcia, late 11 c.
Rome, Biblioteca Alessandrina 173
    Romano-Germanic pontifical, early 12 c., Rome
Vatican City, Biblioteca Apostolica Vaticana Archivio di San Pietro F 14
    Sacramentary, early 12 c., San Salvatore in Primicerio (S. Trifone)
Vatican City, Biblioteca Apostolica Vaticana Santa Maria Maggiore 40
    Sacramentary, ca. 1230, Monastery of Ss. Andrew and Bartholomew, Rome
Vatican City, Biblioteca Apostolica Vaticana Archivio di San Pietro B 78
    Holy Saturday materials, 13-14 c., St. Peter's; Exultet, f. 3
Rome, Biblioteca Vallicelliana B 23, Missal, 12 c., Norcia

D: exudit--includunt
Florence, Biblioteca Riccardiana 299
    Sacramentary-Antiphoner, late 11 c., Rome (not papal?)
Rome, Biblioteca Vallicelliana F 29
    Rituale, 11/12 c.
Subiaco, Biblioteca del protocenobio di Santa Scolastica XVIII
    Missal, first half 12 c., Beneventan melody

E: exudit--instruunt
New York, Pierpont Morgan Library M 379, Missal, 11 c., Foligno

Full text present:
Vatican City, Biblioteca Apostolica Vaticana Barb. lat. 560
    Missal, central Italy, late 10 c.
Rome, Biblioteca Vallicelliana E 15
    Sacramentary, first half 11 c., San Lorenzo in Damaso
Vatican City, Biblioteca Apostolica Vaticana Archivio di San Pietro F 15
    Sacramentary, 12 c., Rome (Spoleto?)

By about 1200 the Exultet was used even at the Lateran, though the pope was not present for the ceremony, as we see from Vat. lat. 12989, a sacramentary from the Lateran.[50] Its rubrics match in most particulars those of the thirteenth-century sacramentary Santa Maria Maggiore 52, and indeed they become standard material in the ordinal of Innocent III.[51] It is the formal adoption of the Exultet not by the churches of Rome but by the Church of Rome—the papal ceremonies—that caused the regularization and abridgement of the full text that had long been used in the suburban churches; this revised text became universal only after the Lateran adopted its version in the thirteenth century.

* * * * *

The use of the paschal candle, a practice of considerable antiquity in some places, was adopted at Rome from the outside in: from the outlying churches of the diocese, the *parrochia*, to the titular churches in the seventh century, and to the Lateran basilica itself only much later. Perhaps the Roman-German Pontifical, made in the tenth century and adopted for papal use somewhat later, partly to fill a great liturgical void in the life of a city in desperate decay, was the vehicle for bringing the paschal candle to the Lateran, to the papal rites themselves. In this case there would have been no intermediate stage at the Lateran where the *Deus mundi conditor* was used to bless the candle. Of this intervening period we know little, however, since we have no specific reference to the candle at the Lateran before the Liber Politicus of Benedict in the first half of the twelfth century.

In the other churches of the city, the adoption of the candle comes first, and then the adoption of the Exultet. We know that *Deus mundi conditor* was used at Rome in the seventh century, and that *Exultet* was used in the eleventh. Our sources for the time between these two are Frankish books, and in them we see the Exultet gradually gain the upper hand. We can only assume, given the dependence of Rome on Frankish books in the tenth century, that the Exultet was adopted in the same gradual way at Rome.

---

50. Rubrics transcribed as Text EE.

51. Compare the edition in Stephen J. P. van Dijk, *The Ordinal of the Papal Court from Innocent III to Boniface VIII and related documents*, completed by Joan Hazelden Walker, Spicilegium friburgense, 22 (Fribourg, Presses Universitaires, 1975) 261-5.

THE MUSIC OF THE EXULTET
The beautiful melody with which the Exultet begins in Stefaneschi's manuscript and in many others is generally considered the melody of the "Roman" liturgy. It has been admired, and deservedly so, for a long time. It is a handsome melody: but its extreme antiquity may be doubted, and its Roman origin is even more dubious. The uniform adoption of the melody sung in the Roman rite of the twenty-first century is essentially the result of the reforms of plainsong practice instituted by Pope Pius X and undertaken by the monks of Solesmes. The present text of the Exultet was adopted into the Roman missal of Pius V (1570), but even then there was still considerable melodic variety from place to place.[52] What we now recognize as the Roman melody of the Exultet, beautiful as it is, is not found in Rome before the thirteenth century.

So far as we know, there is no musical notation for the Exultet anywhere before the tenth century. The oldest melodic indication we have is from ordo romanus 28 (Text M), a Frankish document of about 800, in which the deacon, having completed the first part of the blessing of the candle (whose text is not named), continues with the second part, after *Sursum corda*: "inde vero accedit in consecrationem cerei, decantando quasi canonem." That is, the deacon sings the melody used for the canon of the mass (beginning with the preface). This suggests that what went before, here called a prayer, was sung, if it was sung at all, to a different melody—perhaps that now used for the Roman Exultet?[53]

Bernard, writing about the Lateran in the late 12th century, notes that the Exultet begins in the tone of the preface ("incipit consecrationem cerei decantando in modum prefationis": Text DD¶4): evidently the Roman Exultet-melody was not used there. In fact, the so-called Roman melody is not found in Roman books before the late thirteenth century. This is not necessarily

52. In 1826 there was still printed at Paris a missal for use in Spain which had a special melody as a result of a permission given by Pius V himself on 12 December 1570; see Georges BENOIT-CASTELLI, "Le 'praeconium paschale,' " *Ephemerides liturgicae* 67 (1953), 309-334, at 310.

53. The practice of singing the Exultet to a special melody, and the second portion to the preface-tone, is used widely: in the Ambrosian liturgy, and the various versions of the Frankish-Roman liturgy. Only in southern Italy are both portions sung to a single special melody. On the Beneventan Exultet melody see PM 14: 388-417; PM 4, *Le codex 121 de la Bibliotheque d'Einsiedeln* (Solesmes, 1894, repr. Bern: Lang, 1974), 171-85; KELLY, *The Exultet*, 79-118.

because the melody was not sung before that time: there is simply no melody written.

The oldest Italian source for the Roman melody that I know is the processional Naples VI G 34. The manuscript is in Beneventan script, from the Norman-influenced city of Troia. The same melody is added in a later hand to an Exultet roll of Troia[54] in the late twelfth century. It is possible to postulate a scenario in which the strong Norman influence at Troia gradually brought the use of the Norman Exultet, with a melody which only gradually came to be universally used as the "Roman" melody of the Exultet.

It may be through the adoption of Franciscan books that the melody of the prologue arrived in Rome itself (the preface tone, of course, was already in use); thus Naples VI G 38 may be among the earliest witnesses of the Roman melody in this Franciscan context. In this thirteenth-century missal, cited both by Huglo and Benoît-Castelli, the Exultet is notated in a different and later hand from that which wrote the rest of the musical notation.[55] It is thus not really a very early witness of the melody: Stefaneschi's Exultet may be as early.[56]

This beautiful Roman melody, so universally admired, is probably the last of the many elements of the Exultet ceremonial to be adopted at Rome, and its origin is to be sought elewhere.

54. The melody from Naples VI G 34 is transcribed in KELLY, *The Exultet*, 116; the roll is Troia, Archivio della Cattedrale, Exultet 3; complete facsimile in Guglielmo CAVALLO, *Rotoli di Exultet dell'Italia meridionale* (Bari: Adriatica, 1973), tav. 42-61; and in Guglielmo CAVALLO, Giulia OROFINO, and Oronzo PECERE, eds., *Exultet: Rotoli liturgici dell'Italia meridionale* (Rome: Istituto Poligrafico e Zecca dello Stato, 1994), 191-9.

55. But it is not palimpsest, as is suggested by HUGLO, "L'auteur" (above, n. 28), 336.

56. The sources of the Roman melody of the Exultet is beyond the scope of this discussion. BENOIT-CASTELLI, "Le praeconium", gives the best discussion, the result of comparing some 160 manuscripts and 40 printed version. The Roman Exultet-melody may be the development of either a German or a French tone; the modern tone is found in many Norman and English manuscripts, but not before the twelfth century. The "Norman" tone, found often in Franciscan and Dominican missals, passed from there to the missal of the Roman curia of the fourteenth and fifteenth centuries.

The ceremony: Lumen Christi and the use of the ambo

The introduction of the paschal candle is not the moment of the introduction of the Exultet; and the introduction of the Exultet does not bring with it the various elements of accompanying ceremonial which contribute to the solemnity of the fully-developed rite.

Noteworthy among these added elements is the threefold *Lumen Christi*, often sung in procession, with a variety of intensifiers—singing higher each time; singing a more elaborate melody; holding the candle higher, and so on.[57]

Most of the early witnesses of the paschal candle and the Exultet do not mention the *Lumen Christi*.[58] Still in the twelfth century, San Pietro F 15 makes no mention of *Lumen Christi* (although since the manuscript is not provided with elaborate rubrics we cannot be sure of its absence in the ceremony). And yet by the time of the thirteenth-century codification of the Roman liturgy, it has become a regular part of the ceremonies. The procession with its triple proclamation was introduced at some time between the middle of the tenth century and the middle of the eleventh: a period difficult to document in Rome owing to the scarcity of sources.

The tenth-century Roman-German pontifical, as well as the mid-tenth-century ordo 32, make no mention of *Lumen Christi*. The earliest Roman source is the eleventh-century monastic lectionary of San Saba (Bibl. Angelica 1383, Text U). The manuscript is clearly influenced by the practices of Montecassino,[59] and it is entirely possible that the practice of chanting the *Lumen Christi* came to Rome from the south, where it rapidly attached itself to the rites of the Easter candle.

In southern Italy, the *Lumen Christi* is known from many of the earliest sources of the Exultet, beginning in the tenth century; they include Benevento 33 and Vat. lat. 10673, where *Lumen Christi* is provided in the oldest

57. See texts W, X, Y, DD, EE, FF.

58. They include the Gelasian sacramentary, ordines 17, 27 (MS R), 28, 31, 32, and the 10th-century Roman-German pontifical (Texts E, I, J, M, Q, N, S).

59. The lections of Holy Saturday include versions of the prayer of Jonah, and the two canticles of the Three children, in notated versions which match those of southern Italy, and in particular the practices of Montecassino. See Thomas Forrest KELLY, *The Beneventan Chant* (Cambridge: Cambridge University Press, 1989), 131-33, 158-60; on Montecassino and San Saba, see SUPINO MARTINI, *Roma e l'area grafica*, pp. 140-42; JOUNEL, *Le culte des saints*, 33, 65-66.

Beneventan ordo. A whole series of Exultets from Montecassino, beginning with the Avezzano roll (mid-eleventh century) and continuing with the rolls in London (Br. Lib. add. 30337), the Vatican (Barb. lat. 592), Pisa, and other Cassinese manuscripts,[60] as well as a series of manuscripts from the Dalmatian coast[61] and a number of other Exultet rolls,[62] give evidence of the regular and widespread use of the *Lumen Christi* in southern Italy beginning at least by the end of the tenth century. In the south, however, the *Lumen Christi* is never sung in procession.

The monastic connection between Montecassino and Rome may be seen also in the lectionary of Santa Cecilia in Trastevere,[63] which, like the San Saba lectionary, provides lections *cum cantico* reflecting the practices of Montecassino;[64] this, too, is no surprise given that Desiderius, abbot of Montecassino, was cardinal priest of Santa Cecilia at about the time the manuscript was made.[65] Unfortunately there is no indication of how the Exultet was practiced at Santa Cecilia, though we may suspect that it was similar to that of Montecassino.

A connection between Rome and southern Italy may also be seen in the relation of urban books to those of the important monasteries of the Roman region; Farfa, Subiaco, St. Eutizio in Val Castoriana, and some related man-

---

60. Including Vatican Ottoboni lat. 576, Rome, Vallicelliana C 32.

61. Oxford, Bodleian MSS Canon. bibl. lat. 61 and Canon. liturg. 342; Berlin lat. fol. 920; Vatican Borg. lat. 339.

62. Troia 1, Troia 3, Mirabella Eclano 1. Many incomplete rolls do not allow us to determine whether the *Lumen Christi* was originally present. Facsimiles of all surviving Exultet rolls are in CAVALLO et al., *Exultet*.

63. Now in the collection of S. B. Cron, formerly belonging to Sir Sidney Cockerell.

64. For more detail on these lections and their music, see KELLY, *The Beneventan Chant* , 131-33, 158-60; PM 14, 271-73, 318-21, 417n1.

65. Desiderius, abbot of Montecassino, cardinal priest of Santa Cecilia since 1058, was elevated to the Papacy as Victor III in 1086. Desiderius is Montecassino's greatest abbot, who presided over the renewal of the buildings, the books, and the liturgy of his monastery. That Desiderius should have had some influence on the important activities of eleventh-century Santa Cecilia has often been supposed, but remains to be demonstrated in detail. See the discussion in Thomas CONNOLLY, "The *Graduale* of S. Cecilia in Trastevere and the Old Roman Tradition", *Journal of the American Musicological Society* 28 (1975), 413-58, especially 436-8; Kenneth LEVY, "*Lux de luce*: The Origin of an Italian Sequence", *The Musical Quarterly* 57 (1971), 40-61, at 44.

uscripts. In these manuscripts, missals for the most part, the Exultet has the melody from southern Italy—the melody always used with the Beneventan Exultet and except for these manuscripts known only in the south. These manuscripts show a transitional phase when they give the first part of the Exultet with the Beneventan melody, and the second part (after the *Sursum corda*) with the more-usual—at least in Roman areas—preface-tone.[66] Perhaps they once used the Beneventan text of the Exultet; this would explain the presence of a double melody.

In this same group of monastic manuscripts the *Lumen Christi* is present with a progressively elaborated melody for each of the three announcements; there is no indication of whether they are sung in procession.[67] The same musical elaboration is found also in Vat. lat. 4770, whose connection with southern Italy is made, not through the Exultet (which is not notated here), but through many details of the Beneventan liturgy preserved in this manuscript of the early eleventh century from central Italy (Abruzzo?).[68]

Lumen Christi was known at least in the monastic ambitus north of Rome from the early eleventh century, where it assumed a regular form; this was probably adapted from Beneventan customs, and being present both north and south of Rome by the early eleventh century, we can suppose that it was grafted onto the Roman practices of the Exultet at a time not much later: in the course of the first half of the century.

At the Lateran, however, the *Lumen Christi* was not adopted until some time between 1140 and 1190: it is not mentioned in the ordo of Benedict

---

66. The manuscripts include Subiaco XVIII (19), a missal of the 13th century, which, among other things, contains the complete Good Friday vespers of the old Beneventan liturgy; Vallicelliana F 29 (early 12 c.) from Farfa; Vall B 43 (of undetermined provenance, but not from Subiaco, SUPINO MARTINI, *Roma*, p. 334; it was used at Santa Maria de Ninfa, Rome(?)); Vall B 23 (from Norcia, SUPINO MARTINI, *Roma*, 224), s12; New York, Morgan M 379 (Foligno 11/12 c., SUPINO MARTINI, *Roma*, 225-6 n66). Note that an earlier manuscript of Norcia, Vall B 8, a missal of late 11 c., has a PRG version of the Exultet, inserted into a Gelasian ordo, substituting *Exultet* for *Deus mundi conditor*, and making no reference to *Lumen Christi*. Perhaps significant changes took place there around 1100.

67. This elaborated version is not present in Vall B 43, which has only a single notation for *Lumen Christi*, with an indication that it is to be repeated.

68. On the MS see SUPINO MARTINI, *Roma*, 153-59; on the south Italian connection, see KELLY, *The Beneventan Chant*, 315-16 and index p. 339.

(Text AA); but Albinus, using exactly Benedict's words about 1188 (Text BB), adds the fact that the deacon says *Lumen Christi* three times.

In Rome the candle was not at first blessed from an ambo or pulpit. The Gelasian sacramentary and a long series of *ordines romani*, as well as the Roman-German Pontifical of the tenth century, specify the placement and the blessing of the candle in front of the altar.[69]

Apparently the twelfth century saw the beginning of the practice of ascending the ambo in order to pronounce the Exultet. In the twelfth-century Roman pontifical as edited by Andrieu, a double practice is recorded, which seems to reflect a period of transition. The ordo specifies the triple *Lumen Christi* and the use of the ambo. The same ordo continues, however, with a different custom:

> This [the foregoing] is the custom of the Roman church; but, according to the custom of blessed Pope Zosimus, the great candle which is to be blessed is placed in a candelabrum in front of the altar and, with the clergy and people gathered, the deacon who is to bless the candle comes and with a stylus inscribes a cross and ☐ and ☐ and the year from the incarnation of our Lord. Then humbly bowing to the priest he receives a blessing from him, and then arising and facing the choir he says three times, raising his voice, *Lumen Christi*; and the rest is done as said before. (Text W)

One of these is the current practice of "The Roman Church"—does this mean papal practice?—and the other is a practice of great antiquity, though evidently not the current custom. Perhaps the blessing before the altar is still practiced in some churches, but it is no longer the norm.

Ambos there were, evidently, in many Roman churches. Some churches still preserve the arrangement of two ambones, right and left, with one of which is often associated a paschal candlestick. Arrangements of this kind can still be seen in San Clemente (apparently essentially unchanged since the twelfth century), in San Lorenzo fuori le Mura and in Santa Maria in Cosmedin (both more recent restructurings). That double ambones were once common is asserted in the sixteenth-century description of the Lateran by Onofrio Panvinio:

> In former times in front of the high altar, where now is the sepulchre of pope Martin V, there were two marble pulpits, which are called ambones, just as there are in the basilicas of St Mary Major, Saint Paul, Saints Cosmas and Damian, and as there were in all the city's basilicas, upon which the

69. Ordines 27, 28, 30A, 31, 32, from the seventh through the ninth-tenth centuries; see Texts E, F, J, M, N, Q.

epistle and the gospel used to be read by the deacons and the subdeacons, and the Roman pontiff or one of the cardinal bishops or priests in the presence of the pontiff, used to preach. Between these two pulpits is the canons' choir, with the altar where the canons used to celebrate high mass.[70]

The Exultet began to be sung from the ambo in the churches of Rome in the course of the twelfth century, to judge from the surviving sources. Eleventh-century manuscripts from San Lorenzo in Damaso, San Saba, and the unidentified church represented by Ricciardana 299, make no mention of an ambo (see Texts T, U, V), nor is there any ambo named in the twelfth-century sacramentary of Santa Maria in Trastevere (Text X). In these cases, however, we have only a single source, with laconic rubrics which do not exclude the use of the ambo.

At Saint Peter's we are somewhat better informed. Although the brief rubrics of the late-eleventh-century San Pietro F 12 mention no ambo, San Pietro F 18 (Text Y) make it clear that by the end of the twelfth century an elaborate modern ceremonial is in place: it involves a *Lumen Christi* procession, with genuflexions; and the deacon ascends into the *pulpitum* and blesses the candle; after which the subdeacon ascends the *ambo* to begin the lessons. There are evidently two pieces of furniture, an ambo and a pulpit. As to the presence of a large paschal candle, we cannot tell, since it is not evident whether the *cereus* carried by the deacon is the same as that blessed in the pulpit, nor whether the candle is lit at the beginning or during the Exultet. We do know that the pope accepted pilgrims' offerings in the amount of ten *libras* of wax for the *facula* of Holy Saturday: this seems a large amount for a portable candle.[71]

70. From Philippe LAUER's edition of Panvinio, in *Le palais de Latran. Étude historique et archéologique* (Paris: Leroux, 1911), 436; my translation. On what is known of the ambones of Santa Maria Maggiore see Sible DE BLAAUW, *Cultus et decor. Liturgie en architectuur in laatantiek en middeleeuws Rome. Basilica Salvatoris Sanctae Mariae Sancti Petri* (Delft: Eburon,1987), 195, 470n237; Italian edition, Studi e Testi 355-6 (Vatican City: Biblioteca Apostolica Vaticana, 1994). Citations are from the 1987 editon.

71. The late twelfth-century "descriptio basilicae vaticanae" by Pietro Mallio mentions this sum of wax twice: "Haec sunt, quae domnus papa de consuetudine recepturus est ab illis, qui eunt ad Confessionem beati Petri...et .x. libras cerae pro facula de sabbato sancto..." (Roberto VALENTINI and Giuseppe ZUCCHETTI, *Codice topografico della città di Roma*, 4 vols., Fonti per la storia d'Italia (Rome: R. Istituto Storico italiano per il medio evo, 1940-53) vol. 3 [Scrittori, secoli XII-XIV, 1946]: 425; "Canonici basilicae Beati Petri accipiunt .x. libras cerae pro facula de Sabbato sancto..." [ibid., 427]).

For the location of the paschal candle in St. Peter's we can refer to the 1590 plan of Tiberio Alfarano, which shows, at the nave corner of the North transept, a "Sugestum marmoreum ad evangelium decantandum", a curved ambo with double staircase; and near it, towards the main altar, the "candelabrum eximium pro Cereo Pascali".[72] Whether this sixteenth-century "sugestum" is either of the pieces of furniture referred to as *ambo* or *pulpitum* in the twelfth century can be doubted; but it is surely the ambo from which the paschal candle is blessed at the time of the engraving; and it may be the same medieval ambo of which a curved fragment survives at St. Peter's built into an altar.[73] The curved front of the fragment could be that seen in Stefaneschi's illustrations in San Pietro B 78, and the two angled staircases of B 78 are not inconsistent with the top view of two staircases in the 1590 plan. Unfortunately nothing seems to survive of this candelabrum.[74]

At the Lateran basilica, two ambones (doubtless those described above by Panvinio) are shown on a floor-plan published by Ciampini in 1693: they are rectangular shapes on either side of the tomb of Martin V (the former canons' choir), evidently attached to nave columns.[75] No mention is made, however, of Panvinio's ambones in the twelfth century Lateran ordo of cardinal Albinus (Text BB), nor does Cencius Savelli mention the place from which the candle is blessed in his late twelfth-century ordo. But these descriptions are brief: an ambo is not excluded. Cencius Savelli says: "Then they go into the church, with the new fire placed in a *canna*, and the deacon says *Lumen Christi* three times, and then [the candle] is blessed by the same deacon" (Text CC).

72. The plan, engraved by Natale Bonifacio da Sebenico, is reproduced in Mariano ARMELLINI, *Le chiese di Roma dal secolo IV al XIX* (Rome: Edizioni R. O. R. E. di Nicola Ruffolo, 1942), vol. 2, facing p. 886, and as an added plate in Tiberio ALFARANO, *De Basilicae Vaticanae antiquissima et nove structura*, ed. Michele CERRATI, Studi e Testi, 26, (Rome: Vatican, 1914). A detail showing this portion of the plan is also in Peter Cornelius CLAUSSEN, *Magistri Doctissimi Romani*. Corpus cosmatorum, 1; Forschungen zur Kunstgeschichte und christlichen Archäologie, 14 (Wiesbaden: Steiner,1987), Abbildung 74.

73. Photograph in Claussen, Abbildung 72.

74. For a proposed reconstruction of the ambo of St. Peter's see CLAUSSEN, *Magistri*, 13-6; see also de BLAAUW, *Cultus et decor*, 339-40.

75. Contini's plan, published in Giovanni Giustino CIAMPINI, *De sacris aedificiis a Constantino Magno constructis* (Rome, 1693), is reproduced in LAUER, *Le palais*, 310. See also Figure 7, a reconstruction of the twelfth-century ground-plan, in de BLAAUW, *Cultus et decor*, 624-25.

A "pulpitum" is described—as the only pulpit of the church?—in the late-eleventh-century "Descriptio Lateranensis ecclesiae"; the pulpit is mentioned only in passing: "Pope Alexander III [d.1181] reposes in front of the pulpit (*pulpitum*) of the church, that is, near the way we take when we go to the Curia."[76]

Bernard, in his twelfth-century *ordo officii ecclesiae lateranensis* (Text DD), gives a more detailed account of the blessing of the candle. He is a fussy and worried writer, saying many things twice, and concerned about possible mishaps. The pulpit and the ambo are evidently a single place: the deacon erects the candle near the *pulpitum* after sext; one place, called "ambo", is used for both the Exultet and the readings: this must be the "pulpitum" just described. The twelfth-century Roman pontifical (Text W) matches Bernard's description in most particulars; though giving less detail, it confirms the ambo as the place for the Exultet.

By the end of the century the second ambo is in place, to judge from the ceremonies described in Vat. lat. 12989, a sacramentary of the Lateran of about 1200 (Text EE), which mentions both an ambo and an "ornatum pulpitum", the latter used for the Exultet.[77]

Perhaps the ambo begin to figure large in the ceremonial of the Exultet because the paschal candle became fixed, no longer carried in procession, but lit from another processional candle; it could then be of almost any size, but certainly more important than the already-large processional candle. Such a large candle, if it is to be proportional in size to the deacon, and especially if the deacon (or an assistant) is to light it, is best placed near the ambo so that the deacon can reach to light the candle, and can touch it, and can place incense in it. A candle placed on a base such as began to be seen in Rome in the twelfth century cannot be reached from the floor.

Best known, and earliest, of the surviving free-standing paschal candles in Rome is that of the basilica of St. Paul's outside the Walls, carved in the late twelfth century from re-used spolia, perhaps under the abbacy of Peter

76. "Alexander Papa III jacet ante pulpitum ecclesiae, vel iuxta viam quando imus ad curiam"; ed. VALENTINI and ZUCCHETTI, *Codice topografico della città di Roma*, 3: 350. The pulpit is placed near the entrance to the canons' choir, on a line that joins the choir and the co-called Council door. See LAUER, *Le palais*, 181; DE BLAAUW, *Cultus et decor*, 122.

77. For a summary of the rite and a discussion of the location of the ambo, see DE BLAAUW, *Cultus et decor*, 146-47, and figure 7, p. 624-25.

of Capua.[78] We know little of the specific ceremonial of this church, nor do we have any evidence of its medieval ambones. But such a large base—it is 5.6 meters from the floor to the base of the candle—could not be reached from the ground to light a candle or place incense in it.

Other Roman candlesticks, mostly of the thirteenth and fourteenth centuries, vary in height considerably, from the relative modest one at Santi Cosma e Damiano to the tall early fourteenth-century one at Santa Maria in Trastevere.[79] Particularly noteworthy is the famous arrangement of church furniture at San Clemente, which has been in place more or less continuously since the twelfth century. Here there are two ambones (or an ambo and a pulpit), and the paschal candlestick is attached to the enclosure (the so-called "schola cantorum") in such a way as to be accessible from the ambo: this matches the possibilities envisioned both in the Lateran ordines and in the standardized Franciscan liturgy. But most of the surviving arrangements of two ambones, and most surviving paschal candles, are of a later date than the rubrics we have seen that specify the use of the ambo. They are responses to liturgical change, rather than the instruments of it.

We cannot say why the ambo began to be used, nor where the idea came from; it seems to be part of the Roman renewal of the twelfth century that saw a considerable amount of rebuilding and liturgical expansion.[80]

The practice of blessing the candle from the ambo had long been used in southern Italy, where it is depicted in many of the decorated Exultet rolls. One such roll is now in the Roman area: the roll from Montecassino brought there probably by Leo Marsicanus, monk of Montecassino, author of the

---

78. On Peter see W. MALECZEK, *Petrus Capuanus. Kardinal, Legat am vierter Kreuzzug, Theologe († 1214)* (Vienna, 1988).

79. Other candles include those of Santa Cecilia in Trastevere (ca. 1250); San Lorenzo fuori le mura (ca. 1230), San Lorenzo in Lucina (ca. 1230-50, but perhaps a fake, according to a suggestion by Professor Julian Gardner), Santa Maria in Cosmedin (ca. 1300). On all these and more, see CLAUSSEN, *Magistri doctissimi romani*. Lauer mentions that one or both 13th-century fragmentary twisted columns with mosaic, one of which is supported by a lion, which are preserved in the cloister of the Lateran basilica, may be from paschal candlesticks (LAUER, *Le palais*, 233 fig. 88).

80. See Peter Cornelius CLAUSSEN, "Renovatio Romae. Erneuerungsphasen römischer Architektur im 11. und 12. Jahrhundert", in Bernhard SCHIMMELPFENNIG and Ludwig SCHMUGGE, eds, *Rom im hohen Mittelalters* (Sigmaringen: Jan Thorbecke, 1992), 87-125 with 22 plates.

chronicle of Montecassino, and cardinal bishop of Ostia: the roll is now at Velletri, where he left it.[81]

Such a practice could well have originated in the south and been imitated in Rome beginning in the twelfth century. It does not appear, though, that southern practice was adopted wholesale. We have seen that the *Lumen Christi*, also a possible southern importation, is not always accompanied by the use of the ambo, even though both were the regular practice of the south. And the *Lumen Christi* in the south is nowhere chanted in procession. So the practices, if they were indeed brought from the south, were adapted selectively and separately.

CONCLUSIONS: CONSOLIDATION AND PERSISTENCE

By the time that Vat. lat. 12989 was made for the Lateran basilica about 1200, the liturgical reforms of Innocent III had taken hold, and the rubrics used in 12989 were adopted, with necessary generalization, in a great many manuscripts, from a variety of churches (including Santa Maria Maggiore and Santa Maria *ad Martyres*) as the standard version of the rites of Holy Saturday, with an authority for the church as a whole which goes beyond the description of a localized practice; versions of these rubrics are incorporated into the ordinal of Innocent III and the Pontifical of the Roman Curia.[82]

The developed rite of the Lateran is seen in the late eleventh-century "ordo officiorum ecclesiae lateranensis" of Bernard, the Roman pontifical of the twelfth century, the Lateran missal Vat. lat. 12989, and the ordinal of Innocent III (texts W, DD, EE). They have these elements in common:

(1) A special processional candle (Bernard: "candelas glomeratas"; Pontifical: arundo with triple candle; Vat. lat. 12989: arundo of 3 1/2 cubits with a triple candle);

(2) A procession with *Lumen Christi*, in some cases raising the voice (Bernard, Pontifical) or the hands (12989), and pausing at three places (12989,

---

81. It is now unfortunately fragmentary. On this roll see Pietro FEDELE, "*L'Exultet* di Velletri", *Mélanges d'archéologie et d'histoire* 30 (1910), 313-320 and plates VII-XI; KELLY, *The Exultet*, 253-4.

82. The thirteenth-century pontifical of the Roman Curia omits the details of the blessing of the candle ("Deinde procedatur ad benedictionem cerei, que fit prout traditur in missali"), but the surrounding rubrics correspond to those in text EE; the pontifical is edited in Michel ANDRIEU, *Le pontifical romain au moyen âge*, 4 vols., Studi e Testi 86-88, 99 (Vatican City: Biblioteca Apostolica Vaticana, 1938-41), 2, the relevant portion being found on pp.470-72.

Bernard: entrance to church; entrance to choir; middle of choir—or, for Bernard, near the candle);

(3) Ascent to the ambo (Bernard, Pontifical: ambo; 12989: ornatum pulpitum—as opposed to the ambo mentioned in the same document) for blessing the candle;

(4) A separate large candle (Pontifical, 12989: magnus cereus), presumably in a special candelabrum. This candle will have grains of incense inserted by the deacon, so it must either be in or on the ambo, or near to it and so tall as to be accessible from the ambo.

(5) This candle is lit from the processional candle just before the Exultet (Pontifical, 12989), and the incense grains are placed in it at the words *Suscipe*, etc. (Pontifical); at the words *Qui licet divisus*, etc., seven lamps and two candelabra are lit (Pontifical).

(6) The pope is not present for the blessing of the candle. He arrives in procession from the sacristy during (Pontifical) or after (12989) the blessing, ascends his throne, and is present for the lessons.

The ceremonial just described was reorganized in the Franciscan regula missal of about 1200 (Text FF), and further revised by Haymo of Faversham in the 1240s for use in any church, in particular a Franciscan monastery. Haymo's revised form (Text GG) was widely adopted, in Rome as elsewhere; it is this rite that is depicted in Cardinal Stefaneschi's pictures in Vatican San Pietro B 78, designed for use in St. Peter's.[83] Here the deacon is assisted in the ambo by the subdeacon and two acolytes: it is the subdeacon who carries the triple candle resembling a pitchfork with which the new fire is brought to the ambo, and who lights the paschal candle (not at the beginning, but at *ignis accendit*). Also in the course of the Exultet the deacon inserts the incense at *In huius igitur noctis gratia suscipe sancte pater incensi huius sacrificium*; at *O vere beata nox* seven lamps are lit.[84] Interestingly, Haymo makes no mention of the singing of *Lumen Christi*.

83. The few rubrics contained in this musical document match those of the Haymonian ordo, Text FF.

84. The lighting of the candle during, and not before, the Exultet is specified also in Bernard's ordo (Text DD). There is some disagreement among the sources as to where these three ceremonies—inserting the incense, lighting the candle, lighting the lamps—take place in the course of the text. Compare texts W, DD, EE, FF. Only Bernard seems to have it right: the appropriate words: *incensi, ignis accendit, qui licet sit divisus*, accompany the actions of incense, lighting the candle, and dividing its light among other lamps. The trouble is that in the text *ignis accendit* is followed immediately by *qui licet*: Bernard calls for a pause ("post paululum"), but Haymo prefers to delay the third action, putting it where the text is less appropriate.

Even in the absence of the fuller documentation that would make our task easier, it is possible to trace some basic outlines for the history of this small part of the Holy Saturday ceremonial. Basic elements of the pattern are these:

1. The paschal candle is adopted at Rome, from the outside inward, beginning in the sixth century, and proceeding from the parrochia to the tituli, and finally, but much later, adopted by the Lateran.

2. The widely known text *Exultet iam angelica* is substituted for the earlier Roman *Deus mundi conditor*.

3. The threefold *Lumen Christi*, not originally a part of the ceremony, comes to precedes the blessing of the candle.

4. The deacon begins to bless the candle from the ambo, and a new period of church furnishings in the twelfth century makes this ceremony an impressive and highly visible moment.

5. Finally, an exceptionally striking melody is adopted, perhaps through the Franciscan books influenced by Norman elements.

Other details of the ceremony and later alterations in the rite deserve studies of their own for what they reveal about varying practice: these include (1) the source of the new fire, reserved from Maundy Thursday or struck anew; (2) the means of carrying the new fire into the church—whether with the candle to be blessed, with a triple candlestick, or otherwise; (3) the moment at which the paschal candle is lit; (4) the practice of blessing incense and inserting it into the candle. All these elements are visible in the texts presented here, but they are outside the central purpose of this study.

Even at later stages in this development, after the Exultet is adopted everywhere in Rome, traces of the older history of this ceremony can be detected in the city. We remember that the Roman liturgy, or at least the Papal liturgy, did not employ the Exultet; but that in the rites of the suburban churches of the city a candle was used and blessed as described in the Gelasian ordo and related documents. The Lateran practice of the twelfth century and later reminds us of its history: the pope is not present for the blessing of the candle, for the papal office still begins with the vigil of lessons and prayers, and the Exultet ceremony is in some sense extra-liturgical at the Lateran (Texts DD, EE). Likewise, the Gelasian ordo survives, at least in part, in the prayer *Deus qui divitias* which precedes the first of the lessons of the vigil: a prayer not used in papal ceremonial, and which is expressly forbidden in many documents deriving from papal practice.[85] And yet the Gelasian prayer *does* persist, notably in places not so centrally connected with the great basilicas of the Roman church: San Saba, San Trifone, Santi Andrea e Bartolomeo, and elsewhere.[86] It persists also in Florence, Riccardiana 299, a manuscript attributed to the Lateran,[87] but whose Holy Saturday rite contains so many "Gelasian" elements that an origin in another church of the city seems more likely.

The litanies which begin the rites of Holy Saturday in the Gelasian ordo persist on occasion: they are still used at San Saba in the eleventh century, and at the church where Riccardiana 299 was used. Generally, however, litanies tend to disappear; this is probably because they are replaced with a similar event: the threefold *Lumen Christi* with which the procession reaches the central space of the church. And the pope's entrance, "processionaliter cum silentio", in the twelfth-century Lateran ordines and in the ordo of Innocent III, recalls that the Exultet is not part of the papal ceremonies, and also that the papal (as opposed to the urban) practice is for the entrance to be made, not with a litany, but with silence.

Indeed, even after the consolidation of liturgical practice by the adoption of Franciscan books, and the revision of the ordo of Holy Saturday by Haymo of Faversham, the old Gelasian blessing *Deus mundi conditor*, used in eighth-century Rome but apparently long forgotten since its replacement by the *Exultet*, survives in part: its final section, *Veniat quaesumus omnipotens Deus super hoc incensum*, is included as a blessing of the incense which will be inserted into the candle. This prayer, originally the final paragraph of the Gelasian blessing, referred to the lit candle ("incensum"), but it had been removed as early as the Roman-German Pontifical of the tenth century. By a reinterpretation of the word "incensum," however, the prayer survived for many centuries as a blessing of incense for a ceremony that did not exist, so far as we know, when the *Deus mundi conditor* was used in the churches of suburban Rome in the seventh century.[88]

85. "Et ante *In principio* non dicit orationem": ordo 24, Text B; see also ordines 27, 28, 29, 31, PRG, Bernard ordo (Texts H, J, K, Q, S, DD).

86. It is found in Angelica 1343, San Pietro F 14, San Pietro F 15, Santa Maria Maggiore 40.

87. See SUPINO MARTINI, *Roma e l'area grafica*, 54-55 and n35.

88. The *Veniat* is an integral part of *Deus mundi conditor* in the Gellone, Angoulême, and Phillipps sacramentaries (for editions see above, n. 30). In the Gelasian

THE EXULTET AT ROME   43

What we call the Roman liturgy is not a single thing. It owes its existence to a long period of development, which includes the adoption and adaptation of a variety of practices. Moreover, the customs of the city are not everywhere uniform, even at a given moment in time. The process of accepting and integrating the Exultet, one small moment in the annual round of the Roman liturgy, gives just a brief view onto the complexity of the history of liturgy in the city of Rome.

Sacramentary the *Veniat* is separated from the main prayer, and labeled *Benedictio super incensum*, still presumably referring to the candle (MOHLBERG, *Liber sacramentorum*, no. 429, pp. 69-70). The *Veniat* is lacking at the end of the version of *Deus mundi conditor* transmitted in the tenth-century Romano-Germanic Pontifical (see VOGEL and ELZE, *Le pontifical*, 95-6). In later Roman pontificals, however, the *Veniat* survives as a blessing of incense (see ANDRIEU, *Le pontifical*, 3: 471). See also FRANZ, *Die kirchlichen*, 1: 530-1; SCHMIDT, *Hebdomada sancta*, 2: 638. See Texts EE, FF, GG.

APPENDIX

TEXTS RELATED TO THE EXULTET AT ROME

TABLE OF CONTENTS

VII. Documents describing the practice of the Lateran basilica
AA. Benedict, Liber politicus (c. 1140-43)

BB. Albinus (1188)

CC. Cencius Savelli, late 12th century

DD. Bernard (late 12th century?)

EE. Lateran, c. 1200 (Vat. lat. 12989); S Maria Maggiore (S Maria Maggiore 52); S Maria ad Martyres (Angelica 1606); San Lorenzo fuori le mura (Madrid 730); adopted with revisions into the Orsini sacramentary (Avignon 100), the Ordinal of Innocent III, and the Pontifical of the Roman Curia

VIII. Later, generalized documents
FF. Franciscan Regula missal, as found in Assisi 607 (1225-50) and others (including Rome, Bibl. Corsiniana 376 (c. 1261-64) and Vat. Rossi 199 (14th c.)

GG. Roman curia (Franciscan) missal, as revised by Haymo of Faversham, 1243-44: Vat. San Pietro E 9 (late 13th c.?)

I. PAPAL CEREMONIAL, WITH NO CANDLE

A. Ordo Romanus 23 (700-750)

This ordo describes papal rites, with no evident adaptation for other churches.

1. Sabbato sancto, hora qua[si] VII, ingreditur clerus aeclesiam, nam domnus apostolicus non.

2. Et vadunt ad secretarium diaconi scilicet et subdiaconi in planetis et accendent duo regionarii per unumquemque faculas de ipso lumine, quod de VI feria absconditum est, et veniunt ad altare. Diaconi stant ad sedem et episcopi sedent in choro.

3. Et ascendit lector in ambonem et legit lectionem grecam. Sequitur *In principio*, et orationes et *Flectamus genua* et tract[um].

4. Et dum hoc completum fuerit, descendent ad fontes et dicit scola cantorum letania III vicibus, *Christe audi nos*, et reliqua. Postea benedicit domnus papa fontem et dum venit in eo loco, ubi dicit: *Descendat in hanc plenitudinem*, deponent faculas regionarii qui illas tenent in fontes.

(Michel ANDRIEU, *Les Ordines Romani du haut moyen âge*, 5 vols, Spicilegium Sacrum Lovaniense. Études et documents, 11, 23, 24, 28, 29 (Louvain: Spicilegium Sacrum Lovaniense, 1931, 1948, 1951, 1956, 1961), 3: 272-3)

B. Ordo Romanus 24 (second half of the eighth century)

This ordo adapts the papal liturgy for the use of a bishop in his cathedral. It seeks to reflect the use of the Lateran, making adaptations where necessary. The user is cautioned that there is no prayer before the first lesson: this is the practice of the titular churches, which the compiler evidently knows, but not the practice at the Lateran. The blessing of a candle is omitted here, of course, because it was not practiced at the Lateran. But if candles were regularly blessed at the titular churches, would not the compiler have given us the same sort of warning that he does for the prayer before the first lesson?

Sabbato sancto, veniunt omnes in ecclesiam et tunc inluminantur duo cerei, tenentibus duobus notariis, unus in dextro cornu altaris at alter in sinistro. Et ascendit lector in ambonem. Non pronuntiat: *Lectio libri Genesis*, sed inchoat: *In principio* plane; similiter et illas lectiones omnes. Et ante *In principio* non dicit orationem.

(ANDRIEU, *Les Ordines* 3: 295)

C. Ordo Romanus 30 B (late 8th century)

The source is evidently Roman; note the Constantinian basilica, and the absence of priests; except for the priest who says the collects: this is an adaptation, but keeping very close to the Roman model. The compiler had ordo 30A at hand, but he deliberately omitted the blessing of the candle, based on his knowledge of Rome or of Roman documents.

1. Ordo qualiter in sabbato sancto agendum est. Media nocte surgendum est et, sicut superius taxavimus, ita fiat excepto in luminaribus, sed tantum una lampada accendatur propter legendum.
2. Post hoc vero die illa, octava hora diei, procedit ad ecclesiam omnis clerus seu et omnis populus et ingreditur archidiaconus in sacrario cum aliis diaconibus et mutant se sicut in die sancta. Et egrediuntur de sacrario et duae faculae ante ipsos ancense *(sic)* portantes a subdiacono et veniunt ante altare diaconi, osculantur ipsum, et vadunt ad sedem pontificis et ipsi subdiaconi stant retro altare, tenentes faculas usquedum complentur lectiones.
3. Deinde annuit archidiaconus subdiacono regionario ut legatur lectio prima, in greco sive in latino. Deinde psallit sacerdos infra thronum in dextra parte altaris et dicit: *Oremus;* et diaconus: *Flectamus genua*, et post paululum dicit: *Levate.* Et sequitur oracio *Deus qui mirabiliter creasti hominem.* Deinde secuntur lectiones et cantica seu et oraciones, tam grece quam latine, sicut ordinem habent.
4. Lectionibus expletis, egrediuntur de ecclesia quae apellatur Constantiniana et descendit archidiaconus cum aliis diaconibus, et ipsas faculas ante ipsos, usque in sacrarium qui est iuxta fontes et ibi expectant pontificem... .

(ANDRIEU, *Les Ordines* 3: 471-2)

II. ROMAN BLESSING OF A CANDLE IN TITULAR CHURCHES

D. The Liber Pontificalis: first compiled in ninth century

Duchesne (I, 255) thinks the first edition refers to agni, *only later changed to candle, suggesting that a candle was not blessed when the book was composed, but that the practice was in use by the second edition.*

Andrieu (Les ordines, III, 321n3), points out that both cera *and* cereus *are used of the candle; and also that the use of wax for the* agnus *is itself not evidently early, the earliest witness being Ordo 26.*

(On Pope Zosimus, 417-418, a Greek):
1. Hic multa constituit ecclesiae et fecit constitutum ut diacones leva texta haberent de palleis linostimis per parrochias, et ut cera benedicatur.

(In the second edition, first half of the 6th century:)
2. Hic multa constituit ecclesiae et fecit constitutum ut diacones leva tecta habent de palleis linostimis; et per parrocia concessa licentia cereum benedici.

> (Louis Marie Olivier DUCHESNE, *Le liber pontificalis*, 2d ed., 3 vols, the third ed. Cyrille Vogel. [Paris: E. de Boccard, 1955-7], 1: 225n2)

E. Gelasian sacramentary, seventh century (Vat. Reg. lat. 316)

The chief features to note here, in distinction from the rite at the Lateran, are (1) beginning with a litany; (2) blessing the candle (with Deus mundi conditor, not Exultet); and (3) the presence of a collect before the first lesson (evident in the sacramentary from the arrangement that follows.)

1. Sequitur ordo qualiter Sabbato sancto ad uigiliam ingrediantur.
2. Primitus enim, uiiia hora diei mediante procedunt ad ecclesiam et ingrediuntur in sacrario et induunt se uestimentis sicut mos est.
3. Et incipit clerus laetania et procedit sacerdos de sacrario cum ordinibus sacris. Ueniunt ante altare stantes inclinato capite usquedum dicent *Agnus Dei...*
4. Deinde surgens sacerdos ab oratione uadit retro altare, sedens in sede sua. Deinde ueniens archidiaconus ante altare, accipiens de lumine quod VI feria absconsum fuit, faciens crucem super cereum et inluminans eum, et conpletur ab ipso benedictio caerei. *Deus, mundi conditor...*
5. Post hec surgens sacerdos a sede sua et dicit orationes de uigilia paschae, sicut in sacramentorum continentur.

> (Vatican City, BAV Reg. lat. 316, f. 67v-69, ed. Leo Cunibert MOHLBERG, Leo Eizenhöfer, and Petrus SIFFRIN, ed., *Liber sacramentorum romanae aeclesiae ordinis anni circuli (Cod. Vat. Reg. lat. 316/Paris Bibl. Nat. 7193, 41/56)*, Rerum ecclesiasticarum documenta, Series maior, Fontes 4 (Rome: Herder, 1960), 68-70)

F. Ordo 30A, which repeats Gelasian form (8th century, second half)

This ordo, made for fratres in a church where the celebrant may be a bishop, may have been made for a cathedral. Much is borrowed from ordo 28, but the practice here is very close to the rubrics of the Gelasian sacramentary.

1. Ordo qualiter in sabbato sancto vig[i]l[iae] aguntur. Media nocte in psal[mis], in lec[tionibus] in resp[onsoria], in an[tiphoni]s, in lucernis accendendis vel extinguendis, sicut superius diximus ita fiat.
2. P[ost] hoc, die vero illa, octava hora diei mediante, ad ecclesiam eundum e[st] et ingrediuntur in sacrario et induunt se vestimenta.
3. Et incipit prima letania clerus et procedens sacerdos de sacrario cum ordinibus sacris et veniunt ante altare, stantes inclinato capite, usquedum dic[unt] *Agnus Dei*.

4. Deinde surgens sacerdos ab oratione vadit retro altare sedens in sede sua et veniens archidiac[onus] ante altare, accipiens de lum[ine] q[uod] VI feria absconsum fuit, faciens crucem super cereum et inluminans eum et completur ab ipso benedictio cerei *Deus mundi conditor*.

5. Hoc expleto, incipiunt lec[tione]s legere sicut ordinem habent.

(ANDRIEU, *Les Ordines* 3: 456-7)

III. DOCUMENTS MENTIONING THE BLESSING AS NON-ROMAN

G. Ordo Romanus 26: 3d quarter of the 8th century, made for a church of suburban Rome

Two rites are described here; only "in forensibus civitatibus" is the candle blessed; in "the catholic church within the city of Rome" wax is made into lambs.

1. Ea vero die, hora nona, faciunt excuti ignem de lapide in loco foras basilica; si ibidem oratorium habuerint, super portam ibi excutiunt; sin vero, in loco quo consideraverit prior, ita ut ex eo possit candela accendi. Quae candela in arundine debet poni et a mansionario ecclesiae portari, presente congregatione vel populo. Et de ipso igne continuo, in eadem ecclesia vel loco ubi accenditur, lampada una servetur usque in sabbato sancto ad inluminandum cereum, qui eodem die benedicendus est, ordine quod in Sacramentorum continetur.

2. Et hic ordo cerei benedicendi in forensibus civitatibus agitur. Nam in catholica ecclesia infra civitatem romanam non sic benedicitur.

3. Sed mane prima sabbato sancto in Lateranis venit arcidiaconus in ecclesia et fundit ceram in vas mundum maiore et miscitat ibidem oleo et benedicit ceram et ex ea fundit in similitudine agnorum et servat eos in loco mundo.

4. In octavas vero paschae dantur ipsi agni ab archidiacono in ipsa ecclesia post missas et communionem populo et ex eos faciunt in domos suas incensum accendi ad suffumigandum pro qualecumque tribulatione eis evenerit necessitas. Similiter et in forensibus civitatibus de cereo faciunt.

5. Nam, quod intermisimus, accepit mansionarius prior iam ficta candela in manu sua inluminata in canna, prosequente eum populo cum supplici silentio, ita ut summitas candelae quae inluminatur altare versa inclinata respiciat illa ecclesia quam sunt ingressuri, quae tamen prius absque lumine erit, preparatis ante altare septem lampadibus ita composite, ut, absque ulla impedimenti cuiuscumque retardatione, manu mansionarii cum eadem candela possint acendi. Ac deinceps, preparatis custodibus, omne lumen decoret ecclesiam (*2 of 4 mss: omni lumine decoretur ecclesia*)... .

6. Et hic ordo agitur cena domini mane; sic et in sabbato sancto, sicut in isto die taxavimus, ea vero ratione ut hora nona, feria VI, excuciatur ignis de lapide, sicut diximus, et ab archidiacono portetur; sic in sabbato sancto: sabbato vero sancto ab episcopus iuniore portetur.

(ANDRIEU, *Les Ordines* 3: 325-7, 329)

H. One version of ordo Romanus 28

Ordo 28 (text M, below, ca. 900) specifies a prayer plus the second part of Exultet; one MS, however (Cologne, Bibl. cap. MS 138), adds a text almost identical to that or ordo 26 (text G).

1. ... quia omnis anterior extingui debet. [see text of Ordo 28, below]
2. Et hic ordo cerei benedicendi in forensibus civitatibus agitur. Nam in catholica ecclesia infra civitatem romanam non sic benedicitur.
3. Sed mane primo sabbato sancto venit archidiaconus in ecclesia. Et fundit cera in vas mundum maiore et miscitat ibidem oleum et benedicit cera et ex ea fundit in similitudine agnorum et servat eos in loco mundo.
4. In octabas vero paschae dantur ipsi agni ab archidiacono in ipsa ecclesia post missas et communione populo et ex eis faciunt in domos suas incensum accendi ad suffumigandum pro qualecumque tribulatione eis evenerit necessitas. Similiter et in forensibus civitatibus similiter de cereo faciunt.
5. Nam, quod intermisimus, accipit mansionarius prior candela in manu sua iluminata in canna, prosequente eum populo cum supplicii *(sic)* silentio, ita ut summitas candelae quae inluminatur altare versa inclinata respiciat illam ecclesiam quam sunt ingressuri, quae tamen prius absque lumine erit, preparatis ante altare septem lampadibus ita compositae, ut absque ulla impedimenti cuiuscumque recordatione *(sic)* manu mansionarii eadem candela possit accendi. Ac deinceps, preparatis custodibus, omne lumen decoret ecclesia[m] et sic permaneat inluminata usque ad vigilias.

(ANDRIEU, *Les Ordines* 3:, 404n)

IV. DOCUMENTS IN WHICH THE CANDLE SEEMS A LATER ADDITION

I. Ordo Romanus 17 (late 8th century)

This ordo is odd. It is monastic, with fratres and abbas, and is presided over by a priest. There is no baptism. And the candle seems to be tacked on as a separate ceremony. They come out in procession with litanies. The deacon lights the candle from reserved fire, in the middle of the church, not on the ambo. And he blesses it with a prayer (Deus mundi conditor?) followed by something that begins like the preface: undoubtedly the second part of the Exultet. Then all retire into the sacristy (taking the candle with them?). Then there is a new entrance, with candles lit from that fire, with another litany, for the vigil. There is a prayer before the first reading, which is a Gelasian symptom. Then they exit again. A third litany brings everybody out again, for mass, when a star appears in the sky.

1. In sabbato sancto, hora nona diei, ingrediuntur ad vigilias. Primitus enim induunt sacerdotes, una cum diaconibus, vestibus cum quibus vigilias celebrantur. Et procedunt de sacrario levite tantum cum subdiaconibus, duo et duo inxta se adherentes, sine luminibus accensis, canentibus interrim fratribus letania.

2. Ut autem ante altare venerint, stantes in ordines suos, ille qui cereum benedici debet, stans in medio, postulans eos pro se orare et faciens crucem super cereum et accipiens a subdiacono lumen, quod in parasceven absconditum fuerit, et accenso cyreo dicit: *Dominus vobiscum*. Resp[ondent] omnes: *Et cum spiritu tuo*. Deinde dicit: *Oremus*, et dicit orationem primam. Deinde dicit: *Dominus vobiscum*. Resp[ondent] omnes: *Et cum spiritu tuo*. Iterum dicit: *Sursum corda*. Resp[ondent]: *Habemus a domino*. Et iterum dicit: *Gratias agamus domino Deo nostro*. Resp[ondent]: *Dignum et iustum est*, vel omnia sicut in Sacramentorum commemorat. Benedicto autem cereo, revertuntur in sacrario.

3. Deinde procedant sacerdotis de sacrario cum diaconibus iuxta ordines suos, cum accensis cereis de ipso lumine cum turabulis timiamatum. Iterum canuntur letaniam. Ipsam autem expletam, stantibus vero [diaconis, diaconibus?] et dat sacerdus orationem retro altare, sicut mos est, et sedentibus sacerdotibus in ordines suos. Et ingrediuntur ad legendum. Post unamquamque lectionem, dat sacerdus orationem, sicut in Sacramentorum commemoratur.

(ANDRIEU, *Les Ordines* 3: 189-91)

J. Ordo Romanus 27 (second half of 8th century): Two versions

This is essentially a repetition of Ordo 24 (text B). But two manuscripts of this ordo have different versions for this portion. MS R essentially repeats the Gelasian ordo (but without specifying Deus mundi conditor), and then adds the two candles from the Lateran. The compiler is perhaps trying to include all the ceremonies he knows about.

Sabbato sancto veniunt omnes in ecclesia et tunc inluminantur duo cerei, tenentibus duobus notariis, unus in dextro cornu altaris et alter in sinistro. Et ascendit lector in ambone. Non pronuntiat: *Lectio libri Genesis*, sed incoat: *In principio*, plane. Similiter et illas alias lectiones omnes. Ante *In principio* non dicit orationem.

[ANDRIEU, *Les Ordines* 3: 359]

MS E (Vat. Pal. lat. 47, 9th c.):
Que facienda sint in sabbato sancto. Primitus legantur XII lectiones cum singulis collectis et cantentur tractus. Post novissimum tractum, sequuntur collecte II. Deinde letania; deinde "Gloria in excelsis deo"; deinde collecta ad missam...

(ANDRIEU, *Les Ordines* 3: 358n)

MS R (Paris, BN Lat. 12405, early 10 c.):
1. Sabbato sancto mane reddant infantes symbolum et post hec catecizantur ipsi infantes.
2. Eodem vero die, hora die octava mediante, veniunt omnes ad ecclesiam et ingreditur clerus in sacrarium et induunt se vestimentis sacris sicut mos est.
3. Et incipit clerus letaniam et procedit sacerdos de sacrario cum ordinibus sacris; veniens ante altare stat inclinato capite usquedum dicunt Agnus Dei.

4. Tunc surgens vadit retro altare sedens in sede sua. Deinde veniens archidiaconus ante altare et accipit de lumine quod sexta feris absconsum fuit faciensque crucem super cereum manu sua et inluminans eum, completur ab ipso benedictio cerei.
5. Ac deinceps peraguntur lectiones et orationes de vigilia pasche, sicut in Sacramentorum continetur.
6. Verumtamen quando egreditur de sacrario inluminantur due cerei, quos tenent duo notarii precedentes pontificem, ut, cum ad altare venerint, stet in dextro cornu altaris, unus [a dextris] et alter in sinistro.

(ANDRIEU, *Les Ordines* 3: 359n)

K. Ordo Romanus 29 (ninth century, last quarter)

This ordo, almost all derived from ordo 27 (text J), differs from it substantially here. This passage seems to describe the blessing of the paschal candle after the lessons (as is done at Benevento).

More likely, perhaps, is that the frankish monk who adapted this ordo from his knowledge of Roman practice (without a paschal candle) added the Frankish practice to his ordo, but happened to place it is the wrong order, giving two different ceremonies related to new fire.

1. In nocte vero sancti sabbati surgent ad vigilias hora octava et omnia, sicut in quinta feria ordinavimus, peragantur. Sabbato sancto, hora septima, veniant omnes in ecclesia et excutiant ignem super portam et inluminetur candela et ab abbate portetur, prosequente eum populo cum suppplici silentio, et de ipso lumine duo cerei inluminentur, tenentibus duobus notariis, unus in dextro cornu altaris et alter in sinistro.
2. Et ascendat lector in ambonem, non pronuntians: *Lectio libri Genesis*, sed inchoat: *In principio*, plane. Qua perlecta, dicat sacerdos: *Oremus*; et diaconus: *Flectamus genua*. Et orent quousque diaconus dicat: *Levate*. Et surgant et sacerdos det orationem *Deus qui mirabiliter creasti hominem*. Similiter et illas lectiones omnes. Ante *In principio* non dicat orationem.
3. Expletis lectionibus, regrediantur foras, praecedentibus eum duobus notariis cereos tenentes, et induantur sacerdotes et diaconi et ministri et ceteri clerici dalmaticis et stolis et omni ornament.
4. Et inluminetur cereus, qui eodem die benedicendus est, de igni qui quinta feria excussus est. Et intrent in ecclesiam et benedicatur cereus a diacono, sicut in Sacramentorum continetur.
5. Expleta benedictione cerei, statim veniens unus minister, tenens ampullas in manibus suis, stans in dextro corno altaris, et descendat ipse praecedens pontificem ad fontes... .

(ANDRIEU, *Les Ordines* 3: 443-4)

V. Frankish Documents Using a Candle

L. Ordo Romanus 16 (8th c., third quarter): "candles" are blessed, no text named

This monastic Frankish ordo speaks of blessing CEREI. The ordo, and some of its language, recall the practice of ordines 28 and 32 (texts M and N: procession in silence; priests seated but deacons standing), but without the detail found there.

1. In sabbato sancto, paululum post ora nona, ad vigilias. Primitus autem vestiuntur se sacerdotes una cum diaconibus vestibus suis et procedunt de sagrario cum ceriis vel turribolis et intrant in ecclesia cum silencio, nihil canentis, stantis in ordine suo.
2. Inde vero benedicentur cerei a diacono, ordine quo in Sacramentorum habetur.
3. Et statim accedunt et sedunt sacerdotes in sidilia sua, diaconibus vero tantum permanent stantes iuxta ordinem suum, sive iuxta abb[a]t[em], vel pres[biterum] qui missas celebratur, et incipiunt legere leccionis de ipsa nocte una cum cantica eorum, quas in Sacramentorum commemorat.

(Andrieu, *Les Ordines* 3: 152)

Documents Describing a Combination of Prayer and Preface

M. Ordo Romanus 28: Blessing of candle: prayer plus a preface (the second part of the Exultet?) (ca. 800)

This ordo is based on others, but not in this portion. It combines an opening prayer (perhaps Deus mundi conditor, or the Exultet, or even a blessing of fire); and continues with something sung to the tone of the canon (i.e., the preface). This may be the second part of the Exultet, whose text is however not clear.

1. Hora nona ingrediuntur in sacrarium sacerdotes et levitae et induunt se vestimentis cum quibus vigilias celebrare debent.
2. Et, accenso cereo, procedunt simul omnes de sacrario cum ipso cereo in ecclesia cum silentio, nihil cantantes; et ponitur in candelabro ante altare.
3. Et unus diaconus rogat unum de sacerdotibus vel levitis, qui ibidem revestiti adstant, pro se orare. Et, ut surrexerit, dicit ipse diaconus: *Dominus vobiscum.* Resp: *Et cum spiritu tuo.* Et dicit orationem, sicut in Sacramentorum continetur.
4. Postea sedent sacerdotes in sedilia sua; diaconi permanent stantes.
5. Ipsa expleta, dicit: *Dominus vobiscum.* Resp.: *Et cum spiritu tuo.* Inde: *Sursum corda.* Resp.: *Habemus ad dominum.* Inde: *Gratias agamus domino Deo nostro.* Resp.: *Dignum et iustum est.* Inde vero accedit in consecrationem cerei, decantando quasi canonem.
6. Inde vero accenduntur in duobus candelabris duo cerei et de ipso igne accendunt in omni domo, quia omnis anterior extingui debet.

7. Deinde ascendit lector in ambonem. Non pronuntiat: *Lectio libri Genesis*, sed inchoat: *In principio*, plane; et illas alias lectiones similiter. Et ante *In principio* non dicat orationem.

(ANDRIEU, *Les Ordines* 3: 403-4)

N. Ordo Romanus 32, MS Paris BN Late 14088 (Corbie?, late 9th century)

This ordo, otherwise different, borrows in this manuscript the same text as Ordo 28 (text M), describing the combination of prayer and preface for the blessing of the candle. Here, however, there are Gelasian characteristics: a litany (which however comes after the blessing of the candle); and the collect preceding the lessons. The lessons are not named.

1. ...hora nona ingrediuntur in sacrarium sacerdotes et levite et ind[u]unt se vestimentis cum quibus vigilia sancta celebrare debent.
2. Et, accenso cereo, procedunt simul omnes de sacrario cum ipso cereo in aecclesia cum silentio nihil canentes et ponitur in candelabro ante altare.
3. Et unus diaconus rogat pro se unum de sacerdotibus vel levitis qui ibidem revestiti adstant pro se orare. Et ut surrexerint, dicit ipse diaconus: *Dominus vobiscum.* Resp.: *Et cum spiritu tuo.* Et dicit orationem, sicut in Sacramentorum libro continetur.
4. Postea sedent sacerdotes, diaconi permanent stantes.
5. Ipse expleta, dicit: *Dominus vobiscum.* Resp.: *Et cum spiritu tuo.* Inde: *Sursum corda.* Resp.: *Habemus ad dominum. Gratias agamus domino Deo nostro.* Resp.: *Dignum et iustum est.* Inde vero accedit in consecratione cerei, decantando quasi canonem.
6. Inde vero accenduntur in duobus candelabris duo cerei et de ipso igne accendunt in omni domo, quia omnis ignis anterior extingui debet.
7. Postea canet clerus letania et procedunt sacerdotes vel levite, induti vestimentis cum quibus vigilia sancta celebrare debent.
8. Et stat sacerdos retro altare et dicit: *Oremus*; diaconus: *Flectamus genua.* Et ut surrexerint, dicit: *Levate.* Dicit sacerdos orationem que in Sacramentorum continetur.
9. Ipsa expleta, ad lect[iones] legendum de ipsa nocte et post unamquamque lectionem non dicit: *Dominus vobiscum*, sed tantum: *Oremus*, et diaconus: *Flectamus genua*, una cum cantica eorum.

(ANDRIEU, *Les Ordines* 3: 521-22)

DOCUMENTS SPECIFICALLY NAMING THE EXULTET

O. Ordo Romanus 32, in the version of Cambridge, Corpus Christi College lat. 192 (Brittany, mid of the 10 c.)

There is no mention of lessons. Note that the Exultet is called an oratio: *so the earlier Frankish documents prescribing an* oratio *may refer to the Exultet plus a continuation in preface-tone.*

II

54

1. ...hora nona excutiatur ignis de petra. Et accenso cereo, veniant omnes simul cum ipso caereo in aecclesiam.
2. Et unus diaconus rogat pro se unum de sacerdotibus vel levitis qui ibidem revestiti adstant pro se orare. Et dicat hanc orationem: Benedictio caerei. *Exultet iam angelica.*
3. Postquam autem baptismum finierint, absque ullo cantu revertantur a fonte in sacrarium.

(ANDRIEU, *Les Ordines* 3: 521-23)

P. Ordo Romanus 25, early 9th century

This ordo, interpolated into Ordo 24, appears in only the MS Wolfenbüttel 4175. Andrieu attributes it to the same monk of Wissemburg who adapted other material to Frankish use (ANDRIEU, 3: 301).

Borrowing from ordo 24 and, later, from ordo 26 (which speaks of the candle in forensibus civitatibus, he makes it appear that the Exultet is used at Rome, where in fact he has added it in here himself.

1. Eodem die, sabbato sancto, hora VIII, conveniunt omnes presbiteri tam civitatis quam de suburbanis et omnes cleri cum populo in ecclesia statuta.
2. Et hic ordo cerei benedicendi a diaconibus in suburbanis civitatibus agitur, sicut Sacramentorum continet, his verbis: *Exultet iam angelica turba caelorum,* usque: *implere praecipiat. Per.* Deinde *Sursum corda.* Resp.: *Habemus ad dominum. Gratias agamus domino Deo nostro.* Resp.: *Dignum et iustum est. V. D. vere quia dignum et iustum est ut invisibilem Deum patrem omnipitentem filiumque unigenitum,* usque: *in his paschalibus gaudiis conservare digneris. Per.*

(ANDRIEU, *Les Ordines* 3: 305)

Q. Ordo Romanus 31: Exultet (9th/10th century)

All the lessons are those of the Gregorian sacramentary: four lessons only, ending with Hec est hereditas. This is very close to ordo 28 (text M), which however does not actually name the Exultet. The candle is in front of altar; the Exultet is not sung from the ambo.

1. De ordine cerei benedicendi. Hora octava ingrediantur in sacrarium sacerdotes et levite et induant se vestimentis quibus vigilias celebrare debent.
2. Et accenso cereo benedicendo in sacrario de lumine novo, procedat pontifex cum ordinibus sacris in ecclesia cum silentio et deportetur idem cereus illuminatus ante ipsum et ponatur in candelabro ante altare.
3. Pontifex autem orans, ut surrexerit, deosculetur altare et pergat ad sedem suam.
4. Tunc archidiaconus indutus dalmatica, rogans pro se orare dicat: *Exultet iam angelica turba celorum,* usque ad finem. Inde *Dominus vobiscum.* Et tunc resp.: *Et cum*

spiritu tuo. Dicit: *Sursum corda.* Resp.: *Habemus ad dominum.* Ipse dicit: *Gratias aga-mus domino Deo nostro.* Resp.: *Dignum et iustum est.* Et facit consecrationem cerei, decantando quasi canonem.

5. Qua expleta, accendantur ex eodem cereo duo cerei a duobus notariis staturam ho-minis habentes et tenetur unus a dextro cornu altaris et alter a sinistro et de ipso igne omnia luminaria accendi debent, omni priori lumine extincto.

6. Deinde ascendat lector in ambonem et non pronuntiat: *Lectio libri Genesis*, sed in-choet plane: *In principio creavit Deus celum et terram*, et illas alias lectiones similiter. Et ante *In principio* non dicat orationem.

(ANDRIEU, *Les OAndrieurdines* 3: 500)

R. Amalarius of Metz (second quarter of the 9th century)

Amalarius' 'Romanus libellus' is probably a copy of ordo 26 (text G); he is aware of the differences between urban and suburbican practices, and considers himself as being "in forensibus civitatibus".

1. Hoc est quod dico: reservetur ignis de sexta feria, ut inluminetur cereus qui poni-tur in vice columnae ignis ad benedicendum, qui ab initio benedictionis inluminatus est, et cum benedictus est, ab eo inluminetur secundus cereus. Cetera luminaria ex-tincta permaneant usque ad novissimam laetaniam, quae pertinet ad officium mis-sae de resurrectione Domini; tunc accendantur luminaria ecclesiae… . (*De ordine an-tiphonarii*; Jean Michel HANSSENS, *Amalarii episcopi opera liturgica omnia*, 3 vols., Studi e testi 138-40, (Vatican City: Biblioteca Apostolica Vaticana, 1948-50), 3: 80-81).

2. Romanus libellus narrat eadem die benedici ceram oleo mixtam, indeque fieri agnos, eosque reservari usque in octavis paschae; in octavis vero [post] commu-nionem dari populo ex his incensum adolendum et adsuffumigandum domibus suis; et narrat similiter nos facere debere de cereo consecrato… . (*Liber officialis*; HANSSENS, *Amalarii episcopi* 2: 110.)

3. Romanis ita agentibus [i.e., blessing the *Agnus*], nobis praeceptum est a papa Zosimo benedicere cereum. Ut diximus, cera humanitatem Christi designat. (*Liber officialis*; HANSSENS, *Amalarii episcopi* 2: 111)

4. Cereus propterea benedicitur, quia nisi ex benedictione ministri, non potest ex sua simplici natura transire ad misteria. In misterio cera erat columna ignis. Quod a di-acono benedicitur, morem sequitur romanum. In eo enim archidiaconus conficit agnos. Qui cereus per octo dies neofitorum praecedit pontificem, qui est caput pop-uli, quia columna ignis praecessit populum usque ad terram repromissionis. (*Liber officialis*; HANSSENS, *Amalarii episcopi* 2: 113).

5. Additur etiam in libello memorato alter cereus, ubi dicitur: "Et tunc inluminantur duo cerei, tenentibus duobus notariis", et reliqua. Nos vero hunc ordinem diligenti cura volumus observare, quoniam Christus, lux vera quae inluminat omnem hominem, dixit choro apostolorum: *Vos estis lux mundi.* Sit cereus consecratus in Christi persona, sit alter cereus, inluminatus a primo cereo, chorus apostolorum… .

(Liber officialis; HANSSENS, *Amalarii episcopi* 2: 121)

VI. Roman documents using a candle

S. Ordo romanus 50, taken over into Romano-Germanic pontifical, 10th century

Note that there are five lessons, as in the Gregorian sacramentary. The version of the text of the Exultet omits the passage O felix culpa, *and the praise of the bees.*

1. Ipso die hora septima, ingrediuntur sacrarium pontifex, sacerdotes et levitae et induunt se vestimentis sollemnissimis, cum quibus vigilias sanctas celebrare debent, diaconi dalmaticis, subdiaconi lineis aut sericis albis.

2. Et deportatur lumen, quod quinta feria fuerat excussum de silice vel cristallo, quod deportet prior mansionariorum in manu sua, ut possit ex eo cereus accendi.

3. Et procedunt simul omnes de sacrario foris basilicam ordinatim et, accenso cereo in loco mundo, pontifex sive presbiter, faciens super eum crucem, benedicit eum humili voce, ita ut a circumstantibus possit audiri, scola interim cantante septem psalmos paenitentiae, hoc modo incipiens: *Dominus vobiscum. Et cum spiritu tuo.*

4. Oratio. *Deus mundi conditor*...[in extenso, without final *Veniat*].

5. Alia. *Domine sancte, pater omnipotens, aeterne Deus, in nomine tuo et filii tui domini nostri Iesu Christi et spiritus sancti benedicimus hunc ignem*...

6. Tunc accenditur ex eo cereus positus in harundine et deportatur ab episcopo seu abbate vel praeposito et procedunt simul omnes de loco benedictionis in ecclesiam cum ipso cereo, silentio nihil cantantes, prosequente eum omni populo, sicut supra.

7. Aliqui tamen hic cantant ymnum Prudentii: *Inventor rutili dux bone luminis.*

8. Et illuminantur ex eo septem lampades ante altare, quae tamen prius sine lumine erunt ita compositae, ut absque ullo impedimento possint accendi.

9. Cereus vero magnus, qui benedicendus est, ponitur in candelabro ante altare in medio ecclesiae, congregato hinc inde omni clero seu populo.

10. Deinde veniens archidiaconus facit crucem in eo et illuminat illum de novo igne et humiliter inclinatus rogat unum de sacerdotibus vel levitis qui ibidem reveriti astant pro se orare atque, ut surrexerit, completur ab eo benedictio cerei prima, quasi in modum legentis ita:

11. Benedictio cerei. *Exultet iam angelica turba*...[in extenso] Postea dicit ipse archidiaconus, elevata in altum voce: *Per omnia saecula saeculorum.* Resp.: *Amen. Dominus vobiscum.* Resp.: *Et cum spiritu tuo. Sursum corda.* Resp.: *Habemus ad dominum. Gratias agamus domino Deo nostro.* Resp.: *Dignum et iustum est.*

12. Inde vero accedit in consecrationem cerei, decantando quasi canonem ita: *Vere quia dignum et iustum est invisibilem Deum*... [in extenso; note lack of *O felix culpa*, *O certe necessarium*, and of the praise of the bees]...*Per omnia saecula saeculorum.* Resp: *Amen.*

13. Cereo benedicto, ilico illuminantur ab eodem in duobus candelabris alii duo cerei staturam hominis habentes et de ipso novo et benedicto igne accendunt in omni domo, quia omnis ignis anterior, qui tunc ardebat, extingui debet.

14. Et hic ordo cerei benedicendi in forensibus civitatibus agitur. Nam in catholica ecclesia infra civitatem romanam non sic benedicitur, sed, mane primo sabbato sancto, venit archidiaconus in ecclesiam et fundit ceram in vas mundum maius et miscitat ibidem oleum et benedicit ceram et ex ea fumdit similitudimen agnorum et servat eos in loco mundo.

15. Benedictio cerae. *Benedic, domine Iesu Christe, hanc creaturam cerae...*

16. Alia. *Benedico te, cera...*

17. In octava vero paschae dantur ipsi agni ab archidiacono in ipsa ecclesia post missam et communionem populo et ex eis faciunt incensum accendi ad suffumigandum in domibus suis pro quacumque tribulatione eis evenerit necessitas.

18. Similiter et in forensibus civitatibus de cereo faciunt, qui cereus per octo dies neophytorum praecedit pontificem, qui est caput populi.

19. Cum autem pontifex sive prebiter fuerit paratus, expectet clerus in ordine suo in choro, usquedum eis iussum fuerit obviam illi venire, ut in ecclesiam intret. Eoque veniente ad sedem suam, vel si in sacrario sedere voluerit, alius presbiter dicat orationes ad altare per lectiones.

20. Antea vero quam legantur lectiones, accipiant duo notarii suprascriptos cereos accensos et teneant illos unus in dextro cornu altaris, alter in sinistro, usque ad fontes.

21. Deinde ascendens lector in ambonem legere non pronuntiat: *Lectio libri Genesis*, sed sic inchoat: *In principio creavit Deus*, plane, et omnes alias lectiones similiter inchoat et ante *In principio* non dicit episcopus orationem.

> (ANDRIEU, *Les Ordines* 5: 264-73. Edited from the Romano-Germanic Pontifical in Cyrille VOGEL and Reinhard ELZE, *Le pontifical romano-germanique du dixième siècle*, 3 vols, Studi e testi, 226-7, 229 (Vatican City: Biblioteca Apostolica Vaticana, 1963, 1972) 2: 93-100; from Montecassino 451 and Pistoia 141)

T. San Lorenzo in Damaso, early 11th century: Rome, Vallicelliana E 15

The manuscript is a Sacramentary, made for the church of San Lorenzo (SUPINO MARTINI, p. 119-121).

This is a Roman city rite. The Gelasian prayer before the lessons is present, and the Exultet contains no Germanic abbreviations. There is no mention, however, of the beginning of the ceremonies: whether there is a litany or silence.

1. Incipit benedictio cerei in sabbato sancto.

2. Oratio ad ignem novum. *Deus qui per filium tuum...*

3. Postquam cereum illuminatus est.

4. *Domine Deus noster pater omnipotens, exaudi nos lumen indeficiens...*

5. Tunc facit crucem super cereum. Et veniens archidiaconus ita dicendo *Lumen Christi* .iii. vices. Et respondens omnes *Deo gratias* .iii. vices.

6. Et complentur ap ipsis Benedictio cerei *Exultet...* [in extenso]

7. Sequitur orationes per singulas lectiones. *Oremus. Flectamus genua. Levate. Deus qui divitias... Deus qui mirabiliter...* [thirteen prayers altogether]
(ff. 47-50)

U. San Saba, 11th century: Rome, Angelica 1383

The manuscript is for San Saba, mid-11th c. It has 12 lessons for Holy Saturday, including elaborate canticles for Jonah and the Song of the Three children that are related to south Italian practice.

1. Sabbato sancto hora nona conveniant omnes ad ecclesiam, et induunt se vestimentis sicut mos es, et stent in ecclesia ordinatim. Et TCUN[3] (diaconus?) stet in medio chori, et incipiat letania septena, et chorus alternatim resp[ondit] ...[in extenso].
2.Qua completa, ingrediatur diaconus de sacrario canendo *Lumen xpisti*; resp. chorus *Deo gratias* tribus vicibus. Tunc diaconus incipit benedicere cereum. Quo finito dicat sacerdos *Oremus. Flec[tamus genua]. Levate. Deus qui divitias misericordie tue...*

V. A late eleventh-century Roman church: Florence, Riccardiana 299

*This manuscript is attributed by some to the Papal chapel (*SUPINO MARTINI, *p. 54-55 and note 35); but the persistence of so many non-papal elements (the litany, the prayer before the lessons) makes much more likely its origin in another of the city's churches.*

The rubrics here seem to be an amalgam. The rite of the candle is one unit; the Exultet (where the lighting of seven lamps , ¶7, is repeated from the PRG (text S), ¶ 8) is another; there is a new heading for the lessons ('Incipiunt orationes...'), and the baptismal rite that follows is pontifical, referring often to the pontifex and the members of the schola. It also forbids nursing children before their communion ("parvuli autem non sugant mammillas usquedum communicent"). The mass that follows is celebrated by a priest.

1. Sabbato sancto hora nona conveniunt omnes ad ecclesiam et ingrediantur cleri in sacrarium, et induant se vestimentis sicut mos est, et tunc foris ecclesiam faciant excutere ignem de lapide, ita ut possit ex eo candela accendi.
2. Benedictio ignis. *Deus qui per filium tuum angularem... .*
3. Deinde accendatur cereus ex eo, posito in arundine, et procedat in ecclesiam ille qui tenet arundinem et dicat *Lumen christi.* Respondeant omnes *Deo gratias.* iii. vicibus.
4. Et accendantur ex eo vii. lampade *(sic)* ante altare, que tamen sine lumine sint, et ita composite ut sine impedimento possint accendi, et de ipso igne accendatur in omni domo, quia omnis anterior ignis extingui debet.
5. Deinde canatur letania septena.

6. Qua completa ascendat diaconus in ambonem et incipiat benedicere cereum.
7. *Exultet...* [in extenso, sn; in the course of the blessing: 'hic ponitur incensum in modum crucis'; 'hic accendatur facula'; 'hic accendantur lampades septem ante altare']
8. Finita itaque benedictione diaconus ascendat ad altare permaneat cum sacerdote qui orationes dicturus est.
9. Incipiunt orationes seu lectiones in sabbato sancto, et per unamquamque orationem non dicat sacerdos *Dominus vociscum* sed *Oremus*. Dicat diaconus *Flectamus genua*, Et post paulum dicat *Levate*.
10. *Deus qui divitias... .* Dicta oratione, ascendat lector in ambonem non pronuntiet lectio libri genesis, sed tantum istam lectionem inchoet similiter et omnes alias.

(ff. 63ᵛ-66ᵛ)

W. Roman Pontifical of the 12th century

This text is from Lyon, Bibl. mun. 570 (a 17th-century copy, in the hand of Jean Deslions, Dean of Senlis, of a number of pontificals, including the "Pontifical of Apamea", edited by ANDRIEU: *cf. London, BL add. 57528). Of the other MSS Andrieu uses for this edition, most have no description of the Holy Saturday rite (Grenoble, Bibl. mun. 140 (Grenoble, second half of the 12 c.); London, BL add. 17005 (Mainz, second half of the 12 c.); Vat. lat 7114 (Auch, second half of the 13 c.); Vat. lat. 7818 (Chieti?, 12 c.); Vat. Ottob. lat. 270 (origin unknown, 12 c.); Troyes, Bibl. mun. 2272 (dioc. Pavia?, late 11 c.). Vat. Borghes. lat. 49 (Sora, 13 c.), omits the Exultet, beginning with the lections of Holy Saturday. Vat. Barb. lat. 631 (Monte Cassino, late 11 c.) provides an ordo derived from the Roman-German pontifical, but the candle-blessing preserves a non-Roman Montecassino tradition.*

The rite here describes two different Exultet practices, of which the first, probably the more modern, described as being 'the custom of the Roman church', requires a Lumen Christi *procession, singing the Exultet from the ambo, five grains of incense, and the lighting of seven lamps and two candelabra. The second, 'according to the insitution of blessed pope Zosimus', places the candle before the altar, and the deacon, after inscribing the candle, performs both the Lumen Christi and the Exultet there.*

So how did these new practices, (1) the Lumen Christ, and (2) the Exultet from the ambo, reach Rome? Was it from the south? The Exultet was from the north evidently, in a first wave, but this Lumen and ambo may be a second wave of influence.

1. Magno vero die sabbati sancto ac solemnissino, primo mane ornetur ecclesia et circa tertiam altaria cooperiantur. Hora autem quinta vel sexta, novus ignis, si non fuerit excussus in caena domini, iuxta morem quaramdam ecclesiarum, excutiatur hoc die extra ecclesiam de crystallo, vel etiam alio modo fiat. Postea hora qua ad officium faciendum pontifex intrare debet ecclesiam benedici debet novus ignis a iuniore presbiterorum cardinalium in atrio ecclesiae Lateranensis hoc modo:

2. *Dominus vobiscum. Oremus.* Oratio. *Deus qui per filium tuum angularem…* .
3. Alia. *Domine Deus pater omnipotens, lumen indeficiens…*
4. Alia. *Domine sancte, pater omnipotens, aeterne Deus, benedicentibus…*
5. Alia oratio quae est ad benedicendum incensum quod ponendum est in cereo et ad benedicendum eumdem ignem: *Veniat, quaesumus, omnipotens Deus, super hoc incensum…*
6. Interim autem dum ignis benedicitur, pontifex et prebiteri indui debent in sacrario solemnissimis vestimentis. Diaconi tamen usque ad missam, quae cantatur post reversionem a fontibus, debent indui planetis. In missa autem depositis planetis dalmaticas assumant. Subdiaconi vero a principio officii usque in finem debent habere tunicas.
7. Omnibus igitur sicut diximus in sacrario indutis, antequam ipsi procedant ad altare, benedicto novo igne, iunior diaconus diaconorum cardinalium, iuxta consuetudinem romanae ecclesiae, de ipso novo igne triplicem candelam coniunctam accendat et eam in capite harundinis ponat, ipsam harundinem in manu tenens et processionaliter procedens cum schola cantorum et aliquibus subdiaconis, primum in porta, secundo iuxta quintanas, tercio iuxta ambonem, *Lumen Christi*, vocem singulis vicibus exaltando, decantet, schola cantorum cum subdiaconibus, qui cum ipso procedunt, per omnem vicem *Deo gratias* respondente.
8. Tunc igitur ascendens in ambonem, et magno cereo cum harundine illuminato atque incensato libro, incipit benedictionem cerei decantare. Ubi vero ventum fuerit ad illum versum qui sic incipit: *Suscipe, sancte pater, incensi huius sacrificium vespertinum*, infigat firmiter in ipso cereo quinque grana incensi in modum crucis. Deinde cum debet dicere: *Qui licet sit divisus in partes mutuati luminis detrimenta non novit*, accenduntur ex eo septem lampades et duo cerei in duobus candelabris.
9. Interim autem dum benedicitur cereus, pontifex ad altare procedere debet ordinatim cum omnibus ordinibus suis. Ubi vero cereus fuerit benedictus, iuxta consuetudinem quarumdam eacclesiarum, de ipso novo igne accendunt ignem in omni domo, extincto vetero igne.
10. Haec est consuetudo ecclesiae romanae. Sed, iuxta institutionem beati Zosimi papae, cereus magnus qui benedicendus est ponitur in candelabro ante altare et, clero et populo ibi prope congregato, venit diaconus qui benedicere debet cereum et cum stylo facit crucem im ipso cereo et ⬜ et ⬜ et annum ab incarnatione domini describit. Postmodum vero humiliter inclinatus ad sacerdotum veniens recipit ab ipso benedictionem et tunc surgens et conversus ad chorum dicit ter, vocem exaltando: *Lumen Christi*. Caetera fiunt sicut superius dictum est.
11. Deinde lector ascendens in ambonem absque titulo inchoat: *In principio creavit Deus coelum et terram*, et omnes aliae lectiones similiter debent sine titulo inchoari. Ante primam vero lectionem, oratio non dicitur… .

(Michel ANDRIEU, *Le pontifical romain au moyen âge*, 4 vols., Studi e Testi 86-88, 99 (Vatican City: Biblioteca Apostolica Vaticana, 1938-41) 1: 238-41)

X. Santa Maria in Trastevere, 12th century (Rome, Vall. F 4)

This manuscript uses the same language as Florence, Riccardiana 299 for ¶ 1-2. The differences are interesting: (1) here three candles are lit from the fire and placed in a candelabrum: in Riccardiana 299, a single candle is lit (the same one that will be blessed?); (2) there is no litany here; (3) there is no mention of the ambo here; (4) there is no 'Gelasian' prayer before the lessons.

This manuscript, while in the Roman tradition, is essentially not Gelasian, hence not urban-Roman; it does not, however, borrow from the 10th-century Roman-German Pontifical.

1. Sabbato sancto hora nona conveniant omnes ad ecclesiam et ingrediantut *(sic)* clerici sacrarium, et induant se vestimentis sicut mos est, et tunc extra ecclesiam faciant excutere ignem de lapide in loco congruo, ita ut possit ex eo candela accendi.
2. Benedictio ignis nove. *Deus qui per filium tuum… .*
3. Deinde accendantur ex eo tres candele et ponantur in arundine. Diaconus accipiat illam et intret ecclesiam dicens alta voce *Lumen Christi*, R. omnes *Deo gratias*; postea in medio ecclesie dicat *Lumen Christi*, R. omnes *Deo gratias*; deinde in introitu chori *Lumen Christi*, R. omnes *Deo gratias*.
4. His expletis, diaconus benedicat cereum, *Exultet iam angelica turba celorum.*
5. Finita itaque benedictione, lector ascendat in ambonem non pronuntiet lectio sed incipit legere *In principio creavit.*
6. Finita lectione sacerdos ascendat ad altare et per unaquamque *(sic)* orationem non dicat *Dominus vobiscum* sed *Oremus.*

   (ff. 61ᵛ-62)

Y. St Peter's, 12th/13th century (San Pietro F 18)

This manuscript seems intended for St. Peter's; there is special gold initial for Peter, and special prayers and rubrics for St Peter's on f. 188f. The MS speaks of fratres, and of a bishop or priest singing the Holy Saturday Alleluia, whose music, cued in a Beneventan notation, is closer to Old-Roman than Gregorian. See Bruno STÄBLEIN *and Margareta* LANDWEHR-MELNICKI, *Die Gesänge des altrömischen Graduale, Vat. lat. 5319. Monumenta monodica medii ævi, 2 (Kassel, 1970), 187.*

1. Ordo lectionum et orationum et canticorum in sabbato sancto.
2. Primo excutiatur ignis de lapide vel de cristallo extra ecclesiam, et accensum ignem sacerdos benedicat dicens. *Dominus vobiscum. Oremus. Deus qui per filium tuum angularem… . Domine deus pater omnipotens exaudi nos lumen indeficiens… .* Tunc aspergatur aqua benedicta.
3. Deinde accendatur cereus, et ponatur in arundine quem diaconus indutus dalmatica portat. Cum venit ad limin[em] ecclesie ponens genua alta voce dicat, *Lumen xpisti*. Et illi de processione respondent, *Deo gratias*. Deinde procedens ad introitum

chori, et ponens genua iterum dicat, *Lumen xpisti*, R. *Deo gratias*. Sic faciat et in medio chori.
4. Deinde ascendat in pulpitum, et benedicat cereum. Absolute incipiens *Exultet iam angelica*.
5. Finita benedictione, subdiaconus ascendit ad ammonem, legere incipit sine titulo lectionem.

(f. 51ᵛ)

Z. Monastery of SS Andrew and Bartholomew, Rome, ca. 1230 (Santa Maria Maggiore 40)

Cf. ordo 28 (text M) for the beginning. Cf. also ordo 50 (text S). Note the 'Gelasian' prayer before the collects. But there is no litany at the beginning.

This seems to be a combination of elements; note how the blessing of new fire is inserted later, when it would be better earlier. It is as though there were two beginnings transcribed one after another.

This manuscript also contains SI QUIS CATECHUMINUS EST PROCEDAT, *as in the Beneventan liturgy.*

1. Item ordo qualiter agendum sit in sabbato sancto. Hora nona ingrediuntur sacerdotes, et levite sacrarium, et induuntur vestimentis cum quibus vigilia sancta celebrare debeat, et accenso cereo quem deportat prior mansionarium in manu sua, prosequente eum populo, cum silentio.
2. Eo tamen die hora viii, prius faciunt excutere ignem de lapide in loco foris basilicam, ita ut possit ex eo candela accendi, et benedicitur igni[s].
3. Benedictio ignis novi in pascha. Or. *Deus qui per filium tuum angularem…* . Et accenditur ex eo cereus positus im arundine, et deportatur in ecclesia, et ille qui tenet arundinem cum cereo dicat, *Lumen xpisti*. R. omnes *Deo gratias. Lumen xpisti*. R. *Deo gratias. Lumen xpisti*. R. *Deo gratias*.
4. Et accendantur ex eo septem lampades ante altare, que tamen prius sine lumine erunt, ita composite, ut absque ullo impedimento possint accendi. Et de ipso lumine accendunt in omni domo quia omnis ignis anterior extingui debet.
5. Et dicit diaconus *Dominus vobiscum. Et cum spiritu tuo*. Et incipit benedicere cereum. *Exultet iam* [in extenso, sine notis]
6. Postea procedunt sacerdos et levite indutis vestimentis cum quibus vigilia sancta celebrare debent. Et stat sacerdos retro altare, et dicit sacerdos *Oremus*; diaconus dicit *Flectamus genua*. Et post unamquamque lectionem non dicat *Dominus vobiscum*, sed tamen *Oremus*. Et diaconus dicat *Flectamus genua*, et dicat sacerdos hanc orationem. *Deus qui divitias…*

(ff. 59ᵛ-62ᵛ)

VII. Twelfth-century documents describing the Lateran basilica

AA. Benedict, Liber politicus (c. 1140-43)

Benedict, canon of St. Peter's and former cantor of the papal court, wrote an ordinal in which he describes the rites of St. Peter's. Here, however, he is describing the papal rite at the Lateran.

1. In Sabbato sancto mane surgit archidiaconus et miscitat oleum et crisma annotinum in cera munda; acolitus conficit eam et colat et facit ex ea in similitudinem agnorum, quos domnus pontifex expendit ad missam in sabbato de Albis.
2. Ad sextam sabbati sancti efficitur novus ignis et cereus benedicitur et leguntur XII lectiones latine et XII grece et cantantur tria cantica *Cantemus Domino gloriose, Vinea facta est, Attende celum.*
3. Finito hoc officio, domnus pontifex descendit ad fontem cum diaconis et subdiaconis regionariis cantando letaniam; primicerius cum scola cantando *Sicut cervus* usque in porticum sancti Venantii.

> (Paul Fabre and Louis Marie Olivier Duchesne. *Le Liber Censuum de l'église romaine.* 3 vols (the third, of indices, by Duchesne with Pierre Fabre and G. Mollat), Bibliothèque des Écoles françaises d'Athènes et de Rome, 2d series, VI. Paris, Fontemoing, 1905 (vols 1-2), De Boccard 1952 (vol 3); 2: 151)

BB. Albinus (1188)

Cardinal Albinus' "Ordo Romanus de consuetudinibus et observatntiis Romane ecclesie in precipuis sollempnitatibus" draws heavily on the language used by Benedict of St. Peter's, but not slavishly: here he adds details about the blessing of new fire, and mentions for the first time (becaue it is new?) the singing of Lumen Christi.

1. In Sabbato sancto. Hora VI efficitur novus ignis in atrio ante portas Lateranensis ecclesie et benedicitur a minori diacono cardinali cum incenso et aqua benedicta.
2. Deinde pergunt in ecclesia cum novo igne posito in canna et diaconus dicit: *Lumen Christi*, tribus vicibus. Postmodum [cereus] benedicitur ab ipso diacono. Leguntur XII lectiones latine et XII grece et cantantur tria cantica *Cantemus Domino gloriose, Vinea facta est, Attende celum.*
3. Finito hoc officio, domnus pontifex descendit ad fontem cum diaconis et subdiaconis regionariis, cantando letanias, primicerius cum scola cantando *Sicut cervus* usque in porticum sancti Venantii.

> (Fabre and Duchesne, *Le liber censuum,* 2: 130)

CC. Cencius Savelli, late 12th c.

Savelli, later Pope Honorius III (d. 1227), in his Liber censuum provided a "Romanus ordo de consuetudinibus et observantiis, presbyterio videlicet scolarum et aliis Romane ecclesie in precipuis sollempnitatibus." He owes much to Benedict and Albinus. Note that the pope is not present for the Exultet.

1. Quid debeat domnus papa facere in Sabbato Sancto.

II

64

2. In Sabbato Sancto, hora sexta efficitur novus ignis in atrio ante portas Lateranensis ecclesie, et benedicitur a iuniori presbyterorum cardinalium, cum incenso et aqua benedicta.
3. Deinde pergunt in eclesia cum novo igne posito in canna, et diaconus dicit *Lumen Christi*, tribus vicibus; postmodum [cereus] benedicitur ab ipso diacono.
4. Leguntur duodecim lectiones latine, et duodecim grece, et cantantur tria cantica, *Cantemus Domino gloriose*, *Vinea facta est*, *Attende celum*.
5. Finito hoc officio, domnus pontifex descendit ad fontem cum diaconis et subdiaconis regionariis, cantando letanias, primicerius com sua scola cantando *Sicut cervus*, usque in porticum sancti Venantii; ibi preparato facistorio pontifex sedet.

(Vat. lat. 8486, anno 1192, edited in FABRE and DUCHESNE, *Le 'liber censuum'*, 1: 296-7)

DD. Bernard (late 12th century)

Cardinal Bernard, prior of the Lateran, wote his "ordo officiorum ecclesiae lateranensis" at an undetermined date in the latter part of the twelfth century. Bernard is very loquacious, often describing things twice (note the descriptions of raising the voice for Lumen Christi), and very fussy about detail and concerned about things going wrong (notice his worry about the wind blowing out candles, and about how to be sure that the grains of incense do not fall out of the candle). His description of the Exultet being begun in the preface-tone suggests that the Exultet-melody was not yet in use in his time.

1. Hora uero nona ingrediuntur sacerdotes et leuite, scola et tota curia una cum pontifice ecclesiam sancti Thome et induuntur uestimentis, cum quibus sanctas uigilias celebrare debent. Cardinales enim tam presbyteri quam diaconi uestiuntur planetis, subdiaconi autem tunicis. Postquam autem nona cantata fuerit, ultimus cardinalis indutus pluuiali impositaque stola uenit cum ministris, sicuti mos est, in atrium maioris ecclesie, benedicit ignem de cristallo uel silice ab acolito curie nouiter excussum et aqua benedicta desuper aspergit.
2. Deinde diaconus uidelicet ultimus dalmatica indutus plures candelas in unum glomeratas, ne a uento leuiter extinguantur, ab ipso benedicto igne accensas impositasque arundini ad chorum reportat precedentibus eum ceroferariis cum extinctis faculis in candelabris et turibulo sine incenso.
3. Mox autem ut ecclesiam ingredi ceperit, subsistens paululum dicit mediocri uoce *Lumen Christi*. Et qui cum eo sunt, respondent *Deo gratias*. Dum uero chorum ingredi ceperit, iterum subsistens dicit secundo altiori aliquantulum uoce *Lumen Christi*. Et ministri *Deo gratias*. Interim diaconus progreditur prope cereum et subsistens dicit tertio plus alta uoce *Lumen Christi*. Et ministri *Deo gratias*. Diaconus enim magis exaltat uocem in secunda pronuntiatione quam in prima et in tertia magis quam in secunda ministris similiter consona ei uoce respondentibus.
4. Deinde dans arundinem tenendam acolito et imponens incensum in turibulo ascendit im ambonem et incipit consecrationem cerei decantando in modum prefationis. Conuentus uero stat.

5. Iuxta diaconum autem manent duo ceroferarii cum extinctis faculis et medius sub-diaconus cum fumigante turibulo et ad dextram manum eius stat ille, qui tenet arundinem cum nouo igne prope.

6. Cum igitur diaconus dixerit: *Suscipe, sancte pater, incensi huius sacrificium ues-pertinum*, sint ibi preparata quinque grana incensi purissimi. Que accipiens dia-conus imprimat ea cereo in modum crucis. Que sic infixa hereant, up non facile cadant. Quod ut facilius et aptius fiat, sint prius in ipso cereo quinque loca illa aperte designata et aliquantulum effossa, ut granis impositis fumiget ipsum cereum cum turibulo.

7. Deinde cum dixerit: *Quem in honorem dei rutilans ignis accendit*, porrecta sibi arundine ab acolito de igne nouo accendit cereum. Post paululum autem cum adi-unxerit: *Qui licet diuisus in partes mutuati luminis detrimenta non nouit*, accendun-tur de ipso igne nouo duo supradicte facule in duobus candelabris et VII lampades ante maius altare et reportatur arundo in sacrarium et extinguitur.

8. Interim autem dum cereus benedicitur, domnus papa planeta et aliis sacris uestibus indutus ascendit ad maius altare cum cardinalibus et tota curia, uti mos est, ad celebrandum officium.

9. Post benedictionem cerei quid agatur. Cereo uero benedicto reuertens diaconus in uestiarium cum ministris exuat dalmaticam et indutus planeta reuertatur ad altare et tunc extiuguantur cerei usque ad missam.

10. Statimque post benedictionem cerei accedit lector ad ambonem non pronuntians *Lectio libri genesis*, sed inchoat *In principio creauit deus celum et terram* legens plane et aperte ad intelligendum et alias lectiones similiter.

> (Ludwig FISCHER, *Bernhardi cardinalis et lateranensis ecclesiae prioris Ordo officio-rum ecclesiae lateranensis* (Munich: Datterer, 1916), 60-62).

EE. Lateran, ca. 1200: Vat. lat. 12989; and other Roman churches in the 13th century: S Maria Maggiore (S Maria Maggiore 52); S Maria ad Martyres (An-gelica 1606); San Lorenzo fuori le mura (Madrid 730); also used in Avignon 199 (papal chapel); adopted with revisions into the Ordinal of Innocent III, and the Pontifical of the Roman Curia, in its Gamma recension.

These rubrics, originally evidently for the Lateran, seem to have been used widely. With a few additions they are used in Santa Maria Maggiore 52, but without mention-ing the Lateran. Angelica 1606 is an 18th-century copy, by Antonio Baldani, Canon of S. Maria ad Martyres (the Pantheon), which he transcribes 'ex vetusta codice Mem-branaceo SS Basilicae S. Mariae ad Martyres'. The Holy Saturday ordo is on ff. 54-59. The Pontifical of the Roman Curia adopts ¶1-3, and then skips over the blessing of the candle and the lessons, indicating that they are to be done 'prout traditur in missali"(The relevant portion of the Pontifical edited Andrieu, Le pontifical romain 2: 470-71).

The Ordinal of Innocent III, ca. 1215, reproduces these rubrics; significant additions there are noted below from Stephen J. P. VAN DIJK, The Ordinal of the Papal Court from Innocent III to Boniface VIII and related documents, *completed by Joan*

II

66

Hazelden WALKER. Spicilegium friburgense, 22 (Fribourg, Presses Universitaires, 1975), 261-64.

Note that the pope is not present at the Exultet, but apparently arrives in time for the lessons.

1. Incipit ordo qualiter officium sit agendum in sabbato sancto.
2. Hora sexta conveniunt omnes ad ecclesiam Lateranensem, et facta oratione pontifex cum clero ingreditur sacrarium, ibique eo residente, de cristallo sive de lapide a ministris in atrio ecclesie ignis excutitur et accenditur. Tunc iunior presbiterorum cardinalium sacris indutus vestibus, cum cruce aqua benedicta et incenso, benedicit novum ignem.
3. Benedictio ignis Oratio. *Deus qui per filium ...* alia *Domine Deus pater omnipotens lumen indeficiens...* alia *Domine sancte pater omnipotens eterne deus benedicentibus...* alia (PRC: Benedictio incensi; OrdInnIII: Benedictio incensi quod ponendum est in cereo) *Veniat quesumus.* Benedicto igne, aspergitur aqua benedicta, et adoletur incenso.
4. Deinde diaconus iunior diaconorum cardinalium dalmatica indutus venit, et de manu ministrorum accipit arundinem trium cubitorum et dimidii cubiti, triplicem candelam quam de novo igne illuminatam imponit arundini, comitantibus eum subdiaconibus, cantoribus, et reliquis de clero cum (A1606: *om* cum) populo, precedentibus ministris cum cruce et incenso,
5. et stans in porta ecclesie elevatis paululum manibus, dicit magna voce *Lumen xpisti.* Respondentibus aliis *Deo gratias,* procedit usque ad hostium chori, et elevatis amplius manibus, excelsius dicit, *Lumen xpisti,* et iterum respondentibus *Deo gratias,* procedit usque ad medium chori, et plus elevatis manibus, tertio altius dicit, *Lumen xpisti,* et respondentibus omnibus *Deo gratias,*
6. ascendit adornatum pulpitum, et illuminato magno cereo, et incensato libro, incipit absolute benedictionem cerei, *Exultet...*[in extenso, sn]
7. Interim autem dum cereus benedicitur, pontifex (OrdInnIII adds: dicat tertiam et sextam in camera sua. Nonam vero dicat in ecclesia. Dictis psalmis *Quam dilecta* et ceteris, et calciato,) induitur omni ornatu suo quadragesimali, episcopi pluvialibus, presbiteri et diaconi planetis, subdiaconi vero non planetis sed tunicis induuntur, ut composite induti sint, et magis expediti ad lectiones legendas.
8. Tunc pontifex cum omnibus egressus a sacrario precedente eum subdiacono cum cruce (OrdInnIII: et alio subdiacono cum evangelio) processionaliter cum silentio tam procedit ad altare, et facta reverentia, adornatam condescendit sedem, et circumsedentibus hinc inde iuxta ordinem suum omnibus;
9. subdiaconus finita benedictione cerei, ascendens amonem (A1606: ambonem), incipit legere lectiones sine titulo *In principio creavit deus celum et terram.* Eo vero complente, (OrdInnIII: si dominus papa velit) grecus subdiaconus eandem lectionem grece relegit. qua completa, dicit pontifex *Oremus,* diaconus (Ord InnIII: qui est a dextris) *Flectamus genua,* et post paululum (OrdInnIII: alter diaconus qui est a sinistris) *Levate.* Deinde sequitur oratio et sic per ordinem, duocdecim latine et duodecim grece (OrdInnIII: sicut domino pape placet). vicissim leguntur lectiones.

VIII. Later, generalized documents

FF. Franciscan Regula missal, early 13th century

These missal rubrics are found in Assisi 607 (s13 2/4) and others (including Rome, Bibl. Corsiniana 376 (c. 1261-64) and Vat. Rossi 199 (s14). This is an adaptation of the papal ordo of the Lateran c. 1200 (see text EE), adapted for wider use.

1. Ordo officii de sabbato sancto.
2. Hora sexta a ministris ecclesie ignis excutitur de cristallo sive de lapide et accenditur. Postea sacerdos sacris indutus vestibus cum cruce et aqua benedicta et incenso benedicit novum ignem.
3. Benedictio ignis. Oratio *Deus qui per filium tuum...* . alia oratio *Domine deus pater...* alia oratio *Domine sancte pater...* . Benedictio incensi quod ponitur in cereum alia oratio *Veniat quesumus omnipotens deus super hoc incensum...* Benedicto igne. aspergatur aqua benedicta et adoleatur incenso. Postea dicatur nona et cooperiantur altaria.
4. Deinde diaconus dalmatica indutus venit et de manu ministrorum accipit arundinem trium cubitorum et dimidii cubiti triplicem candelam quam de novo igne illuminatam imponit arundini. comitantibus eum subdiaconibus. cantoribus et reliquis de clero cum populo. precedentibus ministris cum cruce et incenso.
5. Et stans in porta ecclesie. elevatis paululum manibus. dicit magna voce *Lumen Christi*. Respondentibus aliis *Deo gratias*. procedit usque ad ostium chori. et elevatis amplius manibus. excelsius dicit *Lumen Christi*. Et respondentibus iterum *Deo gratias*. procedit usque ad medium chori. et plus elevatis manibus. tertio altius dicit *Lumen Christi*. respondentibus omnibus *Deo gratias*.
6. Et ascendit adornatum pulpitum et. incensato libro. incipit absolute benedictionem cerei *Exultet...et curvat imperia*. Hic ponat incensum in modum crucis in facula. *In huius igitur noctis... rutilans ignis accendit*. Hic accendatur facula. *Qui licet sit...apis mater eduxit*. Hic accendantur lampades ante altare. *O vere beata nox...per omnia secula seculorum. Amen*.
7. Interim autem dum cereus benedicitur. sacerdos induitur omni ornatu suo quadragesimali et diaconus planeta. Subdiaconi vero non planetis sed tunicis induuntur. ut composite induti sint et magis expediti ad lectiones legendas.
8. Tunc sacerdos cum omnibus egressis a sacrario. precedente eum subdiacono cum cruce. processionaliter cum silentio tamen procedit ad altare. et. facta reverentia. adornatam ascendit sedem et circumsedentibus hinc inde iuxta ordinem suum omnibus.
9. finita benedictione cerei. subdiaconus ascendens ad ammonem incipit legere lectiones sine titulo *In principio creavit deus celum et terra*.

(Edited in van Dijk, *The Ordinal of the Papal Court*, pp. 276-77)

II

68

GG. Roman curia (Franciscan) missal, as revised by Haymo of Faversham, 1243-44

Roman manuscripts of this very widespread ordo include Vat. San Pietro E 9 (s13ex?); San Pietro F 16 (s14in). The text transcribed here is San Pietro E 9; F 16 is almost identical. This corresponds to text of the Ordo Missalis of Haymo of Faversham, ed. Stephen J. P. VAN DIJK and Joan Hazelden WALKER, The Origins of the Modern Roman Liturgy, (Westminster, MD: The Newman Press, London: Darton, Longman, and Todd, 1960) 2: 245-46.

1. ...igne excusso de lapide in aliquo vaso a sacrista eidem preparatis benedicit novum ignem dicendo V. *Dominus vobiscum.* R. *Et cum spiritu tuo.* V. *Oremus.* Or. *Deus qui per filium tuum angularem...* Or. *Domine Deus pater omnipotens lumen indeficiens... .* Or. *Domine sancte pater omnipotens et deus benedicentibus nobis hunc ignem...*
2. Deinde benedicat incensum ponendum in cereo absolute dicens Or. *Veniat quesumus omnipotens Deus super...*
3. Et dum benedicitur incensum acolitus assumens de carbonibus predictis ponit in turribulo. Finita vero benedictione incensi, sacerdos ignem benedictum aspergit aqua benedicta et posito incenso in thuribulo ibidem adolet dictum ignem.
4. Interim omnia luminaria ecclesie extinguuntur ut de igne benedictio *(sic)* postmodum accendantur.
5. Deinde dyaconus dalmatica indutus recepta benedictione a sacerdote, cum subdiacono portante in arundine vel baculo trium cubitorum et dimidii triplicem candelam novo igne illuminatam. Una cum quinque granis incensi benedicti, vadit ad ornatum pulpitum, et incensato libro absolute incipit *Exultet iam angelica.* Require infra in fine libri. Asstante ad dextram eius dicto subdiacono. Pervento autem ad *In huius igitur noctis gratia* quinque grana predicta incensi a diacono [here an erasure] infinguntur cereo in modum crucis. In loco autem *Qui licet divisus in partes* accenditur cereus a predicto subdiacono. Et cum dicitur *O vere beata nox* accenduntur lampadas.
6. Completa benedictione cerei sacerdos et ministri vestiti more solito ante altare procedunt. Et facta reverentia in locis suis sedent. Postea legunt prophetie sine titulo. Et in fine prophetiarum dicuntur orationes modo subscripto. [no prayer before lessons].

(ff. 117ᵛ-118)

III

Introducing the *Gloria in Excelsis*[*]

I N THE GREAT ERA OF TROPING, from the tenth to the twelfth centuries, the *Gloria in excelsis* accumulated a repertory of embellishments rivaled in size only by those attached to the Introit and the Kyrie.

The Introit and the Kyrie are natural candidates for troping.[1] The Introit, as the opening chant of the Mass, suggests festal elaboration both because of its prefatory nature—introducing the whole Mass and its liturgical intention—and because its text, often a psalm verse, invites a more specific and objective connection with the feast at hand.[2] Likewise the Kyrie, with its repetitive texts and its possible connections to the litany, invites the creative sympathies of the age to amplify the repeated invocations.[3]

But the *Gloria in excelsis* seems a less likely place for liturgical embellishment. For one thing, it is not always present in the Mass; and secondly, its text is already very long and arranged in short,

[*] An earlier version of this paper was read at the annual meeting of the American Musicological Society, Denver, 1980. I should like to express here my gratitude to Professors Alejandro Planchart and Ruth Steiner for their help in verifying certain manuscript readings.

[1] I must beg the reader's indulgence for the use, here and elsewhere, of the word *trope* to describe a vast array of medieval interpolative chant. We shall, perhaps, never resolve the problem first recognized in the Middle Ages, when books containing tropes, *versus*, prosulae, laudes, and sequences, were called "troparia," as in the following mention from the fourteenth-century Customary of St. Mary's Abbey, York: ". . . si sequentia cantari debet illo die, signum faciet juniori omnibus in choro ut troparia sibi ferat. . . . Quod si Kyrie sit cum versibus, tunc dum introitus cantatur idem signum faciet juveni antedicto et distribuet ut est dictum." *The Ordinal and Customary of the Abbey of Saint Mary, York (St. John's College, Cambridge, MS. D.27)*, ed. The Abbess of Stanbrook and J. B. L. Tolhurst, 3 vols., Henry Bradshaw Society Volumes, 73, 75, 74 (London, 1936, 1937; Maidstone, 1951), I, 99.

[2] A comprehensive edition of the Aquitanian Introit tropes is Günther Weiss, *Introitus-Tropen*, I, *Das Repertoire der südfranzösischen Tropäre des 10. und 11. Jahrhunderts*, Monumenta monodica medii aevi, 3 (Kassel, 1970).

[3] The definition of Kyrie tropes, especially with respect to Latin-texted Kyries, is not at issue here; I mean only to point out the important size of the medieval repertory. A recent comprehensive study of Kyrie tropes is David A. Bjork, "The Kyrie Trope," this JOURNAL, XXXIII (1980), 1–41.

480

varied invocations, which need little adjustment to bring them into line with the aesthetic desiderata of the trope-makers.

Then why should the Gloria have attracted such a large repertory of tropes? Probably because of its special festive nature, which made it appropriate in the Mass only on Sundays and great festivals during seasons of rejoicing. The Gloria is introduced very solemnly, always begun by the celebrant himself. Indeed, the early history of the inclusion of the *Gloria in excelsis* in the Mass indicates that the rank of the celebrant, as well as the solemnity of the day, determined when the Gloria might be used. This is a point to which we shall return.

*   *   *

A Gloria trope, like many Introit tropes, is a phrase-by-phrase interpolated commentary and amplification of a liturgical text. Gloria tropes normally begin after the celebrant's intonation, or after the first choral phrase; a great many of these tropes survive, and they have been studied in some detail.[4]

Attached to this large body of rather grand tropes is a small group of pieces that serve as introductions to the *Gloria in excelsis* as a whole. Unlike the Gloria tropes themselves, these prefaces do not comment on the Gloria text, nor on a specific feast day; instead they introduce the act of performing the Gloria, usually by inviting the celebrant to recite the angelic hymn.

Using the evidence of these Gloria introductions and other pieces, Heinrich Husmann has argued that tropes in general originated as invitations to perform a certain liturgical chant, and that introductions form the earliest layer of the trope repertory.[5] It may be, then, that these small introductory pieces stand at the threshold of the great edifice of troping; they appear in many of the earliest trope manuscripts, and may well predate the larger Gloria tropes with which, as we shall see, they have often been confused.

The typical, and arguably the original, introductory trope of this kind is *Sacerdos dei excelsi*, Example 1.

[4] The principal modern study is Klaus Rönnau, *Die Tropen zum Gloria in excelsis Deo* (Wiesbaden, 1967).
[5] "Sinn und Wesen der Tropen, veranschaulicht an den Introitustropen des Weihnachtsfestes," *Archiv für Musikwissenschaft*, XVI (1959), 135–47, especially pp. 137, 147.

Example 1

Sacerdos dei excelsi, F:Pn, n. a. lat. 1871, fol. 49ᵛ

(O priest of the highest God, come before the sacred and holy altar, and in praise of the King of Kings raise your voice, we humbly beg and pray: speak, *domine*:)

At this point the bishop intones the beginning of *Gloria in excelsis*.

A companion piece to *Sacerdos dei excelsi*, similar in its appeal to the celebrant, is *Summe sacerdos*, Example 2.

Example 2

Summe sacerdos, F:Pn, n. a. lat. 1871, fol. 49ᵛ

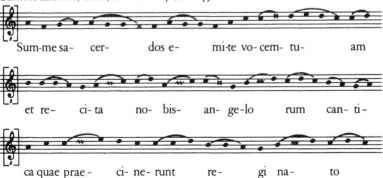

482

do-   mi-   no ei-   a   dic   dom- ne

(O highest priest, send forth your voice and recite to us the song of the angels, which they sang to the Lord, the newborn King, *eia*, speak, *domne*.)

These two pieces in their various versions account for the majority of Gloria introductions, particularly in West Frankish tropers.[6] The way they appear in the sources depends, in part, on the arrangement of the manuscripts themselves. In some sources (as in Paris, n. a. lat. 1871) tropes are arranged by category; and in these manuscripts the introductions, when present, are placed apart from any specific Gloria—usually before the first Gloria trope—to indicate their general applicability to any subsequent Gloria or trope.

In other manuscripts (as for example, Paris, lat. 1118), these chants appear to introduce the Gloria on specific feasts, one serving for Christmas, for example, and the other for Saint Stephen. This is difficult to avoid in Paris 1118 (and elsewhere) since the manuscript arranges tropes by feast, grouping together all the necessary items for Christmas (Introit trope, Kyrie, Gloria trope, etc.) before proceeding to the next feast in the calendar.

Table 1 shows the presence in the manuscripts of what we shall call the "*sacerdos* chants," listing first those that are attached to specific feasts, and then those that are separable, usually as prologue to a group of Gloria tropes. (The presence of other introductions is noted in an indented column; the various textual versions of *Sacerdos dei* are labeled with capital letters and are edited in the Appendix.)

What can we observe from this table? First, these introductions are applied more often to specific feasts than to entire Gloria sections, but

---

[6] Gloria introductions have received only limited attention from scholars. Léon Gautier makes a brief reference to them, noting that they are usually addressed to bishops: *Histoire de la poésie liturgique au moyen âge: Les Tropes*, I (Paris, 1886; repr. Ridgewood, N.J., 1966), 245–47. Some texts are printed in *Analecta hymnica* with brief comments: Vol. XLVII, *Tropen des Missale im Mittelalter*, ed. Clemens Blume and Henry Marriott Bannister (Leipzig, 1905; repr. New York, 1961), pp. 219–20. Rönnau (n. 4 above) notes almost all the introductions in the manuscripts he examines, but he is concerned with tropes in the body of the Gloria, and nowhere presents a discussion of introductions. Alejandro Enrique Planchart, *The Repertory of Tropes at Winchester*, 2 vols. (Princeton, 1977), catalogues appearances of *Sacerdos dei excelsi* (II, 264–66) and transcribes the polyphonic version of the Winchester tropers (I, 314–15).

this may be more a matter of manuscript organization than of the original destination of these pieces. Secondly, we note that *Sacerdos dei excelsi* occurs more frequently and more widely than *Summe sacerdos*, appearing in Northern, English, and Italian manuscripts as well as the Aquitanian tropers; a version of this piece, using the address "Pastor bone," appears regularly in Italy, but only once in the North. This introduction is purely an invitation to intone the Gloria, without specific festival reference; it travels widely and independently, being in many cases the only *sacerdos* chant in a given manuscript.

Summe sacerdos, however, occurs only in Aquitanian manuscripts, and only twice without *Sacerdos dei*. And whenever *Summe sacerdos* is applied to a specific feast, it is always used for Christmas; in fact the three manuscripts that connect it with a specific trope (Paris, lat. 903, 1118, and 779) all couple it with the well-known *Omnipotens altissime deus*.

For two reasons, however, we should not consider *Summe sacerdos* to be a Christmas trope, a sort of occasional opening verse for *Omnipotens altissime*. First, the transmission of the piece is largely independent of the trope. Of the four manuscripts in which the introduction is not attached to *Omnipotens altissime*, all but one (lat. 909) do have the trope in their repertories. And second, although the text of *Summe sacerdos* could be read as referring specifically to the Nativity, it is really an allusion to the historical origin of the *Gloria in excelsis* itself: the angelic hymn overheard by the shepherds at the time of Christ's birth. Hence, despite the fact that *Summe sacerdos*, as it stands, is suitable for any performance of the Gloria, its text sometimes caused it to be applied specifically to the Nativity;[7] and it prompted at least one scribe, as we shall see, to substitute other festival references in the text, even though the results are mild misrepresentations of the biblical account of the *carmen angelicum*. Especially if, as we shall suggest, these introductions are related not so much to a given feast as to the rank of the celebrant, and if this tradition later lost its usefulness, then *Summe sacerdos* might have begun its career as a general introduction, only later emphasizing its textual affinity with Christmas.

---

[7] *Summe sacerdos* is transmitted sometimes without the final "eia dic domne eia." The piece is thus presented in Paris, lat. 1084 and 909 (both without musical notation); and a version in Paris, lat. 887, adds the final words in a later hand. The conclusion that these three versions stem from a single tradition is strengthened by a common textual variant: the use of the word *quam* for *que*. The text of *Summe sacerdos* is edited in the Appendix.

TABLE 1A

Sacerdos introductions for specific feasts

(Letters in parentheses refer to texts edited in the Appendix; an asterisk indicates that only a cue appears)

Manuscript	Feast	Introductory trope	Trope	Rubric
F:Pn, lat. 1240: Limoges, 933–36	Martin	Sacerdos dei, fol. 37ᵛ (A)	Laus tua deus	Ante gloria in ex. Tunc dicat pontifex Gloria
F:Pn, lat. 1120: St. Martial, ca. 1000	Martial	Sacerdos dei, fol. 63ᵛ (A)	—	(Space is provided, rubric is wanting)
F:Pn, lat. 909: St. Martial, early 11th c.	Nat	Summe sacerdos, fol. 11	—	Ante pontificem
F:Pn, lat. 903: St. Yrieix, early 11th c.	Nat	Summe sacerdos, fol. 168	Omnipotens alt.	Ante laudes episcopo dicatur
	Stephen	Sacerdos dei, fol. 169 (A)	Laus tua deus	
F:Pn, lat. 1118: SW France, 985–96	Nat	Summe sacerdos, fol. 13	Omnipotens alt.	Ad rogandum episcopum . . . Deinde dicat episcopus
	Stephen	Sacerdos dei, fol. 19ᵛ (A)	Qui indiges	Ad episcopum rogandum
	Easter	Surrexit Xrs, fol. 5ᵛ	Cives/Xrs surrexit	Item ad gloria
F:Pn, lat. 779: Limoges, late 11th c.	Nat	Summe sacerdos, fol. 3	Cives/Omnipotens	
	Stephen	Sacerdos, fol. 15ᵛ (C)	Cives/Qui indiges	
	Epiphany	Sacerdos dei, fol. 30 (*)	Cives/Laudat in ex.	
	Easter	Xrs surrexit, fol. 38ᵛ	Cives/Xrs surrexit	
	InvHC	O sacer, fol. 63 (F)	Cives/Prudentia	
	Pentec	Sacerdos dei, fol. 68 (*)	Cives/Laus tibi	
F:Pn, lat. 1084: Aurillac, late 10th c.	Nat	Summe sacerdos, fol. 39	—	
F:APT, Ms. 17: Apt, mid-11th c.	Nat	Summe sacerdos, p. 40	Laus tua deus	
	Easter	Sacerdos dei, p. 136 (G)	Cives/Xrs surrexit	
	Pentec	Angelica laudes, p. 217 (H)	Laudat in excelsis	Ad gloriam

			Laudat in excelsis	*Ad pontificem dicant*
F:APT, Ms. 18: SE France, late 10th c.	Easter	*Sacerdos dei*, fol. 35 (B)	——	——
F:CA, Ms. 75: Arras, mid-11th c.	Stephen	*Sacerdos dei*, fol. 8^v (B)	——	*Ad episcopum*
F:Pa, Ms. 1169: Autun, 996–1024	Nat1	*Letentur celi*, fol. 1^v	Quem glorificant	——
	Nat3	*Pastor bone*, fol. 4^v (B)	Pax sempiterna	——
	Easter	*Cives superni*, fol. 20	Christus surrexit	——
I:Ra, Ms. 123: Bologna, early 11th c.	Nat	*Pastor bone*, fol. 191^v (B)	Pax sempiterna	——
	Epiph	*Pastor bone*, fol. 203$_3$ (B*)	Quem novitate	——
	Easter	*Pastor bone*, fol. 214 (B*)	Cives/Xrs surr	——
	Peter	*Pontifex bone*, fol. 239^v (B)	Laudat in excelsis	*Ad pontifex*
I:MOd, Ms. O.I.7: Forlimpopoli, 11–12th c.	Epiph	*Pastor bone*, fol. 27 (B)	Laus tua deus	——
I:Pc, Ms. A 47: Ravenna, *ca.* 1100	Easter	*Pastor bone*, fol. 105^v (B)	Cives/Xrs surr	——
	Easter	*Pastor bone*, fol. 131 (B)	Cives/Xrs surr	——
I:Tn, Ms. G.V.20: Bobbio, 11th c.	Nat	*Pastor bone*, fol. 21^v (B)	Pax sempiterna	——
I:IV, Ms. Boll. LX: Pavia, early 11th c.	Nat	*Pastor bone*, fol. 13 (B)	Pax sempiterna	——
I:PS, Ms. C.121: Pistoia, late 11th c.	Nat3	*Pastor bone*, fol. 16 (B)	Pax sempiterna	——
I:BV, Ms. VI 39: Benevento, late 11th c.	Pentec	*Sacerdos dei*, fol. 95^v (B)	——	——
I:BV, Ms. VI 40: Benevento, mid-11th c.	Pentec	*Sacerdos dei*, fol. 76^v (B)	——	——
D-BAD:BAs, Ms. Lit. 5: Reichenau, 1001	Stephen	*Sacerdos dei*, fol. 33^v (B)	——	*Ad carmen angelicum*
GB:Lbl, Add. Ms. 19768: Mainz, 950–72	(Easter)	*Sacerdos dei*, fol. 39^v (B)	——	(Added in top margin)

TABLE 1B

Sacerdos chants introducing Gloria section
(Letters in parentheses refer to texts edited in the Appendix)

Manuscript	Introductory trope	Rubric
F:Pn, lat. 88: Limoges, S. Martin, before 1031	*Summe sacerdos,* fol. 69ᵛ / *Sacerdos dei,* fol. 69ᵛ (A) / *Domne sacerdos,* fol. 69ᵛ (A)	*Incipiunt laudes de circulo anni maiorum festorum*
F:Pn, n. a. lat. 1871: Moissac, *ca.* 1050	*Sacerdos dei,* fol. 49 (D) / *O sacerdos dei,* fol. 49 (E) / *Summe sacerdos,* fol. 49ᵛ / *Sacerdos dei,* fol. 49ᵛ (A)	(These introductions do not appear among the Gloria tropes)
F:Pn, lat. 13252: Paris, S. Magloire, late 11th c.	*Sacerdos dei,* fol. 26 (B)	———
GB:Ob, Bodley 775: Winchester, *ca.* 1050	*Sacerdos dei,* fol. 64 (A)	*Cantores gemini resonant haec verba dicentes /Sacerdos . . ./ Incipiunt sancti modulamina dulciter ymni quem cecinere chori christo nascenti superni*
GB:Ccc, Ms. 473	*Sacerdos dei,* fol. 58 (A) / (Organal part, fol. 138ᵛ)	*Organa dulcisona docto modulamine compta Ut petat altare resonat laus ista sacerdos*
I:VEcap, Ms. CVII Mantua, 11th c.	*Sacerdos dei,* fol. 35ᵛ (A)	*Tunc veniant duo clerici ante altare et dicant hunc vs*
GB:Lbl, Add. Ms. 19768: Mainz, 950–72	*Sacerdos dei,* fol. 39ᵛ (B)	(Added in top margin: not attached to Gloria section)

III

Both these *sacerdos* introductions, in fact, are independent of any specific Gloria or trope. The manuscripts in Table 1B indicate their general applicability; and Table 1A, whose manuscripts do not arrange Glorias in groups, shows them attached to a variety of feasts and tropes. Likewise there are many Gloria melodies associated with these introductions. In those few cases where the melodic connection between introduction and intonation can be accurately estimated, the nature of the joint varies enough from source to source that we can be sure these introductions are conceived independently of a specific Gloria melody.[8] Their principal function, then, is to petition the celebrant to intone the Gloria. And in some cases at least, judging from the accompanying rubrics, the celebrant must be a bishop.

This episcopal restriction is undoubtedly the impetus for both these introductions, even though the limiting rubric is not always present. A connection with episcopal prerogative exists from the early history of the Gloria; a sketch of this liturgical background can help us to an understanding of these and other Gloria introductions.

The *Liber pontificalis* records that Pope Symmachus (d. 514) ordered the *Gloria in excelsis* to be said on Sundays and on the feasts of martyrs. No restriction is mentioned limiting its use to bishops (Table 2A). But the Sacramentary of Hadrian, brought to France at the end of the eighth century, states in the brief order of Mass that opens the book, "Then is said the *Gloria in excelsis*, if there is a bishop, only on

---

[8] Where introductions are attached to specific Glorias, the melody in most cases is the Medieval "Gloria prima," which Rönnau (n. 4 above) calls "Gloria A," and which is no. 39 in Detlev Bosse's catalogue, *Untersuchung einstimmiger mittelalterlicher Melodien zum "Gloria in excelsis deo"* (Erlangen, 1954), p. 95. This is by far the most widely used melody for troped Glorias. See Richard L. Crocker, "Gloria in excelsis Deo," *The New Grove Dictionary*, VII, 450. For the sake of completeness we list here those Gloria introductions that appear with melodies other than the "Gloria prima" (LU = *Liber usualis*; AM = *Antiphonale missarum juxta ritum sanctae ecclesiae mediolanensis* [Rome, 1954]):

Sacerdos dei:
Bosse, 29: Bamberg, lit. 5
LU, XV: Benevento, VI.40

Cives superni:
LU, IV: Paris, n. a. lat. 1235; lat. 9449; Madrid 19421
LU, XI: Arsenal, 1169; Rome, 1343; Bologna, 2824
AM, 4: Benevento, VI.34; VI.38; VI.40
Bosse, 43 (?): Vatican, Urb. lat. 602

Letentur celi:
LU, IV: Paris, n. a. lat. 1235; lat. 9449
LU, XI: Arsenal, 1169

Sundays and feast days: by priests, however, it is not said at all save only at Easter" (Table 2B).

The *ordines romani*—descriptions of papal ceremonies for those unfamiliar with them—mention the same restriction. The second *ordo*—a supplement to the first, which had arrived in France about 750—gives directions for a Mass when the pope is absent, stating, "And it is done in the same way by a priest when he says a stational Mass, except the *Gloria in excelsis deo*, for it is not said by priests except at Easter" (Table 2C). The fourth *ordo*, from the end of the eighth century, also mentions this restriction (Table 2D).

This state of affairs continued in some measure at least into the eleventh century, when Abbot Berno of Reichenau complained that priests could say the Gloria at Easter, but not at Christmas, when it is particularly appropriate (Table 2E).

The episcopal privilege as regards the Gloria was occasionally granted; Table 2F is the text of the early twelfth-century Pope Calixtus II's permission to one community to use the Gloria on its patronal festival.[9] We know also that certain ("mitred") abbots were granted some episcopal privileges; Table 2G records the ninth-century Pope John IX's concession of the episcopal privilege of intoning the Gloria to the abbey of Monte Cassino.[10]

In the course of the eleventh and twelfth centuries, the distinction between bishop and priest in the matter of intoning the Gloria seems to have disappeared; or rather, the tradition continued in a different degree, in that a bishop retained the right to intone the Gloria whenever he was present at Mass.

Now how is all this liturgical history relevant to our Gloria introductions? The introductory tropes *Sacerdos dei excelsi* and *Summe sacerdos*, preserved as they are only in tenth- and eleventh-century manuscripts, were current when the Gloria was to some extent restricted to bishops. And it seems evident for several reasons that

[9] It is possible that this is a dispensation to sing the Gloria during Lent, as the feast of the Annunciation occurs on March 25.

[10] The document containing this reference is the "Registrum Petri Diaconi," a twelfth-century cartulary compiled by the librarian of Monte Cassino at that time. Peter the Deacon included in this register a great many forged documents that served to increase the apparent power and importance of the abbey. This particular papal privilege seems to be genuine: the right to intone the Gloria would not have been a serious issue in the twelfth century. But even if the document is a fake, we can learn that Peter the Deacon knew of the restrictions placed upon the Gloria in earlier times. On Peter the Deacon and these forgeries, see E. Caspar, *Petrus Diaconus und die Monte Cassineser Fälschungen* (Berlin, 1909); and Paul Meyvaert, "The Autographs of Peter the Deacon," *Bulletin of the John Rylands Library*, XXXVIII (1955), 114–38.

TABLE 2

Some references in nonmusical books to *Gloria in excelsis deo*

A. *Liber pontificalis*: "Hic [Pope Symmachus] constituit ut omne die dominicum vel natalicia martyrum Gloria in excelsis hymnus diceretur." *Le Liber pontificalis*, ed. Louis Marie Olivier Duchesne, 2nd ed. (Paris, 1955), I, 263.

B. *Hadrianum* (eighth century): "Item dicitur Gloria in excelsis deo, si episcopus fuerit, tantummodo die dominico sice diebus festis: a presbiteris autem minime dicitur nisi solo in pascha." Hans Lietzmann, *Das Sacramentarium gregorianum nach dem Aachener Urexemplar* (Münster, 1921; repr., 1967), p. 1.

C. *Ordo romanus*, II (eighth century): "Similiter etiam et a presbitero agitur, quando in statione facit missas, preter Gloria in excelsis Deo, quia a presbitero non dicitur nisi in Pascha. Episcopi, qui civitatibus praesident, ut summus pontifex, ita omnia peragunt." Michel Andrieu, *Les Ordines romani du haut moyen âge*, II (Louvain, 1948), 116.

D. *Ordo romanus*, IV (late eighth century): "Et si presbiter missa debet caelebrare, non dicit Gloria in excelsis Deo, sed tantum psallit et dicit oracione." Andrieu, *Les Ordines romani*, II, 169.

E. *Berno* (eleventh century): ". . . cur non liceat omni die Dominico vel natalitiis sanctorum presbyteros illum hymnum canere, quem nato in carne Domino angeli cecinere, dicentes: *Gloria in excelsis Deo*, etc. quod si concessum est illum cantare in Pascha secundum praetitulationem Missalis non multo minus licitum puto in Nativitate Domini, quando primum coepit audiri ab hominibus in terris qualiter ab angelis canebatur in coelis." Jacques Paul Migne, *Patrologiae cursus completus, Series latina*, CXLII (Paris, 1880), col. 1058.

F. *Calixtus II* (1119-24): "Pro reverentia B. Mariae semper Virginis, cujus nomine locus vester insignis est, in Annunciatione Domini Salvatoris nostri hymnum angelicum inter missarum solemnia abbati et fratribus pronunciare concedimus." Quoted in Edmond Martène, *De antiquis ecclesiae ritibus libri tres*, I, *Tractatus de antiqua ecclesiae disciplina in divinis celebrandis officiis* (Venice, 1783), 132.

G. *John IX* (899; possibly a twelfth-century forgery): "Johannis IX Ragenprando diac. et abb. etc.: confirmat monasterio s. Benedicti et suis pertinentiis libertatem, concedit monachis ius eligendi abbatem ex propria congregatione et episcopum ad sacra ministranda, hymnum angelicum per dies dominicos ad missarum sollemnia dicendum. . . ." Paulus Fridolinus Kehr, *Italia pontificia*, VIII (Berlin, 1935), 127.

H. *Châlons ritual*, thirteenth century (F:Pn, lat. 10579, fol. 8, describing double feasts): "Chorialis regens dextrum chori baculo deposito vadit ad episcopum et ei cantando annuntiat quomodo debeat incipere Gloria in excelsis et continuo repetit locum suum."

I. *Laon ritual*, twelfth century (F:LA, Ms. 215, fol. 48, Christmas midnight Mass): "Cantor dat episcopo Gloria in excelsis et dicitur prosa Sedentem."

J. *Bec customs*, thirteenth century (F:Pn, lat. 1208, fol. 66, Easter midnight Mass): "finita Kyrieleison sine annuntiatio cantoris incipit sacerdos Gloria in excelsis deo."

these introductions were originally addressed to the bishop before he intoned the Gloria. First, the Gloria itself was reserved to the bishops, at least until the ninth century. Second, certain manuscripts make this distinction clear even in the tenth and eleventh centuries (see the rubrics in Table 1A). And third, the exalted form of address to the celebrant (*Summe sacerdos*, etc.) suggests a dignitary of high rank.[11]

Certain passages from later medieval customaries (shown in Table 2 as items H, I, and J) may even be describing this ceremony. The Châlons and Laon rituals may, of course, simply be describing a cantor giving a cue to the bishop (bishops then as now were not chosen on the basis of their singing ability), but the Châlons description seems so ceremonial that we are tempted to wonder whether the cantor does not embellish his duty. And the Bec customs, which directly forbid any announcement by the cantor, are describing the very day when a *sacerdos* introduction would not be used. But even if these customaries are simply describing some behind-the-scenes maintenance of the liturgical machinery, it is easy to imagine how the necessity of cuing the bishop might give rise to a little ceremony, complete with its own music.

The picture given by our sources is not unequivocal. It would be convenient to find, in a troper of early date, a group of *sacerdos* introductions with some such rubric as "One of these tropes may be sung before a bishop only, on any occasion when he is to intone the Gloria." Unfortunately for us, medieval rubrics are for accustomed practitioners, not ignorant latter-day scholars. The situation, as we find it, is that the *sacerdos* introductions that seem applicable to any Gloria (those in Table 1B) mention no episcopal restriction; while those that are limited to bishops are all attached to specific feasts.

Now if these *sacerdos* chants were in fact to be addressed only to a bishop, then clearly they can be used only in the bishop's presence. For a cantor who understands this restriction, the matter is simple: when a bishop is present and the occasion warrants, the cantor turns to the place in his troper where a *sacerdos* introduction is found and causes it to be sung as the bishop approaches the altar. The difficulty arises for the cantor whose troper is arranged by feast, all of today's tropes being conveniently gathered side by side; for in his book there is no convenient way to place a *sacerdos* introduction before a Gloria without suggesting also that it is to be performed only on the day in question. This is the case with the tropers in Table 1A; and, as it happens, these are the only manuscripts that include rubrics limiting the introduction to a bishop. Apparently these rubrics are added to

---

[11] In this connection it might be noted that a similar sung trope, with similar rubric, was occasionally used to request an episcopal benediction. In Paris, lat. 1118, fol. 47, the rubric *Ad episcopum interrogandum* introduces such a piece, which begins "Princeps ecclesie pastor."

indicate the normal function of an introduction when its placement among proper tropes might suggest that it is limited by feast rather than by the rank of the celebrant.

Two of the manuscripts in Table 1A solve this problem in another way: instead of showing the introduction's independence of feast and trope by supplying a restrictive rubric, Paris, lat. 779, and Rome, Angelica 123, provide an introduction among the proper tropes of all feasts when a bishop would normally be expected. Rubrics in Angelica 123 show the presence of a bishop on these occasions;[12] we can only surmise that the same procedure is being followed in lat. 779.

The remaining manuscripts in Table 1A do not fit this pattern; each has a *sacerdos* introduction attached to a specific feast, with no indication of episcopal restriction. It may be that the bishop was expected for the feast in question—but then why not for other feasts as well? These sources, all of them Italian and German, and hence beyond the Aquitanian sphere of influence, where the *sacerdos* chants were normally used, may simply have misconstrued the use of such pieces; or perhaps they do not wish to limit these invitations to bishops alone. We simply cannot tell.

*   *   *

If the *sacerdos* chants illuminate the special prerogative enjoyed by bishops in intoning the *Gloria in excelsis*, the other side of this liturgical coin reveals a second group of Gloria introductions related at its origin to the special case of Easter.

We have seen that the limitation of the Gloria to bishops stipulated in the Sacramentary of Hadrian, the *ordines romani*, and elsewhere, indicates also that a priest may intone the Gloria, but only at Easter. And a trope beginning "Cives superni" has a brief but colorful career as a Gloria introduction connected particularly with that feast.

In its clearest form, *Cives superni* appears as in Example 3. Like the *sacerdos* chants, *Cives superni* refers to the *Gloria in excelsis* as a whole: "The heavenly citizens today announce to the world their festivity and ours; let us all resound the glory of God, Christ arising." But

---

[12] Table 1A shows the four feasts for which Angelica 123 provides a *Pastor bone* introduction; for three of these, a *versus* is provided to be sung before the bishop. The Christmas *versus* is labeled *Incipit versus in natali domini ante episcopum* (fol. 187ᵛ); similar rubrics (and *versus*) are present for the Epiphany (fol. 202) and St. Peter (fol. 238). Significantly, the only feast not so labeled is Easter, traditionally the one day when a priest may intone the Gloria.

III

492

unlike the *sacerdos* chants, this is not an invitation to the celebrant; instead it urges us all to join with the angels—an invitation to choral singing. And except for the ablative absolute attached rather flat-footedly at the end, the text makes no specific reference to Easter; if anything, it might refer to Christmas, since it recalls the angels singing in the sky at the first Gloria performance.

In what we shall call the "Italian version," *Cives superni* appears in many Italian tropers immediately after the intonation of the Gloria; it thus introduces, not the intonation, but the continuation of the performance by the chorus. This Italian version is characterized by

Example 3

Cives superni, I:Rn, Ms. 1343, fol. 9

the presence of the final words "Christo surgente" and by the fact that it always appears with the Gloria trope *Christus surrexit dulcibus hymnis*. These appearances of the Italian version of *Cives superni* are detailed in Table 3A.[13] This Italian version by itself is in no way remarkable; it does not introduce the Gloria, since it follows the intonation; and from these sources there is no reason to treat it as anything other than the first phrase of a widespread Gloria trope for Easter. But there is also a "Northern version" of *Cives superni*—a version that lacks what we might call the "Italian coda": the final words "Christo surgente," which alone make the text proper to Easter.

The Northern version differs also in function, as detailed in Table 3B. In three of these manuscripts *Cives superni* is used just as it is in Italy, except that the Italian coda is lacking. But the remaining appearances of *Cives superni* place it in a category with the *sacerdos* chants as being a special and separable introduction to the *Gloria in excelsis*.

Cives superni is used as a movable introduction, but after the intonation, in the relatively late Aquitanian troper Paris, lat. 779. Here *Cives superni* appears six times, with six tropes, in the course of a manuscript arranged in an annual cycle. In each case *Cives superni* introduces the choral portion of the Gloria, appearing always before "et in terra pax"; and in each case the intonation of the Gloria is preceded by an (episcopal) *sacerdos* introduction, with one notable exception: Easter. At Easter, when, as we remember, priests may intone the Gloria, a special introduction, *Christus surrexit a mortuis*, is used, focusing on the feast and not on the celebrant; the same piece appears in Paris, lat. 1118, also preceding the Easter Gloria. This preface may have originated elsewhere, since it often serves as a trope to the Sequentia.[14]

But in Paris, lat. 779, *Cives superni* is used more than just for Easter: it is a wandering introduction, serving not only for the trope *Christus surrexit dulcibus hymnis* but for five other tropes and feasts as well. The scribe of lat. 779 sees *Cives superni* not as an Easter trope, but as a sort of second-wave introduction, to be applied wherever the Gloria intonation is troped. And the absence here of the Easter Italian coda makes this wider usage perfectly suitable.

[13] In several cases a *sacerdos* introduction appears in the same manuscript, but only in Angelica 123 does a *sacerdos* chant precede a Gloria whose intonation is followed by *Cives superni*.

[14] See Paul Evans, "The *Tropi ad Sequentiam*," *Studies in Music History: Essays for Oliver Strunk*, ed. Harold Powers (Princeton, 1968), pp. 73–82.

TABLE 3A

Cives superni: The "Italian vesion"

Manuscript	*Cives*	Coda?	Trope	Other introductions in MS
I:Rc, Ms. 1741: Nonantola, 11th c.	fol. 25ᵛ	yes	*Christus surrexit*	—
I:Rn, Ms. 1343: Nonantola, 11th c.	fol. 9	yes	*Christus surrexit*	—
I:Bu, Ms. 2824: Nonantola, 11th c.	fol. 7	yes	*Christus surrexit*	—
GB:Ob, Douce 222: Novalesa, 11th c.	fol. 19	yes	*Christus surrexit*	—
I:VEcap, Ms. CVII: Mantua, 11th c.	fol. 39	yes	*Christus surrexit*	*Sacerdos dei*, (A) heading Gloria section
I:Ra, Ms. 123: Bologna, 11th c.	fol. 214ᵛ	yes	*Christus surrexit*	*Pastor bone* (B) precedes this Gloria and three others (see Table 1B)
I:Rvat, Urb. lat. 602: Monte Cassino, 11–12th c.	fol. 50ᵛ	no	*Christus surrexit*	—
I:PS, Ms. C.121: Pistoia, late 11th c.	fol. 34ᵛ	yes	*Christus surrexit*	*Pastor bone* (A), fol. 16
I:BV, Ms. VI34: Benevento, late 11th c.	fol. 124	yes	*Christus surrexit*	—
I:BV, Ms. VI38: Benevento, 11th c.	fol. 48	yes	*Christus surrexit*	—
I:BV, Ms. VI40: Benevento, 11th c.	fol. 21ᵛ	yes	*Christus surrexit*	*Sacerdos dei* (B), fol. 76ᵛ
I:MOd, Ms. O.I.7: Forlimpopoli, 11–12th c.	fol. 105ᵛ	yes	*Christus surrexit*	*Pastor bone* (B) precedes this Gloria and the Epiphany Gloria, fol. 27
I:Pc, Ms. A 47: Ravenna, *ca.* 1100	fol. 131	yes	*Christus surrexit*	*Pastor bone* (B) precedes this Gloria

TABLE 3B

Cives superni: The "Northern version"

Manuscript	Cives	Coda?	Feast	Trope	Other introductions in MS
I. *Cives superni* **as first phrase of Easter trope**					
F:Pn, n. a. lat. 1871: Moissac, *ca.* 1050	fol. 70ᵛ	no	Easter	*Christus surrexit*	Group of four introductions, fol. 49–49ᵛ
F:Pn, lat. 1084: Aurillac, late 10th c.	fol. 107ᵛ	no	Easter	*Christus surrexit*	*Summe*, fol. 39, for Nat
F:Pn, lat. 1118: SW France, 985–96	fol. 51	no	Easter	*Christus surrexit*	*Surrexit Christus* here; *Sacerdos dei* for Nat, Stephen
F:APT, Ms. 17: Apt, mid-11th c.	p. 136	no	Easter	*Christus surrexit*	*Summe*, p. 40, for Nat; *Sacerdos* (G), p. 136, for Easter; *Angelicae* (H), p. 217, for Pentecost
II. *Cives superni* **as movable postintonation trope**					
F:Pn, lat. 779: Limoges, late 11th c.	fol. 3ᵛ	no	Nat	*Omnipotens alt.*	*Summe sacerdos*
	fol. 15ᵛ	no	Stephen	*Qui indiges*	*Sacerdos* (C)
	fol. 30	no	Epiph	*Laudat in exc.*	*Sacerdos dei* (B)
	fol. 38ᵛ	no	Easter	*Christus surrexit*	*Christus surrexit a mortuis*
	fol. 63	no	InvHCross	*Prudentia prud.*	*O sacer* (F)
	fol. 68	no	Pentec	*Laus tibi domine*	*Sacerdos dei* (B)
III. *Cives superni* **as intonation introduction for Easter**					
F:Pa, Ms. 1169: Autun, 996–1024	fol. 20	no	Easter	*Christus surrexit*	*Letentur celi* for Nat1
GB:Lbl, Royal Ms. 8.C.XI: France, 11th c.	fol. 9ᵛ	no	Easter	*Christus surrexit*	*Pastor bone* (B) for Nat3 / none
E:Mn, Ms. 19421: Catania, 12th c.	fol. 23ᵛ	no	Easter	*Christus surrexit*	none

		IV. *Cives superni* as introduction, clearly movable			
		no	Easter	*Christe salus mundi*	
F:Pn, lat. 10508: St. Evroult, early 12th c.	fol. 26ᵛ	no			None elsewhere in MS
F:Pn, lat. 9449: Nevers, 11th c.	fol. 8 / fol. 35 / fol. 47	no / no / no	Nat3 / Easter / Ascens	*Pax sempiterna* / *Laus tua* / *O laudabilis*	*Letentur celi* for Nat1, fol. 5
F:Pn, n. a. lat. 1235: Nevers, 12th c.	fol. 185 / fol. 208 / fol. 216ᵛ	no / no / no	Nat3 / Easter / Ascens	*Pax sempiterna* / *Laus tua* / *O laudabilis*	*Letentur celi* for Nat3, fol. 181ᵛ
		V. *Cives superni* placed at head of Gloria section			
E:Mn, Ms. 288: Sicily, 12th c.	fol. 43	no	—	—	None elsewhere in MS
E:Mn, Ms. 289: Sicily, 12th c.	fol. 18	no	—	—	None elsewhere in MS

The other Northern applications of *Cives superni* do not all work as well. In three manuscripts (listed in Category III of Table 3B), *Cives superni* precedes the intonation of the Easter Gloria; and in all three cases the trope that follows is the familiar *Christus surrexit dulcibus hymnis*. Except for the absence of the coda, this usage is what we know from the Italian sources, with the important difference that *Cives superni* here precedes the intonation. Possibly some imaginative scribe, knowing how to introduce the episcopal Gloria with a special trope, and aware also of the special prerogative of priests with regard to the Easter Gloria, chose to promote *Cives superni* to this prefatory function, even though its text serves better to introduce a chorus than a soloist. But if a transfer was made in this way, it must have happened only after the removal of the Italian coda; for if *Cives superni* introduced only the Easter Gloria (as it does in these three sources) there would be no need to remove a specific reference to that very feast.

So perhaps the scribes of these three manuscripts are preserving a garbled version in which *Cives superni* is confused with a *sacerdos* introduction. If Christmas has an introduction, they reason, why not Easter? Here is *Cives superni*: it sounds like an introduction, so we will move it to where it can serve.

This line of thinking could be followed by the compiler of such a manuscript as Arsenal 1169, which does have two introductions for Christmas Glorias as well as *Cives superni* for Easter. But the other two sources in Group III contain no other Gloria introductions, and this confusion would surely not have originated in a place where the *sacerdos* chants are unknown.

Cives superni in these three sources might be dismissed as a misplaced trope phrase, were it not for a strong tradition, in the two Nevers tropers and in some Norman-Sicilian manuscripts, of using *Cives superni* as a movable introduction like the *sacerdos* chants. These five sources, detailed in Categories IV and V of Table 3B, show varying degrees of independence for *Cives superni*. In the Norman troper Paris, lat. 10508, *Cives superni* introduces one Gloria in the midst of a repertory of troped Glorias; but here the trope is *Christus salus mundi* and not *Christus surrexit dulcibus hymnis* as we might expect, even though the latter trope does appear a few folios later.

The two Nevers tropers (Paris, lat. 9449, and Paris, n. a. lat. 1235) each employ *Cives superni* for several major festivals as an intonation chant. Here *Cives superni* is clearly not a misplaced trope phrase, and there is no connection with the Easter trope *Christus surrexit*. The *sacerdos* chants are nowhere present in these manuscripts; their place and function is taken by *Cives superni*, which serves for three feasts, hence for three different Gloria tropes (none of which is *Christus surrexit*, although this trope is in the repertory).

Like other manuscripts arranged by feast, the Nevers tropers do not show whether *Cives superni* may be extended to other feasts as well; but, like the calendar manuscripts that preserve the *sacerdos* chants, there is a rubrical restriction, in one case at least, to bishops: the Christmas appearance of *Cives superni* in Paris, n. a. lat. 1235 is labeled *antiphona ad episcopum*.

Sacerdos introductions, as we have seen, appear in two ways: attached to specific feasts in manuscripts arranged in an annual cycle, but also preceding a whole section of Glorias in sources arranged by category. And *Cives superni* apes both of these practices; the first we have just seen, and the second is found in two Norman-Sicilian tropers of the twelfth century. Madrid 288 and 289 each have extensive sections of troped Glorias, and in each manuscript the Gloria section is preceded by the trope *Cives superni*, standing here evidently to be applied to any of the following Glorias as an introduction before the intonation.

How does *Cives superni* arrive at playing all these roles? Is it a misplaced Italian trope phrase, brought North, detached, and scattered? Or is it rather a special Northern Gloria introduction associated with Easter, mistaken in Italy for a trope phrase?

Scholars have argued that the trope *Christus surrexit dulcibus hymnis* is of Italian origin; Klaus Rönnau further points out that Paris, lat. 1118, the oldest Aquitanian source of this trope, may have originated in the southeast of France and served to communicate the trope northwards.[15] And since that trope travels with *Cives superni* in Italian sources, it is reasonable to suppose that they would have arrived together in the North—but in this case the Northern usage of *Cives superni* is difficult to explain.

First of all, *Cives superni* would arrive bearing its Italian coda. And since this coda appears nowhere in the North, its removal must be a first step in the hypothetical Italian importation. Since lat. 1118 uses *Cives superni* only for the Easter Gloria, in the normal postintonation position and with the usual trope, there would be no reason to remove a received Easter reference; but the coda is missing in lat. 1118, as it is in every Northern source.

The only good reason for removing the Easter coda is to make *Cives superni* suitable for other feasts; this would be a job for the scribe

---

[15] *Die Tropen zum Gloria in excelsis Deo*, p. 106.

of lat. 779, where *Cives superni* is used six times; or for a Nevers compiler who uses it to introduce several Glorias. And, except in these cases, we should expect *Cives superni* to retain its Italian coda wherever it precedes its parent Easter trope.

Either the Italian coda was removed as soon as *Cives superni* crossed the Alps, or else it is not of Italian origin. And none of our earlier Northern manuscripts give any hint of the *Christo surgente* coda, despite the fact that *Cives superni* is used in them just as it is in Italy, preceding the Easter trope *Christus surrexit*. I think we must conclude that *Cives superni* is not an Italian product at all, that it arose in the same region and at about the same time as the *sacerdos* chants, that, although it does have some special connection with Easter, it is not part of a longer trope, and that the Italian version is a reinterpretation of what was originally not a trope phrase at all. Indeed, we have one Italian source that does not use the Easter coda. But why remove a good reference to today's feast? The coda must not have been there at all.

*   *   *

The repertory of Gloria introductions, as we find it today, presents a confusing picture, owing to two difficulties, one old and one new. There was confusion in the Middle Ages about the changing liturgical nature of the Gloria; and there is confusion nowadays because we lack enough sources to give a clear picture of the accidents of geography and chronology: we are tempted to view everything in one plane, even though we know that fallen leaves do not fully describe the tree.

It is clear that, in the period represented by these tropers, the *Gloria in excelsis* was not restricted to Easter and those days when a bishop was present. All the sources considered here contain significant collections of Glorias and tropes; yet only a few of the manuscripts were used in episcopal churches.

We have argued that the *sacerdos* chants were designed for use when a bishop intoned the Gloria (when only a bishop could intone it); but by the time these pieces appear in the earliest sources, the Gloria had already begun to be extended to persons of lower rank. Even then the *sacerdos* introductions retained their episcopal function, but we also find variants in the form of address, making chants designed for bishops more suitable for priests. Instead of "Sacerdos dei excelsi" we sometimes find "Sacerdos dei," "O sacerdos dei," or

"Pastor bone." And "Summe sacerdos" humbles itself to be known as "Domne sacerdos."[16]

In fact the two textual traditions of *Sacerdos dei* (detailed in the Appendix) may result from this extension of the Gloria to priests. Version A, with the address "Sacerdos dei excelsi," occurs in the earliest manuscripts, beginning with Paris, lat. 1240 (933–36), and is found chiefly in Aquitanian manuscripts of the early eleventh century; its final appearances, in the middle of the century, are in the Winchester tropers and Cambrai 75.

The second version appears only at the beginning of the eleventh century; this is not an Aquitanian text: it is found mostly in Italian and northern French sources. This later text uniformly uses a different and less exalted address to the celebrant: the Italian sources almost unanimously begin "Pastor bone," and the Northern sources generally agree on "Sacerdos dei" (without "excelsi"). Evidently by the middle of the eleventh century the current version of *Sacerdos dei* is one that permits being addressed to a priest; by the latter part of the century this version even finds its way into the Aquitanian manuscript Paris, lat. 779.

Unlike the *sacerdos* prefaces, *Cives superni* was originally intended for use on a certain feast, for liturgical reasons again connected with the rank of the celebrant. As restrictions on the Gloria relaxed, this introduction was occasionally applied to other feasts as well, in a way that sometimes obscured its original purpose and that of other chants.

As the Gloria found wider use in the course of the eleventh century, the functions of these special pieces were assimilated to those of more normal introductory chants: that of celebrating the feast day on which they are sung. This is much of what confuses our picture. There are two trends that illustrate this reorientation: first, the alteration of purposely neutral texts to enhance a specific feast; and second, the composition or adaptation of newer introductions to serve the new function.

In the first case, we can provide two illustrations of this process. Example 4 shows a version of *Summe sacerdos* from Paris, lat. 887.[17] Here, in addition to changing the form of address to the celebrant, the scribe presents two alternate endings to replace the words "regi nato domino"; the first ("resurgenti domino") seems designed for Easter, while the second ("regi magno domino") is even less focused than the

---

[16] Texts of all the *sacerdos* chants are edited in the Appendix.

[17] The problem of diastematic alignment in lat. 887 makes an unequivocal transcription difficult. This example is based on the readings of other sources as well.

Example 4

Summe sacerdos, F:Pn, lat. 887, fol. 69ᵛ

original. Apparently "regi nato" will serve for Christmas, "resurgenti" for Easter, and "regi magno" for everything else.

Paris, lat. 779, in which *Cives superni* is used for six feasts, presents a similar set of adjustments. Four cases present the normal text as in Example 3. But in two others the word "festivitatem" is changed: at Christmas to "nativitatem," and at Easter to "resurrectionem."

Freer use is made of old materials in two versions of *Sacerdos dei excelsi* adapted for specific feasts (listed in the Appendix as Versions C and D). In each case a creative spirit has begun with the musical and textual material of the introduction, made an excursion in praise of Saint Stephen or of the Resurrection, and returned home to close with the familiar "eia dic domne."

The second illustration of changing function is the composition or adaptation of new introductions. An interesting case is *Hodie natus est*, from Paris, lat. 887 (Ex. 5).[18] This clearly occasional piece seems to

---

[18] Lacking other sources, the transcription offered as Example 5, also from Paris, lat. 887, is to some degree speculative.

Example 5

Hodie natus est, F:Pn, lat. 887, fol. 70

stem from the *sacerdos* introductions, ending with the customary
invitatory words "eia dic domne eia." But the introduction is here
presented after the intonation, with the result that the invitation
comes too late. Clearly the function of this piece is confused.[19]

Two other Gloria prefaces, of a local nature, are listed in Table 1.
Letentur celi is a Christmas introduction from the region of Nevers;
celebrating the Nativity, it concludes with an invitation to choral
performance, even though it precedes the intonation.[20] *Christus surrexit a mortuis* introduces the Gloria only in two Aquitanian manuscripts for Easter, but it is frequently found elsewhere as a trope to the
Sequentia.[21] The weight of numbers suggests that this piece is more at

[19] These same invitatory words ("eia dic domne eia") are used in some Italian
tropers at the ends of trope phrases for Offertory verses: see Planchart, *The Repertory of
Tropes at Winchester*, II, 216, 221. Here the invitation is an amplification of the "eia"
(or "eia et eia," or "dicite, eia"), which frequently cues the end of a trope phrase. Such
exclamations are frequently used to warn the choir ("una voce dicentes," "dicamus
omnes," etc.); but these Offertories are evidently sung by a soloist.

[20] Letentur celi celorum et exultet omnis orbis terrarum quia hodie xristus de
virgine maria natus est iubilemus omnes cum angelis clamantes et dicentes: Gloria.
. . .

[21] The text of Paris 1118: "Surrexit xristus a mortuis mortis confractis vinculis
gaudentes angeli voces in altissimis resonant dicentes eia: Gloria. . . ." The version in
Paris 779 reverses the first two words, as do the versions with the Sequentia. For a
discussion of this piece with the Sequentia, and a transcription of the version with a
final *alleluia*, see Evans, "The *Tropi ad Sequentiam*" (n. 14 above).

home with the Sequentia; but since the text refers, as do all the Gloria prefaces, to the celestial song of the angels (who are required to sing *Alleluia* when this piece is attached to the Sequentia), it seems equally plausible that *Christus surrexit a mortuis* originated as a Gloria introduction, only later extended to wider use.

*   *   *

Our picture is thus confused, but in a way that we can understand. From the evidence remaining, we can construct a plausible sequence for the development of this repertory, along the following lines. First, there arise special introductions to the *Gloria in excelsis* that solemnize the bishop's prerogative: the *sacerdos* chants for the bishop himself, and *Cives superni* for the one day when a priest may intone the Gloria. As restrictions relax, these tropes gradually change their focus: sometimes their use is extended by altering the address to the celebrant; sometimes they begin to be assimilated to certain feasts (*Summe sacerdos* to Christmas, for example); and sometimes their original purpose is lost altogether, as when *Cives superni* is substituted.[22] As the original tradition is dissipated, there is a brief flowering of new introductions, with a festival rather than a ceremonial focus, before the practice of introducing the *Gloria in excelsis* dies out altogether.

I cannot resist concluding this study by recalling Léon Gautier's elegant description of the atmosphere of this fleeting ceremonial moment—a description that opens his brief discussion of these introductions in his pioneering 1886 study:[23]

> The bishop has censed the altar, assisted by his archdeacon; he has given the kiss of peace to the deacons, to the assisting priests, to his chaplain. Then, with deliberate steps, he has moved to his throne, which is situated against the wall, behind the altar, in the center of the apse. He has majestically ascended its four steps, and is seated. The Kyrie has just finished; there is a great silence: we are waiting.

---

[22] Indeed, *Sacerdos dei excelsi* wanders so far afield as to be used as an Introit trope for Saint Martin. See Planchart, *The Repertory of Tropes at Winchester*, II, 265–66.

[23] Gautier, *Les Tropes* (n. 6 above), p. 245; my translation: "L'évêque a encensé l'autel, assisté par son archidiacre; il a donné le baiser de paix aux diacres, aux prêtres assistants, à son chapelain. Puis il s'est, à pas lents, dirigé vers son trône, qui est disposé contre la muraille, derrière l'autel, au milieu et au fond de l'abside. Il en a gravi majestueusement les quatre degrés et s'est assis. Le *Kyrie* vient de s'achever: il se fait un grand silence: on attend."

APPENDIX

Texts of *Sacerdos* Introductions

SUMME SACERDOS

1 Summe sacerdos
2 emitte vocem tuam
3 et recita nobis angelorum cantica
4 que precinerunt regi nato domino
5 eia dic domne eia

Paris, Bibliothèque Nationale
lat. 1118, fol. 13
lat. 1871, fol. 49ᵛ
lat. 779, fol. 3ᵛ
lat. 909, fol. 11
lat. 903, fol. 168
    4: *quam*; 5: omitted
lat. 1084, fol. 39
    4: *quam*; 5: omitted
lat. 887
  fol. 69ᵛA:
    4: *quam cocinerunt*
    5: later hand
  fol. 69ᵛC:
    1: *Domne sacerdos*
    3: *carmina*
    4: *quam precinerunt gaudentes regi magno domine*
    5: adds *eia resurgenti domino regi magno domino eia.*

Apt, 17, p. 40
    3: *carmina*

SACERDOS DEI, VERSION A

1 Sacerdos dei excelsi
2 veni ante sacrum et sanctum altare
3 ut in laude regis regum
4 vocem tuam emitte
5 supplices te rogamus et petimus
6 eia dic domne

Cambridge, Corpus Christi, 473, fol. 58
    2: *sanctum et sacrum*
    3: *et (ut)*
    5: *supplices te deprecamur*

Oxford, Bod. 775, fol. 64
    2: *sanctum et sacrum*
    3: *et (ut)*
    5: *supplices te deprecamur*

Paris, lat. 1240, fol. 37ᵛ
    5: *om̄ et petimus*

Paris, lat. 1118, fol. 19^v
    2: *sanctum et sacrum*
    3: *et (ut)*
    6: <u>*om*</u> *eia*

Paris, lat. 1120, fol. 63^v
    1: <u>*om*</u> *excelsi*
    5: <u>*om*</u> *et petimus*

Paris, lat. 903, fol. 169
    5: *deprecamur (rogamus)*
    6: <u>*om*</u> *eia*

Paris, lat. 887, fol. 69^v
    1: *excelse*
    3: *et (ut)*
    6: <u>*om*</u> *eia; domine*

Paris, n. a. lat. 1871, fol. 49^v
    5: *deprecamur (rogamus)*

Verona, CVII, fol. 35^v
    1: *sacerdos dei electe*
    2: *sanctum et sacrum*
    3: *et (ut)*
    5: omitted

Cambrai, 75, fol. 8^v
    2: *sanctum et sacrum*

SACERDOS DEI, VERSION B

1 Sacerdos dei
2 veni ante sacrum et sanctum altare
3 ut in laude regis regum
4 vocem tuam prior emittere digneris
5 supplices te rogamus
6 eia dic domne

Paris, lat. 779, fol. 30, fol. 68
    3: *et (ut)*

Paris, lat. 13252, fol. 26
    2: *asstans (veni)*
    3: *nunc (ut)*
    4: *primum (prior)*
    5: *oramus (rogamus)*

Arsenal, 1169, fol. 4^v
    1: *Pastor bone*
    3: *et (ut)*

Apt, 18, fol. 35
    3: *regem (regis)*

London, British Library, Add. 19728, fol. 39^v
    1: *Sacerdos dei et alme*
    3: *et (ut)*
    4: *dignare (digneris)*

506

Bamberg, Lit. 5, fol. 33^v
    1: adds *excelsi*
    3: *et (ut)*
    4: *dignare (digneris)*
    6: *dicito (dic domne)*

Ivrea, LX, fol. 1
    1: *Pastor bone*

Rome, Angelica, 123
    fol. 191^v
        1: *Pastor bone*
    fol. 203
        1: *Pastor bone* (cue)
    fol. 239^v
        1: *Pontifex bone* (cue).

Pistoia, C.121, fol. 16
    1: *pastor bone*
    4: *voce tua prior*
    5: omitted

Benevento, VI39, fol. 95^v
    3–4: *ut laudes mittere digneris*

Benevento, VI40, fol. 76^v
    3–4: *ut laudem mittere digneris*

SACERDOS DEI, VERSION C (Paris, lat. 779, fol. 15^v):

Sacerdos dei excelsi qui stas ante sacrum et sanctum altare supplices te rogamus ut in laude regis regum vocem tuam emitte ymnum angelicum obnixe precamur per gloriosum martyrem Stephanum ut digneris referre eia dic domne.

SACERDOS DEI, VERSION D (Paris, n. a. lat. 1871, fol. 49)

Sacerdos dei excelsi veni ante sacrum et sanctum altare ut in laude crucifixi qui surrexit a mortuis vocem tuam emitte ymnum angelicum obnixe precamur et petimus eia dic domne.

E: O SACERDOS DEI (Paris, n. a. lat. 1871, fol. 49b)

O sacerdos dei audi preces nostras quas in conspectu tuo supplices fundimus ut stare digneris ante sacrum et sanctum altare et predica nobis angelica ymnum eia recita domne.

F: O SACER (Paris, lat. 779, fol. 63)

O sacer hac sumus domini de more sacerdos
laudibus ecce diu divinis iure moratis
petimus angelicum subnecta primitus himnum
eia dic domne.

G: SACERDOS DEI ECCE RESURGENTEM (Apt, 17, p. 136)

Sacerdos dei ecce resurgentem supernum conlauda et in aula regis regum vocem tuam emittere supplices exoramus eia dic domne.

H: ANGELICAE LAUDES (Apt, 17, p. 217)

Angelicae laudis dic carmina, summe sacerdos, eia.

IV

New Music from Old: The Structuring of Responsory Prosas

MEDIEVAL MUSICAL EMBELLISHMENTS for the liturgical Office hours have, until recently, aroused only passing interest among scholars owing largely to the difficulty of access to the repertoire.[1] It is a particularly interesting repertoire, however, since the limited size of these pieces lets us look closely at the way they are made; their small scale invites a detailed observation of how the medieval composer arranged his material. We can study the progressive development of forms and procedures, which is of particular value as many of the same techniques, used on a larger scale, produce the more familiar Mass tropes and prosas.

In practice, tropes[2] in the Office are used almost exclusively with the great Responsories; these are the only large-scale pieces of Office music approaching the style and complexity of the Graduals and Tracts of the Mass. Responsory tropes are normally placed at the end of the performance, as a final flourish added just before the close of the respond. A Responsory has an *ABA* form owing to the repetition of the respond (or a part of the respond, the *repetenda*) after the verse (or verses), but the respond is normally written only once, to conserve space. Thus, if section *A* includes new material the second time, at least that section which is to differ from the original must be written out. This is, in its simplest form, how we recognize Responsory tropes, melismatic or texted: they are included—sometimes without identifying labels—as an alternative version of the repetenda.

---

[1] Although Mass tropes are conveniently gathered in the medieval compendia called *troparia* or tropers, Office tropes are generally found with the chant they decorate; the extent of the repertoire can be seen only by surveying large numbers of medieval Office books. In the haystack of a faded thousand-page breviary, the needle of a single small prosula can be a real joy! Two recent dissertations have assembled and studied this repertoire: Helma Hofmann-Brandt, *Die Tropen zu den Responsorien des Officiums* (Inaugural-Dissertation, Erlangen-Nürnberg, 1971); Thomas Forrest Kelly, "Responsory Tropes," (Ph.D. diss., Harvard Univ., 1973).

[2] The word "trope" is used here in a general sense to avoid the awkwardness of writing "medieval interpolative chant" or some such term. It would be preferable to reserve the term for the interpolations used for Introits and the like, but in the absence of any accepted general term, it seems simplest to make the same compromise as was made in the Middle Ages, when a book containing tropes, *laudes*, *versus*, prosulas, prosas, and sequentias was generally called a *Troparium*.

IV

In this study, we shall explore the development of textual additions to Responsories by examining two local repertoires. These techniques begin with the simple procedure of adding a syllabic text or *prosula* (i.e., a little *prosa*) to a melisma already present at the end of the respond. More complex procedures include both the expansion of the technique of the prosula and the creation of a prosa to a greater or lesser extent independent of the Responsory's music.

Any prosula, by definition, is restricted in length to the number of notes in the melisma of which it is a texting. If, therefore, a longer texted decoration is thought desirable, more notes must be found to which words can be added. Two principal ways of producing such notes suggest themselves. First, a melisma can be sought that is longer than that available in the Responsory. Some such longer melismas already exist, in fact, as the melismatic tropes used for some Responsories; and these melismas are often found in texted versions.[3] The texting technique, however, is still one of prosulation, of abiding by the musical dictates of a preexistent melisma.

A second and obvious means of finding more notes in order to free the prosula from the restrictions of the respond melisma is simply to produce out of the imagination as many notes as are wanted, that is, to compose words and music together, rather than setting words to a melisma that is already extant. This procedure may seem self-evident, but it is significant and innovative in the light of prosula technique. Furthermore, it can be shown in some cases to be a gradual process, since varying degrees of independence of prosa from respond melisma are to be found. Although these stages do not necessarily represent a chronological development, they do illustrate gradations between two extremes: on the one hand, complete dependence of added text and music on the notes of the final melisma; on the other, complete independence from the music (and also sometimes the sense) of the parent Responsory.

In order to examine this development of prosa technique, I have chosen two repertoires of Responsory prosas, each of which appears in a single manuscript or locality, so as to isolate, as nearly as possible, the efforts of individual creators, or at least individual creative environments. Although these pieces are unique to their parent churches, their techniques are illustrative of a full range of the styles of medieval Responsory prosas.

Manuscript A. 486 in the Bibliothèque municipale of Rouen, a four-teenth-century antiphoner from the abbey of St. Ouen in Rouen, preserves a long and solemn Office for the abbey's patron. The full monastic Office for St. Ouen (Audoenus) occurs only in books from the abbey;[4] The Responsories

---

[3] A catalogue of many of these melismas, with the prosulas which are sometimes added to them, appears in Kelly, "Responsory Tropes," pp. 49–115. See also Ruth Steiner, "Some Melismas for Office Responsories," this JOURNAL, XXVI (1973), 108–31.

[4] See below, pp. 375–76, for other books in which the Office occurs.

have nonbiblical texts which are metrical and rhyming, and the monastic Office has, like many rhythmic Offices, Responsories arranged in consecutive modes. These Responsories appear complete from folios 228 to 229 in the manuscript. Only one has any sort of addition: to the last Responsory, *Beatus Audoenus*, is added the prosa *Christi nostra redemptio*.

A few folios later in the same manuscript—after the Antiphons for psalms at Second Vespers of St. Ouen and before the Antiphon on *Magnificat*—appears a long group of prosas apparently intended for insertion in performances of Responsories of St. Ouen. The placement of this group of prosas is a little odd. This is the normal place for a Responsory at Vespers, if one is used, but no Responsory appears here. Instead are found the incipits of eight Responsories of St. Ouen, with prosas written out for each. We may surmise that at Second Vespers a single Responsory was selected from among those whose incipits are provided, and that this Responsory was performed as it is written for Matins a few folios earlier in the same book, except that the prosa was added at the appropriate place.

What, though, is the reason for providing eight different prosas at a place where only a single Responsory would normally be used? A simple explanation is that they provide a wide choice of Responsories and prosas for Vespers. But why the paucity of prosas at Matins and the almost overwhelming choice at Second Vespers? Such a large group of prosas seems extravagant if used at the rate of one per year. It is more likely that the group, which follows the order of Responsories at Matins, is designed for use as a group in the night Office. Keeping the prosas separate from the Responsories maintains whatever purity and authenticity the Responsories have and also preserves the possible unity of the prosas as a group.

Although the two collections are separated, they are clearly related. The prosas evidently derive their order from that of the Responsories; they also derive their melodic material, to a very great extent, from the music of the Responsory melismas. Hence we may suppose that the composer or composers of these prosas had in mind the complete night Office of St. Ouen.

It may be, of course, that these pieces constitute a personal act of creation, an intellectual or devotional exercise, never intended for liturgical use. It is true that the volume in which they are found appears to be a personal book, too small to be used by more than a single singer. Whatever their purpose, however, these prosas are illustrative of the liturgical Responsory prosas found in other sources. The prosas and the Responsories to which they correspond are listed in Table 1, which shows their relation to the complete night Office of St. Ouen.

Prosas are provided for the first and last Responsories of the first nocturn, for all four Responsories of the second nocturn, and for the first and next-to-last Responsories of the third nocturn. There is no prosa here for the last

IV

TABLE I

THE PROSAS AND THE RESPONSORIES TO WHICH THEY CORRESPOND

Order at Matins	Incipit of Responsory	Mode	Incipit of prosa
1	*Confessor christi Audoenus*	1	*Spiritus sanctus faucis*
2	*O summi viri gloriosa*	2	
3	*Sanctorum sepe potitus*	3	
4	*Rome autem ad confessionem*	4	*Eterna visione Dei*
5	*Pretiosa viri merita*	5	*Christi munere predictus*
6	*In Syon velut tuba*	6	*Corde pio votis*
7	*Digne pater Audoene*	7	*Rex regum gloriose*
8	*Sanctus Audoenus dum iam*	8	*Virtutum gratia*
9	*Dilectus Domini quendam*	1	*Celestis turba*
10	*Quoddam autem*	8	
11	*Pastor bonus Audoenus*	2	*O patris genite*
12	*Beatus Audoenus* (prosa *Christi nostra redemptio* appears with Responsory)	7	

Responsory, presumably because the Matins Office earlier in the manuscript had already provided one.

Do these prosas constitute a single stylistic group? Certainly some connection with the final melisma of the parent Responsory is the rule in all cases, but the relationship is not always exactly the same. Indeed, it is precisely this variation that interests us. The different ways of deriving prosa from melisma show the composer's view of the relationship of words and music and his attitude toward the creation of new music from old.

Since the manuscript provides with each prosa only a brief incipit indicating the appropriate Responsory and its melisma, the examples below provide the full melisma from the end of each Responsory as it appears in the Matins Office.

The first prosa is actually a simple prosula (Ex. 1):

Example 1

Rouen A. 486, fol. 230ᵛ

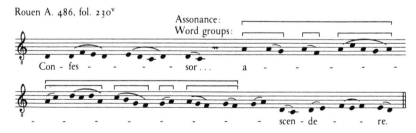

It follows the notes of the melisma closely. Words and syllables are grouped according to the neumes of the melisma to a certain extent, as is shown by brackets above the melisma; larger groups are delineated by assonance with *a*, the vowel of the original text. The omission from the prosula of two notes in the melisma may be scribal error or, as we shall suggest, the prosulator may have had a different melisma for his source than that which appears for Matins in this manuscript.

The prosa *Corde pio votis*, for Responsory 6, is likewise a simple prosula (Ex. 2). But here the prosula is divided into sections, of which the first is

Example 2

Rouen A. 486, fol. 231

marked with the sign ℣, in the same way, as we shall see, as prosas based on repetition. This division may be intended as an indication for the choir to change sides, although antiphonal performance seems somewhat inappropriate for a piece involving no musical repetition. The text is structured so as to fit the neumes with precision; assonance with *o* is used extensively.

The second prosa in the series, *Eterna visione*, has a somewhat more elaborate derivation (Ex. 3). The prosa divides the melisma in half and

IV

Example 3

Rouen A. 486, fols. 230ᵛ–231

repeats the first section with new text, but not the second, producing an *AAB* form from an *AB* melisma. This sort of melodic extension is also frequently found in unprosulated Responsory melismas, where there is no need for more notes simply to accommodate a text. Hence this reduplication is a consciously applied aesthetic principle which creates an order based on repetition where no such order existed.[5] The text is accommodated to this new structure: appropriate assonance with *i* is used in the repetitions, which are marked with the sign ℣. Groups of words and syllables are matched with neumes, and it may be claimed that this correspondence is exact if we consider that the fourth note of the melisma, which is not part of the group, is attached to those notes that follow it (*Vi*-sione) in its first prosulation, to those that precede it (ci-*ves*) in the repetition.[6]

In the third prosa, *Christi munere* (Ex. 4), the prosulator goes twice through the entire melisma, using characteristic assonance and syllable group-ing. Here again, the resulting prosa is divided into sections using the sign ℣; but the division does not correspond to the melodic repetition, even though the assonance and the sense of the words make the latter division a more logical one than what the manuscript offers.

Rex regum gloriose for Responsory 7 (Ex. 5), is produced, like *Eterna visione* (Ex. 3), by reduplication of part but not all of the melisma. Thus an *AAB* form is generated from an *AB* melisma. The resulting prosa is divided

---

[5] See Thomas Forrest Kelly, "Melodic Elaboration in Responsory Melismas," this JOUR-NAL, XXVII (1974), 461–74.

[6] Vertical strokes, which do not appear in the manuscript, have been added to the transcriptions to facilitate melodic comparison.

Example 4

Rouen A. 486, fol. 231

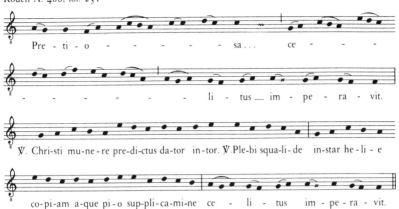

into sections with the points of division occurring at the ends of the repetitions. Much assonance is used, but not necessarily at the same points in corresponding repetitions; neumes are clearly reflected in the text.

The sixth prosa, *Virtutum gratia* (Ex. 6), is produced by dividing the melisma in half and repeating both parts. Division into phrases is according to the melodic repetition. The notes of the prosa correspond to those of the melisma as it appears earlier in the manuscript, but this prosa does not match

Example 5

Rouen A. 486, fol. 231

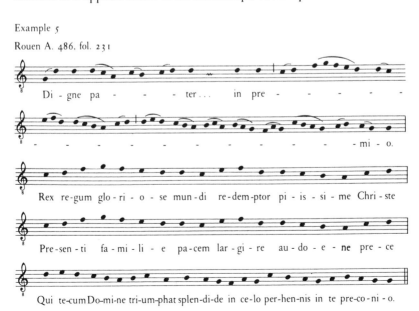

IV

Example 6

Rouen A. 486, fol. 231

San - - - - ctus ... ra - di - a _____
_____ splen - do - - - - re.
℣. Vir -tu-tum gra - ti - a   re - di - mi-tus in - cli - ta. ℣. Chri-sti lu-cer-na splen-di - da
au - do - e - nus per   a - stra   Sa - cre   cru - cis   scig - ma - ta   a - spec - tat
Ca - stra de - si-gnan-ti - a   ful - gi - da   splen - do - - - - re.

the melisma as closely as the other prosas in the group match their parent melismas. The extra notes for the words *Christi* and the missing torculus before the word *splendore* are inaccuracies that may demonstrate that the maker of the prosa used as his model a melisma slightly different from that which appears in this manuscript. Or he may simply have taken liberties with his model.

Celestis turba terrarum (Ex. 7), the next prosa in the group, is formed by a threefold division and repetition of the melisma. Here, as in *Christi munere* (Ex. 4), the division into phrases is not what one would expect from the melodic structure.

The last prosa of the group, *O patris genite* (Ex. 8), apparently introduces a new procedure: the insertion of new melodic material not directly derived from the melisma or its repetition. The first part of the melisma is reduplicated and prosulated; then another versicle pair is added, which begins with the same notes as the continuation of the melisma but goes on with new material, ending in a musical rhyme with the first phrase. The prosa then concludes with the remainder of the original melisma.[7]

---

[7] The prosa is transposed with respect to the original Responsory, ending on *a* instead of *d*, although the original *d* of the Responsory is given in the cue that accompanies the prosa. It is not clear whether the performance of the entire Responsory is intended to begin untransposed and end on *a*, or whether the prosa should be fitted to the pitch of the Responsory, be it *a* or *d*. If this were a simple prosula, we might be tempted to propose simultaneous performance in parallel fifths.

Example 7

Rouen A. 486, fol. 231

This addition of musical material is the important step toward independence by which a great many more extended prosas are created. It is easy to see how this thin end of the wedge allows for the introduction of progressively larger amounts of new material. We shall presently examine the nature and control of such material from another repertoire, but first we should consider the stylistic qualities of the St. Ouen prosas as a group.

Although they are derived in different ways from their parent melismas, all these prosas (except the last) can be described together as a modest expansion of the art of the prosula; that is, they are created by adding syllables of text to the notes of preexistent melismas. This technique is broadened to the extent that several of the melismas are expanded and reshaped by some kind of reduplication to provide a melody of suitable length for the prosulator's purpose. Musically, these prosas stay very close to home, following the melisma in their assonance and grouping of syllables. Although such a relationship is not unusual in prosulas,[8] a very close correspondence might suggest that the neumatic grouping of the melismas is an arrangement expressly made to fit the text. If a music scribe were writing a melisma while thinking of its prosula, he might well group the notes according to the words he already knew.

---

[8] For a general discussion, see Bruno Stäblein, "Die Unterlegung von Texten unter Melismen: Tropus, Sequenz, und andere Formen," *Report of the Eighth Congress [of the International Musicological Society], New York, 1961*, Vol. I (Kassel, 1961), pp. 12–29.

IV

Example 8

Rouen A. 486, fol. 231-231ᵛ

For the St. Ouen prosas, however, it seems fairly clear that some form of the melisma existed before the prosa. In the first place, some of these are not simple prosulations but are the result of reduplications of the melismas—and these, too, reflect the neume groups in their texts. It is difficult to see why a prosulator should burden himself with parallel groupings in versicle pairs where he is not following a melodic original which suggests this grouping. Furthermore, there is no evidence in the manuscript that the melismas are anything other than an integral part of their Responsories, while the prosas clearly play a subservient role. They have no clear liturgical function and cannot be performed without their Responsories. Thus, to argue that the melismas are the abbreviated melodies of these prosas with their texts removed is to go against strong evidence. We must conclude instead that the verbal and musical structures of the prosas are derived from close observation of the melismas.

Despite this evidence of melodic derivation, however, we have noted certain divergences between the notes of the Responsory melismas and their putatively derivative prosas. Though such differences are often to be noted in prosulas, the search for other possible melodic sources for these prosas is rewarding. At least three other manuscripts preserve musical Offices for St. Ouen, though none preserves any of these prosas. Two books are of secular use, presenting only the first nine Responsories of the monastic Office (Paris, Bibl. Ste. Geneviève, MS 2732, a fifteenth-century Rouen breviary; and

Rouen Y. 49, a fifteenth-century life and Office of St. Ouen). Although these books preserve readings that are close to the A. 486 prosas in some details, they introduce discrepancies in other places and are not, therefore, demonstrably closer to the melodies of the A. 486 prosas than are the melismas of A. 486 itself.

A third source is more interesting. Rouen MS A. 531, a thirteenth-century St. Ouen breviary, has the full monastic Office (fols. 281–284) as seen in A. 486. Unfortunately, the manuscript is badly mutilated at this point, so the melisma for Responsory 5 is incomplete, and Responsories 6–9 are wanting altogether. But those that remain show an interesting relationship to the prosas of A. 486 in three melismas.

(1) In *Rome autem* (Ex. 3), the melisma in A. 486 has its *AB* structure reduplicated to generate the *AAB* structure of the prosa. A. 531 includes this *AAB* repetition within the melisma, but the reduplicated portion has been erased, and the melisma now corresponds to that in A. 486.

(2) The two secular sources of *Pretiosa viri* (Ex. 4) have notes which correspond to the prosa's "plebi squalide" (as A. 486 does not). A. 531 has an erasure at this point and is written over so that it now corresponds to the melody of A. 486. Although the relevant page of A. 531 is torn, leaving the melisma incomplete, the melisma breaks off in the middle of a repetition which would, if continued, match the reduplication of the prosa in A. 486. But this repetition, too, is tampered with by erasure.

(3) The melisma for *Pastor bonus* (Ex. 8) in A. 531 provides all the notes found in the A. 486 prosa, but without reduplication. Thus the prosa *O patris genite* of A. 486 is an *AABB* reduplication of the melisma found in A. 531 in the form *AB*. The pitches, however, do not always correspond exactly, and the melisma of A. 531 has been tampered with by a later hand. The prosa of A. 486, therefore, may not actually result from the addition of new musical material but from the reworking of the parent Responsory melisma—albeit a different version of the melisma from that found earlier in the same manuscript.

The evidence available from A. 531 leads us to suggest the following stages of development for the A. 486 prosas. In the thirteenth century or earlier, the prosas of A. 486 were developed from a set of Responsory melismas by a process of reduplication. These melismas were subsequently altered and sometimes simplified; alterations can be seen in progress in A. 531 and are codified without comment in A. 486. The prosas retained the shape of the earlier melismas and were preserved separately in the fourteenth-century MS A. 486 along with the revised melismas, with which they no longer corresponded exactly.

Despite the stylistic consistency of this group of prosas, and despite their probable contemporaneity, a process of increasing complexity can be presumed, moving from simple prosulation to the prosulation of an extended version of the melisma. It is difficult to imagine these techniques proceeding in the reverse order.

We can continue to trace the evolution of independent prosas by examining another consistent local tradition. A twelfth-century antiphoner from St.-Maur-des-Fossées (Paris, Bibliothèque Nationale, MS fonds latin 12044) contains a large repertoire of Responsory prosas; the group is unusually rich in unica, suggesting a consistent local tradition. The few prosas in the manuscript that are known elsewhere are inevitably the best known and most widely disseminated of such pieces. The remaining eighteen prosas in the volume are all unica, with the exception of five which are added in a later hand to another antiphoner of St. Maur from the twelfth century (Paris, Bibl. Nat., lat. 12584). Of these five, three are found in two other Offices of St. Maur. Table 2, below, lists the prosa repertoire of this manuscript, separating the local repertory from those pieces widely known elsewhere.

Of the eighteen "local" prosas, five—marked with asterisks in Table 2— are prosulas, employing the already familiar techniques of assonance and word grouping; one is an imitation of the well-known *Inviolata integra*. The remaining eleven prosas have a paired-versicle structure with considerable independence from the Responsory melisma, showing development beyond the style of the St. Ouen prosas.

The three prosas for the Office of St. Arnulf will serve to illustrate the style of these pieces. The first, *Solus qui permanes* (Ex. 9), is made of three versicle

Example 9

Lat. 12044, fol. 161ᵛ

TABLE 2

THE PROSAS OF PARIS, BIBL. NAT. F. LAT. 12044

Folio	Incipit	Responsory	Feast
	I. The General Repertoire		
9	*Et bonore virginali*	*Confirmatum est*	Nativity
	Other appearances: London, Brit. Lib., Eg. MS 2615, fols. 45, 73–74^v (pr. Wulf Arlt, *Ein Festoffizium des Mittelalters aus Beauvais* [Cologne, 1970]. *Editionsband*, pp. 10–11). Madrid, Bibl. nac., MS 288, fols. 160^v–161; Paris, Ars., MS 279, fols. 107^v–108; Paris, Bibl. Nat., f. lat. 904, fol. 26–26^v (facsm. ed H. Loriquet *et al.*, *Le Graduel de l'église cathédrale de Rouen* [Rouen, 1907]; f. lat. 12584, fol. 210; f. lat. 16903, fols. 41^v–42; Sens, Bibl. mun., MS 46, fol. 25 (pr. Henri Villetard, *Office de Pierre de Corbeil* [Paris, 1907], p. 181—see also p. 120).		
	See also: Henri Villetard, "Une vocalise superbe," *Revue Grégorienne*, IX (1924), 58–63; David G. Hughes, "Liturgical Polyphony at Beauvais," *Speculum*, XXXIV (1959), 194; Peter Wagner, *Einführung in die gregorianischen Melodien*, Vol. I (Leipzig, 1911), p. 292.		
9^v–10	*Tanta nunc* *Familiam custodi* *Fac Deus munda* *Facinora nostra*	*Descendit de celis*	Nativity
	The bibliography on these pieces is too extensive to be cited completely here. See the relevant portions of Hofmann-Brandt and Kelly (fn. 1, above). A recent study dealing with these pieces and others is Ruth Steiner, "The Responsories and Prosa for St. Stephen's Day at Salisbury," *The Musical Quarterly*, XVI (1970), 162–82. See also Bruno Stäblein, "Tropus," *MGG*, Vol. XIII, cols. 797–826.		

TABLE 2 (Continued)

Folio	Incipit	Responsory	Feast
57	*Inviolata integra*	*Gaude Maria*	Purification
	Facsimiles: W. H. Frere, *Antiphonale Sarisburiense* (London, 1901–26; repr. New York, 1966), IV, 402–3; Loriquet, *Le Graduel*, fol. 217–217ᵛ; *Paléographie musicale*, XII, 271–72: XVII (Chartres, Bibl. mun., MS 260, fol. 64ᵛ).		
	Modern editions: *The Liber usualis* (Tournai, 1961), pp. 1861–62: *Variae preces* (Solesmes, 1888), p. 26; Wagner, *Einführung*, 2d ed., Vol. II (Leipzig, 1912), p. 190.		
	See also: J. Pothier, "Inviolata," *Revue du chant Grégorien*, II (1893/94), 19–22; C. Blume, "Inviolata," *Die Kirchenmusik* (Paderborn), IX (1908), 41–48.		
159ᵛ	*Consors merito*	*O beati viri*	Benedict
	Printed: Wagner, *Einführung*, Vol. III (Leipzig, 1921), p. 159.		
	Other appearances: Paris, Bibl. Nat., f. lat. 1089, fols. 2ᵛ, 32ᵛ; f. lat. 1338, fol. 125. See also Ruth Steiner, "Some Melismas for Office Responsories," this JOURNAL, XXVI (1973), 113 f.		
224	*Sospitati dedit*	*Ex ejus tumba*	Nicholas
	Very widely disseminated, often imitated. Some modern prints: Frere, *Antiphonale Sarisburiense*, IV, 359–60; MGG, Vol. XIV, Tafel 89; J. Pothier, "Ex ejus tumba," *Revue du chant Grégorien*, IX (1900/01), 49–52: Hofmann-Brandt, *Die Tropen*, I, 127 (polyphonic).		
	II. The Local Repertoire		

TABLE 2 (Continued)

Folio	Incipit	Responsory	Feast
34ᵛ	*Veloci aminiculo* Chartres, Bibl. mun., MS 89, fol. 183 (facsm. ed. *Paléographie musicale*, XVII); Paris, Bibl. Nat., f. lat. 5344. fol. 55ᵛ; f. lat. 12,584. fol. 245.	*Benedictione postulata*	Maur
41	*Orta de celis* Paris, Bibl. Nat., f. lat. 5344. fol. 56: f. lat. 12584. fol. 245ᵛ: a derivative prosa in f. fr. 5717, fol. 121.	*Sanctus Dominus Maurus	Maur
41ᵛ–42	*Eximie Christi* Chartres, Bibl. mun., MS 89, fol. 184ᵛ (facsm. ed. *Paléographie musicale*, XVII); Paris, Bibl. Nat., f. lat. 5344 56: f. lat. 12584. fol. 245ᵛ.	*Egregius confessor*	Maur
57	*Inviolata nos tua* An imitation of *Inviolata integra*	*Gaude Maria*	Purification
61	*Facere quo duce* Part of the prosa's melody is borrowed—see below, p. 387; see also Steiner, "Some Melismas." pp. 120–26.	*Cornelius centurio*	St. Peter's Chair
124	*O precelsa deitas	*O beata trinitas*	Trinity

TABLE 2 (Continued)

Folio	Incipit	Responsory	Feast
145ᵛ	Prepara Iobannes	Inter natos mulierum	St. John Baptist
	Paris, Bibl. Nat., f. lat. 12584, fol. 304ᵛ; Steiner, "Some Melismas," p. 124, prints the prosa from f. lat. 12044.		
147	*Pastor bone	Post gloriosa prelia	Babolenus
148	Angelica condona	Sanctus Domini confessor	Babolenus
161ᵛ	Solus qui permanes	Romana sancta	Arnulf
	Text pr. Wagner, Einführung, I, 209.		
162ᵛ	Benigne Deus	Conserva famulos	Arnulf
	Text pr. Wagner, Einführung, I, 310. Cf. prosa Maxime Deus, fol. 214; see below, p. 383.		
163	Pro meritis	Beatus martyr Domini	Arnulf
	Text pr. Wagner, Einführung, I, 310. Text and music pr. Stäblein, "Die Unterlegung," p. 19.		
202ᵛ	Perpetua mereamur	Concede nobis Domine	All Saints
	Paris, Bibl. Nat., f. lat. 12584, fol. 385ᵛ. Pr. Willi Apel. Gregorian Chant (Bloomington, 1958), pp. 436–37.		

TABLE 2 (Continued)

Folio	Incipit	Responsory	Feast
213	*Martyr Domini	Post petram	Clement
213	Adjutor omnis Paris, Bibl. Nat, f. lat. 12584. fol. 385ᵛ.	Vernans purpurea	Clement
214	Maxime Deus Cf. prosa Benigne Deus, fol. 162; and see below, p. 383. See also Jacques Handschin, "L'organum à l'église," Revue du chant Grégorien, XLI (1937). 16, fn. 8.	O felix pueri	Clement
214ᵛ	Adeste Domine	Clementis Christi	Clement
219ᵛ	*Culpas nostras	Miles Christi gloriosi	Eligius
224	*Ex eius tumba	Sospes nunc efficitur	Nicholas

pairs. The first versicle is made of the initial notes of the melisma, reduplicated to form a pair and altered to end, like the respond, on *e*. The second pair begins with the next notes of the melisma but continues with additional material. The third pair is not related to the melisma; it presents the same cadence as the other phrases, and though it preserves the original text word *Solamina*, it does not preserve that word's original notes.

Benigne Deus (Ex. 10), the second prosa for St. Arnulf, preserves the whole melisma while adding new material. The first half of the first phrase, together with the third versicle, comprises the full melodic content of the melisma on *beatos*. Thus the opening notes of the melisma serve as nothing more than an impetus for the prosa, lending not even music enough for a whole versicle pair. Though the prosa is quite short, it manages to have more original than derived melodic material, yet it contains, at its beginning and end, the entire melody of the melisma.

Assonance is used at the ends of lines, but the vowel used is not that of the original text word. This same prosa is used in the manuscript as the second prosa for St. Clement. There the Responsory to which it is attached is *O felix pueri*, which has the same melody and the same verse as *Conserva famulos*; the text word for the final melisma is *magnos*, and the opening word of the prosa reflects this difference: the prosa begins *Maxime Deus quem laudant*, but it is otherwise identical with *Benigne Deus*. The assonance with *i*, however, fits neither prosa especially well.

The final prosa for St. Arnulf (Ex. 11) is longer than the others and

Example 10

Lat. 12044, fol. 162ᵛ

Example 11

Lat. 12044, fol. 163

includes much added material. The opening notes of the melisma are used, in reduplicated form, for the music of the first versicle pair. The continuation of the melisma provides the melodic material of the second versicle, which is unpaired, and this same music recurs twice more: as the opening of versicle 7 and as the unpaired last versicle. Except for this opening flourish in versicle 7,

IV

the musical material between the two single versicles is musically unrelated to the Responsory melisma. Hence, a prosa in the form *AAB–CCDDEEFFGG–B* is created from a melisma in the form *AB*. One is tempted to surmise a reduplication *(AABB)* of the melisma, into which is inserted a group of five paired versicles—a sort of prosa within a prosula.[9] This is perfectly accurate for the musical form, but the sense of the prosa makes it clear that any such insertion happened before the addition of text. The unpaired second and eighth versicles, judging from their texts, do not form a matched pair which have been separated by the insertion of new material. The prosa cannot be separated, like the melisma, into original and added elements. The composer of the musical structure must have laid out the music before he (or someone else) set to work on the words.

The prosas unique to St. Maur are a rather close-knit repertoire. For one thing, we have seen that they are made by adding a number of paired versicles to musical material derived from the Responsory melisma. Further, the comparison of the added music from different prosas reveals that a good deal of music is common to the whole repertoire; short melodic contours recur in different prosas as movable cells, not occurring always in the same order.

Some of these melodic groups can be seen in Example 12, which consists of the melodies of four prosas from this manuscript with all but the opening and closing words omitted. Slurs have been provided to show word groupings that occur in both halves of a versicle since the prosas present only individual notes.[10] The sign *d* is used to indicate that a phrase is immediately repeated in the melody; the sign *x* indicates nonrepetition. I have labeled several melodic configurations that are similar.

The most striking of these groups is the little cell *A*, which is characterized both by its melody and its brevity. The other cells may seem more or less fluid to the scrutiny of those requiring note-for-note correspondence, but they are reasonable if viewed as different expressions of a general melodic idea rather than as exact formulas in the manner of a Gregorian Gradual or Tract. They give evidence of a close relationship among all these prosas, as almost all of the prosas from St. Maur contain some melodic material not unique to themselves.[11]

One of the prosas in this manuscript, which has a melodic structure like the others discussed so far—a lengthy addition of melodic material between melisma-derived sections—is unusual in that its added material is a well-known melisma from outside the local repertoire (Ex. 13). The portion of the

[9] See Stäblein, "Unterlegung," p. 19.

[10] It is easy to see how a melisma might come to reflect a known text even when the text is absent!

[11] A similar use, in Responsory melismas, of such melodic cells is discussed in Kelly, "Melodic Elaboration," pp. 472–74.

Example 12

Fol. 214ᵛ

ADESTE

an - ti - sti - - tis.

fol. 148ᵛ

ANGELICA

Do - - mi-num.

fol. 41ᵛ

EXIMIE

ae - ter - no - - rum.

fol. 163

PRO MERITIS

pro me - ru - it.

IV

Example 13

Fol. 61

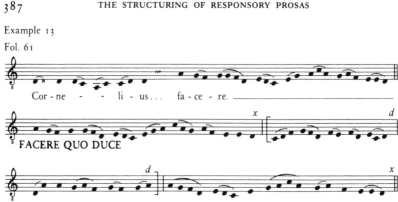

Cor - ne - - li - us . . . fa - ce - re. _____

FACERE QUO DUCE

melody not derived from the Responsory melisma is indicated by brackets. These are the opening phrases of one of the most widely disseminated and frequently used melismas for Responsory elaboration.[12] It is not surprising that a composer borrowing a melody for a first-mode Responsory prosa should choose this one. What is surprising is that any melisma was borrowed at all, considering that all the other prosas from St. Maur seem to employ a local fund of common melodic material.

The melody was borrowed before the prosa was created. It is typical of all the prosas of this group in that the sandwiching of external material between sections of melisma-derived music is accomplished before the addition of words. In this case, it can be determined that the borrowed melody brings along no hint of its many prosulations found elsewhere; the text of the prosa in this manuscript, like that of *Pro meritis* (Ex. 11), runs smoothly from the melisma-derived matter to the added material and back again.

Some of these St. Maur prosas have even less connection with the melodic material of the Responsory than do the examples considered thus far. The three prosas for the feast of St. Maur are each made of paired versicles none of which is derived from the music of the Responsory melisma. Each adds a brief unrepeated final tag including the last word or two of the Responsory's text. The melodies of these prosas are otherwise entirely similar to those already examined and are clearly related to other members of the group. The melodies of two such prosas, *Eximie Christe* (for St. Maur) and *Angelica condona* (for St. Babolenus), are provided in Example 12 as typical illustrations of the melody sharing among prosas in this manuscript.

The prosas considered above form together a picture of increasing musical independence of the prosa from the parent Responsory. The final stage of this development, not seen in the examples above, is the sort of prosa that is

---

[12] For more information on this melisma, see Steiner, "Some Melismas," pp. 120–26.

musically independent of the Responsory and whose text is in metrical rhyming verse, in the manner of the Sequences of Adam of St. Victor. By far, the most widespread of such prosas is *Sospitati dedit egros* for the Responsory *Ex eius tumba* of St. Nicholas, which was widely sung, imitated, and paraphrased.[13] Such prosas characteristically make no reference to the music of the Responsory, sometimes not even returning to the final words of the respond. Prosas of this kind, independently conceived, might almost be separable pieces, entirely effective alone and independent of Responsory performance. But this line of development, so important for the growth of the Sequence, seems to have been little pursued.[14] And these pieces take us beyond our study of developing new music from old.

The examples cited in this study have been arranged to illustrate stages of the prosa's increasing independence from the music of the Responsory. It cannot be conclusively demonstrated, however, that these stages represent a chronological development, although such a process seems in some ways likely. We do know that the earliest Responsory prosas (those for *Descendit de celis*) were prosulations of existing melismas[15] and that metrical rhyming poetry came at a rather later stage of the troping era. But it is not possible, and is probably inappropriate, to insist on the strict chronology of the intervening stages: too much depends on local custom and preference, and on individual creative instincts, as can be seen in our two groups of prosas.

The prosas of St. Ouen appear in a fourteenth-century manuscript, although, as we have seen, the prosas probably date from the thirteenth century; yet they preserve an "earlier" stage of development than the St. Maur prosas, which are found in a manuscript of the twelfth century. Why is their style so "backward"? If we consider the prosa repertoire of the St. Ouen manuscript as a whole, we find that the techniques of the prosas for St. Ouen are unique to that feast. The manuscript contains, besides the well-known prosulas for *Descendit de celis*, only three other prosas. The first of these, *Jesu magne* (for ℞. *Dum transisset*, fol. 101ᵛ) is metrical and rhyming and serves

---

[13] For further information on this prosa, consult Table 2, above.

[14] Tropes were, however, occasionally separated from their Responsories. The nuns of Barking Abbey in the fourteenth century sang *Sospitati dedit egros* in the refectory on St. Nicholas's Day (J. B. L. Tolhurst, ed., *The Ordinale and Customary of the Benedictine Nuns of Barking Abbey*, Henry Bradshaw Society, 65–66, 2 vols. [London, 1925–26], II, 167). *Inviolata* is frequently found in other roles: it serves for the Rogation procession in Sens, Bibl. mun., MS 21, fol. 2; as a Sequence at Mass for the Octave of the Purification in the fourteenth-century manuscript, Paris, Arsenal 595, fol. 292; as a Sequence for Benediction in *The Liber usualis* (Tournai, 1961), pp. 1861–62.

[15] See the references in Table 2 for *Tanta nunc, Familiam*, etc.

as an addition to a *Quem queritis* Easter drama.[16] This prosa is probably a late addition to the repertoire, as it appears in no earlier books. The other two prosas (*Christi nostra redemptio*, for ℞. *Beatus Audoenus*, fol. 229; *Christi Nigasius hostia* for ℞. *Egregius athleta Christi*, fol. 254ᵛ) are also, as it happens, the only prosas to appear in Rouen A. 531 (fols. 284 and 382ᵛ), a manuscript that has been shown to be more nearly contemporaneous with the St. Ouen prosas than A. 486. Hence, these two prosas seem to be regular features of the St. Ouen liturgy.

In both these cases, additional music for the prosa is produced by adding a longer alternative melisma to the end of the respond after the verse and texting this longer melisma as a prosula after the Gloria. From the point of view of prosa technique, this is a simpler procedure than that of the St. Ouen prosas, since it involves only prosulation without reworking the melisma. Thus, A. 486 contains no other evidence of prosulation extended by reduplication. Lacking evidence that their technique was otherwise known locally, we must see the prosas of the St. Ouen Office as being a local or personal inspiration.

It should be noted, however, that if these two longer alternative melismas were not present in A. 486 or A. 531, we might confuse their prosulas with St. Maur-style prosas—long texted additions with little reference to the original Responsory melisma. We should then be tempted to argue that the St. Ouen and the St. Maur prosa types are not successive but simultaneous developments from the simpler technique of the prosula: two different ways— additive and repetitive—of extending a melisma. This is unlikely, though, for two reasons: first, the melismas from which these prosas derive, like most such added melismas, are not made up expressly for the prosa, but belong to a large family of decorative melismas which wander from Responsory to Responsory.[17] Second, the St. Maur prosas do, in fact, often preserve (as these two prosas do not) a significant portion of the original Responsory melisma, often extending it, in the style of the St. Ouen prosas, by reduplication.

At St. Maur, the situation is similar to that at St. Ouen: the local prosas have their own technique. But there is a difference in that the full range of possibilities is available for comparison. In addition to prosulas for *Descendit de celis*, the manuscript contains an added alternative melisma (℞. *O felix sacrorum*, fol. 165ᵛ) and the metrical *Sospitati dedit egros* as well as the equally popular *Inviolata*. If the local prosas keep to a single style, it is not out of dull ignorance of other possibilities; the local technique is clearly the

---

[16] A facsimile of the prosa is printed in Diane Dolan, *Le Drame liturgique de Pâques en Normandie et an Angleterre au moyen âge* (Paris, 1975), facing p. 64. She discusses this drama on pp. 75–100.

[17] See Steiner, "Some melismas."

preferred one, and only the unchallenged favorites from outside are allowed to invade the repertoire.

Although we have been able to trace a line of development in the techniques of Responsory prosas, there is evidently an element of aesthetic preference in both these repertoires. Other possibilities are available but they are rejected. It is clear that no simple rejection of the old in favor of the new, or of the simple in favor of the more complex, operates among the creators of these pieces. The elegance of the prosula is not necessarily exceeded by the breadth of the more independent prosa. In these repertoires we are in the presence of creative intellects that consider possibilities, rejecting some, imitating others, and creating new forms which illustrate the aesthetic temperament of the age.

V

Melodic Elaboration in Responsory Melismas

L IKE THE CADENZA of a Classical concerto, a melisma occurring near the end of a Responsory is a likely place for ornamental elaboration. Such ornamentation is to be found in many Responsories, especially those that end a Nocturn. It can be observed, by the comparison of the same Responsory in different sources, that even though the differences between versions of the Responsory are minor, the differences between versions of the final melisma may be considerable. Such differences seem to be the result of a spirit of ornamental elaboration operating after the composition of the body of the Responsory.

Whether such elaborations ought to be called tropes depends mostly on our own usage of modern divergent terminology. The scribes of manuscripts which preserve such elaborations, far from calling them tropes, seem not to have known that they were preserving material not properly part of the Responsory—or if they added it themselves, they diligently avoided any credit for their work.

Lengthy melismas by themselves are no sure sign of a lurking trope.[1] Cases can be cited where a Responsory has the same long melisma in every source;[2] in other instances, material designed for the embellishment of Responsories is preserved in such a way that a clear distinction is made between the Responsory and the added material. Additions of this sort are not considered here, so that we may focus on some principles involved in elaborating an existing melisma—as distinct from the procedure of adding another, different melisma to the same Responsory.

A few examples will illustrate the way in which these elaborations are made. The use of reduplication as a means of ornamentation is the principal feature to be observed in the comparison of versions of the same melisma. An example of the endings of two (otherwise very similar) versions of the Responsory *Princeps sanctae ecclesiae* shows the simplest form of this reduplication. A portion of the melisma as it appears in Paris, B. n., lat. 903, appears twice in succession in the Worcester

---

[1] Hans-Jörgen Holman, in "Melismatic Tropes in the Responsories for Matins," this JOURNAL, XVI (1963), 36–46, seems to think that any long structured melisma is a trope. Ruth Steiner, in "Some Melismas for Office Responsories," this JOURNAL, XXVI (1973), 108–31, cautions that this view may be too liberal.

[2] An example of a Responsory which has a lengthy melisma from which it seems never to be separated is *Illuminare;* a modern edition is in *Liber responsorialis* (Solesmes, 1895), p. 75.

Example 1

℟. *Princeps sancte ecclesie* Paris, B. n., lat. 903, fol. 134ᵛ

...de - - - - - - - fen - sor...

Worcester F. 160, p. 383

...de - - - - - - - fen - sor...

antiphoner,[3] followed by the rest of the melisma unaltered; what in Paris, lat. 903, appears in form *AB* has the form *AAB* in Worcester (Ex. 1).

Melismas involving direct repetition of melodic elements are found in chants of many sorts, and it is no particular surprise to find them in Responsories;[4] but the frequency with which immediate repetition occurs in chants of relatively late composition suggests that the reduplication found in Responsories may in some cases be the embellishment of earlier pieces according to a more recent aesthetic principle.

Varied repetition—a sort of elaborated reprise—is occasionally found in melismas of form *AAB*, as in Example 2, from the end of the Responsory *Unus panis* as preserved in an antiphoner of Metz. But such varied repetition is much rarer than might be supposed. Scribal errors are unlikely in the immediate presence of the material to be duplicated, and hence the only reason for making any variation must be an aesthetic one. The preference seems to have been vastly in favor of literal reptition.

It might be objected that the doubled version of these melismas which appear sometimes singly, sometimes repeated, is the original, and that the single version represents a sort of "Cistercianism." Examples can be cited from the recent and the not-so-recent past of the removal of melismas and repetitions from the chant by persons with certain aesthetic or

---

[3] This and other examples from the Worcester antiphoner are cited from the facsimile edition in Paléographie musicale, Vol. XII (Tournai, 1922). Vertical dividing lines have been added to this and other examples to help orient the eye to melodic groupings.

[4] Paolo Ferretti discusses repetition as an aesthetic principle and seems to think it is typical of all types of chant; he does not connect it with melismas in particular (*Esthétique grégorienne*, trans. A. Agaësse [Solesmes, 1938], pp. 49 f.). Willi Apel discusses repetitions in melismas for Responsories, Offertories, and Alleluias and concludes that "there can be hardly any doubt that such formations are the product of a relatively late period, and that they appeared first and tentatively in the offertory verses, whence they were adopted for the Alleluias" (*Gregorian Chant* [Bloomington, Ind., 1963], p. 369-70).

V

Example 2

℞. *Unus panis* Metz, Bibl. mun., Ms. 83, fol. 186

... par - - - - - - - - - -

- - - - - - - - ti - ci - pa - mus.

practical ideals: perhaps some earlier zealots were possessed of a similar musical Puritanism with regard to Responsory melismas. Reduplication occurs so regularly in other varieties of chant, with so little evidence of there having been an unreduplicated original for each repetition, that it seems a little odd to suppose that the melodic doubling found in Responsory melismas is founded on different principles.

Examples may be found, indeed, of just such a procedure of removing supposedly superfluous repetition from Responsory melismas: Example 3 shows the versions of the final melisma of the Responsory *Ex ejus tumba* for St. Nicholas from breviaries of Chartres and Vendôme. Note that the Vendôme breviary, by erasures and the addition of notes after erasure, has altered what must have been the original *AAB* melisma and created an *AB* version. But this unreduplicated version occurs nowhere else in the many manuscripts I have examined which preserve this Responsory; reduplication is always present. Indeed, it is likely, because of the late date of the composition of the Nicholas Office, that the

Example 3

℞. *Ex ejus tumba* Vat. lat. 4756, fol. 286

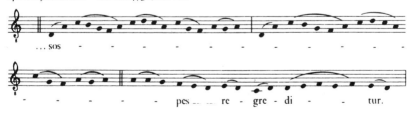

... sos - - - - - pes ... re - gre - di - tur.

Vendôme, Chapter Ms. 17E, fol. 550ᵛ

... sos - - - - - - - pes re - gre - di - tur

464

melisma always existed in reduplicated form; yet in the Vendôme breviary someone has altered not only this but every Responsory of the St. Nicholas Office in a conscious operation on the melismas to remove a seeming defect. Why should we not believe that this is the origin of all the single versions of melismas of which a reduplicated version is also preserved, and that the Vendôme breviary betrays a widespread practice which is elsewhere better concealed?

Example 4, which compares several versions of the ending of the Responsory *O beata trinitas*, argues against this view. The several different ways in which the repeated elements are arranged suggests that none of the reduplicated versions is the source for the others; the version in Metz, Bibl. mun. Ms. 83, could not be the original from which the version in Paris, B. n., lat. 17296, derives its version, and vice versa. The two ways of selecting material for duplication would demonstrate the nature of the common original even if it were not present in Paris, B. n., lat. 1412. The erasures in Rouen, Bibl. mun., 222, are thus an attempt to return to what actually must be the original form of the melisma.

The transmission of melismas involving reduplication sometimes leads to confusion. The presence of a repetition seems not always to be clear to scribes, possibly because they write from memory instead of copying from another manuscript. Example 5 shows three versions of the end of the Responsory *Apparuit caro suo*. Only the scribe of Paris, B. n., n. a. lat. 1236, seems certain that he is writing a melisma of form *AAB*. The versions of Paris, B. n., lat. 12044, and Worcester are progressively unclear about the repetition, so that the Worcester version, although it is evidently recording the same melisma as n. a. lat. 1236, gives a completely unstructured appearance.[5]

It might be argued, of course, that the *AAB* version of this melisma is the reorganization, along reduplication-oriented lines, of an earlier unstructured melisma as found in the Worcester antiphoner; and perhaps the absence of any available unreduplicated form of the melisma corroborates this theory.

A clearer example of an apparently unstructured melisma's being the corruption of an *AAB* form can be seen in Example 6, which compares versions of the final melisma of the Responsory *Circumdederunt*. In the St. Gall melisma[6] may be seen the unreduplicated version of the melisma found doubled in form *AAB* in Metz 83. The same melisma is preserved in the Worcester antiphoner, but in such a form as to conceal the nature of its origin. It seems evident that the unreduplicated version is the

---

[5] The ending of the Worcester version is curious. The rest of the Responsory, including the verse, is pitched just as it is in the other versions.

[6] A facsimile of this manuscript is included in Paléographie musicale, Series 2, Vol. I (Tournai, 1900).

V

Example 4

℟. *O beata trinitas*

Paris, B. n., lat. 1412, fol. 193

Toledo, Arch. cap., 45.9, fol. 114

Metz, Bibl. mun., Ms. 83, fol. 156

Paris, B. n., lat. 17296, fol. 168

Rouen, Bibl. mun., 222, fol. 66ᵛ

V

466

Example 5

℟. *Apparuit caro*

Paris, B. n., n. a. lat. 1236, fol. 50

cum fra - - - - - - - tri - bus tu - is.

Paris, B. n., lat. 12044, fol. 17

cum fra - - - - - - - tri - bus tu - is.

Worcester F. 160, p. 41

cum fra - - - - - - - tri - bus tu - is.

earlier one and hence that the clearly structured melisma of Metz must be closer to its original than the Worcester version.

Example 7 shows some confusion—or disagreement—as to how reduplication should be applied. Three melismas for the end of the Responsory *Terribilis* use differing amounts of material for reduplication. We can imagine an original unreduplicated form of this melisma which is repeated in its entirety and slightly elided to produce the *AA*

Example 6

℟. *Circumdederunt*

St. Gall 390, fol. 9

... vin - - - - di - ca me.

Metz, Bibl. mun., Ms. 83, fol. 109

... vin - - - - - - - di - ca ___ me.

Worcester F. 160, p. 113

... vin - - - - - - - di - ca ___ me.

V

Example 7

℞. *Terribilis*

Hypothetical unreduplicated melisma

Oxford, Bodleian, Bod. 948

Worcester F. 160, p. 317

Charleville 86, fol. 168

form of the Worcester melisma and which produces the Sarum[7] *AAB* form by repeating only the first part of the melisma.

The melisma of the Charleville breviary cannot be generated by reduplication of a portion of this hypothetical original melisma; it is a second-generation reduplication, based on the Sarum form of the melisma by repeating the portions of the Sarum melisma shown in brackets. Thus the Charleville melisma is two steps removed from its original: it is produced by a second reduplication of an already reduplicated melisma.

---

[7] Facsimile in Walter Howard Frere, *Antiphonale sarisburiense*, 4 vols. (London, 1901–25), Plate P.

468

The origins of this impetus to reduplication are impossible to trace; but the melodic repetition characteristic of prosae may have had some effect on repetition-structured Responsory melismas; we can find reduplicated prosae derived from Responsory melismas and reduplicated melodies derived from Responsory prosae.

Prosulation, the process of adding words to a melisma, is a well-known medieval technique.[8] Prosae for Responsories were sometimes made longer than simple prosulae by repeating the music of the final melisma and adding words to both sections. An example of this procedure is the prosa for *Rome autem*, the Responsory which ends the first Nocturn of St. Ouen, from a 14th-century antiphoner of St. Ouen, Rouen (Ex. 8). The Responsory melisma is divided in half, the first section being repeated with new text, but not the second; this produces a reduplicated *AAB* form from an *AB* melisma.

Is it possible that many or all Responsory melismas which show a reduplication owe their structure to this prosa procedure, being prosae from which the words have been removed? Such a suspicion is aroused by Example 9, which shows what appears to be a prosula derived from

Example 8

℞. *Rome autem*

Rouen, Bibl. mun., A. 486, fol. 228

Ro - me au - tem —— in cu - bi - li - bus su - is.

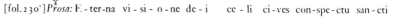

[fol. 230ᵛ] *Prosa:* E. - ter-na vi - si - o - ne de - i ce - li ci - ves con-spe-ctu san - cti

gau - dent in per - pe - tu - is cu - bi - li - bus ____ su - is.

[8] Recent studies dealing with aspects of prosulation are Bruno Stäblein, "Die Unterlegung von Texten unter Melismen. Tropus, Sequenz, und andere Formen," *Report of the Eighth Congress, New York 1961*, I (Kassel, 1961), 12–29; Paul Evans, *The Early Trope Repertory of Saint Martial de Limoges* (Princeton, 1970), especially pp. 15–21; Klaus Rönnau, "Regnum tuum solidum," *Festschrift Bruno Stäblein*, ed. Martin Ruhnke (Kassel, 1967), pp. 195–205; Ruth Steiner, "The Prosulae of the MS Paris, Bibliothèque nationale, f. lat. 1118," this JOURNAL, XXII (1969), 367–93; Joseph Smits van Waesberghe, "Die Imitation der Sequenztechnik in den Hosanna-Prosulen," *Festschrift für Karl Gustav Fellerer*, ed. Heinrich Hüschen (Regensburg, 1962), pp. 485–90; *idem*, "Zur ursprünglichen Vortragsweisen der Prosulen, Sequenzen und Organa," *Bericht über den siebenten internationalen musikwissenschaftlichen Kongress: Köln, 1958* (Kassel, 1959), pp. 251–54.

Example 9

℞. *Videns ergo flentem*

Vendôme, Chapter Ms. 17E, fol. 429

Vi - - dens er - go   re - - - - - -

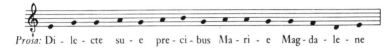

- - - - - - - - su - sci - ta - - vit.

Prosa: Di - le - cte   su - e   pre - ci - bus   Ma - ri - e   Mag - da - le - ne

con - di - tor vi - te La - za - rum de mor - te quar - ta di - e   re - su - sci - ta - - vit.

the notes of the Responsory melisma. This prosula is similar in construction to the prosa which appears above in Example 8; the difference is that the Responsory melisma here has the same reduplicated structure as the prosa. Is this Responsory melisma derived from the prosa and not the reverse? That is, might there originally have been an unreduplicated Responsory melisma, analogous to that in Example 8, from which a prosa "Dilecte sue precibus" was derived and which caused the subsequent alteration of the parent Responsory melisma to a matching reduplicated form? Such an explanation seems unnecessarily complicated in the present instance, but it might serve to explain the impetus to reduplication in many other Responsory melismas.

The evidence does not support this supposition unequivocally. The case would be strengthened if an unreduplicated version of the Responsory melisma of Example 9 could be found; but the several cases of this melisma known to me are always reduplicated.[9] This principle would also seem more plausible if there were a version of the Responsory melisma in Example 8 with a reduplicated structure corresponding to the notes of the prosa "Eterna visione," but such a melisma seems not to exist.

We do know of some melismas for Responsories which appear elsewhere in texted form as prosae.[10] But these prosae are not derived

[9] Paris, B. n., lat. 17296, fol. 349; Rouen, Y. 175², fol. 112; Rouen, A. 393, fol. 134ᵛ.

[10] For an example of such melismas from Laon, Bibliothèque municipale, Ms. 263, see David G. Hughes, "Music for St. Stephen at Laon," *Words and Music: The Scholar's View*, ed. Laurence Berman (Cambridge, Mass., 1972), pp. 137–59.

from the music of the Responsory, and their textless versions are usually so long that they are appended for use as a varied reprise and not disguised as authentic parts of the Respond. Hence we must conclude, in the absence of clear evidence to the contrary, that the relationship between reduplicated Responsory melismas and prosae is not generally a matter of direct derivation of melismas by detexting prosae.

In Responsories and elsewhere, prosulae and prosae were sometimes performed in sections, a texted portion of the melody being repeated immediately in melismatic form; the result is a melody made of reduplicated elements, half of which are texted. The procedure is described in the following rubric from the Exeter ordinal:

R̷. *Sancte dei*. Omnes simul diaconi solempniter et concorditer dicant V̷ *Ut tuo propiciatus* absque *Gloria patri*. Chorus *Funde preces*. Diaconi dicant Prosam ibidem coram altari, et post unumquemque versum respondeat chorus A. vel E. vel O. cum cantu versus precedentis. Hoc eodem modo dicantur omnes Prose per totum annum. . . .[11]

Responsory *Sancte dei*. All the deacons together solemnly and concordantly sing the verse *Ut tuo propiciatus* without *Gloria patri*. The chorus [sings] *Funde preces*. The deacons sing the prosa there before the altar, and after each verse the chorus responds A. or E. or O. with the melody of the preceding verse. In this same way are sung all the prosae for the whole year. . . .

Example 10

R̷. *Sancte dei pretiose*

Ant. Sarisb., p. 60

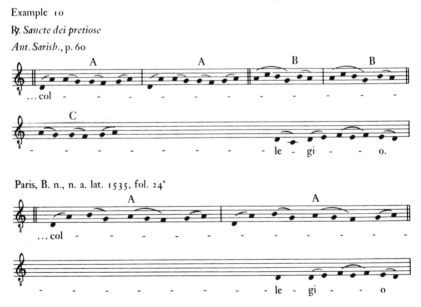

Paris, B. n., n. a. lat. 1535, fol. 24ᵛ

¹¹ *Ordinale Exon.*, ed. J. N. Dalton and G. H. Doble, Vol. I, Henry Bradshaw Society, Vol. XXXVII (London, 1909), p. 69.

Clear and unequivocal directions for this mode of performance are to be found in a number of sources;[12] the effect is the reduplication of

[12] For example, in Cambridge, St. John's College Library, Ms. F. 14, a 15th-century Sarum processional, fol. 6ᵛ: "Chorus post unumquemque versum respondeat prose super ultima vocali, quod in omnibus prosis observeretur"; in Paris, B. n., lat. 975, an ordinal of Toul: ". . . et post finem cujuslibet versiculi prosae respondet chorus neuma super illum versiculum . . ."; in British Museum, Ms. Egerton 2615, fol. 4 (see Wulf Arlt, *Ein Festoffizium des Mittelalters aus Beauvais* [Köln, 1970], Editionsband, pp. 10–11).

smaller segments of the melody of the prosa. But it seems unlikely that this procedure could account for the many reduplications found in Responsory melismas with which no prosa is known to be connected; nor, indeed, do we know of any prosae or melismas which can be shown to be expansions employing the reduplication inherent in this performance practice.

It seems likely, on the whole, that developed melismas found within Responsories are not directly derived from prosae. Although some of the alternative melismas appended to Responsories have close connections with prosae, the melismas within Responsories seem not to be the result but the generators of prosa structure. The large amount of reduplication present within Responsories with which no prosa is thought to be connected suggests that reduplication is an independent melodic principle. But in an indirect fashion the impetus for repetition may have worked both ways: prosa structure suggests the doubling of melismas to produce similar melodies, and the doubling of melodies provides the melodic material and the formal structure of many prosae.

A large group of melismas, mostly within or attached to Responsories ending on D, employ not only repetition but also varying combinations of a number of small melodic cells. Example 10 compares several versions of the ending of the Responsory *Sancte dei pretiose*. Although the melismas differ considerably, they are all made of a small number of melodic inflections, labeled here A, B, C, and D. Unit D, in fact, is typical of this Responsory only and is not a regular member of this group of melodic cells.

Each unit is characterized more by its melodic contour than by the fixity of its notes in different manuscripts. Thus unit A typically rises from *d* to *a* and elaborates the *a*; unit B rises to *c'* and returns to *a*; and unit C falls from *a* to *f* and returns to *a*.

Unit A always begins the melisma. Like each of the other units, it may or may not be reduplicated. Units B and C may be repeated individually, or they may be combined and repeated. Where both B and C are present, B comes first.

In Example 11 are several melismas from other Responsories which demonstrate the use of these same melodic cells. For each of these Responsories, as for *Sancte dei pretiose* in Example 10, there are several versions of the final melisma, of which only a single example from each Responsory is presented here.

The idea that at the origin of all these variants is a basic melisma (like that presented in Example 8 by lat. 17296) consisting of one appearance each of units A, B, and C, must be rejected as not accounting for the frequent omission of B, or C, or both. One might do better to see all these melismas as outgrowths of the melodic impetus provided by the ever-present unit A, with the strength of its characteristic leap of a

Example 11

℟. *Laudemus dominum,*   Paris, B. n., lat. 12584, fol. 320

fifth up to *a*; the rest of the melisma in each case revolves around *a* in an almost-static oscillation before returning to the final *d*. Combined with this melodic contour is the procedure of reduplication—interrupting, delaying, or prolonging the dynamics of the melody. The interaction of these two principles—the ongoing aspects of overall melodic design and the static quality produced by repetition—provides a remarkable variety with very limited means.

It should be noted that the groups of melismas for individual Responsories have a consistency among themselves which is not characteristic of the group as a whole. Thus, the melismas for ℟. *Et valde mane* and those for ℟. *Sancte dei pretiose* form clear groups based on details of melodic contour. This suggests that, although these melismas having a cellular structure are to some extent related, they have been attached to their own Responsories long enough to have had separate developments.

Later Responsories, including many of those for the Offices of local saints, include much reduplication. There is no reason to believe we shall ever find unreduplicated original versions of the melismas in these later compositions. But this does not deny reduplication as a procedure performed on simple melismas, if we think of later composers as knowing, either from experience or from preference, how they think a solemn Responsory ought to sound and creating latter-day echoes.

The sort of ornamentation we have been discussing seems not to have been improvised in Responsories. Almost no marks calling for repetition are to be found in unreduplicated melismas;[13] the only division signs in use[14] are found in melismas which are already doubled, in which the signs are used to indicate a change of side in the antiphonal singing of the melisma. Reduplication seems not to have been available (or to have been thought of) as an extemporaneous ornament, but as a deliberate operation to embellish or solemnify certain Responsories. It was, in short, a conscious aesthetic principle.

[13] An exception is the melisma added to ℟. *Beatissimus Julianus* in the Winchester miscellany (W. H. Frere, *Biblioteca Musico-Liturgica*, Vol. I [London, 1901], No. 126, fol. 212b, reproduced as Plate 6), which uses a *d* to indicate repetitions of portions of the melisma. The repetitions are further illustrated by the prosa "Semper tibi rex," which follows immediately and uses the reduplicated version of the melody.

[14] Such as those found in Lucca 601; see Peter Wagner, "Quelques remarques sur la notation du manuscrit 601 de la Bibliothèque capitulaire de Lucques," *La Tribune de St. Gervais*, XIV (1908), 121-24.

Melisma and Prosula: The Performance of Responsory Tropes

We recognize a Responsory trope usually by its presentation in an Antiphoner or Breviary, as an addendum to the Responsory, giving an alternative version, sometimes of the soloist's intonation, but usually of the final cadence of the Responsory. Such tropes, then, are not additions to a liturgical chant, but replacement parts; they substitute an expanded elaboration for a simpler portion of the chant itself.

The two principal kinds of Responsory trope – melodic and textual, melisma and prosa – are closely bound up together. It is difficult to distinguish between *prosa* (a text-derived composition) and *prosula* (the texting of a melisma) since there is almost always a melodic derivation; and often when no parent melisma is present it can be supplied, as we shall see.

How were these tropes performed? They are written down in various ways, and variations of form, and of time and place, suggest a multiplicity of possibilities and problems.

* * *

The earliest Responsory trope we know is the *neuma triplex* reported by Amalarius as being used in the Responsory *In medio ecclesie* and later transferred to the Christmas Responsory *Descendit de celis*[1]. Although in a few later sources these melismas *were* used with *In medio* (and with a dozen other Responsories), the overwhelming majority of their use is in fact with *Descendit*[2]. The melismas appear as early as the tenth-century Hartker Codex, and prosulas for them appear in the nearly contemporaneous Aquitanian tropers Paris, lat. 1118 and 1084. The Hartker Antiphoner does not supply prosulas, and Lat. 1118 and 1084 provide prosulas but no melismatic versions. Only in later sources do we find the two versions in the same manuscript, as in the eleventh-century Paris, lat. 9449 from Nevers[3].

[1] See J. M. Hanssens, *Amalarii episcopi opera liturgica omnia*, Vol. III [Studi e testi, 140; Vatican City, 1950], p. 54.
[2] See Thomas Forrest Kelly, "Responsory Tropes", unpubl. diss. (Ph. D.), Harvard University 1973, pp. 166–220.
[3] Facsimile in Ruth Steiner, "The Responsories and Prosa for St. Stephen's Day at Salisbury", *The Musical Quaterly*, XVI (1970), 176.

The presence of these melismas in an antiphoner suggests their choral performance, as alternatives to the end of the respond as normally sung by the choir. But the prosulas in lat. 1118 and 1084, included in larger collections of prosulas, are evidently for the use of a soloist: no melisma is present – possibly because the Responsory itself is not notated. Already in the earliest sources, then, we are presented with the same music sung in two ways: the melismatic version by the choir and the texted version by soloists. And so, a central question arises at the outset: were the two versions ever sung at the same time? The matter of simultaneous performance is really a question of whether the choir sings or is silent during the prosula. We shall return to this question after some further stylistic considerations.

This *neuma triplex*[4] seems to represent an early stage of melodic embellishment, for two reasons. First, none of these melismas displays the reduplicated structure which becomes such an esthetic desideratum in slightly later music; and second, the three melismas seem to be imported into the Responsory: they are not expansions of the music of *Descendit de celis* (nor of *In medio ecclesie*) – in fact, one of them is borrowed from an Offertory[5].

This newer melodic style gives rise to both the melodic and textual tropes in later sources; the techniques of immediate repetition permit the construction of lengthy melismas without importation, and a longer trope may be closely related to the music of the parent Responsory. The performance of such pieces is closely bound up with their structure.

A simple melody may be made longer, and perhaps more stylishly repetitive, by repeating its individual elements, as can be seen in the two versions of the final melisma of the Responsory *Sanctissime confessor* in Example 1[6].

[4] The bibliography on this *neuma triplex* and its prosulas is large. Bruno Stäblein presents transcription of several versions in "Tropus", *Die Musik in Geschichte und Gegenwart*, Vol. XIII (Kassel, 1966), cols. 811–816 and Example 9. For some recent studies, see Ruth Steiner, "The Gregorian Chant Melismas of Christmas Matins", *Essay on Music for Charles Warren Fox* (Hackensack, NJ, 1981). pp. 241–253; idem, "The Responsories and Prosa for St. Stephen's Day at Salisbury", *The Musical Quarterly*, LXVI (1970), 162–182; more extentive studies can be found in Kelly, "Responsory Tropes", 166–220 and *passim*, and in Helma Hoffmann-Brandt, *Die Tropen zu den Responsorien des Officiums* (Erlangen, 1971), Vol. I, pp. 56–72 and *passim*.
[5] See Steiner, "The Gregorian Chant Melismas", p. 251 and note 3; Kelly, "Responsory Tropes", pp. 49–50.
[6] Both these examples can be consulted in the published facsimiles of *Paléographie musicale*, Volumes IX (Tournai, 1906) and XII (Tournai, 1922).

EXAMPLE 1

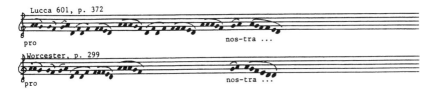

The second melisma is not a trope, in the sense that it is not an externally-applied addition to the Responsory. But its form shows how it was derived from a simpler melisma; and this procedure is one that produces many larger forms, and a variety of modes of performance.

Such reduplication can actually be produced on the spot by repeating each portion of a simpler melisma; I know two examples of such performance.

The elaborate eleventh-century Office of St. Martial in Paris, lat. 909 includes melismatic tropes for the Responsories that end each Nocturn. Each alternative melisma is written in phrases separated by the letter 'd', surely used here to indicate repetition of the foregoing phrase. One of these is reproduced in Example 2.

EXAMPLE 2

The other example is the melisma added to *Beatissimus Julianus* in the eleventh-century manuscript Oxford, Bodley 596[7], which also uses the letter 'd', crossed this time, to indicate doubling of portions of the melisma. The repetitions are confirmed by the prosa *Semper tibi rex* which follows, using as its melody the expanded version of the melisma.

---

[7] W. H. Frere, *Biblioteca Musico-Liturgica* I (London, 1901), no. 126, f. 212 b, reproduced as Plate 6.

Such a repetitive musical style suggests by its very nature the alternation of two singers – or, more likely for a final melisma, two choirs –, the latter singing, perhaps from memory, the music just finished by the former.

A great many such reduplicated melismas are preserved, but almost always fully written out. Occasionally division signs are found in such melismas;[8] unless these are merely analytical marks, they must be used to indicate a change of side in the antiphonal performance of the melisma.

The tendency to reduplication affects textual tropes to Responsories as well. If a simple melody is reduplicated, it follows that a prosula based on it will also have the reiterated melodic structure of the lengthened melisma. But this intervening melodic stage may be omitted, as in Example 3, where the "prosa" expands the original melisma by reduplication. Here the prosa's melody is drawn entirely from the melisma of the Responsory without being identical. The Versicle-signs in the manuscript seem to indicate a change of performer.

EXAMPLE 3

Rouen A.486, f. 227ᵛ

Ro- me au- tem... in cubili-bus su- is.

f. 230v

℣. Eterna visione dei ℣ celi cives conspectu sancti ℣ gaudent in perpetuis

cubili-bus su- is.

A great many other textual tropes for Responsories are to be found in the repertory;[9] and in practically every case the added text, where it is not a prosula, consists of paired versicles of text (in later periods often metrical and rhyming), their sense developed from the words of the Responsory, and usually opening and closing with the boundary-syllables of the Responsory's final

---

[8] Such as those found in Lucca 601 (See Peter Wagner, "Quelques remarques sur la notation du manuscrit 601 de la Bibliothèque capitulaire de Lucques", *La Tribune de St. Gervais*, XIV [1908], 121–124), and in Cambridge, Un. Lib. ms. Mm. ii. 9. (*Antiphonale Sarisburiense*, ed. W. H. Frere [London, 1901–1924, repr. 1966] p. 359).

[9] A discussion of two repertories of such prosas is Thomas Forrest Kelly, "New Music from Old: The Structuring of Responsory Prosas", *Journal of the American Musicological Society*, XXX (1977), 366–390.

melisma. These pieces are in a sense an extension of the prosula technique; though they add more music to the Responsory's final melisma, they generally are related to it. But they also bear a relationship (sometimes a conscious one) to the contemporaneous Sequence, which undergoes a parallel development on a much larger scale[10].

The style of a trope inevitably affects its performance. A melisma made of repeated melodic sections suggests an alternating performance, with two performers or groups dividing the melody. And a prosa of the same melodic type, unaccompanied by a matching melisma, suggests the same performance. A prosula presented in both melismatic and texted version suggests several possibilities: one or the other sung alone; the two sung in order; or both simultaneously.

Most of these performance styles can be documented in the middle ages, and we shall consider them one by one.

* * *

Singing alternately by halves of the choir is used in Responsories both for prosas and for melismatic tropes in reduplicated form.

At Sens the frequent addition of melismas to Responsories has been well documented[11]. We know also that these melismas were sung antiphonally; but the clearest authority is a very late one. Leonard Poisson's eighteenth-century plainchant treatise gives us the following information:

> A Sens on a des neumes, non-seulement pour les Antiennes, mais aussi pour les Répons, dont on ne fait usage qu'aux solemnités: on les a conservées d'un ancien usage non interrompu. Il y a lieu de croire que ces neumes aux Répons étoient autrefois en usage dans toute la Province: on ne les a conservés à Auxerre qu'aux deux fêtes de St. Etienne, et pour la Procession seulement.
>
> Les neumes des Répons étant fort étendues, font aisément sentir les propriétés de chaque Mode. Elles se chantent à deux Chœurs alternative-

---

[10] At least one eleventh-century composer is said to have imitated the Sequence in his composition of an extremely elaborate (and atypical) polyglot Responsory trope. The "Anonymous Haserensis", in his chronicle of the Bishops of Eichstätt, tells us that Reginold, the "optimus hujus temporis musicus", composer of the Office of St. Willibald, added melismas to three of the Responsories ("in fine notulas apposuit") and added to them text after the manner of the Sequence ("eisdem notulis versiculos instar sequentiarum subiunxit"). See *Monumenta Germaniae Historica*, Scriptores VII (Hannover, 1846), p. 257. For a facsimile of this enormous trope, see Hoffmann-Brandt, *Die Tropen*, Vol. I, pp. 19-23.

[11] See Henri Villetard, *Office de Pierre de Corbeil (Office de la Circoncision), improprement appelé "Office des Fous"* (Paris, 1907), p. 133; Kelly, "Responsory Tropes", pp. 86–91.

ment sur une syllabe longue du dernier ou de l'avant-dernier mot du Corps du Répons: après la neume, les deux choeurs se réunissent pour chanter ensemble ce qui reste du Répons[12].

This Sens trandition, which by Poisson's time consisted of a melisma for each mode, can be dated a great deal earlier; we have manuscripts of the twelfth century preserving the same melismas[13]. And since the melismas are found in many sources beyond those of Sens, we may agree with Poisson about the geographical breadth of the tradition.

Poisson continues with an example of a Neume from Sens and the ceremony with which it is sung:

> Les cinq premiers du Choeur, revêtus de Chappes, debout devant l'aigle commencent le Répons, chantent le Verset et le *Gloria patri*, après lequel le Préchantre avec les deux Choristes au milieu du Choeur recommencent le Répons. Pendant que le Choeur chante la répétition, les cinq Dignitaires se partagent et vont, chacun de leur côté, se joindre aux Choristes au milieu du Choeur; là, ils se tournent face à face de la partie du Choeur avec laquelle ils chantent. A la fin du Répons, à la syllabe ou à la note qui précède celle sur laquelle on doit commencer la Neume, tout le Choeur s'arrête, le côté droit commence la Neume, qui se chante alternativement avec le côté gauche: à la fin les deux parties du Choeur réunissent leurs voix pour terminer le Répons[14].

Clearly there is rather a lot of moving about during this final Responsory of Matins; the musical effect of the Neume is of antiphony between sides of the choir (although the five cantors, singing antiphonally but standing in the middle of the choir, may rather have spoiled the stereophonic effect), finished by the whole choir in unison singing the final few syllables of the Respond.

Prosas made of paired versicles may also be sung in choral alternation. In the Everingham Breviary (f. 24 v), a York manuscript of the fourteenth century[15], this rubric precedes the Responsory prosa *Quem ethera*:

> Deinde sequitur prosa alternatim a choro dicenda et incipiatur ab illa parte chori ubi chorus principaliter regitur et sic fiat de aliis prosis a choro cantandis in festis duplicibus contingendis.

---

[12] Léonard Poisson, *Nouvelle méthode, ou Traité théorique et pratique du plain-chant* (Paris, 1745), pp. 379–380.

[13] See the catalogue of melismas in Kelly, "Responsory Tropes", Chapter 2.

[14] Poisson, p. 380.

[15] I am grateful to the Abbey of Saint Pierre de Solesmes for the opportunity to consult their facsimile of this manuscript.

Prosas in this manuscript are not accompanied by melismatic versions; they are performed with the same sort of choral alternation as the Sens melismas.

But not all melismas and prosas performed antiphonally have the paired-versicle structure which lends itself to this mode of performance. For example, if the Everingham instructions above are observed, the prosa *Facture dominans* (for *Descendit*) will have its irregularly-structured melody sung in choral alternation. The prosa is marked off into sections like the others in the manuscript, but the divisions do not show the parallel structure that best suits antiphony. Apparently this is a piece in older style forced into a more up-to-date-performance practice, a bit like waltzing to a minuet.

What may be this same *Facture dominans* melody in its melismatic form is described a being performed antiphonally in a Strasbourg ordinal, according to Martène:

> Ex ordinario Argentino in fine tertii responsorii cujusque nocturni [i. e., of Christmas Matins] non prose, sed tres neumae cantantur, quarum ultima regatur a cantore, qui indutus cappa, et stans in medio chori vertat se ad singulos choros in singulis pausis, quia pausis a choro alternatim cantantur[16].

The cantor here is rather like a choral conductor, turning to left and right as alternate sides of the choir sing the neume[17].

* * *

Many Responsory tropes are sung entirely by soloists. The basic element of this mode of performance is a texted trope – a prosula or prosa – for whose performance solo singers are specified, with no indication of choral participation. An example is found in a fourteenth-century ritual of Bury St. Edmunds (British Libr. Harl. 2977, f. 10):

> XII Responsorium [i. e., of St. Stephen] cantent V diaconi cum magistro diaconorum. Post gloria incipiat precentor in choro Responsorium et cum perventum fuerit ad illum verbum intercede incipiant cantores prosam et prosequunt usque ad illud verbum digneris que canitur a conventu.

---

[16] Edmond Martène, *De Antiquis ecclesiae ritibus*, Vol. III (Antwerp, 1764), p. 34.

[17] Whether the neume has the same melody as the *Facture dominans* sung *alternatim* at York and elsewhere – and this is statistically the most likely third neume for *Descendit* – or another melody, is not clear. There exists another melody which occasionally appears in this position and which has a reduplicated structure more suitable for choral antiphony; a version of it is edited in Bruno Stäblein, "Tropus", *Die Musik in Geschichte und Gegenwart*, Vol. XIII (Kassel, 1966), example 9 d (following col. 816). See also Kelly, "Responsory Tropes", pp. 73–74 and Chapter 4 *passim*; see also Steiner, "The Gregorian Chant Melismas", pp. 244–245.

The Responsory here is undoubtedly *Ecce jam coram te*, often the concluding Responsory for Saint Stephen, and whose respond ends with the specified words *interecede digneris*. The prosa is not named[18]. The choir is instructed to pause after the word *intercede* while the prosa is interpolated by soloists; the prosa ends, like the respond, with the word *digneris*. When the choir resumes (presumably joining the soloists), at *digneris*, the effect is of a complete performance of the respond, suspended in its course for the interpolation of the prosa.

Many other examples can be cited of the naming of soloists for the performance of specific prosas: a fifteenth-century ordinal of Rouen names three deacons for the prosa in the Responsory *O martirum gemma*:

> ... [omnes diaconi] exeant de vestiario cum cereis ardentibus cantando O martirum gemma et ante altare ad modum corone cum et prosa a tribus diaconis fiant. Quo finito incipiatur Te deum[19].

A fourteenth-century ritual of Chalons describes the Responsory *Descendit*, with solo performance of the first two prosas, and (apparently) alternating choral performance of the third:

> Responsum quartum Descendit cantant duo dyaconi cum versu; Et chorus respondet Et exivit usque fabrice. Et duo primi prosam familiam; Et chorus finem decantat fabrice mundi. Deinde idem duo diaconi Gloria patri. Et chorus Lux et decus usque fabrice. Et duo alii primi prosam Fac deus. Et chorus decantat Fabrice mundi. Postea choriales Responsum reincipiunt. Et chorus decantat illud cum prosa Facinora[20].

It is not clear that melismas are also sung. The ritual merely says that the prosas are followed by *fabrice mundi*, which might be either the simple ending of the respond or the elaborate melismas of which these well-known prosulas are texted versions. The third prosa is evidently different from the other two: the first two are sung by soloists, the last by the chorus, perhaps antiphonally.

A practical advantage of solo singing, of course, is that an insertion can be made in any Responsory without having to adjust existing chant-books and

[18] The only prosas I know to have been used with this Responsory before the fifteenth century are *Digne caritatis* in three manuscripts of Meaux (Paris, lat. 1266; lat. 12035; Arsenal 153) and *Sedentem in superne*, a prosa used widely for many Responsories, in Auxerre, Bibliothèque de la ville Ms. 54. Both these prosas have paired-versicle construction, arguably not particularly suited to solo performance. Though neither of these may be the prosa used at Bury St. Edmunds, we shall see that many such prosas were intended for solo performance.
[19] Paris, Bibliothèque nationale ms. lat. 1213, f. 21.
[20] Paris, Bibliothèque nationale ms. lat. 10579, f. 33.

without complicated directions for the chorus: the choral singers simply interrupt their performance at the final melisma, the soloist or soloists insert whatever is desired, and the choir resumes where it had left off.

The presence of verbal Responsory additions in such trope-books as Paris, lat. 1118 and Madrid 288, in sections of music designed for soloists, with all choral parts omitted, suggests this sort of performance.

Such books show, too, that solo interpolations might be used in places where the choral books give no hint of their presence; by interrupting the performance, a soloist, using his own book, can interpolate a prosa, or almost anything he cares to imagine.

Such a practice could be extremely widespread and still leave little evidence. It might be that the prosas which remain to us are only a small part of the practice of interpolation; perhaps their special relationship to a single Responsory, and hence their relative fixity, is what preserves particular tropes in choir-books.

If so, we might expect tropers to contain a relatively large repertory of flexible insertions, and to discover references to this practice in ordinals and elsewhere. In fact, however, the tropers have, not large repertories of unique creations, but very small collections of the best-known prosas, most of them clearly designed for specific Responsories[21]. In ordinals we find no more reference to prosas than is consistent with their frequency in musical manuscripts. Clearly we have not lost a substantial portion of the repertory. However great may have been the importance of individual spontaneous creation in the history of Responsory tropes, the musical remains give little evidence of soloistic improvisation.

* * *

Most Office tropes are in fact closely related to individual Responsories. We have seen how a melody may be expanded; and the process of adding words to a melisma is widespread, as we know from Kyries, Sequences, Alleluias, Offertories, and elsewhere.

Our principal performance problem is what to do with texted and melismatic versions of the same melody when they appear side-by-side, as they do in a great many manuscripts from the earliest period onward. The question was put most recently by Olof Marcusson: "Comment a-t-on chanté les prosules?"[22] The notion of a regular medieval performing style in which a troping

---

[21] There are a few special repertories for local saints, but their sources are not tropers; two such collections are discussed in Kelly, "New Music from Old".

[22] Olof Marcusson, "Comment a-t-on chanté les prosules? Observations sur la technique des tropes de l'*alleluia*", *Revue de musicologie*, LXV (1979), 119–159.

soloist adds his words to the choral performance of the same melody in melismatic form has such fascinating implications for the development of polyphony that scholars have continued to puzzle over it for years[23]. Such a performance style seems to us, perhaps, so desirable a connection between tropes and polyphony that we might tend to be overeager in making the link.

In Responsories, the question of whether text and melisma are sung simultaneously is really a matter of whether the chorus stops singing when the soloists begin the prosula. This is not generally indicated in the sources, even when the singer of the prosa *is* specified. Where the prosa duplicates the melisma which would normally be sung if the trope were not present, the question is a difficult one; it might seem easier, and perhaps more appropriate, for the choir to perform the repetenda in normal fashion, the prosula being overlaid on the usual choral performance of the melisma, than to cause to choir to interrupt their performance – or indeed, to force them to give up part of it altogether. Such incomplete choral performances are not impossible – they are produced, for

[23] The possibility of simultaneous performance of melismas and their prosulations has long interested scholars, probably because of the implications for the development of polyphony. Clemens Blume in 1906 was inclined to see the origin of the motet in the simultaneous performance of melisma and text (*Analecta hymnica*, Vol. XLIX [Leipzig, 1906], 212 and 281–282). Joseph Smits van Waesberghe holds the same view, and sees the simultaneous performance by soloist and choir as particularly important in the growth of polyphony ("Zur ursprünglichen Vortragsweise der Prosulen, Sequenzen und Organa", *Bericht über den siebenten internationalen musikwissenschaftlichen Kongress Köln 1958* [Kassel, 1959], pp. 251–254. See also his remarks in *Bericht über den neunten internationalen Kongress Salzburg 1964*, Vol. I [Kassel, 1964], pp. 68–69). Klaus Rönnau, in an article on prosulas for *regnum tuum solidum*, also argues for simultaneity, citing sources where the melisma in question is divided into sections which follow portions of prosula; if the melisma is sung alternatively with the prosula, he argues, the individual melisma's vowel should change each time a versicle ends in a new vowel ("Regnum tuum solidum", *Festschrift Bruno Stäblein* [Kassel, 1964], Vol. I, pp. 25–35). Other scholars argue that melismas and prosulas are designed for alternative performance in cases where they occur together. Andreas Holschneider suggests that either prosas and melismas are designed for alternative rather than simultaneous performance, or else that melismatic versions are present as notational adjuncts for purposes of clarification in sources with unclear notation. (*Die Organa von Winchester* [Hildesheim, 1968], pp. 90–92.) While the Winchester tropers discussed by Holschneider do indeed present ambiguities with regard to melodic direction, it is difficult to see why a notational adjunct would continue to be employed after the advent of clear diastematic notation. Heinrich Husmann has also attacked simultaneous performance, at least for prosas and sequences, and argued for alternation. ("Das Organum vor und außerhalb der Notre-Dame-Schule", *Bericht über den neunten internationalen Kongress, Salzburg 1964* [Kassel, 1964], Vol. I, pp. 25–35.)

example, in modern performances of Graduals and Alleluias – but the results are vaguely unsatisfactory, owing to the nonsensical incompleteness of the chorus' part.

The available facts, however, seem to show that such simultaneous performance is never intended. On this subject we shall look at evidence of four kinds: 1) the unsuitable nature of many pieces; 2) the evidence of rubrics and ordinals, which is for alternation; 3) comparative sources which clarify readings; and 4) polyphony, which is clearly not an outgrowth of simultaneity, but a decoration of an already alternating performance.

1. Several kinds of texted Responsory trope are in any case not suited to simultaneous performance. When the prosa and the melisma do not match, their concurrent performance is improbable[24]. Often a prosa is an elaborated version of the Responsory melisma, like that in Example 3. In such a case it seems that the prosa must be substituted for – not superimposed upon – its parent melisma, after the fashion of melismatic tropes. In other instances, as we have seen, prosas are specifically intended for choral performance; in these case there can be no question of the chorus performing the melisma at the same time.

2. Often a prosa is presented as texted versicles alternating with corresponding melismas. Such a notational practice might be seen as an attempt to represent simultaneity while preserving the notational integrity of each part; but the evidence of many rubrics and ordinals makes the performance of such pieces clear: the prosa is sung in sections by soloists, each section being repeated melismatically by the choir. Some examples are presented in Table 1.

These directions are unequivocal, but it is only rather late in the development of Responsory tropes that such detailed ordinals are to be found. To make a case for simultaneous performance, the evidence of these manuscripts must be seen as a revision of an earlier practice whose notation is misunderstood. For myself, I see no reason not to accept these witnesses as the continuation of an unbroken performance tradition.

3. Many cases that suggest concurrent performance raise some doubt by small bothersome discrepancies between the notes of melisma and prosula: a simultaneous performance of the notes as they stand often yields difficulties requiring on-the-spot adjustment, or a tolerant ear.

In a few instances we can see that simultaneous performance is not intended even where a manuscript might make it appear possible. Example 4, from a twelfth-century Breviary of Meaux, shows a melisma and a prosa, for the

---

[24] I cannot credit, in these pieces, the sort of immediately-adjusted simultaneous performance ("Halteton–Organum") discussed by Marcusson in "Comment a-t-on chanté les prosules?".

TABLE 1: SOME REFERENCES TO ALTERNATIVE PERFORMANCE

Cambridge, St. John's College F. 14 (Sarum Processional, 15th c.), f. 6 v:
Descendit, prosa *Te laudant*
Item clerici aliam [i. e., the third] prosam. Chorus post unumquemque versum respondeat prose super ultima vocali, quod in omnibus prosis observetur.

London, Br. Lib. Eg. 2615 (Beauvais, 14th c.), f. 4:
Confirmatum est, prosa *Et honore*
Sequitur prosa a prioribus: Et honore ... [with music]; Omnis chorus: O [with melisma]; item primi Que superno ... [With music]; Chorus O [melisma] ... etc.

Paris, lat. 975 (ordinal of St. Epure, Toul, 14th c.), f. 5 v:
XII scilicet Verbum caro debet reiterari hoc modo: Finita repetitione post Gloria patri, cantatur a Cantoribus in medio chori haec prosa: Quem ethera, et post finem cuiuslibet versiculi prosae respondet chorus neuma super illum versiculum, quibus finitis, reincipiatur a cantoribus idem Verbum caro, et chorus prosequitur.

Ordinale Exon., ed. J. N. Dalton and G. H. Doble, Vol I (Henry Bradshaw Society Vol 37, London, 1909), p. 69 (Exeter, 1337):
Sancte dei. Omnes simul diaconi solempniter et concorditer dicant *Ut tuo propiciatus* absque *Gloria patri.* Chorus *Funde preces.* Diaconi dicant Prosam ibidem coram altari, et post unumquemque versum respondeat chorus A. vel E. vel O. cum cantu versus precedentis. Hoc eodem modo dicantur omnes Prose per totum annum ...

EXAMPLE 4

Responsory *Sancte dei pretiosi*. Their notes present approximately the same melody; the differences between them illustrate the small divergences often found in such situations.

Two forms of the same melody, without any indication that the melisma is ever omitted, might suggest that the prosa is added to the melisma when it returns after the verse.

But a contemporaneous manuscript, also from Meaux, removes this possibility. This second manuscript presents the same prosa for this Responsory with the same melody. But the melisma in the respond is considerably different (Example 5):

EXAMPLE 5

In this second case there can be no question of simultaneous performance of prosa and melisma, if what is intended is a neumatic and syllabic version of the same melody. This melisma, while it is clearly another arrangement of the melodic elements found in lat. 12035[25], is definitely not the melodic source of the prosa. If Meaux practice is relatively uniform, then we must conclude that this prosa is not designed to accompany a choral neume, either in Arsenal 153, where the conclusion is obvious, or in lat. 12035, where such a performance might have seemed possible.

4. Polyphonic settings of Responsory tropes survive in substantial numbers, ranging from the earliest note-against note style to settings of the famous texts *Inviolata* and *Sospitati dedit egros* by composers of the Saint Martial and Notre Dame schools, and by Walter Frye, John Taverner, Josquin Despres and

---

[25] A discussion of such melodic rearrangements and developments is Thomas Forrest Kelly, "Melodic Elaboration in Responsory Melismas", *Journal of the American Musicological Society* XXVII (1974), 461–474.

others[26]. While many of these pieces are separate compositions independent of their parent Responsories, some earlier examples remain of polyphony clearly designed for use within the performance of Responsories; and where the trope itself is sung polyphonically the concurrent performance of a melisma is improbable.

An example is a fourteenth-century Lausanne Breviary (Freiburg/Schweiz, Cantons- und Universitätsbibliothek ms. L 61) which contains three prosulas for the Neuma triplex of Descendit de celis in two-voice polyphonic settings, each of which is followed by the melismatic version of the preceding vox principalis[27]. Not only are there discrepancies between the notes of the melisma and the corresponding notes of the polyphonic prosula; but the final prosula, Facinora, is followed by an entirely different, and considerably longer, version of the preceding cantus firmus; the polyphonic voice is composed to fit with the prosula, but NOT with the following melisma.

A similar example is the well-known trope Quem ethera, which is found in ten manuscripts of the Museo Archeologico Nazionale of Cividale, including two 11th–12th century Breviaries of the Aquileian use of Cividale. Four of these manuscripts, of the late fourteenth or early fifteenth century, include archaic two-voice polyphony for the trope[28]. It is evident from Cividale XLVII and LVII that each verse of trope is to be followed by a choral melisma. One section of the prosa, from Cividale XLVII, is Example 6.

The performers are named:"Chorarii" for the polyphonic prosula, and "Chorus" for the following melisma. Clearly the two are meant to follow each other. Alternate notation can hardly represent simultaneity in the presence of

---

[26] Taverner's Sospitati is printed in Tudor Church Music, Vol. III, ed. Percy C. Buck et. al (London, 1924), p. 110; Frye's is printed in Sylvia W. Kenny, Walter Frye: Collected Works, Corpus mensurabilis musicae 19 (1960), p. 17. For some other English settings of Sospitati see Frank Ll. Harrison, Music in Mediaeval Britain (London, 1958), p. 395–397. Inviolata has polyphonic settings from the St. Martial school (Paris, lat. 3549, f. 157), and the eleventh fascicle of W1 (Wolfenbüttel, Herzog-August-Bibliothek ms. 677, f. 211 v); Josquin's Inviolata is edited in A. Smijers et. al., Werken van Josquin des Pres, Motetten Bundel IX (Amsterdam, 1950), p. 111.

[27] See Gilbert Reaney, Manuscripts of Polyphonic Music: 11th–early 14th Century, Répertoire internationale des sources musicales (= RISM) B IV 1 (Munich-Duisberg, 1966), p. 52.

[28] Mss. XXIX, XLI, XLVII, XLIX, LVI, LVII, XCI, XCIII, CI, CII contain Quem ethera. All of these are of the late fourteenth or early fifteenth century except XCI and XCIII, which are Aquileian Breviaries of the 11th–12th century. Polyphonic settings are found in XLI, XLVII, LVI, and LVII. See Kurt von Fischer, Handschriften mit mehrstimmiger Musik des 14., 15. und 16. Jahrhunderts, Vol. II (Munich-Duisberg, 1972), RISM B IV 4, pp. 741–748. See also the remarks by Pierluigi Petrobelli in Bericht über den neunten internationalen Kongress Salzburg 1964, Vol. I (Kassel, 1964), pp. 79–80.

EXAMPLE 6

Cividale XLVII, f. 53v

Chorarii: Quem ethera et terra atque mare non prevalent totum capere

Chorus: E   etc.

polyphonic notation. The later addition of polyphony to the liturgy of Cividale does not affect the performance tradition of the trope itself.

Both polyphony and tropes can be used for the embellishment of the liturgy; but the one is not an outgrowth of the other. Polyphony does not proceed from poorly-performed prosulas. When polyphony is used in a Responsory already decorated with a prosula, the polyphonic voice is added (by adding another soloist) to a procedure that continues to consist of a soloistic prosula followed by a choral neume.

There is evidence, in fact, that melismas were sometimes supplied even where no notation was provided. The Everingham Breviary, which has prosas as Responsory tropes, but not melismas, mentions at one point the practice of making neumes after each versicle of the prosa *Sedentem in superne*:

... et pueri canunt prosam et chorus pneumatizando ad unumquemque versum nisi ad ultimum ... (f. 38).

No melismatic "pneumae" are provided: the chorus presumable "pneumatizes" by repeating in melismatic form the verse just sung by the soloists.

A fourteenth-century manuscript of Palma de Mallorca describes a similar procedure for the performance of intonation prosulas. The long melismatic flourish that opens both verses of the Responsory *Verbum Caro factum* is provided with prosulas; the first prosula, *Olim prophetae*, is performed as follows:

VI. R. *Verbum caro* dicant duo Presbiteri. et alii duo quantum incipiant illos VV. *Olim prophetae*. et primi qui R. inceperunt, dicant tantum de neumate, quantum illi dixerunt de littera ...[29]

* * *

There is, to my knowledge, no clear medieval evidence that prosulas were performed simultaneously with their melismas. Even where the notation

[29] See Higini Anglès, *La Música a Catalunya fins al segle XIII*, Biblioteca de Catalunya, Publicacions del Department de Música, X (Barcelona, 1935), p. 232. Here the

VI

might suggest such a performance, we have seen much evidence that the scribe means exactly what he writes: a prosula followed by a melisma.

In an important sense, though, every texted trope performed in connection with a melisma is a prosula; and every prosula is indeed performed simultaneously with its parent melisma. But the performance takes place, not in church, but in the mind of the creator. For we are sure that prosulas are made with the melisma in mind: the sound of the melisma is used in assonance; the words and phrases are shaped according to the articulations of the melisma; the meaning of the text is derived from, and fitted back into, the sense of the parent melisma's larger text. [These techniques can be studied in Examples 3 and 4.] Who can compose a prosula without singing the melisma? Probably singing to oneself was as rare as silent reading, and it is not improbable that, in composing my prosula, I would ask my neighbor to sing a well-known melisma while I articulate my new words. But in church the prosula itself will be performed before its melisma; it will make time stand still; it will provide a moment for meditation; and it will interpret for the choir their following act of *jubilare sine verbis* in a way that a simultaneous performance would only obscure.

* * *

Melisma, prosula, prosa: the forms vary according to the expressive purpose and the performing medium. But performance practice varies also from place to place, reflecting the fact that different churches prefer different kinds of tropes. Thus three manuscripts of Metz (Metz, Bibl. mun. mss. 83, 461, and 580) illustrated a local practice of embellishing Responsories only with melismas. These melodies were evidently performed chorally without alternation: they contain no division marks, and they are found sometimes as alternative endings, but sometimes also as part of the Responsory itself.

There are many other examples of uniform local practice. Sarum manuscripts use prosas for processional Responsories, alternating sections of text

melisma is performed by soloists rather than by the choir, as is suitable in a Responsory verse. This may be similar to the procedure followed for the Responsory *Quem vidistis* in the Beauvais circumcision office (London, British Library Egerton Ms. 2614, f. 19 v). Here the opening melismatic flourish, labeled "unus", is followed, before the continuation of the respond, by a texted version of the same notes, with the rubric "alter cum eo prosa". The continuation of the repond is labeled "chorus". Whether the "cum" means "alongside" or "concurrent" is not clear; any simultaneity intended is of two soloists and does not involve the chorus. See Wulf Arlt, *Ein Festoffizium des Mittelalters aus Beauvais* (Köln, 1970), Editionsband, pp. 49–50.

with melismas[30]. The York Breviary from Everingham prescribes the regular use of choral alternation in the performance of prosas[31]. The Sens use of long reduplicated melismas in choral alternation has been documented through the eighteenth century.

But despite these examples, it is a misrepresentation of the majority of the evidence to say that regularity in performance style is characteristic of Responsory tropes at any single place and time. In many sources, the presence of several kinds of trope, requiring varying modes of performance, makes complete regularity impossible. The thirteenth-century Antiphoner Vendome 17 E, for example, contains prosulas with their melismas, prosas of all types without melismas, and added melismas without texts. Such a compilation of styles entails a variety of performance techniques.

And a given Responsory trope may be not always be performed in just one way. The Everingham Breviary shows that the prosa *Sedentem in superne* offers three choices. The general rubric cited on page 168 prescribes choral alternation as the normal performance of such prosas. But an additional rubric appended to the Responsory shows two more ways of performing the same trope. If the feast falls on a Sunday, the prosa is performed by three deacons (presumably without alternation or choral intervention); but on a weekday the prosa is performed by boys, each phrase followed by a choral neume:

> Si dominica fuerit dicatur prosa sine repetitione responsorium a tribus diaconis *Sedentem*. Si vero dominica non fuerit repetatur responsum et post repetitione[m] responsorium dicatur prosa et pueri canant prosam et chorus pneumatizando ad unumquemque versum nisi ad ultimum respondeat *Laus tibi domine rex et.* qui a pueris finiatur sine pneuma (f. 38).

This variability emphasizes the difficulty of determining the exact nature of any performance. We are grateful for the few cases where specific directions give a clear idea of the performance of a certain prosa or melisma at a given place and time; for these citations, taken together, seem to present the range of acceptable modes of performance. But these techniques cannot always be applied with certainty where specific directions are lacking. Indeed, although performance is related both to changing style and to local taste, there is every reason

---

[30] See the rubric from Cambridge, St. John's College ms. F. 14 above; Rome, Vat. Ottob. 308, f. 11–1 v ("Chorus vel organa respondeant cantum prose super literam A post unumquenque versum".); Oxford, Bodl. Rawl. lit. d 4, f. 11 ("Chorus vel organa respondeant cantum prose super litteram A. post unumquemque versum.").

[31] See above, p. 168

VI

to believe that variation in style of performance was entirely acceptable, normal, and desirable. And the manner of performance itself, like the use of trope and polyphony, can serve as a means of expression, giving character and individuality to the Office, and distinguishing degrees of solemnity in the regular round of the liturgy.

VII

Neuma Triplex

Amalarius of Metz, writing in the first half of the ninth century, used the term *neuma triplex* to describe a melismatic interpolation in the Responsory *In medio ecclesie* for the feast of Saint John (December 28): "In the last Responsory, that is, *In medio*, contrary to the custom with other Responsories, a *neuma triplex* is sung, and its [the Responsory's] verse and *Gloria* are protracted, by a neume, beyond the normal manner."[1] In *De ordine antiphonarii*, an expository and interpretive treatise on the liturgy of the Office hours, Amalarius goes on to say that modern cantors sing this neume in the Responsory *Descendit de celis*, and on the words *fabrice mundi*.[2]

Neuma triplex: Amalarius uses a singular noun for a melisma, but indicates that in some sense it has a threefold quality. The usage is his alone: the term *neuma triplex* is used nowhere else, as far as I know, for this or any other phenomenon. But what he means seems clear, for a great many later manuscripts – antiphoners, breviaries, and tropers – include three melismas (or their texted versions) as additions to the Responsory *Descendit de celis* at its final words *fabrice mundi*, and occasionally to other Responsories as well (including *In medio ecclesie*).

Amalarius' *neuma triplex* is of continuing interest to scholars.[3] For one thing, Amalarius' statement is among our earliest witnesses of the medieval practice of troping, of enriching the official liturgy with musical and poetic embellishments. Moreover, the manuscript transmission is extensive, permitting a wide view of the use of this *neuma triplex* from the tenth century onward.[4]

---

[1] "In novissimo responsorio, id est 'In medio ecclesiae', contra consuetudinem ceterorum responsoriorum, cantatur neuma triplex, et versus eius atque gloria extra morem neumate protelantur." J. M. HANSSENS, *Amalarii episcopi opera liturgica omnia*, Vol. III = Studi e testi 140 (Vatican City 1950), p. 54.

[2] "Canunt etiam moderni cantores praesens neuma in responsorio Descendit de caelis." HANSSENS, *op. cit.*, vol. III, p. 54.

[3] Many scholars have noted, discussed, and transcribed this phenomenon. Among them are L. GAUTIER, *Histoire de la poésie liturgique au moyen âge: Les tropes* (Paris 1886), p. 166–167; J. POTHIER, *Resp. 'Descendit de coelis'*, in: *Revue du chant grégorien* 11 (1902), p. 65–71; P. WAGNER, *Einführung in die gregorianischen Melodien*, Vol. I, *Ursprung und Entwicklung der liturgischen Gesangsformen* (Leipzig 1911), p. 291–293, and Vol. III, *Gregorianische Formenlehre* (Leipzig 1921), p. 347–348; J. HANDSCHIN, in: *New Oxford History of Music*, Vol. II (London 1954), p. 141–146; W. APEL, *Gregorian Chant* (Bloomington 1954), p. 441–442; B. STÄBLEIN, *Tropus*, in: *MGG* 13 (Kassel 1966), especially cols. 811–816 and Example 9. Some studies focused more directly on the *neuma triplex* are: H. HOFFMANN-BRANDT, *Die Tropen zu den Responsorien des Officiums* (Erlangen 1971), vol. I, p. 12–16, 56–72, and *passim*; Th. F. KELLY, *Responsory tropes*, unpubl. diss. (Ph. D.), Harvard University 1973, p. 166–220; R. STEINER, *The Responsories and Prosa for St. Stephen's Day at Salisbury*, in: *MQ* 56 (1970), p. 162–182; EADEM, *The Gregorian Chant Melismas of Christmas Matins*; in: *Essays on Music for Charles Warren Fox*, ed J. C. Graue (Rochester, N. Y. 1979), p. 241–253.

[4] The controversy between Amalarius and Agobard of Lyons on the subject of Amalarius' new antiphoner seems to have had a significant effect on the transmission and distribution of this Responsory. Though we cannot consider this in detail, we might note that Agobard, in *De antiphonario*, objects to the overblown performance of Resp. *Descendit*: "Considerentur etiam verba alterius responsorii, quod... contra morem nocturni officii ab eminentiori loco pompatice concrepabat: *Descendit de caelis*..." (*Agobardi lugdunensis opera omnia*, ed L. van Acker = Corpus Christianorum, Continuatio Medievalis 52 [Turnhout 1981], p. 341). On this controversy see E. DEBROISE, *Amalaire*, in: *Dictionnaire d'art chrétien et de liturgie* (=*DACL*), Vol. I (Paris 1907), cols. 1323–1350; and IDEM, *Agobard*, in *DACL*, vol. I, cols. 971–979; A. KOLPING, *Amalar von Metz und Florus von Lyon*, in: *Zeitschrift für katholische Theologie* 73 (1951), p. 424–464; A. CABANISS, *Amalarius of Metz* (Amsterdam 1954).

VII

But a century and a half separates Amalarius' verbal description from the tropers, antiphoners, and breviaries that constitute our first musical evidence. By the late tenth century, what Amalarius describes as a single phenomenon appears in a variety of forms:

1. The Hartker antiphoner (SG 390) of the late tenth or early eleventh century presents three melismas on "fabrice mundi" for Resp. *Descendit*; elsewhere the same manuscript (but a slightly later hand) provides a prosula (a syllabic texting) for the third "fabrice" melisma.

2. The Mont-Renaud manuscript, a tenth-century gradual and antiphoner of Saint-Denis, adds three melismas to Resp. *Descendit*; they are written upwards vertically in the margin, and the third melisma is different from Hartker's.

3. Paris 1118, an Aquitanian troper of the late tenth or early eleventh century, provides ten prosae – texted versions of three different melismas – for Resp. *Descendit* (this series of prosae, as we shall see, is found in a number of Aquitanian manuscripts); the Responsory is not present, but each prosa ends with the words *fabrice mundi*. But the third melody is not one of those in the Hartker manuscript; nor does it match those in Mont-Renaud (though it is similar to one of them).

Already in our earliest musical sources, then, we must differentiate between Amalarius's description and what we find: Amalarius describes a *triple neume* for *In medio ecclesie*; but how is it a single entity if its constituent elements may vary? How is it a neume if its melody is often not presented melismatically? And how is it designed for *In medio ecclesie* if it appears almost always with Resp. *Descendit*?

Based on a survey of some 150 manuscripts of the twelfth century and earlier, we shall discuss these questions. Not every relevant manuscript before 1200 could be consulted, but the sampling is large enough to view the general picture of the use and transmission of these seminal Responsory tropes. Manuscripts are indicated in the text by sigla which are expanded in Appendix I (see p. 22).

If this survey's net is a broad one, it is also coarse, and there are many matters that must be deferred to another study. Given limitless space and time, much could be learned from the detailed study of the transmission of music and text; from questions of performance; from a careful study of the curious history of the Responsory *Descendit de celis*; and from the literary and philological scrutiny of the texts. For the present we propose only to survey the geographical and chronological distribution of the *neuma triplex* and its constituent elements so as to learn something of the origin, growth, and distribution of this phenomenon.

At the outset, we present the five melismas that are basic to this study. Although these five never occur all together, they are responsible, in their various groupings, for all the melodic material to be studied here; they are labeled with letters that will be used hereafter to refer to them (see Example 1, next page).

The prosae named in this study are presented in Appendix II (see p. 25).

Example 1

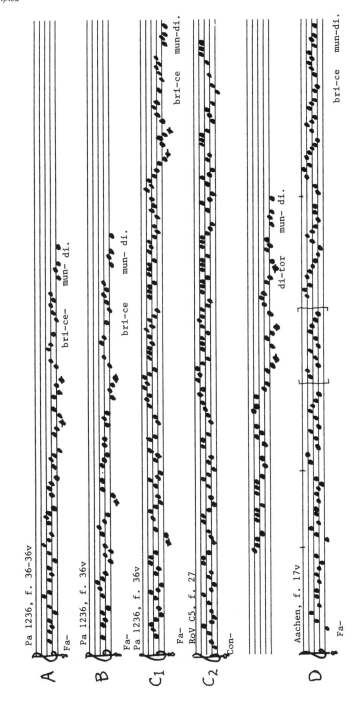

VII

The Responsory

The great Responsories of the night Office include, at least, a verse followed by a full or partial repetition of the Respond; Responsories which, like *Descendit de celis*, end one of the Nocturns have a Doxology, sung to the melody of the verse, and a second partial reprise, which in turn is often followed by a full repetition of the Respond. It is to these repetitions that the melismas of the *neuma triplex* are attached, as alternative forms of the end of the Respond.[5]

By the time of our first surviving musical manuscripts the *moderni cantores* have had their way. The overwhelming majority of melismas associated with the *neuma triplex*, and of prosae related to them, appear with the Responsory *Descendit de celis*.[6] Indeed, the melismas and their prosae are sometimes referred to as "fabrices". (Cai 78, "fabrice in nocte natal. domini;" Pa 1118, "Incipiunt tropos de fabrices; de alia fabrice; de fabrice maiore;" Apt 18, "incipiunt fabrices.")

But Amalarius says the *neuma triplex* came to Resp. *Descendit* from *In medio*, and we must consider the evidence. There remain, indeed, many appearances of these melismas and their prosae with other Responsories; they include Resp. *In medio ecclesie* but are not limited to it.

These *neuma triplex* elements with other Responsories are grouped here according to their relation to Resp. *Descendit*, for all have some connection with it: either they have prosae originally drawn from Resp. *Descendit*; or their melismas are precisely the same as those in the same manuscript for *Descendit*; or their decorations are a subset of those for *Descendit* in the same manuscript. We shall consider these cases, and a few others.

1. In three cases, a Responsory is embellished with a series of prosae clearly designed not for their present use but for *Descendit de celis*:

	Apt 18 (10/11th)	Resp. *Verbum caro factum*
	Prosa	*Familiam plebis* (A)[7]
	Prosa	*Facundie largitor* (B)
	Prosa	*Faciens bonitatis* (C2)

---

[5] Amalarius' description of the performance of a Responsory, in which he contrasts the Roman practice with that of his own church, is much more extensive than what we now consider to be a 'standard' performance. Having described the performance in detail, he says: "And so the succentors sing the Responsory three times, and there is a *tripharium neuma* around the word *intellectus*. It is for the succentors to sing the neume because of the strength of combined voices." (HANSSENS, p. 55) In fact, according to Amalarius' description, the succentors sing the Responsory (or at least that part of it containing the word *intellectus*, the last word of Resp. *In medio*) four times (not three, as he asserts). In any case, none of the surviving sources documents Amalarius' extended performance. It would be wasteful in the extreme to copy out the same music five and a half times; but even where the use of cues makes performance relatively clear, the performance of Responsories in western Europe seems to have been substantially abbreviated by the time of our earliest musical manuscripts.

[6] This Responsory itself has both a curious text and a complex history. Its non-biblical text must have offended what Gautier calls "certaines sensibilités trop délicates" (*Les tropes*, p. 167), and it circulated widely in two forms, the second as a result of an effort at reform. The two texts (as edited in R.-J. HESBERT, *Corpus antiphonalium officii* [= *CAO*], Vol. IV = Rerum ecclesiasticarum documenta, Series maior, Fontes 10 [Rome 1970]) are as follows: "Descendit de coelis, missus ab arce patris, introivit per aurem Virginis in regionem nostram, indutus stolam purpuream, et exivit per auream portam, lux et decus universae fabricae mundi" (*CAO* 6411). The revised text: "Descendit de coelis Deus verus, a patre genitus, introivit in uterum Virginis, nobis ut appareret visibilis, indutus carne humana protoparentis edita: et exivit per clausam portam Deus et homo, lux et vita, Conditor mundi" (*CAO* 6410). See D. CATTA, *Le texte du répons "Descendit" dans les manuscrits*, in: *Études grégoriennes* 3 (1959), p. 75–82; A. BAUMSTARK, *Byzantinisches in den Weihnachtstexten des römischen Antiphonarius officii*, in: *Oriens christianus* 11 (1936), p. 163–187.

[7] Letters in parentheses here and elsewhere indicate the prosa's melodic source. Texts of prosae are edited in Appendix II.

La 263	(12th)	Resp. *Centum quadraginta*
	Prosa	*Dum pectoris* (B)
	Prosa	*Per quem credenda* (A)
Pa 9425	(12/13th)	Resp. *Sancte Stephane protomartyr*
	Prosa	*Familiam* (A)
	Prosa	*Fac deus* (B)
	Prosa	*Facinora* (C1)

In all three cases, prosae are added to a Responsory with which they did not originate; and the original is clearly *Descendit de celis*. The Apt 18 prosae are unique creations, but they are recognizable *Descendit* prosae ending with *fabrice mundi*; likewise the prosae from La 263 conclude, like *Descendit*'s alternate version, with *conditor mundi* (the original presence of a third prosa here is uncertain owing to a lacuna). In Pa 9425 one of the best-known sets of three prosae (see below, p. 13) has been transferred complete to a Responsory with which it is not well matched.

2. In many cases where *triplex* melismas are used for other Responsories, the manuscript contains the same melismas for Resp. *Descendit*, either in precisely the same form, or in an expanded version.

MS	date	Responsory & its melismas		Melismas with *Descendit* in same MS
Rou 164	11th	*Martinus abrahe*	BAC_1	BAC_1
Pa 17296	12th	*Post passionem*	ABC_1	ABC_1
SG 390	10/11th	*Iste sanctus*	D	ABD
RoV C5	12th	*Iste sanctus*	A	C_2BA
Pa 1535	12/13th	*Ecce jam coram te*	C_1	ABC_1
Pa 1028	13th	*Ecce jam coram te*	C_1	ABC_1
Sens 29	14th	*Ecce jam coram te*	C_1	ABC_1
Tol 44.2	12/13th	*In principio*	B	BAC_2
		Felix namque	A	BAC_2
La 263	12th	*In medio*	BAC_1	–
Me 83	13th in.	*In medio*	AB	ABC_2
		In medio	B	ABC_2

We cannot prove from this list that *Descendit* is the source from which these other Responsories received their melismas; but it is suggestive to find that there are so many cases in which the decoration of a second Responsory is a subset of the melismas for *Descendit*. We can even imagine the process, in Tol 44.2, of peeling away first one melisma and then the next, for the decoration of additional Responsories in the manuscript. And in Me 83, from Amalarius' own city, which decorates Amalarius' original Responsory with *triplex* elements, we can envision the opposite process taking place: progessively smaller subsets of a triple neume used for the greater and lesser solemnities on which *In medio* is sung.

La 263, which also provides melismas for *In medio*, is the only manuscript which matches Amalarius' description by assigning three neumes to this Responsory. But though *Descendit de celis* does not appear in La 263, its prosae do, as we have seen above: Resp. *Centum quadraginta* is provided with the same three melismas, and at least two of them have prosae derived from *Descendit*. It seems probable that the melismas in La 263 came to *In medio* through the intermediary of *Descendit*.

3. In several other groups of manuscripts Resp. *In medio ecclesie* bears prosae whose texts are designed for the Responsory but whose melodies are those of *triplex* melismas present earlier with *Descendit de celis*.

In two twelfth-century antiphoners of Klosterneuburg (Kl 1010, Kl 1013) *In medio* is embellished with the prosa *Ante tempus parentis.*[8] The prosa's melody, melisma D, had already appeared earlier in the manuscripts, as part of three melismas (ABD) for Resp. *Descendit*, and it alone was provided with a prosa, *Facture plasmator.* That the final melisma at Christmas is distinguished from the others in this way marks it as separable for embellishing the final Responsory of St. John; and though we shall see that melisma D is often found alone, it seems improbable in these manuscripts that the prosa for *In medio* predates the larger group for *Descendit*.

A similar case is Pa 17296, where Resp. *In medio* is accompanied by melisma C_1 and its prosa *Et intellectus Iohannem.*[9] This is the only Responsory prosa in the manuscript, though both Resp. *Descendit* and Resp. *Post passionem* have triple melismas in order C_1BA. Though the prosa here was certainly not derived from *Descendit*, and though the melismas may well have been assigned by the scribe to several Responsories, nothing here suggests that the melody originates with Resp. *In medio*.

To this category probably also belong the two prosae of melisma B (*Per tuam prolem* and *Permanens virgo*) attached to Resp. *Beata es virgo* in the late twelfth-century Purification office of Mu 23621. The prosae are created with the sense of the Responsory and its final words *permanens virgo* clearly in mind; and yet the melodic source might have been *Descendit*, or it might have been a separately circulating melisma or complex of melismas: we simply cannot tell, for we have only two leaves preserving this fragmentary office.

In a group of English manuscripts of relatively late date (CUL 2602, Ed 13A, Lo 28598, Sa 152, Cdg F.14) a similar phenomenon is to be seen: the addition to other feasts of a single prosa derived from the third *Descendit* melisma. A series of Sarum manuscripts, which have three prosae for Resp. *Descendit* at Christmas, add also a single prosa to the final Responsories of December 26 and 27 (St. Stephen and St. John).

---

[8] The prosa from Kl 1010 is transcribed by STÄBLEIN, *Tropus*, in: *MGG*, example 9; a prosa, *Indutum pro nobis* for the same melody is transcribed there from Prague, Metrop. P. VI, f. 174v–175v.

[9] The prosa and melisma are transcribed by STÄBLEIN, *Tropus*, in: *MGG*, ex. 9c.

The three C_2 prosae are closely related, though their texts connect them to their feasts. The structure of all three is so similar in its phrase-grouping that they are clearly based on the same transmission of the melisma with the articulations from which the text-phrases are derived. The Stephen prosa, *Te mundi climata*, is so closely related textually to the Christmas prosa *Te laudant* that it seems to be modeled on it.[10] Again it seems that the connection of *triplex* elements with Resp. *In medio* (and with other Responsories) comes by way of *Descendit*, and not the reverse.

4. In a few cases, the *neuma triplex* is trasmitted separately and attached to the last Responsory of Christmas Matins in manuscripts where Resp. *Descendit* is unsuitably placed. In Be 377 three melismas (BAC_2) are attached to the last Responsory of Christmas (*In principio*); in this manuscript *Descendit de celis deus verus* is the final Responsory for the Circumcision. In two Italian manuscripts of the twelfth century (Pia 65 and Fl 560) the last Responsory of Christmas, *O regem celi*, is decorated by three *triplex* melismas (C_2BA) and each manuscript contains an undecorated *Descendit de celis* – as the third of four Responsories in the first nocturn in Fl 560, and as a ferial Responsory in Pia 65.[11] The scribe here retains, no doubt from Resp. *Descendit*, a connection with Christmas Matins. This separation of the melismas from the Responsory is just the sort of transfer that Amalarius describes, but away from *Descendit* rather than towards it.

Except for these last three manuscripts, the only examples I know where *triplex* melodic elements are present elsewhere without being present also in Resp. *Descendit* are in two relatively late manuscripts: Cdg F.4.10 has a melisma C_1 for Resp. *In medio* but melisma C_2 (only) for *Descendit*; and Pa 1088 has a melisma C_2 for Resp. *In principio*, but no *triplex* decorations for *Descendit* or elsewhere. I think we must assume that by the fourteenth century the *neuma triplex* elements were well enough circulated that there is no surprise in finding them here.

We have surveyed all the evidence I know of *triplex* elements elsewhere than with Resp. *Descendit*. And although Resp. *In medio ecclesie* has appeared frequently in this discussion, there is no real evidence in these sources of its priority over *Descendit* as the original place of the *neuma triplex*. Indeed, the testimony of the manuscripts points, even if indirectly, in the other direction, towards *Descendit de celis* as the fountainhead of this creative flow. Yet Resp. *In medio* is persistently present in the sources, to an extent that leaves the question open; we shall return to it at the end of this study.

The melismas

Amalarius speaks of a triple neume for Resp. *In medio ecclesie*, and we presume that what he means is the sort of arrangement of three melismas that we often find in connection with Resp. *Descendit*. Although, as we see, there are a great many prosae associated with these *triplex* melismas, they seem to be related to *Descendit*

[10] See the transcriptions and discussion in STEINER, *The Responsories and Prosa*, p. 177–179. Sa 152 has no embellishments for Resp. *Descendit*; facsimiles in W. H. FRERE, *Antiphonale sarisburiense* (London 1901–1924, repr. 1966), p. 60–61, 66.
[11] Both manuscripts also contain prosulae for the verses: see below, note 36.

VII

de celis; hence, if we believe Amalarius' story, the prosae cannot date from the earliest history of these tropes.[12] And so if we seek the survival of the earliest versions of the *neuma triplex* we shall have to look among the neumes – that is, among the melismas attached to these and other Responsories.

Listed below are those manuscripts that employ melismas as tropes to these Responsories; where not otherwise noted the melismas are attached to Resp. *Descendit.* We can see readily that "neuma triplex" may signify three melismas, but not always the same three.

Table 1: *Neuma triplex* melismas

ABC_1			ABD			BA		
Mont-R	10th		SG 390	10/11th		Vro 98	11th	
Mza 75	11th		Ba 24	12th		Graz 211	12th 1/2	(+2 Psae)
Cai 78	11th 2/2		Sz 24	11/12th				
Rou 145	12th		Civ 91	11/12th (+ prosa)				
Rou 175	12th ex.		Civ 93	11/12th (+ prosa)				
Pa 796	12th		SG 388	12th		AB		
Mu 23037	12th		SG 389	12th (+ prosa)		Me 83	13th in.	Resp. *In medio*
Ka 144	12th		SG 416	12th				
Wo 160	13th		Graz 258	12th (+ prosa)		A		
			Ei 83	12th		Tol 44.2	12/13th	Resp. *Felix namque*
BAC_1			Ko 215	12th		Br 3827	13th?	
Be 40047	11th		Pr 4c	12/13th		Rou 226	13th?	
Chia	11th		Br 353	12/13th		Me 580	13th	
Rou 164	11th		Aachen	14th				
La 263	12th					B		
			BAD			Tol. 44.2	12/13th	Resp. *In principio*
C_1BA			SG 413	11th		Me 83	13th in.	Resp. *In medio*
Pa 17296	12th		SG 414	11th				
Val 114	12th		Ox 297	11th		C_1		
			Ba 23	11th		Am 115	12th	
ABC_2			Li 19	11/12th		Pa 1535	12/13th	Resp. *Ecce jam*
Pa 1085	10/11th (+ Psae ABC_1)		Wi 1890	12th (+ prosa)		Cdg F.4.10	13/14th	Resp. *In medio*
Tol 44.1	11th ex. (+ Psae)		Kl 1010	12th (+ prosa)		Pa 1088	14th ex.	
Pa 742	12/13th		Kl 1013	12th (+ prosa)				
Me 83	13th ex.		Ba 22	12/13th		C_2		
			Ba 26	12/13th		Cdg F.4.10	13/14th	
BAC_2			Ox 202	13th (+ prosa)				
Be 377	10/11th Resp.					D		
	In principio					SG 390	11th	Resp. *Iste sanctus*
Dur 11	11th					Me 461	13th ex.	
Pa 796	12th							
Tol 44.2	12/13th							

C_2AB	
Fl 560	12th Resp. *O Regem*
Pia 65	12/13th

$A?A?C_1?$	
To 4	12/13th

[12] But the technique of adding words to melismas was kown in Amalarius' time: see the prosula of ca. 830 reproduced from Munich clm 9543 as Tafel VII, and transcribed on p. 252, of J. SMITS VAN WAESBERGHE, *Zur ursprünglichen Vortragsweise der Prosulen, Sequenzen und Organa,* in: *Bericht über den siebenten internationalen musikwissenschaftlichen Kongreß Köln 1958* (Kassel 1959).

In the left columns above are those manuscripts presenting three melismas; and on the right are combinations of only two or one. We can perhaps best deal with the right column first. Most of the single and double melismas occur in relatively late manuscripts, and we shall mention only the few cases where the melismas are not a subset of a *triplex* group transmitted in the same manuscript.

1. Earliest is Vro 98 (11th c.), which, like Graz 211 (early 12th c.) transmits melismas B and A (Graz 211 also includes two of the three prosae of the "Italian set" – see below, p. 12).

2. Both Am 115 (12th c.) and the relatively late Cdg F.4.10 preserve a single melisma C_1; the latter manuscript uses it with Resp. *In medio*, and uses melisma C_2 for Resp. *Descendit*: this is the earliest and only witness to the use of C_2 alone, and the only manuscript in this survey which contains both these melismas, perhaps as the result of a tardy and mixed transmission.

3. Two relatively late French manuscripts (Br 3827 and Rou 226), which use the "conditor" version of Resp. *Descendit*, decorate the Responsory with a single melisma A.

From these sources we get a first glimpse of ideas that recur through this study: the separability of final melismas; the separate transmission of melismas A and B; and, finally, the independence of melisma A.

Most of the earlier sources present three melismas together, as we see in the left column above. But the variety of arrangements baffles an attempt to get at the unity of the original *neuma triplex*.

There are two main characteristics of these groups of melismas: the pairing of melismas A and B, and the variability of the third melisma. Melismas A and B generally appear together. Their order may be reversed, but they usually are the first two melismas in any group of three. Now A and B are of about the same length, and considerably shorter than any of the other melismas. It has been known for some time (see below, p. 21) that melisma A is drawn from a Gregorian Offertory; this fact is perhaps particularly remarkable in light of the fact that none of the other *triplex* melismas seems to have a similar liturgical origin.

The longest melisma in these triple groups, and the one that usually comes last, may occur in at least three forms (C_1, C_2, D); never does a triple melisma include more than one of these final melodies. And there is a general geographical pattern to be seen in their usage: melisma D is found chiefly in German manuscripts; melisma C_1 mostly in French sources; and C_2, as we shall see, has a particular place in the prosa series of Aquitaine and Italy.

These final melismas raise questions of musical style. Melisma C, in its two versions, is like many Offertory melismas: a shapely melody not structured by large repetitions, though some localized elements may be repeated immediately; though the range is extensive, there are few dramatic intervals or melodic sweeps; and there are substantial passages of relatively static music. The two versions are essentially identical except for a central passage which includes a repetition of the earlier repeated notes on C;[13] this passage makes C_2 significantly longer, though its style is not changed.[14] The question of whether melisma C_1 is the original melisma of which C_2 is a subsequent expansion will be discussed below after texted versions of these melismas have been taken into account.

Melisma D, unlike the other final melismas, is a highly-structured melisma of the "sequence" type, each melodic element being immediately repeated. Such a style is often thought to represent a later melodic aesthetic than that of melisma C,[15] and indeed Bruno Stäblein refers to melisma D as a "substitute melisma for the third neume.[16]"

The generally accepted notion is that the "original" *neuma triplex* consists of melismas A, B, and C_1; that melisma C_2 is a later expansion of C_1; and that melisma D was substituted, at least in some places, for the "normal" third melisma for reasons of aesthetic preference or perhaps suitability for the creation of prosae.

There are many obstacles to accepting such a theory. Why is only one melisma borrowed from an Offertory? Why substitute only one melisma, if the style of all three is old-fashioned? How do we account for the witnesses of all three final melismas in our earliest sources? But before we can deal with these questions, we must consider a third aspect of the *neuma triplex*: the texted tropes.

The prosae

Amalarius does not speak of the technique of adding syllables to the notes of melismas, nor of any verbal additions to the melodies of the *neuma triplex*: probably he did not know of the vast verbal expansion that these melodies were to spawn; and almost certainly prosae were not used at the time and place of which he writes.

In fact it appears that the development of prosae is a later phenomenon; the great majority of prosae, particularly in the earliest sources, are related to Resp. *Descendit de celis*, and hence date from a time after the transfer of the *neuma triplex* to that Responsory. But already as early as the late tenth century (Pa 1118 and related manuscripts) we have substantial collections of verbal additions to these *triplex* melodies.

All of the prosae we shall consider here consist of words adapted, a syllable for each note, to the melody of one or more of the *triplex* melismas.[17] The prosae that survive corroborate much that we have found among the melismas: they are most often grouped in threes; final melismas vary; and there are collections of prosae which circulate in limited geographical areas.

Four sets of prosae are transmitted in groups, and each is related to at least one other group through a common member.

---

[13] In some manuscripts (Me 83, Pia 65, Ut 406, Pa 1338?) this repetition takes places on B-flat.
[14] For a discussion of this longer version see STEINER, *The Gregorian Chant Melismas*, p. 245–249, where she cites some manuscripts not available to me.
[15] On changing melodic style, see Th. F. KELLY, *Melodic Elaboration in Responsory Melismas*, in: *JAMS* 27 (1974), p. 461–474.
[16] „Ersatz-Melisma für das dritte Neuma" (*Tropus*, in: *MGG*, Example 9d).
[17] By this definition they might well be called "prosulae", but we prefer the more general term of "prosa" as being both entirely appropriate and more widely used in the Middle Ages for such pieces.

1. The Aquitanian prosae

Five Aquitanian manuscripts contain collections of as many as ten prosae for *triplex* melismas. In Pa 1118 the presentation of these prosae is clear and melodically logical:

INCIPIUNT TROP‹O›S DE FABRICES	1. *Angelica Christo*	(A)
ITEM ALII	2. *Fabricator extra*	(A)
AŁ	3. *Fabricator descendit*	(A)
AŁ	4. *Felicia angelorum*	(A)
DE ALIA FABRICE	5. *Fabrice mundi polumque*	(B)
AŁ	6. *Aurea stella*	(B)
AŁ	7. *Gaudet beata virgo*	(B)
DE FABRICE MAIORE	8. *Fac domine deus*	(C₂)
ALIOS	9. *Rex regum*	(C₂)
ALIA	10. *Facture tue rex*	(C₂)

Four other Aquitanian manuscripts contain this set or parts of it, though none displays the consistency of rubric or melodic design found in Pa 1118.[18]

> Pa 1084: 5, 1, 7, 8, 2, 3, 6, 8, 10, 4
> Pa 1871: 5, 7, 6, 1, 2, 3, 8, 9
> Pa 1338: 5, 1, 2, 3, 10, 7, 6, 8, 4, 9
> Tol 44.1: 1, 2, 3, 5, 6, 7, 8

Pa 1871 and Tol 44.1 retain some melodic order (though Pa 1871 rearranges the order to BAC₂), but neither has as many prosulas for the final melisma as for the first two.

Peter Dronke[19] has suggested that prosae 1–4 form a coherent poetic entity, and 5–7 constitute another such group. Such a finding confirms the proper ordering of these prosae in Pa 1118, and raises the question of why the C₂ prosae, all of which pose serious textual and poetic problems, were created separately.

Such a collection of prosae seems designed for browsing: for selecting three, one for each melody, to form a triple interpolation in Resp. *Descendit* on a given occasion. This is perhaps demonstrated in the eleventh-century manuscript Wol 79 which presents prosas 1, 7, and 9.[20] Though Dronke's argument of poetic unity for the first seven prosae is persuasive, I find it difficult to imagine a liturgical performance in which all seven, or all ten, of the Aquitanian prosae were performed in the course of a single Responsory. And though the ordering of prosae in Pa 1118 may be poetically convincing, we are about to see that prosae 4 and 5 appear widely and early in East Frankish and North Italian sources as part of an "Italian" group of prosae.

---

[18] Susan Rankin, in an unpublished paper (*The Aquitanian Fabrice prosulae: some editorial comments*) presented at the Second International Conference on Tropes at Canterbury in 1984, has dealt with the ordering of these prosae. Some other later sources can be found in the alphabetical trope catalogue in HOFFMANN-BRANDT, Vol. II.
[19] In an unpublished communication to the Second International Conference of Tropes, Canterbury, August 1984.
[20] In HOFFMANN-BRANDT's trope catalogue, the same manuscript is called Wolfenbüttel 4383.

VII

2. The Italian prosae

Three prosae form a group in a number of early German and Italian sources. Though the prosae are in all cases the same three, there are considerable textual variants among the sources, and the order of prosae is not consistent from manuscript to manuscript.

The prosae are:
1. *Felicia angelorum* (or *Felicitas, Felicitatis*: a version of Aquitanian prosa 4) (A)
2. *Fabrice mundi celum terramque* (a version of Aquitanian prosa 5) (B)
3. *Facinora nostra relaxare* (C_2)

They appear in the following manuscripts, in the order indicated:

Ox 222	11th	Novalesa	BAC_2
Ivr 106	11th	Ivrea	C_2BA
Ox 366	11th ex.	Brescia	C_2BA
SG 614	11/12th	St. Gall[21]	?
Fl s.n.	12th	Florence	C_2AB
Ut 406	12th	Utrecht	ABC_2
Lu 603	12th	nr. Lucca	BAC_2 [C_2 prosa is *Concepit Maria*]
Lu 602	12/13th	Lucca?	BA only: no C
Graz 211	12th in.	Hungary	BA only: no C
Ud 84	12th	Treviso?	prosa A only

These manuscripts generally transmit the melismas as well as the prosae derived from them; in the case of the long C_2 melody the prosa and melisma are alternated by phrases. But despite the additional security that this double notation can provide, the texts and notes of these sources vary considerably.[22]

Here too there is a certain instability in the longest prosa: Lucca 603 has its own unique C_2 prosa; two manuscripts lack any version of a third melisma, transmitting only prosae for melodies A and B; and a third has only a single A prosa. Remember that we have seen this separation of A and B from the third melisma also among the manuscripts transmitting only melismas.

The prosa *Facinora* is a longer version of a similar prosa for the shorter melisma C_1. And this shorter version links this Italian group with the "French" set of prosae.

3. The French prosae

The largest group of prosae, and probably the best known, is the following, found mostly in French manuscripts:

1. *Familiam custodi Christe* (A)
2. *Fac deus munda* (B)
3. *Facinora nostra relaxare* (C_1)

---

[21] The information on SG 614 is from HOFFMANN-BRANDT, and does not permit determining the order.
[22] RoV C5, which contains *Felicitatis* as part of a triple set, is discussed below, p. 18.

They appear in many sources:

Pa 1085	10/11th	Aquitaine	BAC_1 (Melodies BAC_2)
PaA 1169	11th in.	Autun	BAC_1
Pa 9449	11th in.	Nevers	ABC_1
Tr 571	11/12th	Troyes	ABC_1
Rou 135	11/12th	Jumièges	ABC_1
Ma 288	12th in.	Norm./Sic.	ABC_1
Pa 12035	12th	Meaux	ABC_1 (Prosae are in usual order, but melodies A and B are reversed)
PaA 153	13th	Meaux	ABC_1
Pa 1266	14th in.	Meaux	ABC_1
Pa 12584	12th	St. Maur	ABC_1
Pa 12044	12th	St. Maur	ABC_1
Pa 1235	12th	Nevers	ABC_1
Pa 1236	12th	Nevers	ABC_1 (Also an additional C_1 prosa *Facture dominans*)
Pa 1535	12/13th	Sens	ABC_1
Sens 46	13th	Sens	BAC_1
Sens 29	14th	Sens	ABC_1
Pa 1028	13th	Sens	ABC_1
Ve 17C	12th	Vendôme	BAC_1
Ve 17E	13th	Vendôme	BAC_1
Pa 9425	12/13th	Premons.	ABC_1 (Responsory is *Sancte Stephane*)
Vat 4752	13th	Chartres	ABC_1 (C_1 prosa is *Facture dominans*)
LoEll	13th	Langres	BAC_1
Ch 86	13th in.	Paris	BAC_1
PaA 595	13/14th	Châlons	ABC_1
Bari 2	14th	Paris	BAC_1

This is a stable transmission. Only rarely are the first two melismas reversed; in two manuscripts the prosa *Facture dominans* supplements or replaces the regular *Facinora*. The prosae are presented with accompanying melismas only about half the time. Pa 12035 has the curious phenomenon, probably a scribal error, of reversing the first two melodies while leaving the prosae in normal order. Scribal adjustments make it clear, even if the repertory did not, that each prosa has been fitted – with little success – to the other's melody.

The first of these prosae forms a link with the last of our triple sets.

VII

4. The English-Norman prosae

This group of relatively late sources shares one of its three prosae with the French group, and like that group it uses the shorter form of the C-melismas. The prosae are:

1. *Felix Maria mundi regina* (B)
2. *Familiam custodi Christe* (A)
3. *Te laudant alme Rex* (C_1)

Among the manuscripts including this set of prosae are the following:

Pa 904	13th	Rouen
Rou 545	14th	Evreux
Rou 190	13/14th	Fécamp? (Third prosa is *Facta nativitas* [C_2])
*CUL 2602	13th ex.	Sarum
*Ed 13A	13/14th	English
*Lo 28598	13/14th	Sarum
*Cdg F.14	15th	Sarum

The manuscripts marked with an asterisk are those that include additional C_1 prosae for the days following Christmas: *Te mundi climata* (a close relative to *Te laudant*)[23] for Saint Stephen, and *Nascitur ex patre* (or, in CUL 2602, *Facture dominans*) for St. John.[24]

The four prosa sets we have seen here are connected, each to at least one other set, by common members:

Aquitanian	Italian	French	English
Angelica Christo			
Fabricator extra			
Fabricator descendit			
Felicia angelorum ——	*Felicia angelorum*	*Familiam*	*Felix Maria*
Fab. mundi polumque —	*Fab. mundi celum*	*Fac deus*	*Familiam*
Aurea stella	*Facinora* (C_2) ——	*Facinora* (C_1)	*Te laudant*
Gaudet beata			
Fac domine			
Rex regum			
Facture tue rex			

Despite these connections, it is no easy matter to draw conclusions about priorities, ancestors, or derivations. Is one of these sets the "original" set of prosae for the *neuma triplex*?

We should probably eliminate the English prosae as being both tardy and perhaps geographically peripheral; in this case, as in many others, it is easy to imagine the

---

[23] See above, note 10.

[24] Other Sarum manuscripts containing these prosae for Christmas and the two days following are Oxford Rawl. lit. d 4 and Vatican Ottob. 308; prosa *Nascitur ex patre* is transcribed from them in STÄBLEIN, *Tropus*, in: *MGG*, Example 9.

creation of prosae from a received set, either of simple melismas or of completed prosae: one simply saves what is wanted (for the English scribe, the prosa *Familiam*) and uses it as a model from which to expand other melismas in the same fashion.

The Aquitanian prosas are also demonstrably not an "original" version. For one thing, the stylistic distance between the first seven prosae and the last three is marked; indeed, if Dronke is right, the last three prosae will have come to join the orthers at some later date. And the very existence of such a lengthy catalogue suggests an expansion from a somewhat simpler original.

That original may be, of course, the two prosae which Aquitaine shares with the Italian group. These, brought to Aquitaine during or before the tenth century, could well serve as models for further prosae on the same melodies. In such a case it seems that two melodies, not three, must have arrived together; for the lesser quality of the C_2 prosae in the Aquitanian collections suggests that they are not the work of the poet who created the other prosae: yet why should a poet, faced with three melismas, concern himself with only two, leaving the third for a less gifted successor? The third melisma must not have been there at all. Although the Aquitanian poets know the same third melody as the Italians, perhaps this melody – or this version of it – was received in both places separately from the others.

For there are two versions of the C-melody: and there are two similar prosae, using the two versions, which link the Italian and the French groups. If we could show that the longer version was an expansion of an earlier, and shorter, original, we might understand the C_2 melisma as a latecomer to both the Aquitanian and Italian poetic circles. Unfortunately the demonstration is not so clear as would be convenient. Below are the texts of versions of *Facinora*:

A. Arsenal 1169, f. 54

1. Facinora nostra relaxari mundi gloriam
2. Petimus mente devota david regis prolem inclitam
3. virgo quem casta secula maria protulit summi patris gratiam
4. cuius ortus salvat omnes cuncta per secula
5. et die hac nobis dignanter foveat
6. adque omni fabrice mundi

B. "London, Ellis",[25] f. 97v–98

1. Facinora nostra relaxare mundi gloria
2. Petimus mente devota david regis proles inclita
3. virgo quem casta seclo maria protulit mundi patris gloriam
4. cuius ortus salvat omnes cuncta per secula

contempnentes pravam mundi istius vitam
et instanter cassant ob hoc nos tua
complentes jussa ut des quando premia eterna

---

[25] A thirteenth-century Langres breviary whose facsimile at Solesmes is labeled thus; I do not know the manuscript's current whereabouts.

VII

5. et die hac nobis dignanter
6. atque omnia fabrice mundi

C. Oxford, Douce 222

1. Facinora nostra relaxavit mundi gaudia
2. Petimus mente devota regis david prole inclita
3. Quem virgo sacra seculo maria protulit summi patris gloria
4. Cuius ortus salvat omnes cuncta per secula
    a. Ut preclara die ista parcat omnia
    b. Nostra post lavacra
    c. Dignetur pius oriundus famulorum visitare corda
    d1. Piorum mentemque fidelium perpetuumque semper
    d2. [ne regis perirent ovia copia olim data]
        [c]onditor mundi

The first prosa (A) is the version of *Facinora* generally found with melody C_1; like many prosulae, it begins and ends with the syllables ("fabrice mundi") of the melisma from which it is derived, and has frequent assonance on the melisma's vowel, in this case "A".[26]

Prosa B uses the longer melody C_2, and makes a textual interpolation in the shorter *Facinora* prosa, adding new text where melody C_2 diverges from C_1, and returning to the original text where the melismas merge again. This is just the sort of prosa that would demonstrate the derivation of melisma C_2 from the shorter C_1, and the dependence of the longer *Facinora* on the shorter. But the fact is that this prosa B is rather late and very rare: I have seen it only in a single thirteenth-century Langres Breviary (LoEll). It is certainly not the C_2 version of *Facinora* found in the Italian sets of prosae.

The Italian *Facinora* is shown as prosa C; and this is not so clearly a derivation: for it matches the shorter *Facinora* as long as it can – but then, rather than making an insertion and returning to the original text, this prosa simply turns in a different direction, which it follows to the end. There is really no demonstrable precedence here: even though the two prosae share precisely the same text and music for more than half their lengths, they continue as independent creations.

We cannot demonstrate that the longer C_2 prosa is the younger. We can only suspect it.[27] It is not easy, for example, to imagine the abbreviation of a melody in a process whose whole purpose is addition; and there is a certain lack of clarity in the Italian transmission: there are alternative versions of the last line,[28] and the second part in general is much less fixed than the text of the shorter *Facinora*.

---

[26] It is not possible here to consider the finer points of medieval prosula style; for more on the subject, see Th. F. KELLY, *New Music from Old: The Structuring of Responsory Prosas*, in: *JAMS* 30 (1977), p. 366–390; B. STÄBLEIN, *Die Unterlegung von Texten unter Melismen: Tropus, Sequenz und andere Formen*, in: *I. M. S., Report of the Eighth Congress New York, 1961*, Vol. I (Kassel 1961), p. 12–29.

[27] We should note that there exists, in two later manuscripts, an intermediate version of the C-melody, longer than C_1, but not repeating the static passages of C_1 as happens in the longer melisma. This melody can be seen in Cdg F.4.10, and in the melody of the prosa *Facta nativitas* in Rou 190.

[28] The version here is basically that of Iv 106 and Ox 222; the alternative line d2 is that of Ox 366, Fl s. n., and Ut 406.

In any case, the two versions of the C melisma circulated independent of their prosae (see the list of melismas above); if the "Italian" *Facinora* was fashioned from the shorter version, it must have been in the perplexing (or challenging) presence of an unmatching longer melisma; we have seen the same problem solved at Langres by the creator of prosa B.

But then it must also be true that the Italian set of prosae is not an 'original' set: it has been altered before being recorded in the surviving sources. And if the shorter *Facinora* prosa is likely older than the longer, perhaps the French set of prosae has a claim to antiquity, despite its relatively late appearance in the sources.

Actually, however, the clearest conclusion to be made from these prosa sets is that none is the definitive ancestor of another; that each seems to be made from three melismas and at least one textual 'seed' from elsewhere, which is completed by two new prosae.

Five manuscripts whose triple sets of prosae are unique in the repertory show the creative process of generating three prosae from the *triplex* melismas. These compositions date from as early as the late tenth century. They are largely preserved in tropers, a fact which may emphasize their quality as unique creations separate from the normal transmission of Office music.

They include:

1. Apt 18 (10/11th):
   Prosa *Familiam plebis* (A)
   Prosa *Facundie largitor* (B)
   Prosa *Faciens bonitatis* (C_2)

These prosae (mentioned above, p. 4) are attached to Resp. *Verbum caro factum*; but their opening syllables, their assonance, and their final words *fabrice mundi* make it clear that they were originally intended for Resp. *Descendit*.

2. Cai 78 (11th c., 2nd half):
   Prosa *Verbum patris* (A)
   Prosa *Lumen de lumine* (B)
   Prosa *Facture dominans* (C_1)

The last of these prosae is not unique to this manuscript: we have seen it among the "French" group (Pa 1236 and Vat 4752), and we shall see it again shortly: it is a prosa conceived independently and transmitted separately. This prosa set, then, is perhaps made like the others we have seen: a triple set of prosae is made from a single verbal seed.

3. La 263 (12th), Resp. *Centum quadraginta*:[29]
   Prosa *Dum pectoris* (B)
   Prosa *Per quem credenda* (A)
         (lacuna)

---

[29] The prosae and melismas are transcribed in STÄBLEIN, *Tropus*, in: *MGG*, Example 9.

VII

Two prosae (if there was a third it is lost now owing to a lacuna following the written-out melody C_1) each end with *conditor mundi*, and their sense is more suited to Christmas than to the feast of the Holy Innocents; they have been brought here from their original place in Resp. *Descendit de celis deus verus*.[30]

    4. Ox 27 (11th):
        Prosa *De celis venit legem* (B)
        Prosa *Conditor lucis eterne* (D)
        Prosa *Celestis aule rex* (C_1)

This collection of three prosae ending with *Fabrice mundi*, although they are arranged in order and separated by prosae for the Responsory's two verses, are an unusual trio. This is the only manuscript in which prosae for melismas C_2 and D are present together. Like so many sets of prosae, this trio has one member not unique here: the third prosa is found in Leipzig, Univ. St. Thomas 391.[31] Perhaps the combination of an existing prosa with a triple melisma from elsewhere produced a collision in which the wrong melisma was dropped, resulting in a unique case of two "final" melismas designed to be performed together.

    5. RoV C5 (12th):
        Prosa *Ante secla deus* (C_2)
        Prosa *Fari tibi deus* (B)
        Prosa *Felicitas angelorum* (A)

This is another example of a new triple set or prosae grown from a "seed": in this case the seed is one of the prosae (*Felicitas*) from the Italian set; it is known in Aquitaine, as we have seen.

    Isolated prosae are far fewer than triple sets;[32] and with rare exceptions[33] they are textings of the long final melismas.

    Melisma D is given a text in several East-Frankish sources: in these cases, the manuscripts generally transmit a full set (ABD) of melismas, but only a single prosa. In the Hartker Antiphoner (SG 390) a hand of the twelfth or thirteenth century has added the text of the prosa *Auscultate omnes* to the manuscript on page 7, at some distance from where Hartker had written the melisma and its two companions with the Responsory. *Auscultate* appears also in SG 389; and it is transmitted independent of other melismas or of the parent Responsory in the mid-eleventh century SG 380. There the sections of melisma are written in the margin by each phrase: it is easy to imagine how this might lead to the notation of prosae

---

[30] This manuscript borrows many things – mostly Offertory melismas – for use with Responsories; see D. G. HUGHES, *Music for St. Stephen at Laon*, in: *Words and Music: The Scholar's View*, ed. L. Berman (Cambridge, Mass. 1972), p. 137–159; see also KELLY, *Responsory Tropes*, p. 49–60.
[31] According to HOFFMANN-BRANDT, Vol. II, p. 19.
[32] A triple set of prosae from a fourteenth-century Tours manuscript is transcribed in HOFFMANN-BRANDT, Vol. II, p. 62–67.
[33] The Italian AB and A prosae (above, p. 12); two B-prosae in Mu 23621); two isolated appearances of the prosa *Familiam* for melisma A (in the margin of fol. 39 in Civ 93, and in Lo 2615 as a prosa for Resp. *Descendit* for second Vespers); the A-prosa *Factus homo* in PaA 279 ("alia prosa non dicitur versus").

VII

alternating with sections of melisma; a notation that has long raised questions about the possibility of simultaneous performance of prosa and melisma.[34]

The same melisma D provides music for the prosa *Facture plasmator* in seven other East Frankish manuscripts of the eleventh to twelfth centuries (Civ 91, Civ 93, Graz 258, Kl 1010, Kl 1013, SF 384, Li 19[35]). All the manuscripts except SF 384 provide a full set of melismas (ABD) for the Responsory but only a single prosa. The two Klosterneuburg Antiphoners have another prosa for melody D, *Ante tempus parentis*, attached to Resp. *In medio ecclesie*.

Melisma C_1 also has prosae independent of triple sets. We have already seen the prosa *Et intellectus* in Pa 17296 (see p. 6), and the relatively late English prosae for St. Stephen and St. John (see pp. 6 and 14). In addition, the prosa *Facture dominans* has appeared in the "French" set of prosae as an alternate (Pa 1236) or a substitute (Vat 4752) for the usual third prosa. *Facture dominans* is also transmitted independently in a few relatively late sources: PaA 279 ("alia prosa," along with *Facinora* [C_1] for processions); Heref (along with *Te laudant alme* as an alternative), Everin, and Lo 2615. This prosa seems to be a second-stage composition, substituting for or alternating with the more standard prosa *Facinora*.[36]

From the evidence of this survey we can infer the following:

1. Melisma A is the kernel of the *neuma triplex*.
2. Melismas A and B have an early and close association.
3. One of several third melismas came to be associated with these at a later stage.
4. Prosae are added to these melismas largely in association with Resp. *Descendit*, and largely after the establishment of the *neuma triplex* idea: but traces of earlier stages, and of association with Resp. *In medio ecclesie*, are still to be found.

Let us review some of the evidence for these conclusions. First, the third melisma is separate and distinct from the other two. From our earliest sources we see that the

[34] It is impossible to go deeply into performance questions here; but we can say that prosae were probably not intended to be performed simultaneously with their melismas. Some studies of prosula performance (including opposing views) are: Th. F. KELLY, *The Performance of Responsory Tropes*, in: *Liturgische Tropen*, ed. G. Silagi (Bachenhausen 1985), p. 124–143; O. MARCUSSON, *Comment a-t-on chanté les prosules? Observations sur la technique des tropes de l'alleluia*, in: *RMl* 65 (1979), p. 149–159; J. SMITS VAN WAESBERGHE, *Zur ursprünglichen Vortragsweise*, p. 251–254 – see also his remarks in *Bericht über den neunten internationalen Kongress Salzburg 1964*, Vol. I (Kassel 1964), p. 68–69; K. RÖNNAU, *Regnum tuum solidum*, in: *Festschrift Bruno Stäblein* (Kassel 1964), Vol. I, p. 25–35; H. HUSMANN, *Das Organum vor und außerhalb der Notre-Dame-Schule*, in: *Bericht über den neunten internationalen Kongress Salzburg 1964*, Vol. I (Kassel 1964), p. 25–35.
[35] The prosa is written in the bottom margin in a second hand.
[36] The verses (*Tamquam sponsus* and *Gloria patri*) of Resp. *Descendit*, which Amalarius says are extended by melismas, are often accompanied also by prosae. While we cannot study these in detail here, we should note some characteristics of their distribution. Verse prosae are less common than Responsory prosae, and though they occur often in regional repertories they do not always travel with sets of Responsory prosae, and they are clearly not part of sets of five prosae combining Responsory and verses. A German set of verse prosae (*Missus ab arce*/*Gloria pie trinitatis*) is found in Civ 93, Graz 211, Graz 258, Linz, Mza 75 (which however has the Gloria prosa *Laus gloria*), Ox 202, SF 384. There are three Italian sets: *Quem iam Gabriel*/*Laus et gloria* (Cortona 2, Pia 65, Fl 560, RoV C5, Iv 106 [with *Gloria laus nunc*], Ud 84); *Tam gloriosa dies*/*Gloria laus et potestas* (Fl s.n., LoEll, Lu 602, Lu 603), and *Porta quam Ezechiel* (Ox 222, with *Gloria laus nunc*; Ox 366, with *Gloria domino*). A French set, *Tanta nunc*/*Gloria patri ingenito*, is in Pa 12584, Pa 1236, Rou 135, Wol 79, Pa 12044 (without *Gloria*). Unique verse prosae are found in Ox 27 (*Rex omnis*/*Gloria sit venerande*) and, for Resp. *In medio*, in Pia 65 (*Ad conservandam*/*Laudes in celo*).

VII

third melisma is variable; and we have seen the same variety of third melisma both in the transmission of melismas and in the prosa-groups. In some cases, the final melisma is the only one of three to bear a prosa: this is true particularly of the texting of melisma D in many East Frankish sources (SG 380, SG 390, Kl 1010, Kl 1013); in these cases melisma D seems almost to be a vehicle for text, a sequence-structured melisma that exists to be texted; and it is nicely suited to contrast (both in musical style and because of the presence of a text) with the previous two melismas (rather than to complement them, as do the versions of melisma C).

In the troper Ox 27 we see a scribe collecting two final prosae (on melodies C_1 and D), surely from separate sources, and rearranging them, according to principles he clearly did not understand fully, as part of a newly-assembled triple group. And the later evidence of a separate third melisma shows a continuing consciousness of this special relationship. The independent prosa *Facture dominans*; the prose *Et intellectus Johannem* of Pa 17296; and the Sarum practice of C_1 prosae for St. Stephen and St. John, all show this awareness.

Melismas A and B, the two shorter melismas, are a related pair. First of all, they are nearly always transmitted together, almost always side-by-side, whatever the third melisma may be. And sometimes there is no third melisma, as in Vro 98, and in Graz 211, which transmits what may be the earliest version of the Italian group of prosae – a version which, without its third prosa, retains the kernel of two prosae from which the Aquitanian set may have grown. These Aquitanian prosae show poetic evidence that the series of prosae for melodies A and B are a separate unified composition, to which the C_2 prosae must be later additions.

And of this pair, Melisma A is surely the original. First of all, we know it to be derived from an Offertory: it was not composed for a Responsory. Melisma A is a remarkable melody: the striking four-note descending sequential figure would make it jump to the ear. Melisma B, then, is found (in a composer's imagination? – a liturgical source has so far been sought in vain) to complement, in length and style, this first remarkable melisma. It is difficult to imagine the reverse procedure: composing a first melisma and then seeking a mate in the liturgy.

We have seen melisma A transmitted alone.[37] And one of the prosae for this melisma, *Familiam tuam*, is the most widespread of all: in addition to appearing in both the French and English triple sets, it appears by itself in the 11th–12th century Aquileian source Civ 93; and also in the later Lo 2615. Another A-prosa, *Felicitas angelorum*, is shared by Italian and Aquitanian sets; and it travels alone in Italy (in Ud 84, and as the 'seed' prosula for RoV C5: see p. 18).

A third melisma is subsequently joined to balance the combination of the first two; but not always the same melody. Though the third melismas are determined geographically to some degree, the choice of third melisma is partly a matter of taste. Melisma C is designed to complement the others: in both its longer and shorter versions, it has the rough-hewn, not-quite-structured repetitions

---

[37] Albeit in relatively late manuscripts. See the lists of melismas above.

characteristic of the Offertory melismas from which melisma A is drawn; it is roughly equal to the other two in length; and the opening notes use the same shape and range as the first two melismas.

There is little reason to think of melisma D as a substitute: it occurs among the earliest manuscripts. Better perhaps, is to consider it an alternative balancing effort at a time of changing style: a newer, more forceful melisma making a strong contrast to the two shorter melodies, the contrast itself and the angular repetitions of the melody emphasizing newer tastes.

Most of our sources associate these *neuma triplex* elements with the Responsory *Descendit de celis*; this was the norm already in Amalarius' day, as he tells us clearly, so it should be no surprise that all the manuscripts dating from later than his time bear him out.

But should we believe, as some do, that Amalarius, in his well-known zeal to find a mystical or symbolic explanation for any liturgical phenomenon, let himself be carried away with his interpretation of the word *intellectus* on which the neumes fall in Resp. *In medio*,[38] and perhaps overemphasized this Responsory's role in the origin of the *neuma triplex*?

I see no reason to doubt Amalarius. For one thing, melisma A is taken from the Offertory of the first Mass of Saint John the Evangelist.[39] For another, there are just too many puzzling and continuing connections with *In medio* in later sources despite the "transfer," before Amalarius' time, to *Descendit*; and it seems unlikely that the transfer should have worked always the other way – from Christmas to St. John – without involving the feast of St. Stephen as well. (It probably did work the other way in England, and there St. Stephen is included.)

And in fact, though Amalarius does not say so, it is possible that Metz itself, or its region, is the place of origin of this phenomenon. Amalarius is, after all, the first to report it. And the geographical distribution of the various third melismas generally centers in this area. Melisma C_1 to North and West; melisma C_2 to the South; and melisma D to the East.

It is regrettable that we have no early office books from Metz; but from some thirteenth-century manuscripts that we do have we can see a picture remarkably close to the hypothetical development we have sketched for the *neuma triplex*.

In Me 580, melisma A is the only decoration added to Resp. *Descendit de celis deus verus*. Melismas A and B are combined for *In medio ecclesie* in Me 83 (a single B is provided for the reprise of *in medio* for the Octave); and a triple melisma, ABC_2, is provided for Resp. *Descendit de celis deus verus* in the same manuscript. Also at Metz, however, can be found melisma D, as the sole decoration for Resp. *Descendit de celis deus verus* in Me 461.

---

[38] See STEINER, *The Gregorian Chant Melismas*, p. 250; HANSSENS, Vol. III, p. 54.

[39] It can be seen at the end of the second verse ot the Offertory *Gloria et honore* in K. OTT, *Offertoriale sive versus offertorii* (Tournai 1935), and in its reprint, with neumes added, as R. FISCHER, *Offertoires neumés* (Solesmes 1978), p. 135. As Ruth Steiner has pointed out, the Offertory is used in the Middle Ages for a number of saints; but it is normally written out in full only the first time it occurs in a manuscript, generally for the feast of St. John. (See STEINER, *The Gregorian Chant Melismas*, p. 251.)

Amalarius does not mention prosae; and the manuscripts of Metz in no case assign prosae as Responsory decorations. Me 83, although it assigns melismas to a number of Responsories, nowhere uses a prosa. It seems that the Metz practice, even through the thirteenth century, was to exclude prosae from the Office. Any *neuma triplex* melodies coming from Metz, then, would travel without words; and the geographical arrangements of prosa groups is consistent with such a radiating melodic transmission.

A thirteenth-century ordinal of Metz (Paris, Bibl. nat. lat. 990, fol. 17v), which mentions only one melisma for Resp. *Descendit*, prescribes three *notae* for Resp. *In medio*: "In fine ultimi Resp. canitur quaedam nota super sapientie antequam cantetur versus. Post versum alia, post Gloria patri tertia." Could it be that this ordinal and Me 83 preserve the practice actually described by Amalarius? That two melismas, A and B (as provided in Me 83 for *In medio*), along with the Responsory's original notes for *sapientie et intellectus*, are a triple melisma? In such a configuration the final words are sung three times (not four, as is the case with most performances of three additional melismas)? Perhaps Amalarius' *neuma triplex* is that provided by Me 83: the original plus two melismas – and perhaps the form we think of as standard may be a sort of *neuma quadruplex* formed by the addition of another melisma. Of this terminological question we cannot be sure. Whatever Amalarius means, it is clear that three additional melismas rapidly became the norm.

We can now, I think, feel assured about the veracity of Amalarius' testimony; we have a clearer picture of the scope of this phenomenon; and we can rejoice in the variety and richness which remain as witness to the high esteem in which these interpolations were held in their age: they are both a pinnacle of office tropes, and a seminal point for musical and poetical developments to follow.

Appendix I: Manuscripts

This is a list of manuscripts used in this study; it is not a complete list of sources for *neuma triplex* tropes; dates are given here for convenience; they are approximate, and based on no new research. Sources for dates include R.-J. HESBERT, *Corpus antiphonalium officii*, Vol. 5 = Rerum ecclesiasticarum documenta, Series maior, Fontes 11 (Rome 1975), p. 5–18; H. HUSMANN, *Tropen- und Sequenzenhandschriften* = RISM B V[1] (Munich 1964); R. JONSSON *et al.*, *Corpus troporum I: Tropes du propre de la messe, 1: Cycle de Noël* (Stockholm 1975), p. 46–50. In the column "Type", the following letters are used: B = Breviary, A = Antiphoner, G = Gradual, T = Troper, O = Office, P = Processional; lower-case letters indicate whether an office-book is of the secular or the monastic cursus. In addition to the authorities of many of the libraries owning these manuscripts, I am grateful for the kindnesses which allowed me free access to the microfilm archives of Catholic University; The Isham Memorial Library at Harvard University; and the Abbey of Solesmes.

Neuma Triplex　　　　　　　　　　　　　　　　　　　　　　　　　　

Siglum	Manuscript	Type	Date	Provenance
Aachen	Aachen, Münsterarchiv, no number	Bs	13/14th	Augustinian
Am 115	Amiens, Bibliothèque municipale, Ms. 115	Bm	12th	Corbie
Apt 18	Apt, Basilique de Sainte-Anne, Ms. 18	T	10/11th	N. Italy?
Ba 22	Bamberg, Staatsbibliothek, Ms. lit. 22	As	12/13th	Bamberg
Ba 23	Bamberg, Staatsbibliothek, Ms. lit. 23	As	12th	Bamberg
Ba 24	Bamberg, Staatsbibliothek, Ms. lit. 24	As	12th	Bamberg
Ba 26	Bamberg, Staatsbibliothek, Ms. lit. 26	As	12/13th	Bamberg
Bari 2	Bari, Archivio di San Nicola, Ms. 2	Bs	c. 1339	Paris
Ben 21	Benevento, Biblioteca capitolare, Ms. 21	Am	12th	Benevento
Be 377	Berlin, Deutsche Staatsbibliothek, th. lat. 377	Bm	10/11th	?
Be 40047	Berlin, Deutsche Staatsbibliothek, 40047	As	11th in.	Quedlinburg
Br 353	Brussels, Bibliothèque Royale, Ms. 353	Bs	12/13th	Germany
Br 3827	Brussels, Bibliothèque Royale, Ms. II 3827	Am	13th	?
Cai 78	Cambrai, Bibliothèque municipale, Ms. 78	T	11th 2/2	Cambrai
Cdg F.4.10	Cambridge, Magdalen College, Ms. F.4.10	Am	13/14th	Peterborough
Cdg F.14	Cambridge, St. John's College, Ms. F.14	P	15th	Sarum
CUL 2602	Cambridge, University Library, Add. Ms. 2602	As	13th ex.	Sarum
Ch 86	Charleville, Bibliothèque municipale, Ms. 86	Bs	13th in.	Paris
Chia	Chiavenna, Bibl. cap. S. Lorenzo, without no.	As	11th	Chiavenna
Civ 91	Cividale, Museo archeologico nazionale, Ms. XCI	Bm	11/12th	Aquileia
Civ 93	Cividale, Museo archeologico nazionale, Ms. XCIII	Bm	11/12th	Aquileia
*Dur 11	Durham, Cathedral Library, Ms. B iii 11	As	11th	NE France
Ed 13A	Edinburgh, Advocate's Library, Ms. 18.2.13A	As	13/14th	English
Ei 83	Einsiedeln, Stiftsbibliothek, Ms. 83	Am	12th	Einsiedeln
Everin	Everingham, Ms. without shelf number	As	14th	York
Fl 560	Florence, Bib. Med.-Laur., Ms. Conv. soppr. 560	Am	12th	Vallombrosa
Fl s.n.	Florence, Curia arciv., Ms. without number	Am	12th	Florence
Graz 211	Graz, Universitätsbibliothek, Ms. 211	As	12th in.	Hungary
Graz 258	Graz, Universitätsbibliothek, Ms. 258	Am	12th	Germany
Heref	Hereford, Cathedral, Ms. without number	Bs	13th	Hereford
Ivr 106	Ivrea, Biblioteca capitolare, Ms. 106	As	11th	Ivrea
Ka 144	Kassel, Landesbibliothek, Ms. Th. 2° 144	Bs	12th	Fritzlar
Kl 1010	Klosterneuburg, Aug.-Chorherrenstift, Ms. 1010	As	12th	Klosterneuburg
Kl 1013	Klosterneuburg, Aug.-Chorherrenstift, Ms. 1013	As	12th	Klosterneuburg
Ko 215	Köln, Diözesanbibliothek, Ms. 215	Bs	12th	Franconia
La 263	Laon, Bibliothèque municipale, Ms. 263	O	12th	Laon
Li 19	Linz, Bundesstaatl. Studienbibliothek, Ms. Γ. p. 19	Bm	11/12th	Glünik
LoEll	"London, Ellis:" facsimile at Solesmes	Bs	13th	Langres
Lo 28598	London, British Library, Add. Ms. 28598	As	13/14th	Sarum
Lo 30848	London, British Library, Add. Ms. 30848	Bm	11th	Silos
Lo 30850	London, British Library, Add. Ms. 30850	Am	11th	Silos
*Lo 2615	London, British Library, Egerton. Ms. 2615	O	13th 1/2	Beauvais
Lu 601	Lucca, Biblioteca capitolare, Ms. 601	Am	12th	Puteoli
Lu 602	Lucca, Biblioteca capitolare, Ms. 602	As	12/13th	Lucca?
Lu 603	Lucca, Biblioteca capitolare, Ms. 603	Am	12th	S. Maria di Pontetto
Ma 288	Madrid, Biblioteca nacional, Ms. 288	T	12th in.	Norman/Sicilian
Me 83	Metz, Bibliothèque municipale, Ms. 83	Am	13th in.	Metz
Me 461	Metz, Bibliothèque municipale, Ms. 461	Bs	13th ex.	Metz
Me 580	Metz, Bibliothèque municipale, Ms. 580	P	13th	Metz, St. Arnoul
*Mont-R	Private Collection	As	10th	Saint-Denis
Mza 75	Monza, Biblioteca capitolare, Ms. C. 12/75	T	11th	North Italy

Mu 23037	Munich, Bayerische Staatsbibliothek, Ms. clm 23037	Am	12th	Germany
Mu 23621	Munich, Bayerische Staatsbibliothek, Ms. clm 23621	A	12th ex.	fragment; German?
Ox 27	Oxford, Bodleian Library, Ms. Selden supra 27	T	11th	German
Ox 202	Oxford, Bodleian Library, Ms. Can. lit. 202	As	13th ?	South Germany
Ox 222	Oxford, Bodleian Library, Ms. Douce 222	T	11th	Novalesa
Ox 297	Oxford, Bodleian Library, Ms. Can. lit. 297	Bm	1054	Würzburg
Ox 366	Oxford, Bodleian Library, Ms. Can. lit. 366	Bs	11th ex.	Brescia
PaA 153	Paris, Bibliothèque de l'Arsenal, Ms. 153	Bs	13th	Meaux
PaA 279	Paris, Bibliothèque de l'Arsenal, Ms. 279	Bs	13th	Bayeux, for Caen
PaA 595	Paris, Bibliothèque de l'Arsenal, Ms. 595	Bs	13/14th	Châlons
PaA 1169	Paris, Bibliothèque de l'Arsenal, Ms. 1169	T	11th in.	Autun
Pa 742	Paris, Bibliothèque nationale, Ms. latin 742	Bm	12/13th	Ripoll
Pa 743	Paris, Bibliothèque nationale, Ms. latin 743	Bm	11th	St.-Martial
Pa 796	Paris, Bibliothèque nationale, Ms. latin 796	Bm	12th	Montiéramey
*Pa 904	Paris, Bibliothèque nationale, Ms. latin 904	G	13th	Rouen, cathedral
Pa 1028	Paris, Bibliothèque nationale, Ms. latin 1028	Bs	13th	Sens
Pa 1084	Paris, Bibliothèque nationale, Ms. latin 1084	T	11th in.	Aurillac
Pa 1085	Paris, Bibliothèque nationale, Ms. latin 1085	A	10/11th	Aquitaine
Pa 1088	Paris, Bibliothèque nationale, Ms. latin 1088	Am	14th ex.	St.-Martial
Pa 1118	Paris, Bibliothèque nationale, Ms. latin 1118	T	10/11th	SE France
Pa 1235	Paris, Bibliothèque nationale, Ms. nouv. acq. lat. 1235	G/T	12th	Nevers
Pa 1236	Paris, Bibliothèque nationale, Ms. nouv. acq. lat. 1236	As	12th	Nevers
Pa 1266	Paris, Bibliothèque nationale, Ms. latin 1266	Bs	1309	Meaux
Pa 1338	Paris, Bibliothèque nationale, Ms. latin 1338	T	11th 2/2	St.-Martial?
Pa 1535	Paris, Bibliothèque nationale, Ms. nouv. acq. lat. 1535	As	12/13th	Sens
Pa 1871	Paris, Bibliothèque nationale, Ms. nouv. acq. lat. 1871	T	11th 2/2	Aurillac? Moissac?
Pa 9425	Paris, Bibliothèque nationale, Ms. latin 9425	As	12/13th	Premonstratensian
*Pa 9449	Paris, Bibliothèque nationale, Ms. latin 9449	G/T	c. 1059	Nevers
Pa 12035	Paris, Bibliothèque nationale, Ms. latin 12035	Bs	12th	Meaux
Pa 12044	Paris, Bibliothèque nationale, Ms. nouv. acq. lat. 12044	Am	12th	St.-Maur des Fossées
Pa 12584	Paris, Bibliothèque nationale, Ms. latin 12584	Am	12th	St.-Maur des Fossées
Pa 17296	Paris, Bibliothèque nationale, Ms. latin 17296	Am	12th	St.-Denis
Pa 17991	Paris, Bibliothèque nationale, Ms. latin 17991	Bs	11th	Reims
Pia 65	Piacenza, Biblioteca capitolare, Ms. 65	G/As	c.1200	Piacenza, cathedral
Pr 4c	Prague, Universitní knihovna, Ms. VI E 4 c	Bm	12/13th	Prague
RoV C5	Rome, Biblioteca Vallicelliana, Ms. C.5	Am	12th	Norcia, St. Eutizio
*Rou 135	Rouen, Bibliothèque municipale, Ms. U. 135	Frag	11/12th	Jumièges
*Rou 145	Rouen, Bibliothèque municipale, Ms. A. 145	Bm	12th	Jumièges
Rou 164	Rouen, Bibliothèque municipale, Ms. A. 164	Bm	11th	Marmoutier
Rou 175	Rouen, Bibliothèque municipale, Ms. Y. 175[1]	Bm	12th ex.	Jumièges
Rou 190	Rouen, Bibliothèque municipale, Ms. A. 190	Am	13/14th	Fécamp?
Rou 226	Rouen, Bibliothèque municipale, Ms. A. 226	Am	13th?	Rouen, Bonne nouvelle
Rou 545	Rouen, Bibliothèque municipale, Ms. A. 545	Bs	14th	Évreux
SF 384	Saint Florian, Stiftsbibliothek, Ms. XI. 384	Bs	12th	St. Florian
SG 380	Saint Gall, Stiftsbibliothek, Ms. 380	T	c.1054	St. Gall
SG 388	Saint Gall, Stiftsbibliothek, Ms. 388	Bm	12th	St. Gall
SG 389	Saint Gall, Stiftsbibliothek, Ms. 389	As	12th	Sion?
*SG 390	Saint Gall, Stiftsbibliothek, Ms. 390–1	Am	10/11th	St. Gall
SG 413	Saint Gall, Stiftsbibliothek, Ms. 413	Bm	11th 1/2	St. Gall
SG 414	Saint Gall, Stiftsbibliothek, Ms. 414	Am	11th	St. Gall
SG 416	Saint Gall, Stiftsbibliothek, Ms. 416	Bs	12th	St. Gall?
*Sa 152	Salisbury, Chapter Library, Ms. 152	As	15th	Sarum

Sz 24	Salzburg, St. Peter, Ms. a. V. 24	Bm	11/12th	Salzburg
Sens 29	Sens, Bibliothèque municipale, Ms. 29	Bs	14th	Sens
*Sens 46	Sens, Bibliothèque municipale, Ms. 46	Off	13th	Sens
Tol 44.1	Toledo, Biblioteca capitular, Ms. 44.1	Am	11th ex.	Aquitaine
Tol 44.2	Toledo, Biblioteca capitular, Ms. 44.2	As	12/13th	Aquitaine?
Tr 571	Troyes, Bibliothèque municipale, Ms. 571	Bs	11/12th	Troyes, St.-Loup
To 4	Turin, Biblioteca nazionale, Ms. F.IV.4	Am	12/13th	Bobbio, St. Colomba
Ud 84	Udine, Biblioteca arcivescovile, 84 (olim fol. 25)	As	12th	Treviso
Ut 406	Utrecht, Rijksuniversiteit Bibliotheek, Ms. 406	A	12/15th	Utrecht, St. Mary
Val 114	Valenciennes, Bibliothèque municipale, Ms. 114	Am	12th	St.-Amand
Vat 4752	Vatican City, Bibl. Ap. Vaticana, Ms. lat. 4752	Bs	13th	Chartres
Ve 17C	Vendôme, Archive of La Trinité, Ms. 17C	Bs	12th	Vendôme dioc.
Ve 17E	Vendôme, Archive of La Trinité, Ms. 17E	Bs	13th	Vendôme dioc.
Vro 98	Verona, Biblioteca capitolare, Ms. XCVIII	As	11th	?
Wi 1890	Vienna, Österreichische Nationalbibliothek, Ms. 1890	Bm	12th	German
Wol 79	Wolfenbüttel, Herzog-August-Bibliothek, Ms. Guelph 79 Gud. lat.	T	11th	Limoges
*Wo 160	Worcester, Chapter Library, Ms. F. 160	Am	13th	Worcester

*Dur 11: Facsimile as *Pars antiphonarii* (London 1923).
Lo 2615: Edition of relevant portion as W. ARLT, *Ein Festofficium des Mittelalters aus Beauvais*, 2 vols. (Köln 1970).
Mont-R: Facsimile as *Paléographie musicale* 16.
Pa 904: Facsimile as H. LORIQUET, J. POTHIER, and A. COLETTE, *Le graduel de l'église cathédrale de Rouen au XIII* siècle*, 2 vols. (Rouen 1907).
Pa 9449: Facsimile of *Descendit* melismas and prosae in R. STEINER, *The Responsories and Prosa for St. Stephen's Day at Salisbury*, in: *MQ* 56 (1970), p. 176.
Rou 135: Facsimile in R.-J. HESBERT, ed., *Les manuscrits musicaux de Jumièges* = Monumenta musicae sacrae 2 (Mâcon 1954), plate XXV.
Rou 145: Facsimile *ibid.*, plate XXXII.
SG 390: Facsimile in *Paléographie musicale*, Series 2, Vol. 1. See also R. STEINER, *The Gregorian Chant Melismas of Christmas Matins*, in: *Essays on Music for Charles Warren Fox*, ed. J. C. Graue (Rochester 1979), p. 243.
Sa 152: Facsimile of relevant portion of MS in W. H. FRERE, *Antiphonale sarisburiense* (London 1901–1924, repr. 1966), plates 1–5.
Sens 46: Edition in H. VILLETARD, *Office de Pierre de Corbeil* (Paris 1907).
Wo 160: Facsimile as *Paléographie musicale* 12.

Appendix II: Prosae

These are the texts of the prosae to *neuma triplex* melodies before the thirteenth century, with a few additional texts whose earliest witnesses are after 1200. Each text is the reading of a single manuscript; no attempt has been made at a critical edition. Prosae are arranged according to the melismas of which they are settings, and within each group they are ordered alphabetically.

I. Prosae to Melisma A

Angelica christo canant agmina
Qui restauravit quod crearat
ut potenter ut astancium bina
Lustra claruit
  Fabrice mundi (Pa 1118, f. 117v)

Fabricator extra polum conditor
Ex astra vegit ut descendat
splendidaque regionis introeat
Gloriosus rex
  Fabrice mundi (Pa 1118, f. 117v)

VII

Factor celi descendit de superos
Ex astra celi carne clara
iam indutus salus vera hodierna
Refulsit stella
    Fabrice mundi (Pa 1118, f. 117v–118)

Factus homo est pro nobis hostia
infernus erit comunitus
eruet vide captivos cum gloria
ad celestia
    Fabrice mundi (PaA 279, f. 85)

Familiam custodi christe tuam
quam natus alma de Maria
redemisti morte tua ut cognoscat
te conditorem
    fabrice mundi (Pa 1236, f. 36–36v)

Familiam plebis refovens credulam
venit miseranter relaxara
lacrimosa gencium suspiria qui est et
erat rex omnis
    fabrice mundi (Apt 18, f. 95v)

Felicia angelorum gaudia
hodie celi stillaverunt
hominibus vernantia in secula
deo per alta
    conditor mundi (Ox 222, f. 3v–4)

Per quem credenda hominibus
mente devota plus ceteris
sacramenta aperuit celestia sublimius
divine vocis
    conditor mundi (La 263, f. 110v)

Verbum patris sol inaccessabilis
deus de deo lux de luce
matris factor est editus in seculo
cum patre conditor
    fabrice mundi (Cai 78, f. 49–49v)

II. Prosae to Melisma B

Aurea stella fulgens per tempora
audite vox quam preclara
Xristus in quo de sede patris in terrisque est venturus
    Filius dei (Pa 1118, f. 118)

De celis venit legem implevit
promissum replevit verbum
ipse est rex prepotens conditor atque salvator
    Fabrice mundi (Ox 27, f. 60)

Dum pectoris de fonte divini
illum mente debriavit
altius danda superna carismatum dona
    conditor mundi (La 263, f. 110v)

Fabrice mundi polumque terre
Te conlaudat et adorat
Quia tu pater filio sedem dedisti de sacro
    Fabrice mundi (Pa 1118)

Fac deus munda corpora nostra
et animas die ista
ut tui protecti dextra conlaudemus auctorem
    fabrice mundi (Pa 1236, f. 36v)

Facundie largitor inclita
cuius fulga [*corr. to* fulget] nativitas
laudes nostre vocis addat eius larga potestas dans lumen
    fabrice mundi (Apt 18, f. 95v)

Fari tibi deus laude digna
possit semper nostra lingua
qui funestos venistis redimere a maledicto lux vera
    (RoV C5, f. 27v)

Felix maria mundi regina
te collaudant universa
celorum agmina stelle mirandaque structura
    fabrice mundi (Ed 13A, f. 25v)

Gaudet beata virgo maria
gignens factorem e vulva
Quem celica pre eius quibant et seculi frustra Huic tulit
    Fabrice mundi (Pa 1118, f. 118)

Lumen de lumine coeternum
corde patris ructutarum
patri consubstantialis conditor et reparator
    fabrice mundi (Cai 78, f. 49)

Permanens virgo sancta maria
inter choros angelorum
pro nobis derexa (?) semper dominum iesum christum
    (Mu 23621, f. 258v)

Per tuam prolem nos te rogamus
beata virgo maria
qui meruisti portare dominum salvatorem mundi factorem
    (Mu 23621, f. 258v)

III. Prosae to Melisma C_1

Celestis aule rex et glorie deus aeternae
Cui laus ab angelicis ordinibus sonant iugiter
Volens pro nobis homo fieri hodie natus est ex virgine
Quem ovantes celi cives terris predicant
Quem syderis novi splendor annuntiat opificem
    fabrice (Ox 27, f. 60v)

Et intellectus johannem quem elegerat virginem
ex omni populo quemcumque plasmavit χριstus redemptor
et moriturus pendens in cruce
mariam pretiosam parentem
discipulo castitatis prerogativa
precunctis ornato conmisit et claro sapientia
    intellectus (Pa 17296, f. 36)

VII

Facinora nostra relaxari mundi gloriam
Petimus mente devota david regis prolem inclitam
virgo quem casta secula maria protulit summi patris gratiam
cuius ortus salvat omnes cuncta per secula
et die hac nobis dignanter foveat adque omni
    fabrice mundi (PaA 1169, f. 54)

Facture dominans potestatis atque principans
virtute non adjectiva sed nativa et substantiva
condolens namque diva bonitas
hominem quem creaverat ad vitam
fraude hostis incurrisse mortis discrimina
dictavit consilium admirabile atque necessarium
    Fabrice mundi (Pa 1236, f. 37)

Nascitur ex patre zebedeo matre maria
Et volat ante alios in domini theologia
Nomine et de dei gratia
Asiana vicit gignasia
Vas penale Jus letale Pathmos exilia
Vocatur christi presencia senex ad convivia
    (Ed 13A, f. 36v–37)

Te laudant alme rex tellus pontus celi sydera
Qui primus ad vota tue majestatis condens omnia
Hodie natus ante secula
Filium per virginis viscera
Nasci mundo Voluisti Tua clementia
Ut pelleres orbis crimina veniens lux aurea
    fabrice mundi (Ed 13A, f. 25v)

Te mundi climata protomartyr laudant omnia
Qui primus ad martyrii gloriosa currens bravia
Hodie sacra plenus gratia
Domini sequeris vestigia
Quem videre Meruisti Patris in gloria
Ut pelleres lapidantium crimina supplicans de venia
    (Ed 13A, f. 33–33v)

IV. Prosae to Melisma C_2

Ante secla deus est in sua patrisque gloria
omnia in ipso constant esse facta idem tellus freta
ex limo humi plasmavit adam
ac rationalem illi animam
ad eternam condonavit perfruenda [3 *syl.: MS torn*]
atque fasces paradysi arte deceptus
mox diabolica cecidit de gloria que demum
prole prius tenuit in sidus
usque dum redimi venient illa dei filius lux vera
    conditor mundi (RoV C5, f. 27–27v)

Concepit maria ventre verbi semine fide
Quem totus orbis non baiula continens puelle viscera
Radix [ ] iesse virga [ ]
Edidit partum virgo fecunda
Partum tulit Et intacta Perseverans Presepe ponit

Auctorque extitit
Lucis protulit cum patre olymphum
Condidit panno sub matre induit
Lucem dedit Que seculo Cuius precepta decem sunt
dignando factus est homo esse subditus legis mundi
    Et exivit... (Lu 603, f. 20–20v)

Fac domine deus quia verbum tuum χριste rex
Processit de virgineo genitricis dei marie
Continens namque sua virtute
Hicnam que in gremio in caelum
Terram in se Hoc regentem Virgo genitrix est
Confirmatum cor virginis
In quo divina narrantes te rex
Domine deus alme dei deo
Regi χρisto redemptor mundi
Conserva hoc populum χριste quod tuum est
Alme ihesu a principe mundi (Pa 1118, f. 118–118v)

Faciens bonitatis sue misericordiam celi celsa
cum ordinaret simul cum patre sidera missus ad
terras tali gratiam hominem fraude captum maligna
homo factus ut salveret mundum clemens ab ira
et qui culpa protoplasti sede fuerat laupsus a
celica huius per carnem nova liberaret vetustate
pulsa nativitas et mundi principe devicto in secula
rex maneret tocius
    fabrice mundi (Apt 18, f. 96)

Facinora nostra relaxare mundi gloria
Petimus mente devota david regis proles inclita
virgo quem casta seclo maria protulit mundi patris gloriam
cuius ortus salvat omnes cuncta per secula
    contempnentes pravam mundi istius vitam
    et instanter cassant ob hoc nos tua
    complentes jussa ut des quando premia eterna
et die hac nobis dignanter atque omnia
    fabrice mundi (LoEll, f. 97v–98)

Facinora nostra relaxavit mundi gaudia
Petimus mente devota regis david prole inclita
Quem virgo sacra seculo maria protulit summi patris gloria
Cuius ortus salvat omnes cuncta per secula
    Ut preclara die ista parcat omnia
    Nostra post lavacra
    Dignetur pius oriundus famulorum visitare corda
    Piorum mentemque fidelium perpetuumque semper
    [c]onditor mundi (Ox 222, f. 4–4v)

Facta nativitas hodierna christi per regna
regina sancta maria quem edidit nobis in terra
nostra caterva quem summe laudat
per secla sit salus summa angelica
cui canit laus deo gloria
et in terra perpetua hominibus pax
qui det nobis vera gaudia per eterna secula et ultra in eterna
    fabrice mundi (Rou 190, f. 51)

Facture tue rex fulget sacrata dies ista
Cum virgine fecundata sidereum honnus innuba
Rerum creator opus implevit
promissum intemerate conserva
sidera lux nova mundo toto polo gracia
Sponsus ovans speciosus formans talamum hominum figura
Nos quoque ipsum regem conlaudemus
veneremus voce humillima
Nos elevet summa gaudia fluenta caelestia
    Fabrice mundi (Pa 1118, f. 119)
Rex regum ab alta χοistus petens a terestria
Regesque potestates et tirannorum fregit tartara
Claustra inferni virtus impera
Corusque angelorum proclamat
Sanctus deus Sanctus fortis Sanctus et inmortalis
Deus alme Vite pie Tu sanctificas Nostrorumque vota
Lux vera decus honor tibi χοiste
permanebit cuncta in secula
Nosque simul merite vite et sedule
Maneat χοistusque in
    Fabrice mundi (Pa 1118, f. 118v–119)

V. Prosae to Melisma D

Ante tempus parentis congenite
Procreate ex matre in tempore
Qui super accline pectusculum
Dilectum potasti discipulum
Ex eiusde sapientie purissimo flumine
Nos per ipsum consitientes perfundere digneris
    Et intellectus (Kl 1013, f. 40–40v)
Auscultate omnes ubique fideles
Propagator noster et autor eternus
Dolens male nosmet perisse
Et patria longe exulasse
Coeternum sibi filium misit ut eriperet hominem
Idcirco jubilet domino circus universe
    (SG 390, p. 7)
Conditor lucis aeterne deus
fons sapientiae astra creans
arva regens mari et imperans
factor matris natus hic de matre
procedens hodie thalamo patris in gracili
nascitur presepio angeli psallebant in celis
laudes in excelsis domino deo nostro (Ox 27, f. 60)
Facture plasmator et conditor
Cunctorum et angelorum sator
Qui celos cum patre confirmarat
Cum sanctoque spiritu crearat
Quique nunc hominem patrie factum imagini similem
Hunc iungens sibimet retulit hostis quem ceperat
    (Civ 91, f. 99–99v)

VIII

Modal Neumes at Sens

In his treatise on plainsong of 1745, entitled *Nouvelle méthode, ou Traité théorique et pratique du plain-chant*, Léonard Poisson writes: 'At Sens there are neumes, not only for Antiphons, but also for the Responsories; these are used only on solemn feasts. They have been retained from an ancient and uninterrupted usage.'[1] Indeed there were neumes for responsories at Sens in Poisson's day. Plate 17.1 shows the neumes for responsories, arranged by mode, as they are printed in the Sens processional of 1756. But what about the second part of Poisson's statement, about the ancient and uninterrupted use of them? That is the subject of this investigation: the relation of this list of neumes to the medieval tradition of the great primatial see of Sens.

What is a neume for a responsory? Substantial recent scholarship has investigated this phenomenon, and a word or two of background might be useful here.[2] The great responsories of Matins often end with some sort of melismatic flourish at the end of the main section before the verse begins. This is a perfectly normal musical event, and such melismas, even when they are quite long, are most often an integral part of the responsory.[3] It sometimes happens, however, that when the responsory is repeated in whole or in part after the verse, a longer melisma is substituted. This added melisma (or neume) is performed at the last singing of the repetenda. Some of these melismas were retained in the Solesmes *Processionale monasticum* of 1893.[4]

Melismas added to responsories have been known for a long time. Amalarius of Metz refers to the famous *neuma triplex* used for the office of St. John and which 'moderni cantores' sing with the responsory *Descendit de celis*;[5] versions of this *neuma triplex* are found in the Hartker antiphoner and the Mont-Renaud manuscript, and texted versions are found in Paris, BNF lat. 1118, of the late tenth or early eleventh century, so the phenomenon dates at least from the tenth century.[6]

Amalarius' triple neume is far from being the only melismatic addition to responsories. There are a variety of kinds of melisma which have been used at one place and time or another to embellish the end of a responsory.[7] Some melismas seem to be composed for use with a single responsory, and never appear anywhere else. Many responsories, as I have said, contain sizeable melismas at their ends, but when these are not varied in the repetition of the responsory – that is, when a different, or lengthened, melisma is not substituted – they are, so far as we can tell, an integral part of their parent chant.[8] It is the provision of a special neume for the end, different from what appears in the body of the responsory, that constitutes, in most cases, an addition to the responsory, a sort of melodic trope.

N.B. This article was Chapter 17 in the original publication. To avoid unnecessary changes, the original numbering of the plates and tables has been retained.

cciv   *Numes des Répons.*

Quand on fait la Nume, le ℣. du Répons ne se dit point, s'il n'est autrement marqué.

La Nume se chante sur une seule syllabe du dernier ou pénultième & même antepénultième mot du Répons, & elle se commence à l'endroit du ℟. où se trouve cette marque ✴ suivant le mode du ℟. l'Orgue joue, & le Chœur chante alternativement.

La Nume étant finie, le Chœur acheve le Répons, en reprenant ce qui est après l'astérisque. ✴

POUR LES RÉPONS du 1. 2. & 4. & l'astérisque. ✴

MEL 1A

Le reste du Répons après l'astérisque.

[*Si à l'astérisque ✴ on ajoute cette marque † on commence ainsi la Nume.*

MEL 1B

Le reste du Répons après l'astérisque.

POUR LE RÉPONS du 3.

MEL 3

PROCESSIONAL
DE SENS

IMPRIMÉ PAR L'ORDRE
DE SON EMINENCE

MONSEIGNEUR

LE CARDINAL DE LUYNES,
ARCHEVÊQUE VICOMTE DE SENS,

Primat des Gaules & de Germanie, Premier Aumônier de Madame la Dauphine, &c. & du consentement des Doyen & Chapitre de ladite Eglise.

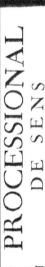

A SENS,

Chez ANDRÉ JANNOT, Imprimeur de son Eminence, & du Clergé.

M. DCC. LVI.

AVEC PRIVILEGE DU ROI

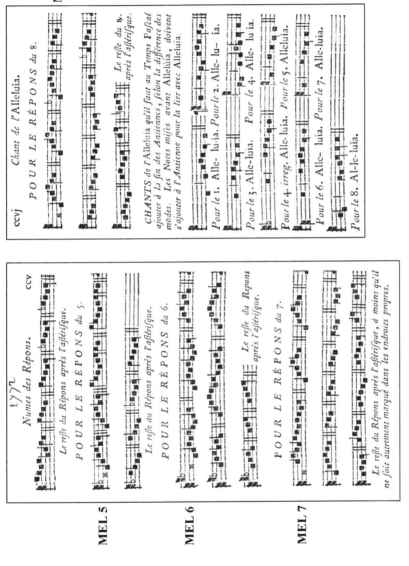

Pl. 17.1 *Processional de Sens*, 1756: title page and neumes for responsories, pp. cciv–ccvj; the neumes numbered for reference

Melismas added to an original responsory can be recognized, in the first instance, by their presentation: they are given as alternatives, usually written after the verse or the Gloria and indicating their substitution for the earlier ending. This is a practice used widely, including in the earliest books of office music from Sens. Plate 17.2, from Paris, BNF n. a. lat. 1535 (a late twelfth-century antiphoner of Sens), shows a melisma added to the end of the responsory *Precursor* for St. John the Baptist. We will come to know it as Melisma 8.

An added melisma may also be detected when it appears only in some manuscripts, while others show a shorter melisma. A third way of identifying an addition is to recognize the melisma itself as being familiar from another context. The borrowing of melismas for use with responsories is a relatively common phenomenon, and closely related to the practice at Sens.[9]

A number of melismas used in responsories at Sens, at Laon and elsewhere have been borrowed from Offertories. I say borrowed from Offertories, rather than the other way around, because the melismas in question are almost always present in the Offertory, but used only sometimes with responsories.[10] These are generally melismas with the characteristic not quite clearly articulated repetitions that set Offertory melismas apart from many others.

Other melismas added to responsories are melodies in what seems to be a later style. Such melismas, with a regular AABBCC structure like little Sequences, serve as the melodic basis of many of the prosae that also are used to decorate the same place in responsories; and when a responsory presents the melody only of a very famous text, like *Sospitati dedit egros*, or *Inviolata integra et casta*, it is difficult not to imagine that the melisma in these cases is a wordless prosa. Indeed, texted additions have been used as long as melismas for the embellishment of responsories. Sometimes melismatic and texted versions appear together, which raises questions as to how they should be performed.[11] But here we want to concentrate on the use of added melismas like those of Sens.

Neumes for responsories may come from a variety of places: composed, transferred from another piece, or summarizing a texted piece. How does it happen that Sens has a set of melismas for use in each mode? Were they all composed together in a similar style? And when?

The Sens melismas are, so far as I know, the only practical evidence of passepartout responsory neumes for use in each mode. Modal melismas for antiphons, on the other hand, were long in use. They are mentioned by theorists, presented in tonaries, prescribed in ordinals, and evidently were in regular use from at least the tenth century. These neumes for antiphons are usually found attached to the echematic formulas, NOEANE etc., or to the modal formulas 'Primum querite regnum dei', etc., and are used as attachments to certain antiphons, usually the Gospel antiphons of major feasts.[12]

These modal neumes for antiphons are very widespread, and relatively uniform. It may be that their existence suggested a similar process for responsories. If so, the idea did not catch on very widely, since I know of no modal neumes for responsories except for those of Sens, with one exception: the list of 'caudae' or 'versiculi' provided by Jacques de Liège in his early fourteenth-century *Speculum musicae*. These are melodies to be sung to the

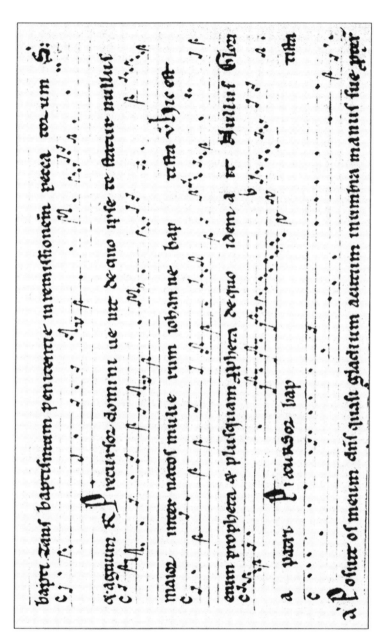

Pl. 17.2 The responsory *Inter natos* with added melisma, from Paris, BNF n. a. lat. 1535, fol. 87[v]

text 'Amen' at the ends of responsories, and there is a different versiculus for each mode. The melody for Mode 1 is reproduced here as Pl. 17.3 from Roger Bragard's edition of Jacques.[13]

These melodies are apparently unique to this treatise. Their style is not typical of the chant nor of its later additions; they resemble nothing so much as the charming two-voice pieces often called 'ductia' found in London, BL Harley 978.[14] Structured in puncta, AABBCC, like some reponsory prosae, Jacques's melodies have open and closed endings, which are not normally found in responsory melismas or indeed elsewhere in the chant. They also have some suggestion of rhythmic performance, and look in some cases as though they might be polyphonic. These are melodies to study on another occasion, for they are more nearly related to contemporaneous secular musical practice than to widely known ecclesiastical chant. They are wondeful melodies, but they appear nowhere else.

The Sens list of neumes, then, is the only one known from practical sources of the chant. But it dates from the eighteenth century. What about medieval Sens? We can show that from medieval times Sens regularly added melismas to responsories, and used the same melismas for a variety of responsories in the same mode. But it does not follow that an eight-mode system of neumes for responsories was in place at Sens from an early date. As we shall see, that systematization came much later.

The oldest source of office music from Sens is Paris n. a. lat. 1535, an antiphoner from the last quarter of the twelfth century.[15] Appendix §A summarizes the additions made to responsories in that manuscript. Neumes are not the only way to embellish responsories, and the use of melismas here is not systematic. In the course of the year, the clergy of Sens sang just about every known sort of responsory embellishment. They sang the most famous prosae (at least two of them): *Inviolata* and a set of 'Fabrices' (for some reason we do not have *Sospitati* for St. Nicholas).[16] They sang a variety of melismas, some of them borrowed from Offertories. They were already accustomed to using the same melisma for more than one responsory; note that the melisma marked MEL 7 is used twice, as is that marked MEL 1A. But they were not restricted to mclismas. Some responsories were embellished with a prosa, not a melisma; and sometimes melisma and prosa were combined for the same responsory.

Essentially, then, the earliest evidence we have of embellishing responsories at Sens appears to be inclusive. There is a bit of everything, probably gathered from here and there as occasion offered and as taste dictated. There is no evidence that one particular way of decorating responsories is preferred or insisted on – using only prosae, for example, or only melismas, as is the case in some other places.[17] There does, however, appear to be a tendency to use melismas alone, and to repeat them in more than one responsory. Although there is no evidence of a system of modal neumes, three of the neumes that appear in the eighteenth-century list are already present in Paris 1535 (melismas 1A, 7 and 8).

A late twelfth-century ordinal of Sens matches the practice observed in the antiphoner, though not in every detail. This ordinal, summarized in Appendix

²⁵ Item pro singulis tonis ponantur hic "amen" vel caudae quae dici possunt in solemnitatibus, vel quando chorialibus amplius cantare placet in fine alicuius antiphonae, responsorii vel sequentiae, seu prosae, et fit ad cantus primi <toni> finis talis:

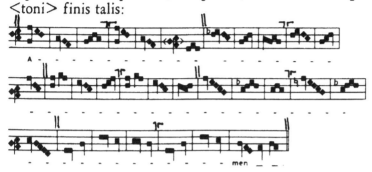

Pl. 17.3 Mode 1 melisma from Jacques de Liège, *Speculum musicae*, ed. Roger Bragard. Division marks have been added

§B, does not use notation. It indicates the presence of a melisma for a responsory, but does not tell us what melisma it is. The prosae, however, can be identified since their incipits are specified. We can see that most of the prosae are those of the antiphoner of Appendix §A; *Sospitati* for St. Nicholas has joined the group, while *Inviolata* is absent, owing to a rearrangement of the office of the Assumption. Some additional responsories have melismas: ones for Lent, the Assumption, John the Baptist, All Saints and St. Martin. We should note here that the ordinal specifies the repetitions of many responsories – with their melismas or prosae – at second Vespers on principal feasts.

A thirteenth-century notated breviary of Sens, Paris, BNF lat. 1028, has a similar repertory, detailed in Appendix §C. Notice the presence here of both versions of melisma 1 – that is, 1A and 1B – both of which appear among the modal neumes of the eighteenth century. This manuscript also adds a number of prosae imitated from older ones: versions of *Sospitati* for St. Katherine and for All Saints, and *Fabrice* imitations for the Assumption (these last were already present in the ordinal).

Later sources of Sens use do not add much to the picture. Manuscripts summarized in the Appendix (at §§ D–J) add no new melismas to the repertory used at Sens, though occasionally a new prosa appears.[18] In fact, to judge from Paris 1535 (Appendix §A), a wider variety of melismas was available in the twelfth century than was used later. Even so, and even though we might wish to detect a trend over time toward the increasing use of melismas instead of prosae, and toward a restricted number of increasingly mobile melismas, such trends are difficult to support with the evidence available. It might be worth noting that two sources of particularly local interest use melismas that will appear in the eighteenth-century modal list. These are the Office of Saints Savinianus and Potentianus, and the famous Circumcision office, both edited by Villetard.[19] In general it looks as though Sens used a variety of embellishments, adding new ones when they came along.

How then does the Sens modal list come into being? It is clearly not a medieval phenomenon. I should like to suggest a way in which it might have arisen that essentially has to do with typography. The answer, or an answer, lies in the Sens printed antiphoner of 1552, which announces the presence of neumes on its title page.[20] The neumes and prosae in this antiphoner are shown in Table 17.1. There are five different neumes here, most of them printed more than once. Although there are still some prosae, it does appear that neumes are a relatively regular feature of the solemnities at Sens in the sixteenth century. In this printed antiphoner, neumes for responsories are sung at Vespers, but not at Matins. Consequently, the neumes are printed at Vespers, while the responsories with which they are sung are printed at Matins. The result is that the neume appears as a separate element, and might seem to be separable from any specific chant. Any printer might wonder why he prints the same neume several times.

Plate 17.4 shows part of a folio from the 1552 antiphoner, with a portion of Vespers from the office of Saints Savinianus and Potentianus. The rubrics indicate that the antiphons at Vespers are those of Lauds, with psalms of one martyr. The capitulum *Sancti et iusti in domino* is followed by the responsory *Athletam domini*, with the rubric 'et reincipitur cum neumate sequente'. Only the intonation of the responsory is given, and the neume is provided with the text of the end of the responsory.

Printing neumes this way, separately and repeatedly, easily leads to the idea of printing each neume only once; if the printer had chosen to save space by making a table of neumes for this printed antiphoner, five neumes would have been needed: those listed in Table 17.1 as 'Cor', 'Fabrice C', the two versions of Melisma 1, and Melisma 7. It might seem a simple step to assign a melisma to each mode, and print them only once. This is of course what has happened in the eighteenth-century neume table (Pl. 17.1). But that table does not consist only of neumes known in medieval Sens, nor does it include all the neumes that were used in earlier sources. The omission of medieval neumes from the neume table seems to be done on the basis of style, since the three neumes not retained are two that are borrowed from Offertories and the long Fabrice C melisma. These have in common the absence of a reduplicated structure that would lend itself to antiphonal performance by the two sides of the choir or by choir and organ.

Three of the neumes in the neume table, however, do have a long history at Sens. These are neumes 1A/1B, 7 and 8. These accommodate responsories in five of the eight modes, and are used for these five modes in medieval manuscripts.

Neume 1 is the first neume in the eighteenth-century neume table, and it comes in two versions. The shorter version (1A) is of unknown origin, but its reduplicated form suggests that it may have come from a prosa. The longer version (1B) adds more music to the beginning of this melisma; this added

Table 17.1 Melismas and prosae in the printed antiphoner of Sens, 1552

The neumes are separated from their responsories to show their use at Vespers. The folio numbers here are those on which the responsory is found.

Fol.	Feast	Mode/Text	Addition
17ᵛ	De scss. sacr.	1 Unus panis	MEL 1A
73ᵛ	Dedicationis	1 Terribilis	MEL 1B
80ᵛ	Ioh. baptistae	1 Inter natos	MEL 1B
87ᵛ	Petri	4 Petre amas me	MEL ('cor'?, pasted over)
107ᵛ	M. Magd.	2 Felix Maria unxit	MEL 1B
121	Germani	8 Gloriosus domini	pr. *Pacis perpetue*
128ᵛ	Inv. Stephani	2 Igitur dissimulata	MEL 1B
131	Inv. Stephani	7 Lapides torrentes	MEL 7
132ᵛ	Inv. Stephani	1 Ecce iam coram te	MEL [Fabrice C]
147	Laurentii	2 Beatus Laurentius	MEL 1B
158	Assumptionis	1 Virginitas celum	pr. *Benedic/Benedicat/ Benedictus*
175	Decoll. J. Bapt.	4 Metuebat	MEL 1B
179	Lupi	1 O venerandum	pr. *Insignis de Christo*
179ᵛ	Lupi (Vespers)	1 O venerandum	MEL 1A
216	Sav. et Poten.	1 Athletam domini	MEL 1A
224	Omn. Scorum	1 Ecce iam coram te	MEL [Fabrice C]
225ᵛ	Omn. Scorum	1 Concede nobis	MEL 1A
233ᵛ	Martini	1 Martinus Abrahe	MEL 1A
249ᵛ	Katherine	1 Ex eius tumba	pr. *Sospitati*

music corresponds to the opening notes of the Alleluia *Posuisti*, and in this longer form the melody as a whole serves as the melodic basis of the prosa *Sedentem in superne*, which is used in the Sens Circumcision office and is widely known elsewhere, attached to one of several responsories.[21]

This melisma 1 in its two forms is often used at Sens. It may seem odd that a single melody should be used for three different modes in the later printed sources, but it was used for those same modes in medieval sources. The melisma's insistence on the note *a*, which is the tenor of fourth-mode psalmody, makes its use for responsories in the fourth mode plausible, especially when we remember that the melisma does not provide the final note of the performance, but is inserted shortly before the end of the original responsory, so that the responsory itself provides the final, whether *D* (for Modes 1 and 2) or *E* for Mode 4.

Neumes 7 and 8, both used in medieval Sens, are again two versions of the same melody. Melisma 7 is found also in the Offertory *Gressos meos*;[22] Melisma 8 is a transposed version of Melisma 7, without its first eleven notes. In this transposed form it is used in twelfth-century Sens for an eighth-mode responsory,[23] so the idea of transposition, and of using the same melisma for more than one mode, is not an eighteenth-century invention. The notion of

Pl. 17.4 Antiphoner of Sens, 1552, fol. 217 (detail): the melisma for the responsory *Athletam* for use at Vespers

using the same melisma for multiple modes does make one wonder, however, how Poisson in his treatise can say the following: 'The neumes for responsories, being much extended, make the properties of each mode easily understood.'[24]

With two medieval melismas the compiler of the Sens list manages to provide neumes for five modes. Only three more melismas are needed to provide melismas for every mode. One of these, the melisma for mode 6, was already known at Sens and elsewhere; it is found at the end of the processional antiphon *Ibo michi ad montem* (in Paris 1535 it is found at fol. 93ᵛ); with an added verse the antiphon with its melisma serves as a responsory in Paris, BNF lat. 12044, fol. 177 (St-Maur-des-Fossés, twelfth century). The same melisma is replaced by a prosa (*Alle resonemus omnes*) in the Circumcision offices of Sens and Beauvais.[25]

The Sens melismas for Modes 3 and 5 are as yet unidentified in medieval sources. Judging from the process involved in selecting the other melodies of the neume table, it would not be a surprise to find that these two neumes appear somewhere in the music books of Sens, but I have not succeeded in finding them. They both have the not quite exactly reduplicated structure that is characteristic of some Offertory melismas, but they do not seem to appear in any known Offertories. In any event, these last two neumes are used very little. In the 1756 processional (Table 17.2), the melismas for modes 3 and 5 are used once each.

When did this modal arrangement take place? Clearly the modal neumes were arranged at some time between the sixteenth-century printed antiphoners and the eighteenth-century printed versions. But between the two there is a great deal of political and ecclesiastical history.

Table 17.2 *Processional de Sens*, 1756: list of responsories sung with neumes

Page	Feast	Responsory	Mode
12	Natalis	Cantate Domino	6
16	Vespers of Christmas, at the cathedral	Stephanum virum	1
19	Stephani	Cum esset Stephanus	3
31	Epiphanie	Stella antecedebat	1
35	Reliquarum	Haec dicit Dominus	1
196	Purificationis	Benedixit illis Simeon	6
200	Annunc.	Virtus altissimi	6
228	Joh. Bapt.	Quid existis in desertam	1
231	Petri et Pauli	Quid sunt suae olivae	7
234	Petri et Pauli, in churches dedicated to St. Peter	Simon Joannis	?
252	Assumptionis	Apertum est templum	1
263	Lupi archiep.	Sapientia a peccatoribus	7
273	Sav. & Pot.	Laudemus viros	1
277	Omn. scorum	Laudebunt piae	5
xxij	Com. angel.	Audivi vocem angelorum	1
xxiv	Com. ang. gard.	Non accedet ad te malum	1
xxvj	Com. apost.	Non sunt loquelae	7
xxviij	Com. 1 mart.	In fraude circunvenientium	1
xxxij	Com. pl. mart.	Hi sunt qui veniunt	1
xxxvj	Com. 1 pont.	Ipse est directe	1
xl	Com. pl. pont.	Beati servi illi	2
xlij	Com. 1 doct.	Juxta manum Dei	1
xlvij	Com. Abb. & mon.	Perfectio tua et doctrina	1
l	Com. scorum laic.	Dispersit dedit pauperibus	4
lij	Com. virginum	Gaudeamus et exultemus	7
lvij	Com. non virg.	Erat in omnibus	1
lx	Poenitentiorum	Benedic anima mea	6
lxiij	Dedicationis	Si conversus populus	1

440

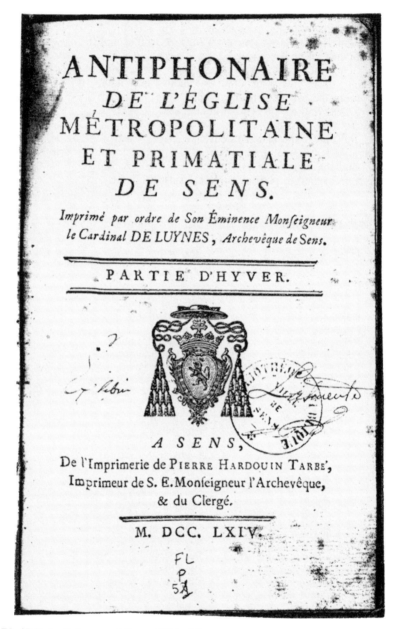

Pl. 17.5 Antiphoner of Sens, 1764, title page

ijn

PROCESSIONNAL
DE SENS,
IMPRIMÉ PAR L'ORDRE
DE SON ÉMINENCE

MONSEIGNEUR

LE CARDINAL DE LUYNES,
ARCHEVÊQUE VICOMTE DE SENS,

*Primat des Gaules & de Germanie, Abbé-Comte
de Corbie, Commandeur de l'Ordre du Saint-
Esprit, &c. & du consentement des Doyen &
Chapitre de ladite Église.*

Nouvelle Édition.

A SENS,

Chez Pierre-Hardouin TARBÉ, Imprimeur
de Son Éminence, & du Clergé.

M. DCC. LXXII.
AVEC PRIVILEGE DU ROI.

Fl
uう5

Pl. 17.6 Processional of Sens, 1772, title page

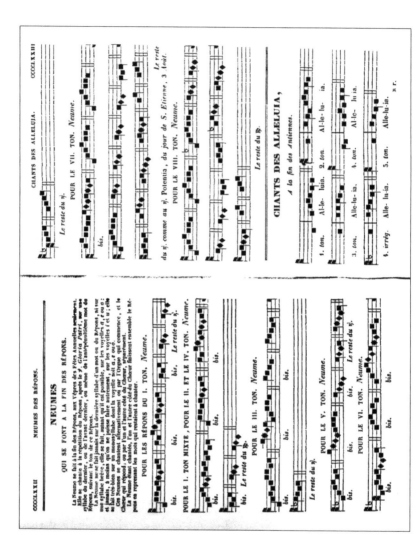

Pl. 17.7 Neume table from *Processional, Graduel, Antiphonaire et Psautier à l'usage de l'église primatiale et métropolitaine de Sens* (Sens: Thomas-Malvin, 1844)

It seems probable that the neumes were introduced when the Gallicanized chant was adopted. The 1756 processional, which uses all the melismas, has responsories that are Neo-Gallican (see Table 17.2); these responsories are found also in the printed breviary of 1780,[26] where they proudly show their biblical sources. These are the responsories used also in the antiphoner of 1764–5 (Pl. 17.5), and the Processional of 1772 (Pl. 17.6). They are a regular feature of the newly revised Sens liturgy, perhaps a proudly archaizing one.[27]

The considerable revision of the liturgy was the likely moment of systematizing the melismas; the neume table purges the liturgy of all its prosae, with their non-biblical texts, but retains traditional, unobjectionable melodies from the Sens tradition. These melismas, in tabular form, still appear in the printed processional-Gradual-antiphoner of 1844 (Pl. 17.7),[28] where the description of neumes and their performance is reprinted from the eighteenth-century books. One wonders how long these neumes remained in use: perhaps until the reforms of the Second Vatican Council? I have asked senior clerics at Sens, but have yet to meet someone who remembers singing these neumes.

The moment of singing of the neume was an important event in the office of the great feasts. Its choreography, if we might call it that, is described in Poisson's treatise, and it involves movement, vestments and dignitaries that lend weight to what has become a musical high point of the office:

> The five leaders of the choir, vested in copes, standing before the lectern begin the responsory and sing the verse and the *Gloria patri*, after which the Precentor with the two Choristers in the middle of the choir re-intone the Responsory. While the choir sings the repetition, the five Dignitaries divide and return, each to his side, to stand with the Choristers in the middle of the choir. There they turn to face the side of the choir with which they sing. At the end of the Responsory, at the syllable or the note which precedes the one on which the neume is to begin, the whole choir stops, the right side begins the neume, which is alternated with the left side: at the end, the two sides of the choir unite their voices to finish the Responsory.[29]

This investigation, undertaken to discover an antique practice suitable for a collection of essays on chant in the first millennium, turns out to have as its subject a codification that appears to date from about a thousand years too late. But the result is interesting in itself, I think, for what it says about the invention of tradition, and about how readily elements of an ancient practice can be recombined and reinvented to produce something that has almost nothing to do with tradition.

Appendix

Prosulae and Neumes for Responsories in Medieval Manuscripts of Sens

pr.:	prosula whose incipit follows
MEL:	an added melisma, identified by one of the Sens modal melismas or otherwise
'Cor meum':	Offertory *Benedictus es*, verse 3, *Viam iniquitatis* (*Offertoriale*, ed. Ott, 30).
'meminero':	Offertory *Super flumina*, verse 2, *Si oblitus* (*Offertoriale*, ed. Ott, 121).
Fabrice C:	the third element of the *neuma triplex* added most often to the responsory *Descendit de celis* (see Kelly, 'Neuma triplex')

A. Paris, BNF n. a. lat. 1535; antiphoner (secular) of Sens, twelfth century (last quarter)

Fol.	*Feast*	*Mode/Text*	*Addition*
5	Nicolai	5 Qui cum audisset	pr. *Clementem*
19	Natalis	1 Descendit	pr. *Familiam/Fac/Facinora*
20	Natalis	7 In principio	MEL 7
20v	Natalis	2 Sancta et immaculata	pr. *Beata es virgo*
23v	Stephani	7 Lapides torrentes	MEL 7
24	Stephani	1 Ecce iam coram	MEL [Fabrice C]
24v	Stephani	4 S. Stephane sydus	MEL ['cor meum']
25	Stephani	2 O martyrum gemma	pr. *Qui scis infirma*
46	dom2inXL	6 Oravit Iacob	MEL [unknown: Offertory?]
80	Assumptionis	6 Gaude Maria	pr. *Inviolata*
85v	Ioan. bapt.	8 Precursor domini	MEL 8
89	Petri	4 Petre amas me	MEL ['cor meum'] + pr. *Psallat in isto die*
101	Lupi	1 O venerandum	MEL 1A + pr. *Insignis de Christo*
101v	Lupi	7 Dum beatus Lupus	MEL ['meminero']
126	Paule	1 O admirabilem	MEL 1A

B. Paris, BNF lat. 1206; ordinal of Sens, twelfth century (last quarter)

Fol.	*Feast*	*Mode/Text*	*Addition*
44	Natalis	1 Descendit	pr. *Fac deus/Facinora*
44	Natalis	1 In principio	cum neumate
44	Nat. (ad. proc.)	1 Descendit	cum prosis sicut est ad matut.
48	Stephani	7 Lapides	cum neumate (repeated at procession and Vespers)
48	Stephani	1 Ecce iam	cum neumate
47v	S. reliquarum	7 Lapides	cum neumate
	S. rel. (7 Feb)	1 Concede nobis	cum neumate sed sine versu (Sunday procession)

Fol.	Feast	Mode/Text	Addition
57ᵛ–	Pascha		(The Alleluias of the Mass with their sequences are sung at Vespers during Easter week)
66ᵛ	Nicolai	1 Ex eius tumba	cum prosa *Sospitati* (repeated at Vespers)
67	Inv. reliquarum	1 Concede	cum neumate (repeated at Vespers)
68	Purificationis	6 Gaude Maria	cum prosa *Inviolata* (repeated at Vespers)
70	Ioan. Bapt.	1 Inter natos	cum neumate
70ᵛ	Petri et Pauli	4 Petre amas	cum prosula sua *Psallat* (repeated at Vespers)
71ᵛ	Germani	8 Gloriosus	cum prosula sua *Pacem perpetue*
72	Inv. Stephani	7 Lapidesᵃ	cum neumate (repeated at Vespers)
		1 Ecce iamᵃ	cum neumate
		4 Sancte Stephaneᵃ	cum neumate
72ᵛ	Assumptionis	1 Virginitas celum	pr. *Benedic/Benedicat/ Benedictus* (repeated at Vespers)
73	Assumptionis	?Virgo thurifera	cum neumate
74	Lupi	1 O venerandum	cum prosula sua *Insignis* (repeated at Vespers)
76	Omn. scorum	1 Concede	cum neumate (repeated at Vespers)
76ᵛ	Martini	1 Martinus Abrahe	cum neumate (repeated at Vespers)

ᵃ These responsories are the next to last of each nocturn (nos. 3, 7, 11).

C. Paris, BNF lat. 1028; breviary (secular) of Sens, thirteenth century

Fol.	Feast	Mode/Text	Addition
50ᵛ	Natalis	1 Descendit	pr. *Familiam/Fac/Facinora*
51	Natalis	7 In principio	MEL 7
54	Stephani	7 Lapides torrentes	MEL 7
24	Stephani	1 Ecce iam coram	MEL [Fabrice C]
24ᵛ	Stephani	4 S. Stephane sydus	MEL 1B
79ᵛ	Epiphanie	1 Concede nobis	MEL 1A
120	Pascha	1 Et valde mane	pr. *Ortum predestinatio*
173	Dedicationis	1 Terribilis	MEL 1A
177	Nicolai	1 Ex eius tumba	pr. *Sospitati*
188ᵛ	Pauli	1 O admirabilem	MEL 1A
193	Annuntiatione	6 Gaude Maria	pr. *Inviolata*
204	Ioan. bapt.	1 Inter natos	MEL 1B
216ᵛ	Marie Magd.	2 Felix Maria	MEL 1B (internal)

446

Fol.	Feast	Mode/Text	Addition
221ᵛ	Germani	8 Gloriosus domini	pr. *Pacis perpetue*
233	Assumptionis	1 Virginitas celum	pr. *Benedic/Benedicat/ Benedictus*
243	Lupi	1 O venerandum	pr. *Insignis* (= MEL 1A)
263	Martini	1 Martinus Abrahe	MEL 1A
293ᵛ	Katherine	1 Ex eius tumba	pr. *Sospitati . . . Katherina*
309	Omn. scorum	1 Concede nobis	pr. *Sollemniter* (*Sospitati*) + MEL 1A

D. Auxerre, BM 60; breviary (secular) of Sens, late thirteenth century, pars aestivalis

Fol.	Feast	Mode/Text	Addition
175	Ioan. bapt.	8 Precursor	MEL 8
176ᵛ	Ioan. bapt.	1 Inter natos	MEL 1B
188ᵛ	Petri	4 Petre amas me	MEL ['cor'] + pr. *Psallat*
221ᵛ	Germani	8 Gloriosus domini	pr. *Pacis perpetue*
234ᵛ	Inv. Stephani	7 Lapides torrentes	MEL 7
37	Inv. Stephani	1 Ecce iam coram	MEL [Fabrice C]
240	Inv. Stephani	4 S. Stephane sydus	MEL ['cor']
266	Assumptionis	1 Virginitas celum	pr. *Benedic/Benedicat/ Benedictus*
308	Lupi	1 O venerandum	pr. *Insignis* (= MEL 1A)
370ᵛ	Omn. scorum	1 Ecce iam coram	MEL [Fabrice C]
372	Omn. scorum	1 Concede nobis	pr. *Sollemniter* (*Sospitati*) + MEL 1A
385ᵛ	Martini	1 Martinus Abrahe	MEL 1A
409	Katherine	1 O mater nostra	pr. *Sospitati . . . Katherina*
411	Kather. (ad vesp)	1 Ex eius tumba	pr. *Sospitati . . . Katherina*

E. Sens, BM 6; 'precentoris norma', thirteenth century

(This manuscript gives only incipits, the neumes being cited only in rubrics.)

Fol.	Feast	Mode/Text	Addition
32	Natalis	1 Descendit	pr. *Familiam/Fac deus/Facinora*
34ᵛ	Stephani	7 Lapides	cum suo neumate
48	Stephani	1 Ecce iam	cum pneumate
59	dom2inXL	6 Oravit Iacob (ad vesp.)	cum neupmate
71ᵛ	Pascha	1 Et valde mane	pr. *Ortum predestinatio*[a]
72–	Pascha		The Alleluias of the Mass with their sequences are sung at Vespers during Easter week
108ᵛ	Nicolai	1 Ex eius tumba	cum prosa *Sospitati* (at Vespers only)

Fol.	Feast	Mode/Text	Addition
111ᵛ	Inv. reliq.	1 Concede	cum neumate (at Vespers only)
117	Paule	1 O admirabilem	cum prosa *Ad sacrum* (at first Vespers)

(this list is provisional)

ᵃ This prosula begins the Easter drama: the prosula is preceded by the rubric *Representatio Mariarum*.

F. Sens, BM 29; breviary (secular) of Sens, early fourteenth century

Fol.	Feast	Mode/Text	Addition
190	Natalis	1 Descendit	pr. *Familiam/Fac/Facinora*
193	Natalis	7 In principio	MEL 7
202ᵛ	Stephani	7 Lapides torrentes	MEL 7
204ᵛ	Stephani	1 Ecce iam coram	MEL [Fabrice C]
206	Stephani	4 S. Stephanus sydus	MEL ['cor meum']
234	8 Stephani	2 O martirum gemma	pr. *Qui scis infirma*
412	Pascha	1 Et valde mane	pr. *Ortum predestinatio*
507	Nicolai	1 Ex eius tumba	pr. *Sospitati*
552	Inv. Stephani	7 Lapides torrentes	MEL 7
554	Omn. scorum	1 Concede nobis	MEL 1A
579	Purificationis	6 Gaude Maria	pr. *Inviolata*
660	Com. non p.	1 Laudemus dominum	MEL 1A

G. Rome, BAV Vat. lat. 153; breviary (secular, no notation) of Sens adapted to Provins, fourteenth century

(In this manuscript without notation the neumes are not indicated.)

Fol.	Feast	Mode/Text	Addition
120	Natalis	1 Descendit	pr. *Familiam/Fac/Facinora* (repeated at Vespers)
197ᵛ	Pascha	1 Et valde	pr. *Ortum predestinatio*
198–	Pascha		(The Alleluias of the Mass with their sequences are sung at Vespers during Easter week)
299	Nicolai	1 Ex eius tumba	pr. *Sospitati*
301ᵛ	Conc. BMV	? O Maria clausa porta	pr. *Stella maris O Maria*
332	Purificationis	6 Gaude Maria	pr. *Inviolata*
354ᵛ	Cyriaci Martyr	? Christi pretiosus	pr. *Apposito salutis*
371ᵛ	Petri et Pauli	4 Petre amas me	pr. *Psallat in isto die*
398ᵛ	Germani	8 Gloriosus domini	pr. *Pacem perpetue*
417	Assumptionis	1 Virginitas	pr. *Benedic/Benedicat/Benedictus*
434	Lupi	1 O venerandum	pr. *Insignis de Christo*
492	Katherine	1 Ex eius (Vespers)	pr. *Sospitati*

H. Rome, BAV Vat. lat. 182; breviary (secular, no notation) of Sens, fourteenth century

(In this manuscript without notation the neumes are not indicated; only Vespers responsories are named, whence the absence, e.g., of R. *Et valde* of Easter.)

Fol.	Feast	Mode/Text	Addition
117ᵛ	Natalis	1 Descendit	pr. *Familiam/Fac/Facinora* (at Vespers)
145ᵛ–	Pascha		(The Alleluias of the Mass with their sequences are sung at Vespers during Easter week)
175ᵛ	Nicolai	1 Ex eius tumba	pr. *Sospitati*
188	Purificationis	6 Gaude Maria	pr. *Inviolata*
197	Cyriaci	? Martyr dei pretiosus	pr. *Apposito salutis*
202ᵛ	Petri et Pauli	4 Petre amas me	pr. *Psallat in isto die*
210	Germani	8 Gloriosus domini	pr. *Pacem perpetue*
221ᵛ	Assumptionis	1 Virginitas	pr. *Benedic/Benedicat/ Benedictus*
227	Lupi	1 O venerandum	pr. *Insignis de Christo*
245	Katherine	1 Ex eius	pr. *Sospitati*

I. Sens, BM 46A; office of the Circumcision, fourteenth century (ed. Villetard)

Fol.	Text	Addition
2	*Letemur gaudiis, Christus manens* [beginning of first Vespers]	MEL 1A
3	Descendit de celis	pr. *Fac/Familiam/Facinora*
9	In principio	MEL 7
10ᵛ	Te laudant angeli	MEL (similar to 1A)
12	Veni sancte (Alleluia verse, on *ignem*)	MEL 1B
14	[as Versiculus]	pr. *Sedentem* (similar to 1B)
23ᵛ	[as Versiculus]	pr. *Qui scis infirma*
24ᵛ	Gaude Maria	pr. *Inviolata*
25	[as Versiculus]	pr. *Sancta Dei genitrix*

J. Rome, BAV Vat. lat. 577 (Office of SS. Savinianus and Potentianus)

Fol.	Text	Addition
93	Athletam domini	MEL 1A

Notes

1 'À Sens on a des neumes, non-seulement pour les Antiennes, mais aussi pour les Répons, dont on ne fait usage qu'aux solemnités: on les a conservées d'un ancien usage non interrompu.' Léonard Poisson, *Nouvelle méthode, ou Traité théorique et pratique du plain-chant* (Paris: P. N. Lottin & J. H. Butard, 1745), 379. According to Henri Villetard (*Office de Saint Savinien et de Saint Potentien, premiers évêques de Sens* (Paris: Picard, [1956], 103, n. A), Poisson was curé of Marsangis in the diocese of Sens. Villetard's publication includes the most complete list of the liturgical manuscripts of Sens: 'Catalogue des livres liturgiques de l'ancien diocèse de Sens', 91–114.
2 Research on neumes and prosulae in the office include the following: Hans-Jörgen Holman, 'Melismatic Tropes in the Responsories for Matins', *JAMS* 16 (1963), 36–46; Helma Hofmann-Brandt, *Die Tropen zu den Responsorien des Officiums*, 2 vols. (diss., University of Erlangen, 1971); Ruth Steiner, 'The Responsories and Prosula for St. Stephen's Day at Salisbury', *MQ* 56 (1970), 162–82; ead., 'Some Melismas for Office Responsories', *JAMS* 26 (1973), 108–31; ead., 'The Gregorian Chant Melismas for Christmas Matins', in Jerald C. Graue (ed.), *Essays on Music for Charles Warren Fox* (Rochester, NY: Eastman School of Music, 1979), 241–53. All three of Steiner's articles have been reprinted in Steiner, *Studies in Gregorian Chant* (Aldershot: Ashgate Publishing, 1999). See also Thomas Forrest Kelly, 'Responsory Tropes' (Ph.D. diss., Harvard University, 1973); id., 'Melodic Elaboration in Responsory Melismas', *JAMS* 27 (1974), 461–74; id., 'New Music from Old: The Structuring of Responsory Prosas', *JAMS* 30 (1977), 366–90; id., 'Melisma and Prosula: The Performance of Responsory Tropes', *Liturgische Tropen: Referate zweier Colloquien des Corpus Troporum in München (1983) und Canterbury (1984)*, ed. Gabriel Silagi (1985), 163–80; id., 'Neuma Triplex', *Acta musicologica*, 60 (1988), 1–30.
3 This is not, however, the view of Holman, 'Melismatic Tropes', who sees almost any responsory melisma as a trope.
4 Solesmes: Abbaye Saint-Pierre, 1893. Neumes may be seen there for *Descendit de caelis* (27–8); *Ecce jam coram te* (31–2); *In medio* (227–8).
5 *Amalarii episcopi opera liturgica omnia*, ed. Jean Michael Hanssens, vol. 3 (Vatican City: Biblioteca Apostolica Vaticana, 1950), 54. See Kelly, 'Neuma Triplex'.
6 Hartker's antiphoner, St. Gall, SB 390–391 (ca. 1000), is published in facsimile in PM, ser. 2, vol. 1 (Solesmes: Abbaye Saint-Pierre, 1900; new edn, ed. Froger, 1970); the so-called manuscript of Mont-Renaud (tenth century), privately owned, is published in facsimile in PM 16 (1955–6). On the triple neume in these manuscripts, see Steiner, 'The Gregorian Chant Melismas', 241–4 and *passim*; Kelly, 'Neuma Triplex', 1–2 and *passim*.
7 For lists, see Hofmann-Brandt, *Die Tropen*; Kelly, 'Responsory Tropes'.
8 An example is the responsory *Illuminare*, which has a lengthy melisma from which it seems never to be separated; a modern edition is in *Liber responsorialis* (Solesmes: Abbaye Saint-Pierre, 1895), 75.
9 On melismas borrowed from other chants, see Steiner, 'Some Melismas'; Kelly, 'Responsory Tropes', 49–66; David G. Hughes, 'Music for St. Stephen at Laon', in Laurence Berman (ed.), *Words and Music: The Scholar's View. A Medley of Problems and Solutions Compiled in Honor of A. Tillman Merritt By Sundry Hands* (Cambridge, Mass.: Harvard University Press, 1972), 137–59.

450

10 Indeed, one of the melismas of the *neuma triplex* seems to have started life in the Offertory *Gloria et honore*. See Steiner, 'The Gregorian Chant Melismas', 251 and n. 3; Kelly, 'Responsory Tropes', 49–50.

11 On performance, see Kelly, 'Melisma and Prosula', and the literature cited there.

12 See Terence Bailey, *The Intonation Formulas of Western Chant* (Toronto: Pontifical Institute of Mediaeval Studies, 1974).

13 Jacques de Liège, *Speculum musicae*, ed. Roger Bragard, 7 vols. in 8 (Rome: American Institute of Musicology, 1955–73), iii, 256. Jacques's label for the first mode indicates that the melisma may be appended to antiphons, responsories, sequences or prosas; for the other seven modes only responsories are mentioned. The labels for the other modes read: 'Responsoria secundi [tertii, etc.] toni sic [for mode 5, 'sicut'] sunt terminanda versiculo sequente.'

14 On this manuscript, see Christopher Hohler, 'Reflections on Some Manuscripts Containing 13th-Century Polyphony', *Journal of the Plainsong and Mediaeval Music Society*, 1 (1978), 2–38; facsimiles of the polyphonic 'ductiae' are conveniently found in Willi Apel, *The Notation of Polyphonic Music 900–1600* (Cambridge, Mass.: The Mediaeval Society of America, 1942 and later edns), facsimile 49, 247 (the numbers vary with the edition); transcriptions in Timothy J. McGee, *Medieval Instrumental Dances* (Bloomington: Indiana University Press, 1989), 126–9.

15 On the manuscript see Steiner, 'Some Melismas', 108 n. 1; in the same article, 109, Steiner prints a facsimile of the responsory *Sancte stephane sydus* with its neume from this manuscript.

16 The prosa *Inviolata* can be seen in modern editions in *LU* (1961), 1861–2; *Variae preces* (Solesmes: Abbaye Saint-Pierre, 1888), 26; Peter Wagner, *Einführung in die gregorianische Melodien* (2nd edn, Leipzig: Breitkopf & Härtel, 1911–21; repr. 1962), ii, 192. Published facsimiles include *Antiphonale Sarisburiense*, ed. Walter Howard Frere (London: PMM Society, 1901–24; repr. edn, 6 vols Farnborough, Hants, England: Gregg Press, 1966), iv, 402–3; Henri Loriquet, *Le Graduel de l'église cathédrale de Rouen au XIIIe siècle* (Rouen: J. Lecerf, 1907), fol. 217^r–v (Paris, BNF lat. 904); PM 12: 271–2 (from Worcester F.160); PM 18 (Chartres, BM 260), fol. 64^v. See also Joseph Pothier, 'Inviolata', *RCG* 2 (1893–4), 19–22; Clemens Blume, 'Inviolata', *Die Kirchenmusik*, 9 (1908), 41–8. On the 'Fabrice' melismas, see above, n. 6. For some modern prints of *Sospitati dedit egros*, very widely disseminated and imitated, see *Antiphonale Sarisburiense*, ed. Frere, iv, 359–60; *MGG* 14 (1968), Tafel 89; Joseph Pothier, 'Ex ejus tumba', *RCG* 9 (1900–1), 49–52. On some later imitations of *Sospitati* see most recently Kay Brainerd Slocum, 'Prosas for Saint Thomas Becket', *PMM* 8 (1999), 39–54.

17 Some manuscripts that provide only melismas as additions to responsories include Rouen, BM A.164, an eleventh-century monastic breviary of Marmoutier, and Metz, BM 83, an early thirteenth-century monastic antiphoner (destroyed). Examples of manuscripts that provide only prosae as embellishments for responsories include three secular breviaries of Meaux (Paris, Bibl. de l'Arsenal 153, thirteenth century; Paris, BNF lat. 1266, ca. 1300; Paris, BNF lat. 12035, twelfth century), and the twelfth-century monastic antiphoner of St-Maur-des-Fossés, Paris, BNF n. a. lat. 12044 (see Kelly, 'New Music from Old'). On the repertories of these manuscripts see Kelly, 'Responsory Tropes', app. 2.

18 I have not been able to consult for this study the breviary of c.1300, perhaps from Sens, MS W. 108 in the Walters Art Gallery, Baltimore, cited in Steiner, 'Some Melismas', 108 and n. 1.

19 Villetard, *Office de Saint Savinien et de Saint Potentien*; id., *Office de Pierre de Corbeil (Office de la circoncision) improprement appelé 'Office des fous'* (Paris: A. Picard, 1907).

20 *Antiphonarius ad ritum et consuetudinem Metropolitis ac Primatialis Senon.*
   ecclesie . . . ex integro officia cum tonis ac pneumatibus (Sens: Franciscus Girault,
   1552).

21 This melody and its prosula have been the subject of considerable discussion.
   See Steiner, 'Some Melismas', 120–22; Wulf Arlt, *Ein Festoffizium des Mittelalters
   aus Beauvais in seiner liturgischen und musikalischen Bedeutung*, 2 vols. (Cologne:
   Volk, 1970), Darstellungsband, 99–100, Editionsband, 55 (transcription of
   'Sedentem' from London, BL Egerton 2614), 223; Kelly, 'Responsory Tropes',
   74–7, 428–9.

22 The melisma appears on the words *iniustitia* at the end of the verse *Cognovi
   domine*. See *Offertoriale sive versus offertoriorum*, ed. Carolus Ott (Paris: Desclée,
   1935), repr. with additions as *Offertoires neumés* (Solesmes: Abbaye Saint-
   Pierre,1978), 40. In addition to its appearances at Sens, the melisma is attached
   to the responsory *Lapides torrentes* in Paris, BNF n. a. lat. 1236 (a twelfth-century
   antiphoner of Nevers), fol. 46 in a later hand; Paris, BNF 17296 (twelfth-century
   antiphoner of Saint-Denis), fol. 30; and Metz, Bibl. de la Ville 461 (a breviary
   of the later thirteenth century), fol. 118. See Kelly, 'Responsory Tropes', 50–52.
   The melisma is attached to the reprise (on *collocaret*) at the end of the versus
   Christus manens, which in turn is attached to *Letemur gaudiis*, an Offertory
   prosula here used independently, in Sens, BM 46A (see Villetard, *Office de Pierre
   de Corbeil*, 133). On *Christus manens*, found also in the Beauvais Circumcision
   office, and its polyphonic settings, see Arlt, *Ein Festoffizium*, Darstellungsband
   67–9, 231–3, 259–71; Editionsband, 6, 169–73, 196, 263–5; David G. Hughes, 'The
   Sources of *Christus manens*', in Jan LaRue et al. (eds), *Aspects of Medieval and
   Renaissance Music: A Birthday Offering to Gustave Reese* (New York: Norton,
   1966), 423–34.

23 See Appendix §A, responsory *Precursor domini*.

24 'Les neumes des répons étant fort étendus, font aisément sentir les propriétés de
   chaque Mode.' Poisson, *Nouvelle méthode*, 379.

25 See Villetard, *Office de Pierre de Corbeil*, 131 n. B; Arlt, *Ein Festoffizium*,
   Editionsband, 19, 204–5 (citing further manuscript appearances).

26 *Breviarium senonense*, 4 vols. (Sens: Tarbé, 1780).

27 On the 'Neo-Gallican' reforms, see David Hiley, *Western Plainchant: A
   Handbook* (Oxford: Clarendon Press, 1993), 618–21.

28 *Processionnal, Graduel, Antiphonaire et Psautier à l'usage de l'église primatiale et
   métropolitaine de Sens* (Sens: Thomas-Malvin, 1844).

29 'Les cinq premiers du Choeur, revêtus de Chappes, debout devant l'aigle
   commencent le Répons, chantent le Verset et le *Gloria Patri*, après lequel le
   Préchantre avec les deux Choristes au milieu du Choeur recommencent le
   Répons. Pendant que le Choeur chante la répétition, les cinq Dignitaires se parta-
   gent et vont, chacun de leur côté, se joindre aux Choristes au milieu du Choeur;
   là, ils se tournent face à face de la partie du Choeur avec laquelle ils chantent.
   À la fin du Répons, à la syllabe ou à la note qui précède celle sur laquelle on
   doit commencer la Neume, tout le Choeur s'arrête, le côté droit commence la
   Neume, qui se chante alternativement avec le côté gauche: à la fin les deux parties
   du Choeur se réunissent leurs voix pour terminer le Répons.' Poisson, *Nouvelle
   méthode*, 379–80.

Structure and Ornament in Chant:
The Case of the Beneventan Exultet

Even before my days as a student of David Hughes I was fascinated with those manuscript fragments that we all used to treat so casually: the framed page of an antiphoner that hangs over the photocopy machine in a departmental office that I won't name; the drawerful of uncatalogued vellum leaves used to illustrate "the medieval manuscript" in another music department; and the two pages that I must confess to owning myself. The fascination, of course, lies in wondering why one particular page, or one manuscript, should survive; in the amazing durability of medieval book-production as compared to modern efforts; in the contrast between what such a page's original purpose was and what it is doing hanging over a photocopy machine.

So it seemed particularly meaningful, when a friend of mine was recently dismembering a tenth edition of the *Encyclopaedia Britannica* (for reasons best known to himself), that I should be presented with a fragment including the article entitled "Plain Song." I was then beginning a study of the Exultet, and this fragment shared my enthusiasm for the subject. The author, the eminent William Smyth Rockstro, speaks of the Exultet as being "of extreme antiquity, and beautiful beyond all description. The melody of the Exultet is, indeed, very frequently cited as the finest example of plain song in existence."[1]

But despite Rockstro's admiration for the Roman Exultet, and indeed despite its undoubted beauty, we cannot be certain any longer about its extreme antiquity, particularly as we know that the Exultet was sung variously in different regions, and we have no evidence that the Roman Exultet is older than some others.[2]

In fact, it is a non-Roman melody that will occupy our attention here: the melody used in southern Italy, the Beneventan melody—which is not beautiful beyond description. It is a simple recitation on three pitches; and although it is not "frequently cited as the finest example of plain song in existence," it is a fine example of a highly-structured reciting tone with opening formulas, a flex, an intermediate cadence, and a final cadential phrase. An example of this melody can be examined in example 1.

Example 1
The Beneventan Exultet melody

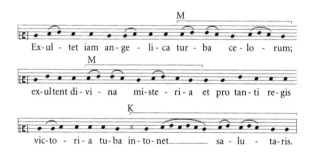

The Exultet—the extended praise of the Paschal candle sung by the deacon at the Easter Vigil—has a particular importance in the old Beneventan liturgy. Whereas the Exultet elsewhere is normally the first event of the Paschal Vigil, in the Beneventan liturgy it comes after the reading of the

[1] *Encyclopaedia Britannica*, 10th ed., s. v. "Plain Song," by William Smyth Rockstro.

[2] On the history of the Exultet and its ceremony in general see Jordi M. Pinell, "La benedicció del ciri pasqual i els seus textos," *Scripta et documenta* 10: *Liturgica* 2 (Montserrat: Abadia de Montserrat, 1958), 1–119; Georges Benoît-Castelli, "Le 'Praeconium paschale,'" *Ephemerides liturgicae* 67 (1953): 309–34; Bernard Capelle, "La procession du *Lumen Christi* au Samedi-Saint," *Revue bénédictine* 44 (1932): 105–19; Hermanus A. P. Schmidt, *Hebdomata sancta*, 2 vols. (Rome: Herder, 1956–57).

Table 1

Musical sources of the Exultet in southern Italy, in roughly chronological order

This table lists musical versions of the Exultet; thus some sources are included more than once, when they contain two texts (as do the fragments of Farfa and Trento), or when they were substantially revised from an earlier form to provide a later text (as were Vat. lat. 9820, Bari 2, and others).

(LS = Lower script; US = Upper script)

	Date	Deposit	Text	Type	Provenance
1.	10ex	Vat. lat. 9820	Ben	Exultet roll	Benevento
2.	10/11	Benevento, Bibl. cap. 33	Ben	Missal	provenance unknown
3.	11in	Vat. lat. 10673	Ben	Gradual	provenance unknown
4.	11in	Manchester, Rylands 2	Ben	Exultet roll	provenance unknown
5.	11in	Bari, Duomo, Exultet 1	Ben	Exultet roll	Bari
6.	11	Farfa-Trento A	Ben	Gradual	Veroli?
7.	11	Farfa-Trento B	Rom	Gradual	Veroli?
8.	11	Mirabella Eclano Exultet 1	Ben	Exultet roll	Benevento?
9.	11	Gaeta, Duomo, Exultet 1 (LS)	Ben	Exultet roll	Gaeta?
10.	11	Montecassino Exultet 1	Ben	Exultet roll	Amalfi (?)
11.	11med	Avezzano, Curia vescovile	Rom	Exultet roll	Montecassino
12.	11	Capua, Bibl. arcivescovile	Rom	Exultet roll	Capua? Montecassino
13.	11	Gaeta, Duomo, Exultet 2	Rom	Exultet roll	Gaeta?
14.	11	Pisa Duomo, Exultet 1	Rom	Exultet roll	Montecassino
15.	11 2/2	Vat. lat. 3784	Ben	Exultet roll	Montecassino
16.	11 2/2	Troia, Duomo, Exultet 1	Ben	Exultet roll	Troia
17.	11 2/2	Rome, Vall. C 32	Rom	Ritual	Montecassino?
18.	11 2/2	Mirabella Eclano Exultet 2	Rom	Exultet roll	Mirabella? Benevento?
19.	11ex	Bari, Duomo, Exultet 2 (LS)	Ben	Exultet roll	Bari
20.	11ex	Velletri, Museo capitolare	Rom	Exultet roll	Montecassino
21.	11ex	London, BL add. 30337	Rom	Exultet roll	Montecassino
22.	11ex	Oxford, Bodl. Can Bibl lat 61	Rom	Evangelistary	Zadar
23.	11ex	Vat. Barb. lat. 592	Rom	Exultet roll	Montecassino
24.	1082	Vat. Borg. lat. 339	Rom	Evangelistary	Dalmatian
25.	11/12	Gaeta, Duomo, Exultet 3	Rom	Exultet roll	Gaeta
26.	11/12	Paris, B.N., n.a. lat. 710	Rom	Exultet roll	Fondi
27.	11/12	Rome, Vall. F 29	Rom	Ritual	Farfa
28.	11/12	New York, Morgan M 379	Rom	Missal	Foligno
29.	12in	Troia, Duomo, Exultet 2	Ben	Exultet roll	Troia
30.	1106-20	Montecassino Exultet 2	Rom	Exultet roll	Sorrento
31.	12 in	Rome, Vall B 23	Rom	Missal	Norcia
32.	12 1/2	Berlin, Staatsb. Lat. Fol. 920	Rom	Missal	Kotor
33.	12	Subiaco XVIII	Rom	Missal	Subiaco
34.	12	London, BL Eg 3511	Rom	Missal	Benevento
35.	12	Troia, Duomo, Exultet 3 (LS)	Rom	Exultet roll	Troia

36.	12	Rome, Casanat. 724	Rom	Exultet roll	Benevento
37.	12	Vat. lat. 6082	Rom	Missal	Montecassino?
38.	12	Rome, Vall. B 43	Rom	Missal	Central Italy
39.	12ex	Naples VI G 34	Rom	Processional	Troia
40.	12ex	Bari, Duomo, Exultet 3	Rom	Exultet roll	Bari
41.	12/13	Salerno, Duomo, Exultet	Rom	Exultet roll	Salerno
42.	12/13	Vatican Ottob. lat. 576	Rom	Missal	Montecassino
43.	12/13	Vatican Barb. lat. 603	Rom	Missal	Caiazzo?
44.	13	Oxford, Bodl. Can. lit. 342	Rom	Missal	Dubrovnik
45.	13	Bari Exultet 2 (US melody 1)	Rom	Exultet roll	Bari
46.	13 2/2	Bari Exultet 2 (US melody 2)	Rom	Exultet roll	Bari
47.	13?	Naples VI G 38 (LS)	Rom	Missal	Franciscan
48.	14	Vat. lat. 3784A	Rom	Exultet roll	Naples
49.	15	Salerno 3	Ben	Missal	Salerno
50.	15	Salerno 4	Ben	Missal	Salerno
51.	15	Rome, Casanat. 1105	Rom	Missal	Montevergine

lessons and before the procession to the baptismal font.[3] Also peculiar to southern Italy is the phenomenon of the Exultet roll: some twenty-four surviving scrolls contain the text of the Exultet and its music, the oldest of them from the late tenth century.

An Exultet roll is made by sewing lengths of parchment together. Often pictures are painted on the roll, of three sorts: images from the text; or liturgical scenes of the ceremony at hand; or pictures of the ecclesiastical and secular rulers named in the Exultet. The illustrations are often painted upside-down with respect to the script so that viewers can see the pictures as they unroll from the top of the ambo (see plates 1–4).

These Exultet rolls have been given much scholarly attention, principally from art historians studying the beautiful illustrations they contain.[4] But scholars have often overlooked the many other appearances of the Exultet in southern Italy in missals, graduals, processionals, and the like (my own list of musical appearances of the Exultet in southern Italy appears as table 1); and nobody pays much attention to the music.

In what follows we shall give some close consideration to the melody of the Beneventan Exultet, and from it we can learn some simple but important facts about melodic transmission and about the process of embellishment. But even before that, I propose a brief survey of the surviving witnesses of the Exultet in southern Italy, for there is much to be seen of history and politics in this one occasional chant. In the space of less than two hundred years and in a limited area, the Exultet underwent many

[3] On the liturgical placement of the Exultet in the south Italian literature see René-Jean Hesbert, "L' 'Antiphonale missarum' de l'ancien rit bénéventain" (part 6, 'Le Samedi-Saint'), *Ephemerides liturgicae* 61 (1947): 153–210; idem, *Paléographie musicale* 14: *Le codex 10673 de la Bibliothèque Vaticane* (= *PM* 14, Tournai, 1931; repr. Bern, 1971), 240–60, 418–26.

[4] The art-historical bibliography on the south Italian Exultet rolls is vast, and will not be cited comprehensively here. The classic study is found in Émile Bertaux, *L'art dans l'Italie méridionale* (published as Tome 1; Paris, 1904); under the general direction of Adriano Prandi, Bertaux's work has been expanded and brought up to date as *L'art dans l'Italie méridionale: Aggiornamento dell'opera di Émile Bertaux*, 4 vols. (numbered IV–VI plus *Indici*; Rome: École française de Rome, 1978). Myrtilla Avery has published the surviving miniatures from Exultet rolls in *The Exultet Rolls of South Italy* (publ. as vol. II; Princeton: Princeton University Press, 1936); and more recently the Italian paleographer Guglielmo Cavallo has published a study and facsimiles of the rolls from Bari and Troia (*Rotoli di Exultet dell'Italia meridionale*; Bari: Adriatica, 1973) with substantial bibliography, 239–51. Additional facsimile volumes include Herbert Douteil, ed., *Exultet: Codex Vaticanus lat. 9820, Vollständige Facsimile-Ausgabe in Originalformat des Codex Vaticanus lat. 9820 der Biblioteca Apostolica Vaticana* (Graz: Akademische Druck- u. Verlagsanstalt, 1974), and Guglielmo Cavallo and Lucinia Speciale, eds., *Die Exultetrolle Codex Barberini latinus 592*, Codices e Vaticanis selecti 76 (Zurich: Belser, 1988), including essays by Cavallo and Speciale; for all the manuscripts cited here that are in Beneventan script, further bibliography can be found in Elias Avery Loew, *The Beneventan Script: A History of the South Italian Minuscule*, 2nd ed. Virginia Brown, 2 vols., Sussidi eruditi

Plate 1: Bari, Archivio del Duomo, Exultet roll 1 (detail). The deacon, on the ambo, sings the Exultet from a scroll while an attendant holds the Paschal candle. Note that the illustrations are reversed with respect to the text. Reproduced by permission.

Plate 2: Montecassino, Archivio della Badia, Exultet roll 2 (detail). Two pieces joined together with a parchment strip. The illustration of Christ harrowing Hell is reversed so that it will appear right side up at the proper time. Reproduced by permission.

Plate 3: Troia, Archivio del Duomo, Exultet roll 3 (detail). Portraits of ecclesiastical and civil rulers for whom God's blessing is implored (Pope, Bishop, King); the roll concludes with the so-called Norman finale: "Qui semper vivis, regnas, imperas, necnon et gloriaris. . . ." Courtesy of the Istituto centrale per il catalogo e la documentazione, Rome.

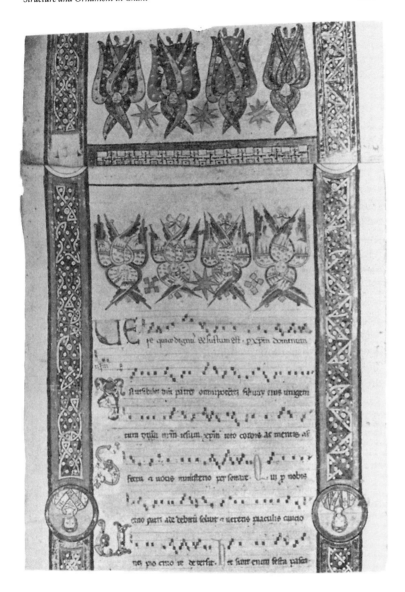

Plate 4: Bari, Archivio del Duomo, Exultet roll 2 (detail). The original Beneventan script is visible for the first portion of the preface, but is erased beginning with *te invisibilem patrem;* the original notation has been erased throughout and replaced with square staff notation. Note the initial letters of the Beneventan text preserved on the left even though they no longer correspond to the substituted text. Reproduced by permission.

changes. Each new version, each alternative, owes its existence to a choice which reflects something of local history, and of cultural and even of political traditions.

Exultet rolls contain one of two texts, which we might call the Beneventan and the Roman versions (what Bannister called the *Vetus Itala* and the *Vulgate*).[5] The Beneventan text is a survival of the ancient liturgical rite of the area, associated with the Lombard duchy of Benevento at least as far back as the eighth century, and almost completely suppressed in the course of the eleventh century under the joint forces of Papal reform and Norman invasion. The Vulgate text reflects the rites of the church of Rome, whose authority only gradually asserted itself in southern Italy during the ninth and tenth centuries. Hence when we see, as we do in so many of the Exultet rolls, the old Beneventan text erased and the newer Roman text substituted, we see also the decline of Lombard power in the South and the increased importance of the Roman church.[6]

We notice also that Montecassino seems almost to be a factory for Exultet rolls with the newer Vulgate text. Montecassino, reaching the height of her power in the eleventh century, and no longer dependent on Lombard princes, is producing bishops, cardinals, and popes for the universal church: when a monk of Montecassino was made a bishop, the monastery often sent him out with a beautiful Exultet roll—using the Roman text—for use in his new diocese. Exultet rolls now at Velletri, Avezzano, the Vatican, the British Library, and probably others, are part of this phenomenon.[7] Montecassino, under Frankish and Papal influence, seems to have embraced all things Roman rather sooner than other places in the South, and these Exultets are an aspect of Montecassino's public stance.

The melody used for the Exultet in southern Italy is also clearly associated with the old Beneventan liturgy.[8] So it is no surprise that the oldest

33–34 (Rome: Edizione di storia e letteratura, 1980); see also Thomas Forrest Kelly, *The Beneventan Chant* (= *TBC*; Cambridge: Cambridge University Press, 1989), 46–48, 59–60, and Appendix 3 (298–319).

[5] Henry Marriott Bannister, "The *Vetus Itala* Text of the Exultet," *The Journal of Theological Studies* 11 (1910): 43–54, edits the Beneventan text, but incompletely and with errors. The Beneventan text is conveniently available in *PM* 14, 385–86, and in Cavallo, *Rotoli*, 26.

[6] On the Roman and Beneventan liturgies in the history of southern Italy see Kelly, *TBC*, 6–40; a classic article which deals with the changing role of the church at Benevento is Hans Belting, "Studien zum beneventanischen Hof im 8. Jahrhundert," *Dumbarton Oaks Papers* 16 (1962): 141–93, plus plates.

[7] The Exultets in question are Velletri, Museo capitolare, Exultet without shelf-mark (displayed under glass); Avezzano, Curia vescovile, Exultet without shelf-mark; Vatican City, Biblioteca Apostolica Vaticana MS. Vat. lat. 3784; London, British Library Additional MS. 30337.

[8] The demonstration that the melody considered here, and exemplified in example 1, is a melody from the old Beneventan liturgy, requires more space than is available here. Briefly, the

surviving Exultets have the local text and the melody associated with the regional liturgy; and these are among the very earliest musical documents in the area.

But because Exultet rolls are very beautiful and not easily replaced, they are not discarded, like so many other outmoded liturgical documents, when needs change. As a result, the Exultet rolls together, and many of them separately, reveal several layers of influence.

In cities which preserve more than one Exultet roll—Bari, Troia, Gaeta, and Mirabella Eclano—the successive documents reflect changing needs (these multiple rolls are summarized in table 2). The oldest roll in each city has the Beneventan text. This is, of course, a reason for the existence of multiple rolls in these cities, since the Beneventan text is soon replaced with the more widespread Vulgate. Sometimes, as at Bari and Troia, a second roll is designed probably to clarify the musical notation of the older Beneventan Exultet.

At some point in the late eleventh or early twelfth century, each center creates a new Exultet roll using the Roman text (these are Bari 3, Troia 3, Gaeta 2, Mirabella 2); but often—and here the musicologist can help the art historian in detecting Lombard conservatism—often the new text retains the old Beneventan melody.

At a still later stage, an older roll is sometimes re-used to fill the need for a "Roman" melody and a Vulgate text. Thus two old rolls were altered— Bari 2 in the thirteenth century, Gaeta 1 in the fourteenth—to preserve their illustrations while rejecting both their text and their melody. Similarly, Troia 3, whose text was already the Vulgate, had its Beneventan melody altered in the fourteenth century.

These two, separate, stages of transition—from the Beneventan to the Roman text, and from the Beneventan to the Roman melody—are to be seen also in many of the individual documents in other cities. The scribes of some of the Vulgate Exultets show a transitional stage when they include, in their new document, parts of the older Beneventan text: a south Italian roll now at Pisa, a Dalmatian gospel-book at Oxford, and an Exultet at Montecassino[9] all show a combination of texts. An intermediate stage in

---

use of the same melody for a variety of other functions specific to the Beneventan liturgy makes the connection clear. The melody of the Exultet is used also for a reading from the book of Jonah used either for Maundy Thursday or the Easter Vigil; for the introductory verses to the canticle of Azarias and the canticle of the Three Children from the book of Daniel, sung on Good Friday or Holy Saturday; and for the prayer of Jeremiah. See Kelly, *TBC,* 131–32. See also *PM* 14, 271–74, 318–21, and 417 n.1.

[9] These are Pisa, Duomo, Exultet roll without shelf-mark (now on display in the Museo dell'Opera del Duomo); Oxford, Bodleian Library MS. Canonici liturg. 342; and Montecassino, Archivio della Badia, Exultet 2.

Table 2

Cities with Multiple Exultets

Bari

11in	Bari 1	Beneventan text and melody
11ex	Bari 2	Beneventan text and melody; clearer notation
12ex	Bari 3	Roman text, Beneventan melody elaborated
13	Bari 2	revised, in Gothic hand (for those portions of text not matching Roman version) to Roman text, and elaborated melody on staff

Troia

11 2/2	Troia 1	Beneventan text and melody
12in	Troia 2	Beneventan text and melody, clearer notation
12	Troia 3	Roman text with Norman finale, Beneventan melody
14	Troia 3	Beneventan melody replaced with Roman

Gaeta

11	Gaeta 1	Beneventan text and melody
11	Gaeta 2	Roman text, Beneventan melody
11/12	Gaeta 3	Roman text, Beneventan melody
14	Gaeta 1	text and melody altered to Roman

Mirabella Eclano

11	Mirabella 1	Beneventan text and melody
11 2/2	Mirabella 2	Roman text, Beneventan melody

Other Later Alterations to Exultets

1. Vat. lat. 9820 (s. 10ex, Benevento) erased and reversed for Roman text, s. 12.
2. Farfa-Trento (s. 11 gradual) contains Beneventan and Roman texts together.
3. Vat. lat. 3784 (s. 11 2/2 Montecassino) amputated (s. 14) after prologue, replaced with Roman text and melody.

melodic change may be the twelfth- or thirteenth-century missal Vatican, Barberini lat. 603, whose Vulgate Exultet begins and ends with the Beneventan melody, but whose central portion has the now-usual preface-tone. A particularly interesting transitional stage is seen in four fragmentary folios, now divided between Farfa and Trento, from a single eleventh-century gradual which contained *two* versions of the Exultet—the one Beneventan with the usual melody, and the other Vulgate with a unique melody.[10]

One brutal way to change the text is simply to chop off the parts of an old roll that do not correspond to the Vulgate text, and to append new text and music; this is the fate of the Montecassino roll now Vatican, Barberini lat. 3784. A similarly drastic measure was taken with the Exultet of St. Peter's convent *extra muros* in Benevento (now Vat. lat. 9820), which in the twelfth century was erased and reordered to become a Roman text; by reversing the scroll the original pictures were now presented upside-down (that is, right-side-up to viewers), and in fact the initial letters of the older text survive upside-down in the present right margin.

A further layer of textual alteration is the so-called Norman finale of the Exultet, apparently imported into southern Italy and Sicily by the Normans in the later eleventh century.[11] This is an alternative ending to the Roman text, related, with its "qui semper vivis, regnas, imperas," to the Frankish *Laudes regiae;* it appears occasionally in Beneventan script, as in the processional Naples VI G 34; more often, however, it comes from the periphery of the Beneventan zone, where the confluence of traditions may be seen in many ways. An example is manuscript M. 379 in the Pierpont Morgan Library—a missal in ordinary minuscule that in many ways resembles those of Subiaco. The Exultet has the Roman text, but the melody is the old Beneventan one—at least at the beginning: but it switches to the Roman preface tone in the middle, at just the place where the two texts diverge. The Morgan missal may well reproduce an earlier source that physically substituted the Roman melody for the Beneventan, as in the amputated roll at the Vatican. And at the end comes the Norman finale. The rubric that follows demonstrates the foreign origin of what has preceded: "benedictione cerei

---

[10] These two fragments are Farfa, Biblioteca dell' Abbazia MS. AF.338 Musica XI (formerly AB.F.Musica XI) and Trento, Museo Provinciale d'Arte, s. n. (formerly Lawrence Feininger collection); the Farfa fragment is reproduced in *PM* 14, pls. XXVI–XXVII (in the first printing erroneously labeled "Cava"); the Exultet melodies from this manuscript are studied and transcribed in *PM* 14, 390–99.

[11] The name was coined by Ernst H. Kantorowicz in "A Norman Finale of the Exultet and the Rite of Sarum," *Harvard Theological Review* 34 (1941): 129–43; see also Eileen L. Roberts, "The Exultet Hymn in Twelfth Century Sicily as an Indicator of Manuscript Provenance," *Ecclesia orans* 5 (1988): 157–64.

finita, secundum teutonicum ordinem." It is not clear what is Teutonic about the foregoing: is it the Norman finale?

Is it possible, in fact, that the arrival of the Normans in the eleventh century, and their imposition of imported liturgical customs—including the Norman finale—provided the impetus for the change to the Roman melody? Evidently not: although the processional Naples VI G 34, one of only two sources in Beneventan script which have the Norman finale, uses the Roman melody, the third Exultet roll of Troia, which also has the Norman finale, was originally written with the Beneventan melody throughout; only in the fourteenth century was Troia 3's old notation replaced with the Roman melody. Three related missals from central Italy (Subiaco XVIII, Morgan M. 379, and Rome, Vallicelliana B 23) all have the Norman finale, and all use the Beneventan melody. These are sources peripheral to the Beneventan zone, written in ordinary minuscule; but they use the Beneventan melody for the first part of the Exultet, and the Roman preface-tone thereafter. The Norman conquest of south Italy, of which the Norman finale of the Exultet is a very small side effect, was not also the impetus for the change to the Roman melody. The cause for this change must be sought elsewhere; perhaps in the thirteenth-century standardization of Roman books by adopting Franciscan models.

All of these details contribute to underscore a single simple but important observation: for these scribes at least, changing the text does not necessarily mean changing the music. The Beneventan melody survives later and more frequently than its associated text. The arrival of the Vulgate text is not the moment of change to the Roman melody; we have already seen, in Bari, Troia, Gaeta, and Mirabella, that the earliest version of the Roman text retains the Beneventan melody. A new text, even if it arrives clothed in a new melody, can be selectively received, adapted to a well-known melodic formula, and the useless melody discarded. Melody and words can be, and are, transmitted separately. The older Beneventan melody survives for a long time—and because it is a formulaic reciting-tone it adapts easily to the needs of changing texts.[12]

---

[12] This facile reception of new texts is possible only when the melody is relatively formulaic—that is, adaptable to a variety of texts. A notable example of this is the adoption in most Gregorian chant traditions of the Gallican Psalter for formulaic verses such as those accompanying Introits, while retaining the Roman Psalter for all those pieces with more specific melodies; it is worth noting, however, that the southern Italian tradition either resists the Gallican Psalter, or never receives it in the chant tradition. See *PM* 14, 145–51.

This Beneventan melody deserves a little more of our attention. It is isolated in time and place, and in most of its appearances remarkably uniform; but in a few later sources, singers have developed, and scribes have recorded, ornamented versions of the Beneventan Exultet melody, and these can teach us much about how musicians of the time thought of embellishment, how they carried it out, and—what is often difficult to observe in other contexts—what precisely is the base material on which the embellishment is mounted.

The standard Beneventan Exultet tone is limited to the three pitches of a major third, reciting on the central pitch.[13] The music is arranged in periods, each of which ends with a characteristic final cadence (marked K in example 1 on p. 250); an intermediate cadence (marked M) divides the longer period into—usually—three phrases. Each phrase begins with an intonation, a special intonation being reserved for the opening of each period. In longer phrases, a descent of a tone precedes the *podatus* which marks occasional accents in the text, evidently for breathing pauses.

The final and medial cadences are based on a single accent, and vary only according to whether the final word is a paroxytone or a proparoxytone. For the final cadence (K) this is simply a matter of adding a single note at the end; but the medial cadence has two versions, in which the characteristic *torculus* of the paroxytone "caelorum" is subdivided for the proparoxytone "misteria." The rest of the cadential figure is applied to the syllables preceding the final accent without regard to their accentuation.

This melody is quite strictly applied to the text in almost 40 manuscripts. There are, of course, the occasional small variants which we find in almost all chant transmission, as in example 2, which shows the beginning of nine Exultets; all different, but all designed to emphasize the first accent of the text.

The first four are from the "standard" group presenting the original melody, but they are chosen to show a variety of openings. The leap of no. 1 is in fact the only leap in this otherwise entirely stepwise melody. The melody leaps a third, emphasizing the opening accent, before settling to the tenor on the central pitch. No. 2 compresses this leap to a single syllable, giving the further weight of length to the accented syllable. No. 3 keeps the weight but avoids the leap by filling in the third. No. 4, by beginning a step higher, eliminates the third altogether, but keeps the weight of the accent. No. 5 can be viewed as filling in the leap as presented in no. 2; and no. 6,

---

[13] The structure of the Beneventan Exultet was analyzed as long ago as 1894 by Dom Mocquereau in vol. 4 of the *Paléographie musicale* (Solesmes, 1894, 171–85), and considered also by Dom Hesbert in vol. 14, 388–90.

Example 2

Openings of selected Exultets

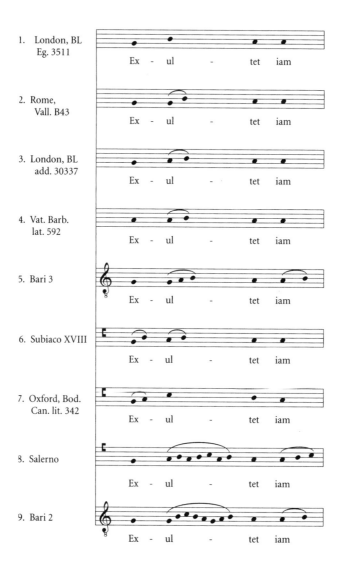

1. London, BL
   Eg. 3511

   Ex - ul - tet iam

2. Rome,
   Vall. B43

   Ex - ul - tet iam

3. London, BL
   add. 30337

   Ex - ul - tet iam

4. Vat. Barb.
   lat. 592

   Ex - ul - tet iam

5. Bari 3

   Ex - ul - tet iam

6. Subiaco XVIII

   Ex - ul - tet iam

7. Oxford, Bod.
   Can. lit. 342

   Ex - ul - tet iam

8. Salerno

   Ex - ul - tet iam

9. Bari 2

   Ex - ul - tet iam

perhaps related to No. 3, creates a new leap on the first syllable, anticipating the high note of the second syllable. The last three openings are from later, consciously-embellished Exultets. No. 7 leaps beyond the range of the traditional Exultet on its first accented syllable; and nos. 8 and 9 use this high note as part of an extended flourish.

A comparative look at the principal cadences of elaborated Exultets will show many of these same principles at work. Example 3 shows typical cadences from eight Exultets. The two versions of the intermediate cadence appear in columns M1 through M9, and the final cadences in columns K1 through K8. I have selected a Montecassino Exultet of the late eleventh century, British Library Additional MS. 30337, as representative of the "standard" version of the melody, and its cadences are transcribed at the top.

In arranging these versions in order of ascending complexity it is important to avoid viewing them as a single development. Each version is, of course, a single way of singing the Exultet on a given occasion, and is not necessarily based on one or another slightly less decorated melody in another source. A better approach, in most cases, is to consider each version in comparison with the "standard" melody, whose widespread familiarity is certain.

The Dalmatian missal Berlin 920 is quite close to the standard melody. It does, however, alter the typical *torculus* in column M5 to provide an anticipation of the final; and in column K3 it sometimes, but not always, extends the range to the upper fourth. Subiaco XVIII, also a peripheral manuscript, uses in column M5 the same anticipation as seen in Berlin 920, and extends the range, not upward, but below the final at the end—in columns K6 and K7. The second Exultet of Troia extends the range in both directions: in the medial cadence at column M3 it precedes the standard *clivis* with another providing upper and lower auxiliaries and reaching the upper fourth; and in the final cadence the subfinal is reached by continuing the scale at K3, and the subfinal is repeated, at K7, in proparoxytone endings.

With the second and third Exultet rolls of Bari we are lucky to be able to study the progressive development of the Exultet melody in the same place: the three melodies of Bari are clearly related to one another. The first Exultet of Bari[14] is one of the oldest extant witnesses of the traditional melody and the Beneventan text. Later in the eleventh century, as we have

---

[14] Bari, Archivio del Duomo, Exultet roll 1 is reproduced in full in Cavallo, *Rotoli*, pls. 1–11, and discussed on 47–55; see also Avery, *The Exultet Rolls*, 11–13 and pls. 1–11; most recently, see Penelope C. Mayo, "Borders in Bari: The Decorative Program of Bari I and Montecassino under Desiderius," in *Monastica IV: Scritti Raccolti in memoria del XV centenario della nascita di S. Benedetto (480–1980)*, Miscellanea cassinese 48 (Montecassino: Pubblicazioni cassinesi, 1984), 31–67.

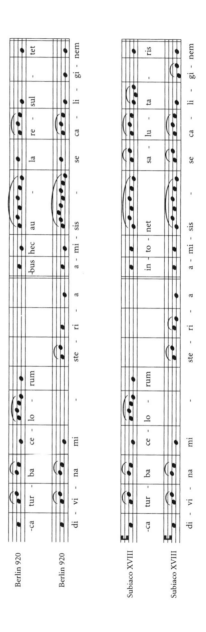

Example 3a: Cadential formulae of selected Exultets.

Example 3b: Cadential formulae of selected Exultets (continued).

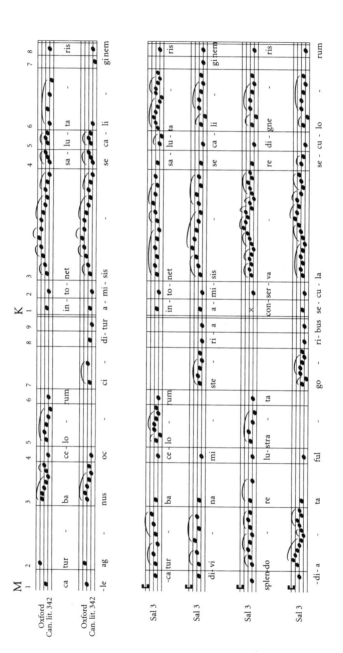

Example 3c: Cadential formulae of selected Exultets (continued).

seen, a second Beneventan Exultet was made at Bari with a clearer musical notation.[15] This second roll, however, was altered at a later date—somewhere around the turn of the thirteenth century; the Beneventan portions of its text were erased to provide for the Roman text in Gothic script, and its standard Beneventan melody was replaced throughout with a more elaborate version in an awkward square notation (see plate 4).

Bari also preserves a third Exultet roll, usually dated earlier than the revision of Bari 2, but whose melodic version clearly is a later development. This third roll has been little studied because it has no pictures; it is made, not too carefully, from an older scroll which once contained a Greek liturgical text (see plate 5).[16]

Example 4 compares these three Bari melodies. It is important to remember that, although Bari 2 and Bari 3 present embellished forms of the melody, they still follow the standard formal procedures for the Exultet: the formulas are regular, and consistently applied.

Bari 1 presents the "standard" melody—you may wish to compare it with the British Library roll in example 3. Noteworthy here, though, is the *quilisma* in column K4, which is not typical. Bari 2 shows a development of this basic melody. The intermediate cadence M reaches beyond the third at column M2, continuing the upward motion. On the word "celorum" (column M5), the typical *torculus* is divided, its first note given to the preceding syllable. This produces, by analogy, the *podatus* at the corresponding place in the proparoxytone cadence ("Misteria"), even though this version of the cadence lacks the original *torculus;* and the extra syllable allows a move to the upper fourth on the second syllable of "misteria"; this upper fourth is reached *only* on the three-syllable proparoxytone cadence. Bari 2 never reaches this upper fourth in the closing formula K. Instead, there is an elaboration of the figure at K3 with an opening *torculus* and a final scalewise continuation down to the subfinal. Bari 2's arch at K4, replacing the *quilisma* of Bari 1, has the effect of inverting the figure at K5. Note that the subfinal returns at the final cadence, but only where there is an extra syllable, as on "caliginem," column K7.

As for the melody of Bari 3, a glance will confirm that it is a development of what we have just seen in Bari 2, and not an independent branch from the original melody of Bari 1. One of the most striking developments is the "feminine ending" of the medial cadence (columns M6, M9),

---

[15] Cavallo, *Rotoli*, pls. 17–23 and pp. 99–102; Avery, *The Exultet Rolls*, pls. 17–23 and pp. 14–15.

[16] Avery, *The Exultet Rolls*, pl. 24 and pp. 15–16.

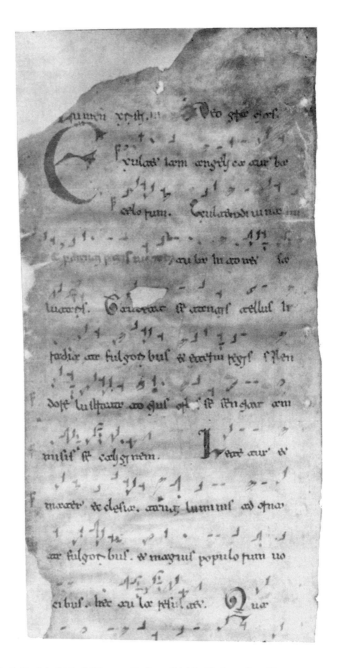

Plate 5: Bari, Archivio del Duomo, Exultet roll 3 (detail). Reproduced by permission.

Example 4

Cadences from Exultets of Bari

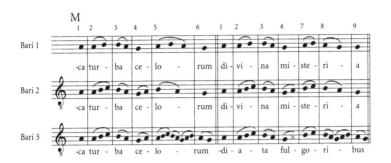

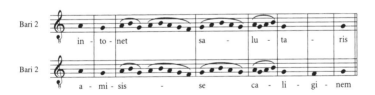

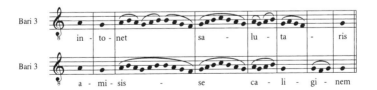

achieved by a reallocation of the last three pitches, giving two of them to the final syllable. The elaborated figure in column M5 surrounds the two-note figure of Bari 2 with two rising three-note *scandicus*. The result is, in fact, that the last two syllables are a reprise of the whole phrase: or more exactly, of the precise notes of "turba celorum" in Bari 2. The similar figure in column M8 (on "fulgo*rí*bus") is simpler because the phrase has already risen to the upper fourth on the previous syllable.

The final cadences of Bari 3 show some typical developments from Bari 2. On "intonet," column K3, Bari 3 fills in a gap in the version of Bari 2. The arched figure at K4 is taken one step higher in Bari 3, to the upper fourth; and the final cadence, in both its accentuations, elaborates the subfinal, which in Bari 2 was only used in the three-syllable cadence.

Two further versions of the Exultet remain to be considered. These are the thirteenth-century Dalmatian missal now in the Bodleian Library, Canonici liturg. 342, and the Exultet preserved in two fifteenth-century missals of Salerno. Both of these differ from the versions presented so far in that they show a loosening of the formulaic understanding of the melody and present rather extravagant and florid melodies. The Oxford version was studied in some detail by Dom Hesbert,[17] so we will concentrate here on the Salerno missals, which until recently were inaccessible.

These twin missals,[18] though they are written in Gothic script with occasional square notation, seem to be retrospective books, representing the liturgy of the twelfth century at Salerno, probably the liturgy as reorganized by archbishop Romualdo Guarna.[19] They contain many elements of the old Beneventan rite for Holy Week—including, as it happens, one antiphon

---

[17] *PM* 14, 399–416.

[18] Salerno, Archivio del Museo del Duomo, manuscripts without shelf-number. They will here be referred to as Salerno 3 and Salerno 4, according to the order in which they are described in Arturo Capone, *Il Duomo di Salerno* (Salerno, 1927–29), 2:261–63 ("Capo 3"), 265–66 ("Capo 4"); the Exultet from these missals was described, and partially transcribed, in Agostino Latil, "Un 'Exultet' inedito," *Rassegna gregoriana* 7 (1908): cols. 125–34; facsimiles of both manuscripts, including the complete Exultet from Salerno 4, appear in Thomas F. Kelly, ed., *Les témoins manuscrits du chant bénéventain*, Paléographie musicale 21 (Solesmes: Abbaye St. Pierre, 1992).

[19] An *ordo officii* (Capone no. 6) in the Salerno library carries the incipit "Incipit compendiosa pronuntiata officii ecclesiastici secundum salernitanae ecclesiae quam dominus Romualdus venerabilis Salernitanus archiepiscopus cum voluntate sui capituli ordinavit." According to Capone (2:271–72) this is Romualdo II Guarna (116?–1181); the *ordo officii* was copied by the same Guglielmo da Roma who copied Salerno 3 in 1431; this group of fifteenth-century manuscripts may represent a codification of the twelfth-century liturgy as then preserved and understood.

whose melody is known nowhere else.[20] The Exultet has the Beneventan text—extremely unusual for the fifteenth century, but not so rare for the twelfth; and the Exultet is placed, in Beneventan fashion, after the lessons. The Beneventan antiphons and tracts transcribed in these missals are not so different from those preserved in eleventh- and twelfth-century manuscripts—except for the Exultet, whose exuberance probably represents not so much the development of several centuries as it does a Salerno practice of great virtuosity on the part of the deacon (see illustration in plate 6).

Some typical cadences are transcribed at the end of example 3. Despite the melodic prolixity, and the fact that the cadences are not identically formulaic, we can see elements of the basic Beneventan melody. The decoration in column M5 and the elaborations in K3 occur at places where the Beneventan melody has its longest figures. Indeed in column K3 we can recognize the original Beneventan melody in the first six notes of three of the cadences.

But the Salerno melody seems more attentive to accented syllables than is the standard melody. The original Beneventan final cadence is entirely oriented to the single accent in column K6, though the syllable itself is an undecorated arrival on the final; but the Salerno singers give the accented syllable an extended figure. They do the same in column M2 for a syllable which is often, but not always, accented, and the results are not always happy.

The Salerno Exultet, then, follows the outline, and the general formulaic shape, of the Beneventan melody. But it does not limit itself to repeating the same formula when the same situation recurs. Indeed it seems a part of the singer's duty to vary these inflections as his virtuosity makes possible. Some clear examples of this process of immediate variation and development are transcribed in example 5, the Salerno versions of the threefold "Lumen christi," and the passage in the Beneventan text beginning "Flore utuntur," whose short repetitive phrases surely seem to cry out for virtuosity, at least to a singer in the Salerno style.

This is virtuoso solo singing. Indeed, even the standard Beneventan Exultet is no easy matter to sustain. The singer must be an expert, and it is easy to imagine a temptation to embroider the melody at hand. One wonders how many of the "standard" Exultets were sung precisely as written; perhaps in the hands of an adventurous and capable deacon the Beneventan melody served only as a framework for extempore embellishment. Perhaps

---

[20] This is the antiphon *Transivimus per ignem et aquam*, which was formerly known only from a rubric in the Farfa fragments ("postea pergat sacerdos vel episcopus ad altare canente antiphona haec: Transivimus per ignem et aqua"): see *PM* 14, pl. XXVII.

Plate 6: Salerno, Archivio del Museo del Duomo, manuscript without shelf-number (Capone 3), fol. 136ᵛ. Missal, 15th century; beginning of the Exultet. Reproduced by permission.

IX

Example 5

From the Salerno Exultet.
Salerno, Archivio del Museo del Duomo,
manuscript without shelf-number (Capone 3)

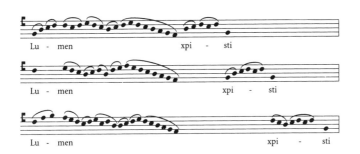

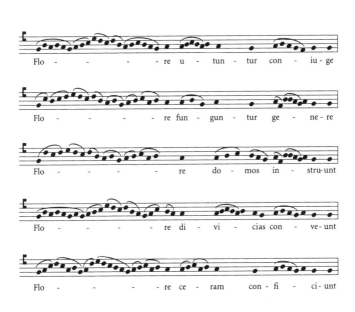

IX

it is a change of writing habit, not of performance style, that gives us our few decorated melodies. They are perhaps records of a singer's performance, rather than the framework on which he builds.

In any case, the survival of these ornamented melodies allows us to consider at close range the nature of medieval musical elaboration. It is remarkable how often we speak of a decorated melody, of a melodic embellishment—and how seldom we actually can compare framework and ornamentation. This melody gives us such an opportunity, and it is a rare one. With further study we may come closer to a medieval, rather than a modern, appreciation of this and other music; and the music of the Exultet rolls of southern Italy may once again take its rightful place with the illustrations in our esteem for the beauties of these extraordinary documents.

X

The Liturgical Rotulus at Benevento

Long after writing in the West was regularly transmitted in the form of the codex, the practice of assembling parchment membranes into *rotuli* survived in a limited way, usually for specific reasons. Sometimes the purpose was practical: documents which might need to be lengthened (rent rolls, obituary rolls, and the like) or documents whose illustrative contents suggested a longwise form (maps, genealogies, and so on) continued to made as scrolls. For the most part, however, scrolls in the later Middle Ages, as today with doctoral diplomas and honorific citations, had an archaizing, ceremonial, and solemn purpose.[1] For many of the same reasons, scrolls were used for solemn moments in the liturgy. Just as ecclesiastical vesture is based on earlier modes of dress and liturgical language tends towards the archaic, the conservatism of the liturgy suggests the archaic form of the roll for particular solemn moments.

Rolls for use in the liturgy, often of sumptuous manufacture, survive in the greatest number in southern Italy.[2] Two tenth-century rolls of Benevento preserve pontifical offices and are illustrated with pictures of liturgical ceremonies being performed. Rome, Biblioteca Casanatense MS 724 (i) contains a series of pontifical blessings: of doorkeepers, lectors, exorcists, acolytes, subdeacons, deacons, and priests.[3] Its

---

1 For an introduction to the use of the roll in the Middle Ages, and in the liturgy in particular, see Thomas Forrest Kelly, *The Exultet in Southern Italy*, forthcoming (Oxford University Press), Chapter 1. In what follows I make no distinction among the terms "roll", "scroll", "roll", and "rotulus". Although some rolls are written so as to be opened sideways, and others to be held vertically, there is no clear reason to apply one term to one form of scroll.

2 Although there are literary references to rolls used by bishops, pontifical rolls from north of the Alps seem not to survive from before the thirteenth century; see Kelly, *The Exultet*, Chapter 1.

3 Commentary by Beat Brenk and facsimile in Guglielmo Cavallo with Giulia Orofino and Oronzo Pecere, *Exultet. Rotoli liturgici del medioevo meridionale* (Rome: Istituto Poligrafico e Zecca dello Stato, 1994) (hereafter cited as *Exultet*), 75-85; partial facsimile in Myrtilla Avery, *The Exultet Rolls of South Italy* (Princeton: Princeton University Press; Oxford: Oxford University Press; The Hague: Nijhoff, 1936), plate CVI; on this very important roll see Elias Avery Lowe, *The Beneventan Script; A History of the South Italian Minuscule*. Second Edition prepared and enlarged by Virginia Brown, Sussidi eruditi 33-34 (Rome: Edizioni di storia e letteratura, 1980; hereafter Lowe/Brown, TBS2), II, 122 and the literature cited there; particularly important is the study in Hans Belting, *Studien zum beneventanischen Malerei* (Wiesbaden: Franz Steiner, 1968), 144-52.

X

The Liturgical Rotulus at Benevento

companion, Biblioteca Casanatense MS 724 (ii), contains material for the blessing of fonts.[4] There is a further pontifical roll for the blessing of baptismal water from eleventh-century Bari.[5]

Best known of the liturgical rolls of southern Italy are, of course, the Exultet rolls, scrolls containing the text ("Exultet iam angelica turba ...") and music for the blessing of the paschal candle on the vigil of Easter. Some twenty-six illustrated Exultet scrolls survive from southern Italy; in most cases the illustrations are painted upside-down with respect to the writing.[6] Two of these rolls are from the city of Benevento. The oldest of all the surviving Exultet rolls, Vatican Vat. lat. 9820,[7] made at Benevento in the last quarter of the tenth century for the convent of St. Peter *extra muros*, is a copy, as Hans Belting has shown, of a roll originally commissioned by archbishop Landolf, perhaps in 969.[8] A twelfth-century Exultet roll of Benevento is based on the illustrative model of Vat. lat. 9820, but with the Franco-Roman text of the Exultet and with the pictures reversed; this is Rome, Biblioteca Casanatense 724 (iii)[9], kept together with the two Beneventan pontifical rolls mentioned above.[10]

4 See Lowe/Brown, TBS2, II, 122-3; commentary by Beat Brenk and facsimile in *Exultet*, 87-100.

5 Facsimile in Guglielmo Cavallo, *Rotoli di Exultet dell'Italia meridionale* (Bari: Adriatica, 1973), tav. 12-17; commentary by Francesco Magistrale, bibliography, and facsimile in *Exultet*, 143-50; Lowe/Brown TBS2 II, 15.

6 The surviving Exultets, along with the pontifical rolls of Benevento and Bari, are reproduced in color and accompanied by scholarly commentary and bibliography in the recent catalogue *Exultet* (see note 3).

7 Bibliography by Rosalba Zuccaro in Adriano Prandi, ed., *L'art dans l'Italie méridionale. Aggiornamento dell'opera di Emile Bertaux* (hereafter *Aggiornamento*), 4 vols numbered IV-VI plus Indici (Rome: École française de Rome, Palais Farnèse, 1978), 442-46; Avery, *The Exultet Rolls*, 31-34, 46-49, plates CXXXV-CXLVI; Enrico [Henry] Marriott Bannister, *Monumenti vaticani di paleografia musicale latina* (2 vols., Leipzig: Harrassowitz, 1913), no. 345 (pp. 118-19), pl. 68; Belting, *Studien*, 167-80, 234-36; Émile Bertaux, *L'art dans l'Italie méridionale. Tome premier. De la fin de l'Empire Romain à la conquête de Charles d'Anjou* (Paris: Albert Fontemoing, 1904), 221-24; Beat Brenk, 'Bischöfliche und monastische «Committenza» in Süditalien am Beispiel der Exultetrollen', in *Committenti e produzione artistico-letteraria nell'alto Medioevo occidentale (4-10 aprile 1991) Settimane di studio 39* (Spoleto: Centro italiano di studi sull'alto Medioevo, 1992), 275-302; *Exultet. Codex Vaticanus lat. 9820. Vollständige Facsimile-Ausgabe in Originalformat des Codex Vaticanus lat. 9820 der Biblioteca Apostolica Vaticana* (Graz: Akademische Druck- und Verlagsanstalt, 1974: complete facsimile); Thomas Forrest Kelly, *The Beneventan Chant* (hereafter TBC; Cambridge: Cambridge University Press, 1989), 316; Lowe/Brown, TBS, II, 153; Valentino Pace in *Exultet*, 101-18 with complete facsimile.

8 Belting, *Studien*, 168-80.

9 On this roll see *Aggiornamento*, 454-5; Avery, *The Exultet Rolls*, 29-30, pl. CXVIII-CXXIX; Beat Brenk in *Exultet*, 319-339 with facsimile; Kelly, TBC, 310; Ernest Langlois, 'Le rouleau d'Exultet de la Bibliothèque Casanatense', *Mélanges d'archéologie et d'histoire* 6 (1886), 466-82; Lowe/Brown, TBS, II, 123.

10 In addition to Exultets, other liturgical rolls from southern Italy include the pontifical and benedictional rolls in the Biblioteca Casanatense; the eleventh-century benedictional roll of Bari (see note 5); a fragment of a later twelfth-century roll at Montecassino with portions of the solemn prayers for Good Friday (Montecassino, Archivio della Badia, Compactiones XVI; see Richard Francis Gyug, 'A Fragment of a Liturgical Roll at Montecassino (Compactiones XVI)', *Mediaeval Studies* 52 (1990), 268-77, 2 plates); Francesco Magistrale in *Exultet*, 477-9 with facsimile). There is now no trace, however, of the roll that was among the possessions of the monastery of Santa Maria de Fontanella, Amalfi, in 1007; it contained penitential material, the blessing of water, and the blessing either of wax

168

X

The Liturgical Rotulus at Benevento

The Exultets in the Vatican and the Casanatense, along with the Casanantense pontifical rolls, are among the chief glories of Beneventan production; but the use of the liturgical roll at Benevento evidently continued for a long time. The fifteenth-century inventory of the Cathedral library shows the presence of a large number of rolls, some of which survive to this day.

The inventory of the Chapter Library of the cathedral of Benevento made by Bartolomeo Pantasia between 1436 and 1447, and reviewed by the librarian Luigi Theuli in 1447, includes what seem to be at least twelve rolls (if we can assume that a *carta* in this context is a roll). They include the following (numbers have been added here for convenience):

1. Item carta una cum notis pro processione sancti Bartholomei.
2. Item liber constitutionum antiquarum capitularium dicto [sic] ecclesie.
3. Item Rotus unus cum orationibus pro letaniis
4. Item Rotus unus cum letania.
5. Item Rotus unus cum orationibus adorande crucis in parasceue.
6. Item Roti duo cum ympnis pro processionibus
7. Item alius Rotus magnus cum ympnis pro processionibus
8. Item alius Rotus cum letania
9. Item quaternus consitutionum quondam Gasparis archiepiscopi beneventani
10. Item sacca una...
11. Bulla una...
12. Item carta processionis crismatis que incipit *o redemptor*
13. Item carta lectionis palmarum que incipit *lectio libri exodi*
14. Item carta ubi est *exultet iam angelica.*
15. Item carta una ubi est rotus cum lectione *noueritis fratres charissimi.*
16. Item instrumentum unum...[11)]

This collection of rolls is extensive, but it does not seem to include any of the early illustrated rolls now in the Vatican and the Casanatense libraries. In this inventory the documents in Beneventan script are listed separately, and the portion transcribed here is from the list of books in modern, Frankish, writing. Thus no. 14, "carta ubi est *exultet iam angelica*", is clearly an Exultet roll, but equally clearly is neither of the rolls in Beneventan script mentioned above.

The liturgical rolls in this list seem in many cases destined for use in procession.

or of the paschal candle — perhaps the Exultet? ("Rotulum unum de penitentia cum benedictione da fonti et alia benedictione de ipse cirio." From a list of donations of 1007; Matteo Camera, *Memorie storico-diplomatiche dell'antica città e ducato di Amalfi* (2 vols., Salerno, 1876, repr. Salerno: W. Casari-Testaferrata, 1972), I, 221-2.) Another such roll, now lost, was given by Duke Gregory of Gaeta to the church of St. Michael in Planciano, described in 964 as "unum rotulum ad benedicendum cereum et fontes": Mauro Inguanez, *Catalogi codicum casinensium antiqui (saec. VIII-XV)*, Miscellanea cassinese 21 (Montecassino, 1941), 62.

11 Alfredo Zazo, 'L' 'Inventario dei libri antichi' della Biblioteca capitolare di Benevento (sec. XV)', *Samnium* 8 (1935), 5-25 at 10, but with errors. The list above is transcribed from the original inventory as corrected by Theuli. That the then librarian of Benevento was named Theuli (and not Feoli as Zazo and others record) see Jean Mallet and André Thibaut, *Les manuscrits en écriture bénéventaine de la Bibliothèque capitulaire de Bénévent. Tome I: manuscrits 1-18* (Paris: Éditions du CNRS, 1984), 10, n. 1.

X

The Liturgical Rotulus at Benevento

This is a sensible use for a roll, since a small occasional portion of the liturgy can be written down and carried about much more easily than can a large choir-book. No. 1 in the list above includes music for St. Bartholomew, a patron of Benevento and of the Cathedral since the translation of his relics to Benevento in 832. The singing of hymns in procession is facilitated by rolls no. 6 and 7. The special procession of chrism on Maundy Thursday is accompanied by the hymn *O redemptor sume carmen* sung from roll no. 12.

Equally important is the use of rolls for litanies. Roll no. 3 includes prayers for litanies, evidently said by a celebrant; rolls nos. 4 and 8 contains the litany (or litanies) themselves; on many occasions, and in many churches, litanies are sung in procession, and the practice of using rolls at Benevento suggests that the rolls are carried about as the litany proceeds.

Roll no. 5, including "prayers for the adoration of the cross on Good Friday", may actually be a roll including the solemn prayers which are said as part of the liturgy of Good Friday, though in fact these prayers normally precede the adoration of the cross (which is usually accompanied by singing, not by prayers).[12]

The other liturgical rolls in this list are also for special occasions in the liturgical year. The reading from the book of Exodus used at the ceremony of the blessing of the palms on Palm Sunday is written on roll no. 13; this ceremony normally takes place outside the main church, and the texts needed for this part of the liturgy might well be written on a roll. The Exultet, sung from the ambo by the deacon on Holy Saturday, is written on roll no. 14, and it stands in a long south Italian tradition of Exultet rolls (though this particular roll seems not to survive). The reading "Noveritis fratres carissimi" is also an occasional piece, sung yearly on the feast of the Epiphany to announce the date of Easter and the moveable feasts dependent on that date.[13]

Most of the fifteenth-century library of the Chapter of Benevento is now lost. Of the books detailed in Theuli's inventory, almost none can be identified today with items listed there.[14] Nevertheless, a number of liturgical scrolls do survive, some of which may be identified with items in the fifteenth-century inventory.

A paper envelope kept in the locked manuscript cabinet of the Biblioteca capitolare contains eight small scrolls, each of which is labeled on its dorse. The rolls have no shelf-marks, and the letters assigned here are provisional. These rolls are the following (titles in inverted commas are those written on the rolls themselves).

A. "Concilium provinciale viij Archiepiscopi della Casa": Acts of 1548 synod, in Italian.
B. "exemplum articulorum ... pro Ecclesia Arcipresbyteriali S. Marie oppidi Montenarie de notis Marci Clarutii de Tarano S. Palatii Arci(episcopalis?) Notarii": 16th century.

---

12 The solemn prayers were sung from a roll also at Montecassino, to judge from the fragmentary survival of an eleventh-century roll; see above, note 10.

13 See Jean Claire, 'L'évolution modale dans les récitatifs liturgiques', *Revue grégorienne* 41 (1963), 127-51 at 141 and Tableau Jc.

14 For an introduction to the library and its vicissitudes, see the introduction to Mallet and Thibaut, *Les manuscrits*, I.

170

C. "Exemplum variae Scripturae pro juribus et redditibus S. Marie de Vitulano": 14th-15th century.
D. "Variae collectae sanctorum": later 14th century.
E. "Sequentia Stabat Mater, etc.": 14th/15th century.
F. "Hymni a dominica Passionis ad festum Corporis Christi.": 14th/15th century.
G. "Hymni canendi tempore Paschali, et in die Ascensionis": 14th/15th century.
H. "Antiquus Hymnus: Signum salutis": 17th century?

The first three rolls are notarial documents, but a further five are liturgical scrolls, standing at the end of a long tradition of the use of such scrolls at Benevento and in southern Italy.

Scroll D, written in a single vertical column on one side of the roll, contains a series of collects labeled with liturgical feasts, mostly feasts of saints (see the list in the Appendix). This is clearly a Beneventan series of prayers. It includes collects for major saints in the Beneventan calendar: St. Barbatus, bishop of Benevento (here promoted to archbishop); the translation of St. Bartholomew from Lipari to Benevento; St. Mercurius, whose relics were enshrined in the ducal church of Santa Sofia in the eighth century. The second membrane may be an addition to the first, as it contains (with the exception of a collect for St. Katherine) prayers from the common of saints. Added to this membrane is a series of prayers for the Annunciation and for more recent feasts: (Dominic, Francis), with some additional prayers not included in the surviving portion of the first membrane. The rewriting of one of the prayers (for St. Sebastian) indicates that the roll was still in use as late as the seventeenth century.

The added membrane includes materials that may have been intended for use in processions in time of war: a series of antiphon texts (now mostly illegible), versicles and responses, and a prayer for the protection of this city ("ut ponas in omnes fines istius ciuitatis pacem").

It is possible that this roll is identical with the prayer roll listed in the fifteenth-century inventory and cited as no. 3 above ("Rotus unus cum orationibus pro letaniis"); we do not know that litanies were sung in procession on all these feast-days, nor that these particular prayers were said as part of the litanies; but this roll, and the one listed in the inventory, both contain collects, and perhaps the inventory gives us an idea of the function of a roll containing a single prayer for each feast.

Scroll E is really two separate documents sewn together; each membrane contains a single item, and they are written by different hands. Membrane 1 contains the sequence *Stabat mater dolorosa*, without musical notation; to it is attached a devotional lyric in Italian, addressed by the sinner to the Virgin. Whether such a scroll was intended for liturgical use, at least in its present form, may be doubted; but its purpose was certainly devotional, and the first membrane, by itself, might have had a liturgical function for the singing of the sequence which it contains. This roll cannot be identified with any of those listed in the old inventory.

Scroll F, evidently complete, contains a series of fourteen hymns, in roughly liturgical order. The hymns are generally well-known compositions for major feasts of the proper of the time: there are no specifically Beneventan elements. For each hymn the first strophe is given with musical notation, successive verses being written without notation.

Scroll G is now incomplete; the surviving portion duplicates the closing portion of scroll H: the same hymns, in the same format; one roll might be a copy of the other.

Scrolls F and G may be among the three rolls with hymns (numbers 6 and 7 above) inventoried in 1547; if so, they are probably the "Roti duo cum ympnis pro processionibus" listed as no. 6. Scrolls F and G are about the same size, and neither of them is very large: the other roll with hymns, the "Rotus magnus cum ympnis pro processionibus", must now be lost. The inventory makes it clear that hymns were sung in procession, and these rolls seem likely candidates for use in this way; the presence of two copies suggests choral usage, and perhaps also the alternation of strophes between two groups of singers.

Scroll H, including the Sapphic hymn *Signum salutis*, may not have a specifically liturgical function; it contains no music; the hymn implores God's protection for our dwellings and for our city. It would be entirely suitable for a procession, for a devotional service, or for individual use. The scroll seems to be written in a very late hand, perhaps of the seventeenth or eighteenth century, in imitation of earlier writing. This is a remarkably late persistence of the tradition of using scrolls.

There was a long and tenacious tradition of liturgical scrolls in the city of Benevento. Three rolls survive from the tenth century, an Exulet from the twelfth, and five devotional or liturgical roll from later centuries; the fifteenth-century inventory indicates regular use of rolls in the liturgy of the city. The long use of rolls at Benevento, and the particular uses to which they are put, contribute to what we know about liturgical scrolls in south Italy, and ought for a moment to be considered in this larger context. How does it happen that such scrolls were regularly in use at Benevento and in southern Italy?

The origin of the liturgical scrolls of southern Italy has concerned scholars for a long time, particularly with regard to the south Italian Exulet rolls.[15] The best and most carefully-considered discussion of this matter is by Guglielmo Cavallo,[16] who surveys the liturgical rotulus, east and west, including notice of their use at Milan. Cavallo doubts whether the Exulet-rolls came from an existing Western liturgical tradition; he strongly rejects Baldass's notion of a lost tradition of Exultets descending from Augustine or Ambrose, of antique "Gründtypen" passed on as a patrimony of southern Italy.[17] Surveying Byzantine rolls, Cavallo demonstrates Greek influence in southern Italy; he concludes that the Exulet roll is a phenomenon related to Byzantine practice. "It is probable, that is to say, that hymns or consecration-formulae of the 'Beneventan' liturgy then in use were extracted from the Sacramentary and transcribed

---

15 For surveys of the literature see *Aggiornamento*, 461-3; and the bibliography in *Exultet*.

16 Especially in his article 'La genesi dei rotoli liturgici beneventani alla luce del fenomeno storico-librario in Occidente ed Oriente', *Miscellanea in memoria di Giorgio Cencetti* (Milano: Bottega d'Erasmo, 1973), 213-29 and 4 plates.

17 Peter Baldass, 'Die miniaturen zweier Exultet-Rollen. London add. 30336; Vat. Barb. lat. 592', *Scriptorium* 8 (1954), 75-88, 205-19, pl. 2-7., esp. 215-19; see also Cavallo, *Rotoli*, 43, n. 86.

on rotuli in imitation of a practice far from unknown to Greek ritual".[18] Cavallo sees it as unlikely that Exultet rolls were used before the tenth century, and proposes a Beneventan origin for the Exultet rolls, perhaps under bishop Landolf I (952-82).

Cavallo's survey is measured and well-considered, and I would only add some observations which may broaden the view of this remarkable phenomenon arising from the cultural crossroads of medieval southern Italy.

First, Cavallo's discussion is related mostly to the phenomenon of the Exultet roll, which is really a single aspect of the larger tradition of the liturgical rotulus in the south; the situation at Benevento, where rolls are regularly used for a variety of functions, may be similar to that of other places; we know that at Bari and elsewhere rolls were used for the Exultet and for other functions as well.[19]

Second, I should prefer to emphasize, not the Byzantine connection, but the importance of the link between Milan and Benevento, between the liturgy of the Lombard north and south.

The relation between the old Beneventan liturgy and the rites of Milan has been shown to be a close one, based on musical and textual links.[20] This connection was well known to the scribes and liturgists of the tenth and eleventh centuries, for when they referred to their regional liturgy (that which we call 'Beneventan') they called it 'Ambrosian'; Pope Stephen IX knew it and tried to suppress it in 1058;[21] and there are many more references, in chant books and elsewhere, to the 'Ambrosian' rite as practiced in southern Italy. One of them refers to the Beneventan practice of the Exultet.[22]

Unfortunately we do not have complete books of texts and ceremonies for the Beneventan rite, so we cannot compare difference in ceremonial and usage between it and the Ambrosian practice of Milan; but the closeness of musical and textual practice, and the awareness in southern Italy of the link with Milan, give special importance to what we can learn about the use of the rotulus in the rites of Milan.

Rolls were regularly used in the Ambrosian liturgy of Milan, and surviving sources give a clear view of their employment in worship. The twelfth-century ordinal of Beroldus, the contemporaneous Codex Metropolitanus, and the thirteenth-century

---

18 Cavallo, 'La genesi', 224; my translation. It is not obvious that the Exultet roll should be considered as an extract of the sacramentary. The Exultet is a single text for a unique occasion, not suitable for collection in larger groups; and thus when collections came to be made (from *libelli* or other individual sources) and gathered into sacramentaries, lectionaries, pontificals, rituals, and the like, there is no specifically evident place for the Exultet. The Exultet as a single document is really its most logical form. Further discussion on this subject in Kelly, *The Exultet*, chapter 7 .

19 For some other rolls, see above, note 10.

20 See Kelly, TBC, 181-203; Terence Bailey, 'Ambrosian Chant in Southern Italy', *Journal of the Plainsong & Mediaeval Music Society* 6 (1983), 1-7.

21 *Chronica monasterii Casinensis [Die Chronik von Montecassino]*, ed. Hartmut Hoffmann, Monumenta Germaniae Historica, Scriptores 34 (Hannover: Hahn, 1980), II, 94.

22 "Lectio hec est hereditas que quinta est ordinata secundum romanum legatur hic; secundum ambrosianum legatur post benedictionem cerei" (Vatican City, Bibl. Apostolica Vaticana, Vat. lat. 10673, ff. 34-34v), an explanation of the divergence in lessons for Holy Saturday and the placement of the Exultet between the Roman and the local rites. Kelly, TBC, 181-82 cites all known references in the south to 'Ambrosian' practice.

The Liturgical Rotulus at Benevento

"Beroldus novus" all describe the use of the rotulus in the Milanese liturgy. The rotulus contained collects which the archbishop or his vice-presbyter said at the office hours, and at supplications called *litaniae*. At vespers, for instance, a *rotulus orationum* is placed on the altar by the *minor custodum*, and the priest takes it up to say the prayer; the same *custos* takes it back from the priest later.[23] When the archbishop himself is present, his *rotularius* holds the roll for him while he says the prayer.[24] There are references also to a *rotulus letaniarum*, which is perhaps a different document from the *rotulus orationum*.[25] Indeed, according to one passage there seem to be at least three separate litany-rolls, for use in three separate weeks.[26] A rotulus is also used for the Exultet at the Easter vigil, as is made clear both in Beroldus and Beroldus novus:

> ...et unus subdiaconus ebdomadarius debet portare rotulum similiter indutus alba, et debet tenere ipsum rotulum ante diaconum, donec legerit, et benedixerit ceram et ignem [here "Beroldus novus" clarifies by adding] dicendo sic: *Exultet iam*, etc.[27]

Because of the close connection of the Milanese liturgy with the Beneventan liturgy of south Italy, we cannot ignore their relationship as regards the rotulus and the Exultet. In the circumstances the Milanese liturgist Marco Magistretti justly regretted that no trace of any one of these Milanese rotuli seems to have survived.[28] It may be, of course, that one day a fragment may be discovered in a binding or a flyleaf, disguised by the survival of only a page-sized fragment. There are reports that such rolls do survive. Huglo and his colleagues report that manuscript Z 256 sup. of the Biblioteca Ambrosiana consists of two rolls with litanies for the last days of holy week;[29] and Niels Krogh Rasmussen has remarked that the inventory of the Biblioteca

---

23 Marcus Magistretti, *Beroldus sive ecclesiae ambrosianae mediolanensis kalendarium et ordines saec. XII* (Milan: Josephi Giovanola, 1894), 55-6.

24 "... sed si archiepiscopus adfuerit, rotularius ejus porrigit ei": Magistretti, *Beroldus*, 57; "Sed si archiepiscopus aderit, idem custos porrigit rotulario, et rotularius archiepiscopo": *Beroldus*, 59.

25 This is not easy to determine, since the *rotulus orationum* is specifically referred to as lying on the altar at Vespers (Magistretti, *Beroldus*, 55), while the *rotulus letaniarum* (*Beroldus*, 57, 89, 91) is also referred to as a *rotulus letaniarum et vespertinum* both in the Beroldus ordinal (*Beroldus*, 59) and in the Codex Metropolitanus (*Beroldus*, 84); this rotulus might be the same document, then, containing prayers and the necessary materials for the litanies.

26 *Beroldus*, 89.

27 *Beroldus*, 110; the passage from "Beroldus novus" is cited in Marcus Magistretti, *Manuale ambrosianum ex codice saec. XI olim in usum canonicae vallis travaliae*, Monumenta veteris liturgiae ambrosianae 2-3 (Milan: Hoepli, 1904-1905), II, 198, n. 1.

28 "Dolendum quod nullum exemplar huiusmodi *rotuli* ambrosiani ad nos pervenireret": Magistretti, *Manuale*, II, 7; however, a libellus of litanies (London, British Library, Egerton 3762, of the early 11th century) may be a descendant of the separate rotulus: see Klaus Gamber, *Codices liturgici latini antiquiores* (= CLLA), Spicilegii Friburgensis Subsidia 1 (2 vols. in 3 parts, Freiburg Schweiz: Universitätsverlag, vols. 1,1 and 1,2, 2nd edn. 1968; vol. 1A [Supplementum], 1988); no. 577, p. 281-2.

29 Michel Huglo, Luigi Agustoni, Eugène Cardine, Ernesto Moneta Caglio, *Fonti e paleografia del canto ambrosiano*, Archivio ambrosiano 7 (Milan: n. p., 1956), 259. I have not been able to verify the content of this document.

capitolare mentions several rolls for the use of celebrants in the cathedral.[30]
The documents describing the Milanese use of the rotulus date only from the twelfth century and later, but they are the oldest surviving ceremonial descriptions from a liturgy very much older; although they may represent a re-arrangement of an older ordo (accounting in part for differences between Milan and Benevento), it seems unlikely that the archaizing rotulus should be adopted at Milan only in the twelfth century. Much more likely is that it had been in regular use for a long time. One use of the roll, for litanies, might have a long ancestry; the litanies of Pentecost week can be traced back to the time of bishop Lazarus (438-49),[31] and perhaps the litany-rolls were used continuously ever since.

The use of the rotulus in southern Italy has many similarities to its use at Milan:

1. **Rolls have a regular place in the liturgy**. The Milanese documents make clear that the liturgy regularly requires the use of a rotulus for vespers, for litanies, for prayers said by the archbishop, for the Exultet. Although there are occasional witnesses to the use of rolls in the liturgy elsewhere in Latin Europe, the largest suviving collection from the earlier middle ages is of southern Italian origin: several pontifical rolls (two from Benevento, one from Bari), a roll of prayers for Good Friday (at Montecassino), and twenty-six Exultet rolls. In addition to these, the liturgical rolls inventoried at Benevento in the fifteenth century (of which three were used for litanies), suggest the frequent and continuous use of rolls in the liturgy there.

2. **The use of the roll is focused on the (arch)bishop**. The liturgical rolls of southern Italy are also closely related to the bishop or archbishop. Not only are there specifically pontifical rolls from Benevento and Bari, but the Exultet rolls themselves often have a very close relation with the bishop, and seem in some sense to be his property.[32]

3. **A roll is used for the singing of the Exultet**. Nowhere else in Europe is the Exultet regularly sung from a roll, so far as we know, except for Milan and southern Italy: that is to say, in the two related liturgies of the Lombards.[33] We have no surviving Milanese Exultet rolls, but we know that the Exultet was sung from a roll. The Beneventan Exultet rolls survive doubtless because of their beautiful illustrations: we can surmise that the Milanese rolls were not items of such luxurious production — but they *were* rolls.

4. **The roll is laid upon the altar before being used**. At Milan it is the custom to

---

30 'Les pontificaux du haut moyen âge. Genèse du livre de l'évêque' (unpubl. diss., Institut Catholique de Paris, 1977), 425, n. 32. Giovanni Mercati thought that perhaps the Ambrosian dedication ordo appended to Lucca, Bibl. capitolare, 605 (edited in Giovanni Mercati, *Antiche reliquie liturgiche ambrosiane e romane*, Studi e testi 7, Roma: Typografia Vaticana, 1902, 5-27), might be the transcription of a roll (p. 15). Alberto Turco has kindly informed me that the Biblioteca capitolare now contains no rolls.

31 Gamber, CLLA, 281.

32 See Brenk, 'Bischöfliche'; Kelly, *The Exultet*.

33 The only Exultet rolls not in Beneventan script are two from Pisa (where a Beneventan Exultet roll has lain since the eleventh century: see Anna Rosa Calderoni Masetti in *Exultet*, 457-75) and the late Neapolitan Vat. lat. 3784A, in Gothic script (see Lucinia Speciale in *Exultet*, 445-55 with facsimile).

place the roll on the altar, whence it is taken by the priest or the the rotularius.[34] The similar practice of laying the Exultet on the altar at Montecassino and related churches[35] may well be more than coincidence.

In view of these facts it seems hardly necessary to posit a Byzantine influence to explain the existence of liturgical rolls in southern Italy in the tenth century. Byzantine influence there undoubtedly was, and scrolls were indeed used in the Byzantine liturgy — though not usually for the same functions as in the West.

There is clearly a tradition in Lombard lands, north and south, of using rolls in the liturgy. These traditions are related in their practices, and they reflect the link of the northern and southern Lombards before the fall of the northern Lombard capital of Pavia to Charlemagne in 774 and the consequent establishment of an independent Lombard state ruled from Benevento. The ultimate origin of such a practice might well go back to a time when rolls were much more common; there might well be Greek influences in the tradition; but the phenomenon is not so much south Italian as it is Lombard.

That the cathedral of Benevento should preserve this tradition actively, elegantly, and prolongedly, is a mark of the conservatism of this ancient Lombard capital. The same city that preserved the older Beneventan liturgy (itself related to Lombard practices) made beautiful pontifical and Exultet rolls in the earlier Middle Ages, and continued the use of rolls for litanies, prayers, hymns, and the Exultet, for a longer time than we had previously imagined.

Appendix: Rolls at the Biblioteca Capitolare, Benevento

The following rolls are kept in the armored cabinet ("armoire blindée") in the Biblioteca capitolare; they are in a paper envelope, and are not numbered. The numbers below are provisional. Titles given below in inverted commas are those written on the outside of the roll in a later hand.

A. *"Concilium prouinciale uiij Archiepiscopi della Casa"*: Acts of 1548 synod, in Italian.
12 membranes glued together, 13-15mm wide by 28.5 + 47.5 + 51 + 46.5 + 45.5 + 50+ 47.5 + 52.5 + 51 + 65.5 + 64 + 51 mm.

B. *"exemplum articulorum . . . pro Ecclesia Arcipresbyteriali S. Marie oppidi Montenarie de notis Marci Clarutii de Tarano S. Palatii Arci(episcopalis?) Notarii"*: 16th century.

34 "Et notandum, quia antequam vesperum incipiatur, minor custos ebdomadarius ponit rotulum orationum super altare ...": Magistretti, *Beroldus*, 55; "Sed praesciendum quia minor custos ebdomadarius ponit rotulum letaniarum super altare uniuscujusque diei ..." *Beroldus*, 57.

35 Many documents from Montecassino, Benevento, Montevergine, and elsewhere contain the direction "Tunc diaconus postulata benedictione a sacerdote tollat benedictionem cerei desuper altare". Sources include Paris, Bibl. Mazarine, 364 (1099-1105); Vatican Urb. lat. 585 (1099-1105); Montecassino 198 (ordinal, s12/13); Vatican Barb. lat. 631, p. 75-76 (Pontifical, s11ex); Montecassino 127 (Missale, s11ex); Montecassino 198 (ordo officii s12/13); Montecassino 562 (ordinal, s13); Benevento 66 (ordinal, S Pietro, Benevento, s12); Malibu, J. Paul Getty Museum, IX. 1 (ordinal, anno 1153). Modern editions of this portion of the text are found in Teodoro Leutermann, *Ordo casinensis hebdomadae maioris*, Miscellanea cassinese 20 (Montecassino: Badia di Montecassino, 1941); from Vat. Barb. lat. 631 ed. Michel Andrieu, *Le pontifical romain au moyen-âge*, Studi e testi 86-88, 99 (Vatican City: Biblioteca Apostolica Vaticana, 1938-41), I, 292-3.

The Liturgical Rotulus at Benevento

8 membranes glued together, incomplete at beginning, 15 mm wide x 26 + 36 + 48.5 + 40 + 37 + 35 + 47 + 69 + 15 mm.

C. *"Exemplum uariae Scripturae pro juribus et redditibus S. Marie de Vitulano"*: 14th-15th century.
4 membranes sewed together, the first (15 wide x 12 mm) smaller and in a different writing from the four following, which measure 19 mm wide x 54.5 + 39 + 79.

D. *"Variae collectae sanctorum"*: later 14th century.
2 membranes sewed together (14.5-15 mm x 46 + 45 mm), with a third piece (13 mm wide x 31.5 mm) attached, writing-side-up, at the bottom of the second membrane so as to cover a portion of the second membrane. The two original pieces, much rubbed, are repaired with paper. The third piece is also much worn. The roll is incomplete at the beginning. It includes collects for feasts of saints, including:

Membrane 1
de Angelis
de sancto Petro
de sancto Paulo
de sancto Jacobo
translationis sancti Bartholomei de Lipari
    Beneuentum
alia oratio (for St. Bartholomew)
De sancta Maria
de sancta Maria post pascha
in Ramis palmarum
de sancto Andrea
de sancto Donato
de sancto Thoma
de sancto Augustino
de sanctis apostolis Symone et Iuda
de sancto Mercurio
de sancto Iohanne apostolo et euangelista
de sancto Barbato archiepiscopo et
confessore Beneventano
    De sancto Ianuario
    De sancto Stephano prothomartire

Membrane 2
    de sancta Katherina

de plurimorum apostolorum
de uno martire pontifice
de plurimorum martirum
de confessore pontifice
de confessore non pontifice
    si fuerit abbas
pro uirgine et martire
pro uirgine et non martire
[additions in later hand:]
in annunciacione beate marie uirginis
de sancto Dominico
de sancto Francisco
de sancto Iohanne baptiste
pro sancto Petro apostolo
pro sancto Laurencio
[in a third hand, written over earlier writing:]
pro sancto Sebastiano
[in a fourth hand:]
O mira refulsit gratia martir inclitus
sebastianus [with musical notation].

Membrane 3
Added, in a fifth hand: antiphons, versicles, prayers, (in time of war?)

E. *"Sequentia Stabat Mater, etc."*: 14th-15th century.
2 membranes sewed together, 11.5 mm wide x 43 + 38, incomplete at the end. Sewing marks at the top of the first membrane indicate that it was joined to another membrane, and was thus attached to another roll or is itself the continuation of a roll whose beginning is lacking.

The roll is really two separate documents attached together; each membrane contains a single item, and each is in a different hand. Membrane 1 contains the sequence *Stabat mater dolorosa*, without musical notation.

Membrane 2 contains a devotional metrical text in Italian. A Latin title, "Dicunt peccatores beate Marie" is prefixed at the end of membrane 1. The beginning of the poem is mutilated by a repair in the parchment; the opening strophe reads:

Maria virgo pia
pace virgene maria
non guarda(te?) nostri cuori
maria anda[...] gridando

maria non [...]dando
maria [...] clamando
Maria a lo peccatore
The poem is incomplete at the end, breaking off in the middle of the nineteenth stanza. I have not identified this text; it is not found in Fabio Carboni, *Incipitario della lirica italiana dei secoli XIII e XIV*, 2 vols., Studi e testi 277, 288 (Città del Vaticano : Biblioteca apostolica vaticana, 1977-1980; idem, *Incipitario della lirica italiana dei secoli XV-XX*, 10 vols. to date, Studi e testi 297-299, 299 bis, 321, 330, 334-335, 349-350 (Città del Vaticano: Biblioteca apostolica vaticana, 1982-); nor in the several volumes of trecento devotional poetry I have been able to consult. I am grateful to Professor Robert Kendrick for his help in seeking other sources for this text.

F. *"Hymni a dominica Passionis ad festum Corporis Christi"*: 14th-15th century.
3 membranes, 20-21 mm wide x 52 + 48 + 47.5 mm. The membranes are glued together, and have been repaired with paper and parchment.
This roll, evidently complete, contains a series of hymns. For each hymn the first strophe is given with musical notation, sucessive verses being written without notation. The hymns contained here, with their rubrics, are:
Dominica de Passione hymnum. *Vexilla regis prodeunt*
Hymnum. *Pange lingua gloriosi prelium certaminis*
Ym. *Lustris sex qui iam peractis*
In tempore paschali ymnum. *Ad cenam agni prouidi*
Hymnum. *Rex eterne glorie* (melody of *Ad cenam agni*, but the first note is missing in the notation to match the text, even though all subsequent strophes require it).
Ymnus. *Aurora lucis rutilat*
Hymnus. *Ihesu nostra redemptio*
Eterne rex altissime
In Pentecostes hymnum. *Veni creator spiritus*
Hymnum. *Iam Christus astra ascenderat*
Hymnus. *Beata nobis gaudia*
In festo Corporis Christi hymnum. *Pange lingua gloriosi corporis misterium*
Ymnum. *Sacris sollempnis uincta sint gaudia*
Hymnum. *Verbum supernum prodiens*

G. *"Hymni canendi tompore Paschali, et in die Ascensionis"*: 14th-15th century
Two membranes sewed together, 26.5-27 mm x 55.5 + 55 mm. The roll begins incomplete, and stitching marks indicate that it was sewed to a previous membrane.
This roll contains a series of hymns. For each hymn the first strophe is given with musical notation, sucessive verses being written without notation. The hymns contained here, with their rubrics, are:
Lustris sex qui iam peractis (begins incomplete)
In tempore paschali ymnus. *Ad cenam agni prouidi*
Ymnus. *Rex aeterne glorie*
Ymnus. *Aurora lucis rutilat.*
In ascensione domini ymnus. *Ihesu nostra redemptio*
Ymnus. *Eterne rex altissime*
These hymns are the same, in the same order, as those found on Roll F. Perhaps more than one copy was used at a given time.

H. *"Antiquus Hymnus: Signum salutis"*: 17th century?
One membrane, 8.5 x 52 mm. Damaged and repaired at both ends.
This single strip contains the text of the hymn *Signum salutis* without musical notation.

Fig. 1: Benevento, Biblioteca Capitolare, Roll A. "Concilium provinciale viij Archiepiscopi della Casa". Acts of 1548 synod, in Italian.

179

The Liturgical Rotulus at Benevento

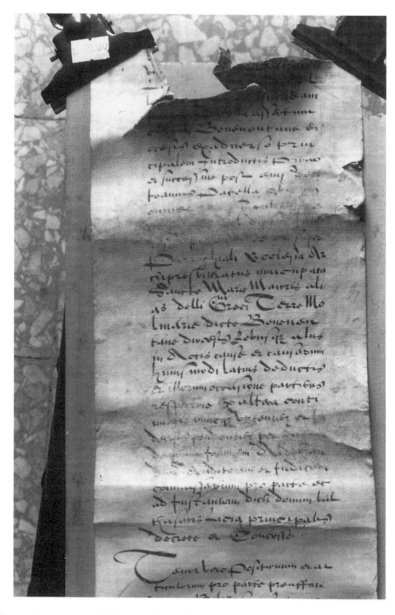

Fig. 2: Benevento, Biblioteca Capitolare, Roll B. "exemplum articulorum . . . pro Ecclesia Arcipresbyteriali S. Marie oppidi Montenarie de notis Marci Clarutii de Tarano S. Palatii Arci(episcopalis?) Notarii", 16th century.

The Liturgical Rotulus at Benevento

Fig. 3: Benevento, Biblioteca Capitolare, Roll C. "Exemplum variae Scripturae
pro juribus et redditibus S. Marie de Vitulano", 14th-15th century.

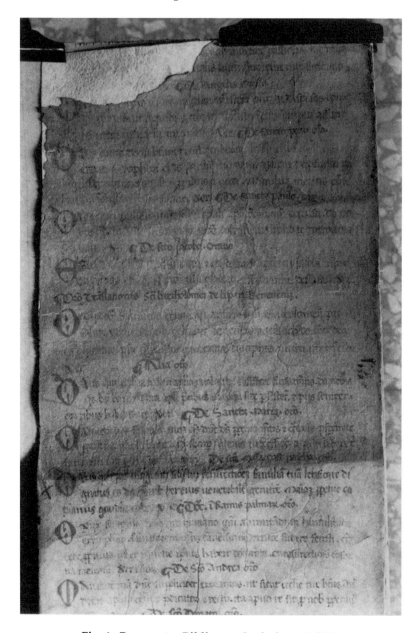

Fig. 4: Benevento, Biblioteca Capitolare, Roll D.
"Variae collectae sanctorum", later 14th century.

The Liturgical Rotulus at Benevento

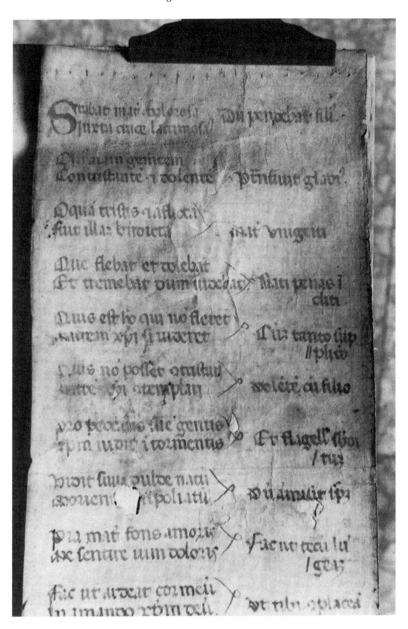

Fig. 5: Benevento, Biblioteca Capitolare, Roll E.
"Sequentia Stabat Mater, etc.", 14th/15th century.

X

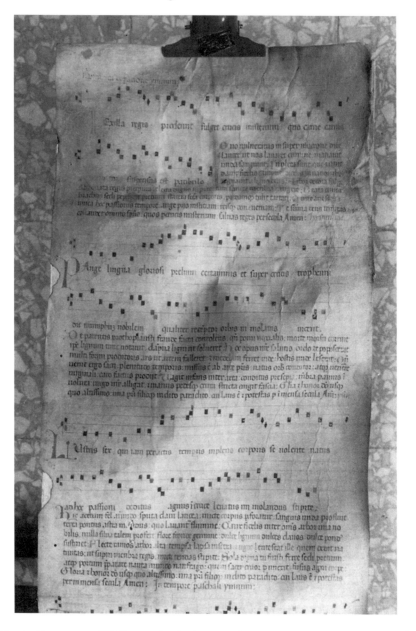

Fig. 6: Benevento, Biblioteca Capitolare, Roll F. "Hymni a dominica Passionis ad festum Corporis Christi", 14th/15th century.

The Liturgical Rotulus at Benevento

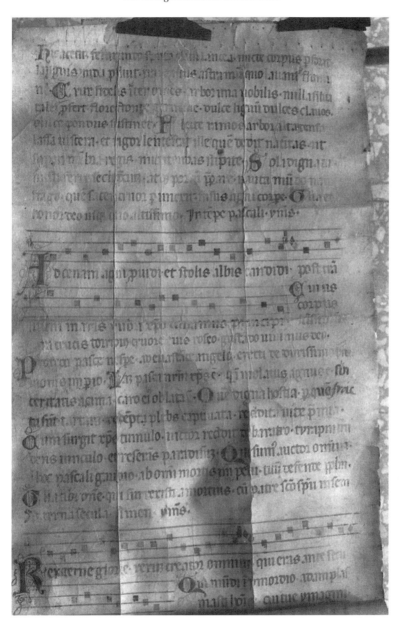

Fig. 7: Benevento, Biblioteca Capitolare, Roll G. "Hymni canendi tempore Paschali, et in die Ascensionis", 14th/15th century ?

X

The Liturgical Rotulus at Benevento

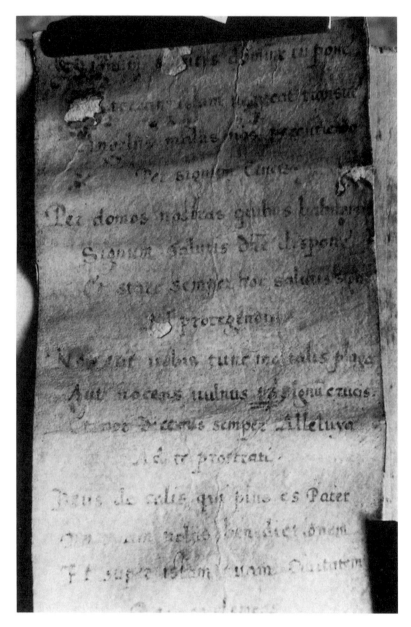

Fig. 8: Benevento, Biblioteca Capitolare, Roll H.
"Antiquus Hymnus: Signum salutis", 17th century?

XI

A MILANESE PROCESSIONAL ROLL AT THE BEINECKE LIBRARY

Manuscript 810 of the Beinecke Library, acquired in 1995, is a rotulus made about 1300 containing music for use in the three-day litany processions of the Ambrosian liturgy of the region of Milan. This is the only complete roll of this kind,[1] and it is a record of the musical items required for these processions. It is a highly important witness of the use of rolls in the Milanese liturgy, and its specific contents confirm and increase our understanding of this specific Milanese practice.

MEDIEVAL ROLLS

The roll (or scroll or rotulus) is an unusual form in the middle ages.[2] Although rolls were the standard way of recording a long text in the ancient world, in Egypt, and in the Middle East, by the fourth century the codex had become the usual form for organizing a long text on parchment. The codex has clear advantages: instant access to any place in the text; the use of both sides of the parchment; and relatively small size, and the codex has been the standard for literary texts until our own day. It remains to be seen whether the return to the scroll on the modern computer will affect the way texts are perceived and duplicated.

In the middle ages, then, to make a roll was to choose an unusual format. There are, however, several hundred surviving medieval rolls, and there is generally a clearly discernible reason for choosing the unusual format of the roll.

Medieval rolls generally can be said to fall into one or more of the following categories, each of which has to do with the relation of the text to be written with the format chosen:

Documents indeterminate with respect to length. Many notarial and archival documents are recorded on rolls. Rent-rolls, inventory rolls, and the like can be formed by adding a membrane to a growing series. (To "enroll" is to add to a list.) The medieval obituary rolls of French and other monasteries were designed to be lengthened by written condolences as the traveling roll-bearer brought the written news of a death to a succession of destinations.

Documents whose format suggests roll-form. Maps, pilgrims' guides, histories, and genealogies are all sometimes written in roll form, to give a visual representation of space, physical or chronological. Some, such as the fifteenth-century genealogies of the English crown, or the many exemplars of Peter of Poitiers's *Compendium historiae*, are among the most lavishly illustrated rolls of the middle ages.

Archaizing ceremonial documents. As modern diplomas are written on rolled vellum, so a certain mark of distinction was given by the use of roll form in medieval documents. Certain liturgical texts for the use of high ecclesiastics or in special liturgical ceremonies are written on scrolls. The Byzantine liturgy regularly used scrolls for the text of the eucharistic liturgy, and the magnificent illustrated Exultet scrolls of southern Italy are the best-known examples of this ceremonial genre.

Portable documents. Actors' parts ("rôles"), poems to be recited, songs, and charms to be worn around the neck, were sometimes written on scrolls. Scrolls of the life of Saint Margaret were used as a protection during pregnancy and childbirth; and there were amulet-scrolls of the precise length of the body of Christ. Portability was also the intent of many liturgical scrolls which contain the chants used for certain processions or the prayers used in special ceremonies, particularly when these actions took place outside the normal ecclesiastical setting.

The Beinecke roll is an example of the last of these categories. It contains chants to be sung for the three-day series of processions known as *Letaniae* in the Ambrosian liturgy. Since these processions went from place to place over the course of three days, it was convenient to assemble the necessary liturgical materials in a form easy to carry from church to church. But since the ceremonies in which the roll was used were of great antiquity and solemnity, the use of the roll surely has an archaizing and ceremonial significance as well.

Rolls in the Liturgy of Milan

Although the Ambrosian rite of Milan used the rotulus in a number of its special rites, almost none of these rolls survives. The Beinecke manuscript is thus one of the very rare witnesses of a practice that is reported to us in other documents but whose physical evidence is much strengthened by the discovery of this new document.

The Carolingian imposition of the Roman rite on the entire realm, with the purpose of insuring uniformity and cohesion, swept away much evidence of the many local liturgical practices that had been a characteristic feature of the early-medieval ecclesiastical landscape. Despite their suppression, evidence of these earlier local or regional practices survives from the Old Spanish liturgy, the Beneventan liturgy, and the so-called Gallican liturgy. Only the Ambrosian rite, jealously protected in the area of Milan, was never suppressed, and it continues in limited use to this day. Under the protection of Saint Ambrose, bishop of Milan, the local rite was able to hold its own against the influence of the rite whose music was identified with Pope Gregory the Great. The Gregorian liturgy was elsewhere essentially universal by the end of the eleventh century, but at Milan the local liturgy and its chant were maintained.

A wealth of medieval books gives us a clear idea of what the Ambrosian liturgy was like. In particular, we know that scrolls were regularly used for particular places in the Milanese liturgy. The twelfth-century ordinal of Beroldus (Milan, Biblioteca Ambrosiana MS I. 152. inf.), along with the contemporaneous Codex Metropolitanus (Milan, Biblioteca Capitolare S.N.) and the thirteenth-century "Beroldus novus," all give evidence of how rolls were used.

On Holy Saturday a roll was used for the singing of *Exultet*, the blessing of the pashcal candle:[3]

> ... and one of the weekly subdeacons should carry the roll likewise vested in an alb, and should hold that roll before the deacon, while he sings, and blesses the wax and the fire, saying thus: *Exultet iam angelica turba coelorum*, etc.[4]

At vespers a roll (the *rotulus orationum*) was placed on the altar so that the officiant might use it to say the prayer:

> And note that before Vespers begins, the lesser *custos* of the week[5] places the rotulus of prayers on the altar, unless there be proper prayers. And the priest takes up the same rotulus from the altar, when he says the prayer.[6]

A *rotulus letaniarum* was used by a deacon for the ceremonies called letaniae which replaced the *Gloria in excelsis* on Lenten Sundays.[7] And what is probably the same litany-roll (or rather, a set of litany-rolls) is used on Ash Wednesday and on Wednesdays and Fridays of Lent for litany-processions.[8] The same litany ceremonies are performed on three weekdays before Christmas.[9]

The litany-rolls are also used on the vigils of important feasts, when a procession is made to the church of the saint who is celebrated. On these occasions the archbishop himself, if he is present, says the prayer from the roll, which is handed to him by his *rotularius*.[10]

These litany-rolls, used on several occasions throughout the year, are principally designed for use in the three great processions known as the *triduum letaniarum*, and it is for these days that the Beinecke rolls are designed.

The Letaniae Triduanae of Milan

The three-day litanies of the Milanese church are related to the so-called lesser litanies, or Rogation Days, an ancient Gallican practice.[11] They consist of a three-day series of processions in which litanies, antiphons, and other types of music are sung. These are from early times days of fasting, prayer, and repentance.[12] The greater litany is associated with 25 April, the ancient Roman festival for the renewal of the earth. The lesser litanies, observed in the Roman rite in the week before Ascension Day, are observed at Milan a week later, in the week before Pentecost, where they are called "Letaniae triduanae"; they are not considered "lesser" at Milan, even though the litanies of 25 April are also observed there.[13]

The three-day litanies consist of a series of processions that involved the whole clergy and city of Milan.[14] Centering on the cathedral, it involved a long procession on each of three days; each day's procession followed a different route, visiting some thirty-two churches of the city; each day's procession concluded with the celebration of mass at one of the city's churches: the first day at St Ambrose, the second at St Nazarius, and finally at St Lawrence. A map of the three processional routes is shown on page 18.[15]

In each church visited, the procession entered the church while a *psallenda* was sung in honor of the saint to whom the church was dedicated; then followed a ceremony essentially consisting of a fore-mass: a litany proper to the church; a prayer, a reading from the Old Testament, a responsory, and a Gospel-reading.[16]

The ceremonies accompanying these processions were elaborate, and involved most of the functionaries of the Milanese cathedral and its clergy. The description of the ceremonies and the funtionaries in the *Beroldus* ordinal includes the following:[17]

> On the first day of the litanies, the two major custodes and eight of the lesser should gather clean and sifted ashes, which the ebdomadarius priest should bless, and of the said custodes two should be ebdomadarii, then the two others that follow [in seniority?] should get the ashes and perform the other tasks. The blessing of the ashes: *Omnipotens et misericors Deus*. When the blessing is finished and the litanies begun, one of the mentioned custodes offers ashes to the archbishop, who himself imposes ashes in the form of the cross on the foreheads of majorum clericorum and the primicerii of the priests and the archdeacon. Then the primicerius of the priests imposes ashes on the heads of the priests and the clergy under his jurisdiction. For the remaining, laity and women, the said custos continually carries and imposes ashes until [the church of] Saint Simplicianus. And the same custos with his associate always hands the gospel to the deacon [levitae], and after the gospel is read he takes it back, and places it on the altar, and says *Silen-*

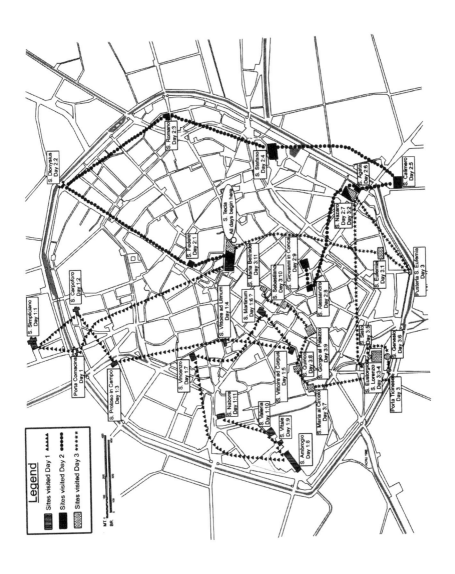

tium habete, in the church of St Ambrose, and St Nazarius, and St Lawrence, before *Parcite fabulis*, and after the salutation of the deacon.

And in these three days the ebdomadarius and the chief doorkeeper take turns carrying the golden cross before the cardinal priests and deacons, and one of them should always dine with the archbishop, but on the third day, both of them. And the two persons who are behind them who carry the ashes, should carry one cross before the subdeacons, and another before the notaries, and should dine with them. And the two lesser ebdomadarii likewise should carry a cross before the primicerius of the priests, one of whom on the third day will dine with them, and will give twelve denarii. Likewise two lesser doorkeepers shall take turns carrying a cross before the viscount, and one of them on the third day shall dine with him.

Note further, that the archbishop in these two days takes the gospel-book from all the altars at which he prays, and gives it to the subdeacon—it having previously been placed there by the same subdeacon—and likewise all the subdeacons in turn carry the gospel-book and the staff [baculum] of St Ambrose to all the churches; and the ordinarioli [=notarii?] likewise take turns carrying the pallium, and they cover the altars, except for the ebdomadarius.

And be it known, that the secundicerius reads the first lection, and the notarius sings the responsory; then the notarius reads the second lection, and the lector the responsory. And thus they continue to take turns reading and singing until the last [lection], except the four lections of the primicerius of the lectors, namely at St Victor *ad corpus*, and at St Stephen, and at St Eustorgius, and at St George. And the deacons likewise take turns reading the gospels. And the *rotularius* of the archbishop always carries the rotulus, and ministers to the archbishop; but if the archbishop is absent, he who carries the golden cross carries the same rotulus, and places it on the various altars, from which the priest takes it and says the prayers.

And the chaplain of St Michael *de domo* offers to the archbishop a chalice and two unconsecrated hosts, and the primicerius decumanorum [gives him] two denarios, which the archbishop places with the chalice on the altar of each church, and says: *Requiem etarnam dona ei, Domine. Et lux perpetua luceat ei. Anima eius requiescat in pace.* And the deacon who is to read the gospel in the next church goes with the archbishop to the individual altars to pray, with the subdeacon who carries the gospel-book and the staff.

In those same days everything is from the daily office at matutinum and vespers, except a proper responsory at vespers on the first and second day. When the litanies are finished, *Benedicat et exaudiat nos Deus* is not said on the first or second day, but rather the mass is begun, and it is said without proper chants [*sine officio*] except for the canticum. On the third day, however, they [the litanies] conclude with *Benedicat et exaudiat nos Deus*.

During the procession from church to church a great many musical pieces were sung, and this is the music contained on the Beinecke rolls. The music consists of a long series of antiphons, generally of a penitential cast; in the course of these antiphons, responsories are included for singing at the ceremonies within each church.

This music for the processions themselves seems to be a standard series in the Milanese liturgy of the later Middle Ages. The Beinecke rolls preserve the same music that is indicated in other sources for the litany processions. Musical sources used for comparison in this paper include:

London, British Library MS Egerton 3763, a richly illustrated booklet of the early 11th century including portions of the psalter, and a complete set of litanies, prayers, and music for the litany processions.[18]

Milan, Biblioteca del Capitolo metropolitano MS 2102, a *manuale* from Val Travaglia of the 11th century.[19] A "handbook" of the Ambrosian liturgy, rich in ceremonial rubrics. The *manuale* names the series of processional antiphons, and also describes the processional route by indicating which music is to be sung on the way to the next church, naming each church in turn. Litanies, prayers, and responsories for use in each stational church are also given.

Oxford, Bodleian Library MS lat. liturg. a.4. An Ambrosian chant-book of the late 14th century. Like most such books, this one contains all the music for mass and office for half the year. The antiphons and responsories are given in full with musical notation, and they are essentially the same series as in the Beinecke rolls.

Vendrogno, the Muggiasca manuscript, a complete Ambrosian antiphoner copied 1398-99 for the church of St Lawrence, Muggiasca.

Milan, Biblioteca Ambrosiana MS Z 256 supra. Two rolls of the 14th-15th century containing music for the litany processions.[20] Unlike the other sources, these rolls include, in addition to the processional music, the *psallenda* to be sung at the entrance to each church in honor of its titular saint.

The Beinecke Rolls

The three Beinecke MS 810 rolls constitute the only complete set of rolls for the processional music for the Ambrosian litanies, each containing the music for one of the three litany processions. The roll was originally a single document, as is evident from the irregular cutting of membranes which fit together perfectly. The original roll measures some 676 cm in length, and varies in width between about 15 cm at its outer end and 16.5 cm toward its center.

The roll is made of 16 membranes, attached end-to-end with glue. The membranes are roughly 45 centimeters in length, except for the first and the last three, which are about 37 cm long. (Adding the total length of the membranes does not measure the length of the roll, since each membrane is overlapped by about 2 cm with its neighbors.) To the top of the roll is sewn a piece of dark-brown leather serving as a cover, and the end of the roll is attached to an apparently original wooden umbilicus. The worn edges of the roll are repaired here and there with medieval parchment. The membranes were assembled before writing (except where blank space is left at the end of membrane 10 and the beginning of membrane 11) so that nothing is written on the overlapping portions.

Vertical rules are drawn in light-brown ink at the left and right, leaving a margin of about 1 cm on each side, and providing a writing space 14 cm wide. Evenly spaced text-rules are drawn in the same light-brown ink; a system of six lines is used for text and music, five lines being used for the musical staff and the sixth for aligning the text. A system of six lines occupies 2.6 cm. A dark-brown ink is used for text and musical notation, and is sometimes much rubbed and worn. Red ink is used for rubrics and to label musical pieces "a" (for antiphon) and "R" (for responsory); the same red ink is used to indicate the level of the musical pitch F by inking in the appropriate line in the musical staff. Traces of a yellow pitch-line for the note C are occasionally visible.

The text is written in an Italian Gothic hand, and the musical notation is characteristic of the notation of the region of Milan around 1300.

The roll was written, as is typical, on one side only, beginning with what would be the outside end; evidently membranes were joined before writing. Perhaps the full length of the roll was assembled and glued before writing began, since the length of the roll is not sufficient for the complete music for these ceremonies; and at the end of Roll C, the scribe turned the roll over and wrote the rest of the text and music on the back, beginning at the beginning of membrane 11, and writing in the same direction as the front.

This means that the rolls could not have been used as separate documents, cut apart as they are now; at least the third day of the litanies is not complete on Roll C. The continuation of the third day begins in the middle of the back of Roll B, and continues on the back of Roll C. The following diagram may help to explain this system:

Roll A: *Die primo letaniarum*
        Membrane 1   37 cm
        Membrane 2   44 cm
        Membrane 3   44 cm
        Membrane 4   44 cm
        Membrane 5   44 cm
        Membrane 6   44 cm
        Membrane 7   33.5 cm
Roll B: *Die secundo letaniarum*
        Membrane 7,
           continued   9.5 cm

Membrane 8	43.5 cm
Membrane 9	46.2 cm
Membrane 10	43.5 cm
Membrane 11	40.75 cm (continuation of *Die tertio* begins on back)
Membrane 12	45 cm
Membrane 13	23 cm

Roll C: *Die tertio letaniarum*

Membrane 13, continued	22.5 cm
Membrane 14	37 cm
Membrane 15	37 cm (*Die tertio* ends on the back of this membrane)
Membrane 16	37 cm

These rolls contain the antiphons to be sung as the procession moves from one church to another; and they also contain the responsories sung, after a lection and before the gospel, as part of the stational liturgy in each church. (They do not contain, as do the rolls in the Biblioteca Ambrosiana, the psallendae proper to each church which were sung at the beginning of each stational liturgy.)

A later hand has added to the responsories in the Beinecke rolls an indication of the functionaries who are to sing the responsories. The Beroldus ordinal cited above indicated that the responsories are to be sung by turns:

> And be it known, that the secundicerius [the second-ranking of the lectors] reads the first lection, and the notarius sings the responsory; then the notarius reads the second lection, and the lector the responsory. And thus they continue to take turns reading and singing until the last [lection], except the four lections of the primicerius of the lectors, namely at St Victor *ad corpus*, and at St Stephen, and at St Eustorgius, and at St George. And the deacons likewise take turns reading the gospels.[21]

There is thus an alternation between those who hold the office of *lector* and those who are *notarii*, taking turns with reading the first lection and the singing of the following responsory. Here a lector reads, a notary sings; and in the next church, the next notary reads and the next lector sings, and so on. This alternation is indicated in the Beinecke roll by the additions of abbreviations ".L.", ".N.", etc) indicating which dignitary is to sing which responsory. On three occasions, however, the alternation is interrupted by subdeacons or deacons who are to sing, at the churches of St Protasius in Campo (Day 1), St Stephen and the basilica of the Apostles at St Nazarius (Day 2). With the exception of St Stephen, these are not the churches where a full mass is sung, nor (again with the exception of St Stephen) are they the churches where the Beroldus ordinal specifies a special privilege of the *primicerius lectorum*. Evidently there has been some change in the ceremonial between the Beroldus ordinal and the time of the Beinecke roll.

The portability of this roll is one of its chief uses. The books containing the Ambrosian Chant are normally very large, and include the complete musical texts and notation for the entire year. They are not conveniently carried in procession.[22] The Beinecke roll permits all the music needed to be conveniently carried and referred to. This seems to be a document for someone who leads the singers. It includes not only the antiphons sung by all the choir, but it also includes the responsories, sung by soloists, used in each stational church—pieces not required by choir-singers. This roll might be handed to the series of notaries and lectors who were to sing these responsories, though it might also have remained in the possession of the functionary whose duty was to see to it that the music was sung in the proper order and in the correct way.

Clearly other rolls, as well as this one, were used during the litanies. Perhaps most of the singers sang from some sort of written notation, in which case we might imagine a dozen or so rolls, similar to the Beinecke rolls, having been carried by the singers. The *rotulus letaniarum* was brought from church to church, and from it were said the prayers that were part of each stational liturgy.

Many Ambrosian rolls seem to have been lost. We know from other evidence that they once existed, but the difficulty of conservation of rolls—they cannot be arranged on shelves like codices—probably accounts for the almost complete disappearance of the rotuli that were once a significant feature of the Ambrosian liturgy of Milan. The Beinecke roll, the only complete surviving roll from the Ambrosian liturgy, is thus an incomparable treasure.

1. The only other such roll is a later document, Milan, Biblioteca Ambrosiana MS Z 256 supra. It is incomplete, consisting of two (of three) rolls of the 14th–15th century. See the description below, p. 26.

2. There is no comprehensive modern study of the medieval rotulus. The discussion below is summarized from Chapter 2 ("The Rotulus") of Thomas Forrest Kelly, *The Exultet in Southern Italy* (New York and Oxford: Oxford University Press, 1996), pp. 12–29, where substantial further references may be found.

3. The use of a roll for the *Exultet* is a characteristic shared with the old Beneventan liturgy, and is one of the many features which link these two non-Roman rites. Both descend perhaps from an original common Lombard practice. See Thomas Forrest Kelly, *The Exultet in Southern Italy*, pp. 25–29, 208–11.

4. ". . . et unus subdiaconus ebdomadarius debet portare rotulum similiter indutus alba, et debet tenere ipsum rotulum ante diaconum, donec legerit, et benedixerit ceram et ignem" (Marcus Magistretti, *Beroldus sive ecclesiae Ambrosianae mediolanensis kalendarium et ordines saec. 12* [Milan: Giovanola, 1894], p. 110). The thirteenth-century "Beroldus novus" names the text by adding here "dicendo sic: *Exultet iam angelica turba coelorum*, etc." (Magistretti, *Beroldus*, p. 110n).

5. The *custodes*, literally (Door-)keepers, were clergy in minor orders. There were sixteen custodes, under their cimilarcha: 8 maiores, divided into 4 cicendelarii and 4 ostiarii, and 8 minores.

6. "Et notandum, quia antequam vesperum incipiatur, minor custos ebdomadarius ponit rotulum orationum super altare, nisi sint propriae orationes. Et presbyter suscepit eumdem rotulum ab altari, quando dicit orationem" (Magistretti, *Beroldus*, p. 55).

7. "Alius [subdiaconus] idest observator portat rotulum ad letanias faciendum. . . . Et in dominca de Abraham, et de Coeco, et de Lazaro similiter. Et hoc facto subdiaconus ponit rotulum super altare, et archiepiscopus porrigit illum diacono ad letanias faciendas, quem ille sumens osculatur manus ejus" (Magistretti, *Beroldus*, p. 91).

8. The ordinal does not specifically mention a roll for Ash Wednesday, but since rolls are always used elsewhere for litanies, we can assume its presence: "In primo die quadragesimae archiepiscopus cum toto clero vadat ad ecclesiam sancti Ambrosii cum processione, cantando antiphonas et cum suis versibus primi diei letaniarum; et faciunt letanias in ecclesia S. Georgii" (Magistretti, *Beroldus*, p. 83). The Beroldus ordinal does mention the rolls for the Wednesday and Friday processions: "Et sciendum est, quia ante tertiam cantatam minor custodum ebdomadariorum ponit rotulum letaniarum super altare, primum in prima ebdomada, secundum in secunda, tertium in tertia. In quarta feria, finita tertia, presbyter tollit rotulum ab altari, et dicit orationem ante altare, et primicerius lectorum incipit letanias; et pergunt in ecclesiam aestivam, cum rotolo presbyter, cicendelarius ebdomadarius cum pallio, et ponit illud super altare" (Magistretti, *Beroldus*, p. 89). The first, second, and third rolls are those of the three days of the great litanies, the days for which these rolls are principally intended, and for which the Beinecke rolls were made, as is discussed below.

9. "In sexta ebdomada letaniae secunda et tertia et quarta feria celebrabuntur" (Magistretti, *Beroldus*, p. 69).

10. "In vigiliis sanctorum, quando ordinarii canunt psalmos, semper canunt tertiam in ecclesia hyemali, deinde proficiscuntur ad festum cum processione, cantando cantus letaniarum secundum diem, cui ipsa ecclesia festi ipsius data est. Si primo data est, incipiunt *Domine deus virtutum*; si secundo, *Quem deprecamur*, si tertio, *Dei genitrix*. Et primicerius lectorum semper incipit psallentium in letaniis, sequentibus suis. Sed praesciendum quia minor custos ebdomadarius ponit rotulum letaniarum super altare uniuscujusque diei, sicut competit, deinde presbyter tollit illum ante processionem, et dicit orationem, sed si archiepiscopus adfuerit, rotularius ejus porrigit ei. . . ." (Magistretti, *Beroldus*, p. 57).

11. For an introduction to the history of the Rogation Days and the Roman rogation of 25 April, see Terence Bailey, *The Processions of Sarum and the Western Church* (Toronto: Pontifical Institute of Mediaeval Studies, 1971), pp. 93–98.

12. On the origins of the Milanese litanies, see Pietro Borella, "Le Litanie Triduane Ambrosiane," *Ambrosius* 21 (1945), 40–50.

13. See Magistretti, *Beroldus*, pp. 122–23; since the processional music for the 25 April litanies (called "letaniae s. Gregorii" in the Beroldus ordinal) includes many pieces used for the three-day litanies, we can presume that processional rotuli were also used.

14. On stational liturgy in general, and especially as regards Jerusalem, Rome, and Constantinople, see John F. Baldovin, *The Urban Character of Christian Worship. The Origins, Development, and Meaning of Stational Liturgy.* Orientalia Christiana Analecta, 228 (Rome: Pont. Institutum Studiorum Orientalium, 1987). An introduction to stational liturgy at Milan is Christian Troelsgard, "Stational Liturgy and Processional Antiphons in the Ambrosian Rite," in Eva Louise Lillie and Nils Holger Petersen, *Liturgy and the Arts in the Middle Ages. Studies in Honour of C. Clifford Flanigan* (Copenhagen: Museum Tusculanum Press, 1996), pp. 85–94.

15. The processional routes are determined from the indications in Marcus Magistretti, *Manuale ambrosianum ex codice saec. XI olim in usum canonicae vallis travaliae.* 2 vols.

Monumenta veteris liturgiae ambrosianae, 2–3 (Milan: Hoepli, 1904–05), 2: 245–75, where musical pieces are indicated as serving for the portion of the initerary "usque ad portam Civitatis"; "usque sanctum Simplicianum"; etc.; these are confirmed, to the extent that they are complete, by the indications in Milan, Biblioteca Ambrosiana MS Z 256 supra (which, however, has an additional station at St Vitus on the third day: see the appendix); on these processional rolls, see below.

16. Magistretti, *Manuale* 2: 246n2; Magistretti, *Beroldus*, p. 220.

17. Magistretti, *Beroldus*, pp. 118–20.

18. The manuscript is described, and its texts edited, in Odilo Heiming, "Ein Benediktinisch-Ambrosianishes Gebetbuch des frühen 11. Jahrhunderts," *Archiv für Liturgiewissenschaft* 8/2 (1964), 325–435.

19. Edited in Magistretti, *Manuale*, vol. 2.

20. A typewritten description by Ernesto Moneta Caglio which accompanies these rolls indicates that there are two rolls, for the second and third days of the litanies. The microfilm generously provided to me by the Ambrosiana Project at the University of Notre Dame includes only the roll for the third day, and the description here is based on that.

21. Magistretti, *Beroldus*, p. 119.

22. There are, however, alternatives to the rotulus. Several small (portable) manuscripts of the fifteenth and sixteenth centuries include the music for the processions. They include: Milan, Bilioteca capitolare U.4.43 (late 14th c.; cf. Michel Huglo, Luigi Agustoni, Eugène Cardine, and Ernesto Moneta Caglio, *Fonti e paleografia del canto ambrosiano*. Archivio ambrosiano, 7 [Milan: n.p., 1956], no. 246, p. 231); Milan, Biblioteca capitolare U.4.39 (15th c.; Huglo et al., no. 247, p. 231); Solesmes, Abbaye St. Pierre MS 64 (15th–16th c.; Huglo et al., no. 139, p. 75); Milan, Biblioteca capitolare E.1.25 (1507, responsories of the third day; Huglo et al.; no. 140, p. 77); Milan, Biblioteca Trivulziana N5 (15th c.; Huglo et al., no. 141, p. 77); Milan, Biblioteca capitolare U.4.41 (late 15th c.; Huglo et al., no. 245, p. 231); Rho, Collegio degli Oblati s.n. (1492; Huglo et al., no. 248, p. 231). In addition, the printed processional of 1633 and 1752, and perhaps also that printed in 1494, contain the music of the litanies: see Huglo et al., p. 75.

Appendix
THE MUSIC OF THE *LETANIAE TRIDUANAE* OF MILAN AS FOUND IN THE
BEINECKE ROLL COMPARED WITH OTHER SOURCES

B: Beinecke 810.

L: London, British Library MS Egerton 3763; ed. Odilo Heiming, "Ein
Benediktinisch-Ambrosianishes Gebetbuch des frühen 11. Jahrhunderts," *Archiv für Liturgiewissenschaft* 8/2 (1964), 325–435;
this MS includes litanies and prayers, which are omitted here.

M: Milan, Biblioteca del Capitolo metropolitano MS 2102, a *manuale*
from Val Travaglia of the 11th century; ed. Marcus Magistretti,
*Manuale ambrosianum ex codice saec. XI olim in usum canonicae val-
lis travaliae.* 2 vols. Monumenta veteris liturgiae ambrosianae,
2–3 (Milan: Hoepli, 1904–05), vol. 2.

O: Oxford, Bodleian Library MS lat. liturg. a.4, an Ambrosian antiphoner, *pars aestiva*, made in 1399 for the church of Sant'Ambro-
gio, Milan; cf. Michel Huglo, Luigi Agustoni, Eugène Cardine,
and Ernesto Moneta Caglio, *Fonti e paleografia del canto ambrosiano.* Archivio ambrosiano, 7 (Milan: n. p., 1956), no. 64, pp. 52–
53.

V: Vendrogno, the Muggiasca manuscript, a complete Ambrosian
antiphoner copied 1398–99 for the church of St Lawrence, Muggiasca; cf. Huglo et al., *Fonti e paleografia*, nos. 62–63, pp. 50–52.

Z: Milan, Biblioteca Ambrosiana MS Z 256 supra (*die tertia* only); cf.
Huglo et al., *Fonti e paleografia*, no. 141 bis, p. 77. Note that this
roll has a somewhat different format, omitting the responsories
said in each church, and instead providing a proper psallenda
sung at the entrance to each church.

Additions to roll		Notes
	Die primo in letanis	L: *Die I. Processio de ecclesia estiva*
	a. Convertimini ad me	M: *usque ad portam Civitatis*
		L: *oratio ad Portam Cumanam*
	a. Domine deus virtutum deus israhel	M: *usque ad sanctum Simplicianum*
not	R. Convertimini ad me dicit	O: *in sancto Simpliciano*
	dominus	
	v. Attendite populus	
	a. Peccavimus ante te deus ne des nos	M: *usque ad sanctum Carpoforum*
.L.	R. Tibi domine placeat	L: *in sancto Carpoforo*
	v. Rogamus te domine	
	a. Misereris omnium domine	M: *usque ad sanctum Protasium in Campo*
sub.	R. Rogamus te domine deus quia	L: *in sancto Protasio in Campo*
	v. Vita nostra in dolore	
	a. Qui fecisti magnalia in Egypto	
	a. Circumdederunt nos mala	M: *usque ad sanctum Victorem ad Ulmum*
.L.	R. Peccantem me cotidie	L: *in sancto Victore ad Ulmum*
	v. Quoniam iniquitatem	
	a. Si fecessimus precepta tua	M: *usque ad sanctum Victorem ad Corpus*
.N.	R. Convertamur ad dominum	L: *in sancto Victore ad Corpus*
	v. Convertamur	
	unusquisque	
	a. Iniquitates nostras agnoscimus	B: added in later hand; M: *usque ad sanctum Martinum*
.L.	R. Peccavi domine peccavi super	L: *in sancto Martino*
	v. Peccavi domine peccavi	
	a. Vide domine afflictionem	M: *usque ad sanctum Vincentium*
.N.	R. Numquid domine peccatorum	L: *In sancto Vincento*
	v. Voce mea ad dominum	
	a. Liberator noster de gentibus	M: *usque ad sanctum Ambrosium*
.L.	R. In te domine sperabunt omnes	L: *in sancto Ambrosio ad Corpus*
	v. Vere dico vobis	
	a. Tu vir dei ora pro nobis	M: *usque ad sanctum Vitalem*
.Not	R. Domine miserere nobis et libera	L: *in sancto Vitale*
	v. Qui regis israhel	
	a. Ne avertas domine hominem	M: *usque ad sanctam Valeriam*
.L.	R. Quo ibo domine a spiritu	L: *in sancta Valeria*
	v. Si ascendero in celos	
	a. Memento domine quoniam pulvis	M: *usque ad sanctum Naborem*
.Not	R. Domine non secundum peccata	L: *in sancto Nabore*
	v. Peccavimus cum patribus	
	a. Fac nobiscum domine	
		L: *usque ad Porta Vercellina*
	a. Civitatem istam tu circunda	M: Plebem istam
	a. Gemitus noster domine ad te	M: *usque ad sanctum Victorem ad refugium*
.L.	R. Transeat a me delictum	L: *in sancto Victore ad refugium*
	v. Averte faciem tuam	
	a. Populus meus si unus	
	a. Propter peccata nostra deus	

a. Serviamus domino in timore
a. Adiutor noster esto ne derelinquas
a. Dies tribulationis et ire

M adds: Kyrie. Kyrie. Kyrie. *sequitur*
Agnus dei.
L M O add: *Ad missam Cant.* Conserva
me, domine. O *adds: Ad vesperas*
. . . (music in extenso)
V adds: *in Mag.* Magnificat anima. *v.*
Et exultavit spiritus. *Sequitur .xij.*
Kyrie.

ad   R. Appropinquet oratio nostra
vesper-   v. Intret postulatio nostra
um

Die secundo letaniarum

   a. Convertamur unusquisque   M: *usque ad sanctum Fidelem*
.L.   R. Domine secundum actum meum   L: *in sancto Fidele*
       v. Peccavi domine peccavi
   a. Quem deprecemur qui te mittiget

                L: *Item ad porta nova oratio . . .*
                post Kyrie foris muros
                M: *foris muros, post Kyrie*
   a. In te speraverunt patres nostri   M: *usque ad sanctum Dionysium*
Not.   R. Recordare domine testamentum   L: *in sancto Dionysio*
       v. Exaudi domine voces
   a. Media vita in morte sumus
   a. Anima mea cessa iam peccare   M: *usque ad sanctum Romanum*
.L.   R. Scio culpas in me domine   L: *in sancto Romano*
       v. Ego autem ad flagella
   a. Peccavimus domine peccatum
   a. Aufer iram tuam a nobis   M: *usque ad sanctum Stephanum*
Subd.   R. Commovisti domine terram   L: *in sancto Stephano . . . respon-*
       v. Deus repulisti nos   *sorium subdiaconi*
   a. Peccavimus peccavimus ante faciem
   a. Domine si inquiras cordis nostri   M: *usque ad sanctum Kalimerum*
Lect.   R. Precamur domine ut audias   L: *in sancto Kalimero*
       v. Nos quoque oramus
   a. In te domine speramus   M: *usque ad sanctam Agatham*
Not.   R. Liberet nos domine manus tua   L: *in sancta Agatha*
       v. Peccavimus tibi domine
   a. Dominus non sumus digni   M: *usque ad basilicam Apostolorum*
                ad sanctum Nazarium
diac.   R. A facie furoris tui deus   L: *in basilica apostolorum*
       v. Dies mei sicut umbra
   a. Domine si iratus fueris
   a. Muro tuo inexpugnabile   L: *usque ad Portam Romanam*
                M: Fine tua . . . *ad sanctum*
                Alexandrum
Not.   R. Includite elemosynam in sinu   L: *in sancto Alexandro*
       v. Bona est oratio
   a. Exaudi domine voces servorum   M: *usque ad sanctum Iohannem ad*
                concam
Lect.   R. Angelus tuus domine circundet   L: *in sancto Iohanne ad conca*
       v. Noli claudere

a. Peccavimus domine peccavimus
parce
a. Erigat nos dextera tua
a. Domine inclina aurem tuam

M adds: Kyrie. *sequitur* Agnus dei.
Ad missam Cant. In convertendo.
L adds: *in ecclesia estiva ad missam
cantus* In convertendo.
V adds: *In Mag.* Quia fecit. *Sequitur
.xij.* Kyrie

.L. ad
vesper-
um

R. Fiant aures tue intendentes
v. De profundis clamavi

L: *responsorium in choro* Fiant aures
tue v. De profundis
M: *Ad vesperas . . .* (music in
extenso)

Die tertio letaniarum

L: *processio de ecclesia estiva
usque ad sancta Euffimia*

a. Converte israhel ad dominum
a. Deus noster exaudi nos peccatores

M: *post Kyrie, foris muros*
L: *usque ad posterlam s. Eufimie
foris muros post Kyrie*
M adds after this antiphon: *usque ad
sanctam Eufimiam*

a. Convertimini et agite penitentiam

LMOVZ: *this antiphon comes before*
Deus noster
Z adds: *psallenda* Eufemie virgo
humilis

.L.

R. Spem in alio numquam
v. Confitebimur tibi
a. Terribile est Christe iudicium

L: *in sancto Eufimia*

M: *usque ad sanctum Celsum*
Z adds: *psallenda* Nazarius et Celsus
ipsi sunt vasa sacra

.Not.

R. Abscondi tanquam aurum
v. Averte faciem tuam
a. Rex sanctorum deus converte

L: *in sancto Nazario in campo*

M: *usque ad sanctum Nazarium*
Z adds: *psallenda* Beatus Nazarius
una cum Celso

Lect.

R. Domine non posuisti
penitentiam
v. Flecto genua cordis mei
a. Non despexisti multum misericors
a. Propitiare domine creature tue
a. Dum indignaretur dominus
a. Super flumina Babilonis

L: *in sancto Celso*

M: *usque ad sanctum Eustorgium*
Z adds: *Ad sanctum Eustorgium ps.*
Confessor sancte sacerdos magne
beate Eustorge

.Not.

R. Hec dicit dominus non cessabo
v. Si custodierint filii tui
a. Impetum inimicorum
a. Peccata nostra diviserunt inter nos
a. Propitiare domine populo tuo

L: *in sancto Eustorgio*
Z omits this piece

M: *usque ad sanctum Lauretium*
Z adds: *ad sanctum Laurentium ps.*
Gratia dei sum.

*continuation on back of membrane
11, Roll B*

*[singers of responsories are no
longer noted in B]*

R. Sacerdotes et levitae principes   L: *in sancto Laurentio . . . responso-*
   v. Universa multitudo   *rium diaconi*
                        Z omits this piece

a. In tribulatione nostra invocamus   M: *usque ad sanctum Systum*
   R. Pater peccavi celo et coram te   L: *in sancto Xisto*
     v. Surgam et vadam   Z omits this piece
                        Z adds: *Ad sanctum Genesium ps.*
                        Generatio et generatio laudabit

a. Petite et accipietis   M: *usque ad sanctum Yenesium*
   R. Qui iudicas omnem mundum   L: *in sancto Salvatore*
     v. Domine exaudi orationem   Z omits this piece
                        Z adds: *Ad sanctum Vitum ps.* O
                        quam beatus Vitus

a. Nolite timere quoniam deus
a. Deprecamur te domine in omni   L: *usque ad porta Ticinese*
                        M adds before this antiphon *Infra*
                        civitatem, post Kyrie; and after it
                        usque ad sanctam Mariam ad
                        circulum
   R. Ascendat domine oratio nostra   L: in sancta Maria ad circulum
     v. Domine exaudi orationem   Z omits this piece
                        Z adds: *Ad sanctam Mariam ad cir-*
                        culum ps. Sub tuam misericor-
                        diam confugimus

a. Dei *[MS: Sci]* genitrix que   M: *usque ad sanctum Quiricum*
a. Sicut promisisti omnipotens   M omits this antiphon
   R. Peccata mea multa sunt domine   L: *in sancto Quirico*
     v. Ego sum domine   Z omits this piece
                        Z adds: *In sancto Quirico ps.* O
                        quam beatus Quiricus *require in*
                        sancti Viti

a. Illuxisti domine dies in qua
a. Exaudi domine fletum *[illegible]*   M: *voces fletus*
                        O: *vocem fletus*
                        LZ: *vocem fletu*
                        M adds: *usque ad sanctum Georgium*

continues on back of roll C
   R. Nolite tardare converti   L: *in sancto Georgio*
     v. Nolite sperare   Z omits this piece
                        Z adds: *In sancti Georgii ps.* Sancte
                        Georgi martyr

a. Propitiare peccatis meis   M: *usque ad sanctum Sebastianum*
a. Videns vidi afflictionem   LMOVZ: *this antiphon comes before*
                        Propitiare
   R. Miserere domine supplicantibus   L: *in sancto Sebastiano*
     v. Pacem rogamus domine   Z omits this piece
                        Z adds: *In sancti Sebastiani ps.*
                        Sebastianus dixit Marceliano

a. Gemitus populi tui deus   M: *usque ad sanctam Mariam*
                        Bertrade
                        V omits this piece
a. Peccavimus deus malum coram te   M omits this antiphon
   R. Ne recorderis peccatum meum   L: *in sancta Maria Bertrade*
     v. Cui monti dicturus   Z omits this piece
                        Z adds: *In sancta Maria beltradis ps.*
                        Virgo dei genitrix quem totus

a. Nunc exequuntur de toto corde   LM: *exequimur*
a. Desiderium pauperum

a. Nisi acceleraveris Christe liberare
a. Angustiati per singulos dies   LMOVZ omit this antiphon
a. Non expandimus manus nostras
a. Inclina domine aurem tuam
a. Respice in servos tuos et in opera
a. Exurge libera deus de manu mortis
a. Ascendant ad te domine preces
a. Criste tuis famulis subveni
a. Miserere nobis domine miserere
a. Non est aliud refugium nisi in te
a. Ne obliviscaris domine voces
a. Deus qui conteris bella
a. Liberati serviamus domino deo
a. Agnus dei qui tollis peccata mundi   L: Kyrie Kyrie Kyrie. Agnus dei, qui
   miserere nobis.   tollis peccata v. 1. Gloria patri et
                                             filio. v. 2. Sicut erat in principio.
                                             2. Agnus dei, qui tollis v. 3. Sus-
                                             cipe deprecationem nostram. 3.
                                             Agnus dei, qui tollis peccata.
                                             Ad missam cantus Laudate domi-
                                             num. v. Quoniam. *Ad vesperum*
                                             resp. Precatus sum faciem v.
                                             Legem pone.
                                          M: *Post* Kyrie. Kyrie. Kyrie. *excelsa*
                                             voce sequitur Agnus dei qui tollis
                                             peccata mundi miserere nobis.
                                             Alia Suscipe deprecationem nos-
                                             tram, qui sedes ad dexteram
                                             patris. *Alia* Agnus dei. *Sequitur*
                                             Gloria patri. *Alia.* Agnus dei.
                                          O: *Post* Kyrie. Agnus dei qui tollis
                                             peccata mundi miserere nobis. v.
                                             Gloria patri. v. Sicut erat in.
                                             euouae. *Item* Agnus dei. v. ij.
                                             Suscipe deprecationem nostram,
                                             qui sedes ad dexteram patris.
                                             Item. Agnus dei.
                                          MO: *Ad missam cantus* Laudate
                                             deum omnes gentes. v. Quoniam.
                                             Ad vesperas . . .
                                          V: Kyr. Kyr. Kyr. *post Kyrie* Agnus
                                             dei qui tollis peccata mundi miser-
                                             ere nobis. v. Sicut erat in principio
                                             . . . amen. v. ij. Agnus dei. iij.
                                             Suscipe deprecationem nostram
                                             qui sedes ad dexteram patris. iiij.
                                             Agnus dei. *cantus* Laudate domi-
                                             num. v. Quoniam [notated
                                             in extenso]. Ad vesperum . . .
                                          Z omits this section

XII

MEDIEVAL COMPOSERS OF
LITURGICAL CHANT

> ... e se licito è dir il vero, voi stesso e noi altri
> tutti molte volte, ed ora ancor, credemo piú
> alla altrui opinione che alla nostra propria. E
> che sia 'l vero, non è ancor molto tempo, che
> essendo appresentati qui alcuni versi sotto 'l
> nome del Sanazaro, a tutti parvero molto eccel-
> lenti e furono laudati con le maraviglie ed
> esclamazioni; poi, sapendosi per certo che er-
> ano d'un altro, persero súbito la reputazione e
> parvero men che mediocri. E cantandosi pur in
> presenzia della signora Duchessa un mottetto,
> non piacque mai né fu estimato per bono, fin
> che non si seppe che quella era composizion di
> Josquin de Pris. Ma che piú chiaro segno volete
> voi della forza della opinione?
>
> Baldesar Castiglione, *Il libro del cortegiano*,
> Bk. 2 cap. 35

Many readers will know the story from Castiglione's *Il libro del cortegiano* in which works of art are given higher value when they are thought to be the work of a famous poet or composer, a Sannazaro or a Josquin.

In the study of medieval liturgical chant we are accustomed to works without composers, to a timeless repertory that takes its value from its context, from its appropriateness, and sometimes even from its intrinsic beauty. But we do not normally deal in musical personalities. We are not concerned to identify early, middle, and late styles of musical artists, or to distinguish individual creations on the basis of style; there is not much connoisseurship involved in the study of medieval chant, little in the way of attribution to individual composers. Those are concepts more suited to the music, and the musicology, of the nineteenth and twentieth centuries.

Scholarly discussions of chant tend more to matters of genre, of formula, of mode, of accentuation. The question of composition is seldom raised, by us or by the writers of the middle ages.

XII

The value attached to tradition and authority kept the liturgical repertory stable and strong, providing relatively little space, or need, for new music.

And yet, when we consider the creation of music in the later middle ages, the addition of material to a hallowed repertory, we find that there are occasional indications of composition. We sometimes learn the name of a person who "composuit," or "dictavit," or "invenit," or "compilavit" an office, or a hymn, or some other liturgical item. Such composers are sometimes high prelates, sometimes poets, but only rarely are they musicians. We are well aware, I think, that many ascriptions are made to very unlikely composers, and some such ascriptions are made very much after the fact. The attribution of the terrifying antiphon *Media vita* to Notker goes back, it seems, no farther than the seventeenth century.[1]

Although we continue to use the term "Gregorian Chant," we are aware that its ascription to Gregory the Great is a convenience useful throughout history – useful to John the Deacon in the ninth century, and useful to those who illustrated Gregory's divine musical authority, from Hartker of St Gall, whose antiphoner includes a portrait of Gregory,[2] to the editors of the Vatican gradual, who begin their volume with the famous "Gregorius praesul."[3]

It does sometimes happen that medieval composers are remembered and even celebrated. In the choir of the principal church at La Verna – the site of St Francis' stigmatization, and now a Franciscan center – the choir stalls includes a series of nineteenth-century *intarsie* of persons important in the Franciscan order; among them is Julian of Speyer, composer of the Office of St Francis.

I am grateful to Evan Angus McCarthy for his assistance in this project.

[1]   To a certain J. Metzler, historian of St. Gallen, in 1613, according to David Hiley in "Notker," *The New Grove Dictionary of Music and Musicians,* 2d edition, vol. 18, p. 201. I have not been able to locate Metzler or his reference.

[2]   Hartker's antiphoner is reproduced in facsimile in *Paléographie musicale,* Series II, vol. 1.

[3]   *Graduale sacrosanctae romanae ecclesiae de tempore et de sanctis SS. D. N. Pii X. pontificis maximi jussu restitutum et editum* (Rome: Typis Vaticanis, 1908), p. 1; on the prologue, see Stäblein, "*Gregorius Praesul;* der Prolog zum römischen Antiphonale," in *Musik und Verlag: Karl Vötterle zum 65. Geburtstag* (Kassel: Bärenreiter, 1968), pp. 537-561; on the tradition of such illustrations, see L. Treitler, "Homer and Gregory: The Transmission of Epic Poetry and Plainchant," *The Musical Quarterly* 60 (1974), 333-72. Repr. with additions in L. Treitler, *With Voice and Pen; Coming to Know Medieval Song and How it Was Made* (Oxford: Oxford University Press, 2003), pp.131-185

I have assembled a provisional list of composers of medieval liturgical song, and it is presented here as Table 1; this list is surely both incomplete and inaccurate: it should not be relied on to determine who actually composed what melody. The list merely reports what has been said about persons who composed, or made, or found, or compiled, music. Where possible, I have indicated the source of the earliest ascription of chants to the composer; and where there is an interesting text about composition, I have excerpted it in a separate series. I have tried to limit myself to the middle ages, and so I have not included such composers of chant as Henry Dumont, Abbé Lebeuf, Joseph Pothier, and others whose contributions to the official liturgy have been substantial. And I have not included composers of non-liturgical music, Latin or vernacular, nor of polyphonic versions of already-existing liturgical items. I could not resist including Guillaume Dufay, and I therefore define the middle ages as including the fifteenth century. What follows here, then, will consist of some observations that arise from compiling this list. I hope that readers will provide additions and corrections to this list. There is, as you can see, much more to be done.

Many composers are remembered and celebrated, but few of them are composers in the sense of being creators of new music. Those whom we suspect not to be composers in our modern sense are usually either poets or persons in high authority. In both these cases we should think carefully about why these attribution exist, and what they may tell us about the place of music in the spirit of the times.

Poets are often named as composers – and sometimes in fact they are the composers of the music to which their text is sung; more often, probably, they are not, at least in our modern understanding of composition. Creating the text is the essential thing, and in a sense the text is in itself the liturgical item, however it is sung. Perhaps that is part of the phenomenon that gives us also so many chant books without notation, even in the late middle ages – missals and breviaries which provide what we would call the texts without the music. Perhaps the users of these books, like the users of the graduals edited in René-Jean Hesbert's *Antiphonale missarum sextuplex*, felt that the music was indeed present, inherent in the words. It is not surprising, then, that music is rarely attributed to anyone other than the author of the text.

A great many hymns are ascribed to authors famous and unknown. Martin Gerbert, in *De cantu et musica sacra*, has a long list, from Popes to abbots, kings to archdeacons, but unless there

97

Table 1. *Medieval Composers of Chant: Attributions*

Name	Attributed composition	Source of attribution; remarks	Bibliography (see list at end)
Abbo, ab of Fleury, 945?-1004	Off of St Stephen		Gerbert II: 35, citing Lebeuf, 19; Valère, 5
Adam Easton, d1397	Off of Visitation (AH 24, 29)	Words only; melodies from Off of St Francis by Julian von Speyer	Hughes, BRO 250; Strohm, 19
Adam of St Victor, d1146?	Sequence texts, "probably" also a few melodies (Fassler 137)		Fassler, *Gothic*, 183-4, *passim*
Adelmus, Engl bishop, 8c	"compositiore cantuum ecclesiasticorum clarus fuit."	William of St Lô, ab of St Victor, d. 1349	Gerbert II: 29 and Lebeuf, 18, both citing Mabillon saec. IV
Adémar de Chabannes, c988-1034	Liturgy of St Martial 1029; Off of St Valeria and St Austroclinianus		Emerson; Grier, "Roger;" Grier, "Ecce."
Ainard (from Mont-S Cath. Nr Rouen, later ab in Bayeux), s11	Off of St Catherine, St Kilian	Orderic Vitalis, bk. IV, ch. 24 *Texts M, N	Wagner I: 315, citing Gerbert II: 36; Pothier, 50; Ord. Vit. (PL 188, col. 369)
Alfanus, abp of Salerno, 1054-1085	Off of St Sabina (AH 24, no 96), of tr St Matthew (AH 25, no 85)	Words only?	Wagner I: 316 Migliavacca
Ambrose of Milan, d397	Hymns		Pothier, 52; Delaporte, 53; Lebeuf, 21-22
Angelramus (Angerlan), s11	Off of St Riquier; St Valery; St Vulfran		Gerbert II: 39, citing Pez, *Thesaurus*, bk. IV
Arnaldus, Belgium, 1141	"in partibus Belgii ita in *musica* clarus effulsit, ut Sanctorum cantus ab ipso compositi raptim a vicinis ecclesiis peterentur."		
Arnaut du Pré	Off of St Louis, s13 (AH 13, no 71)	Words only?	
Arnold Heimericius	Off of St Victor of Xanten, d. 1491 (AH 50, no 420)	Words only?	LMLO
Arnold of St Emmeran	Off of St Emmeran, c1030		Hiley, *Historia Sancti Emmerammi*
Arnoul of Chartres, s11	Off of St Evroult	He taught it to 2 monks of St Evroult	Fassler, "Chartres;" Delaporte, 53; citing Clerval
Benedict of Peterborough, d1193	Off of Thomas of Canterbury, comp. 1170-1177 (AH 13,93)	A chronicler of Peterborough *Text R	Hughes, "Chants;" Hughes, BRO 275; Hunt; "Notes."

Name	Attributed composition	Source of attribution; remarks	Bibliography
Bernard of Clairvaux, 1090-1153	Off of St Victor		
Berno of Reichenau, s 1047	3 hymns, trope, 3 seq, Off of St Ulrich	Words only?	Oesch, Wagner I: 315, Gerbert II: 36
Birgerus Gregorii, abp Uppsala, d1383	Off of St Birgitta, AH 25 no58, of St Botuido, (AH 25, no 62)	Words only?	Schlager, "Reimoffizien," 296
Bonaventure, d1274	Off of Passion (Christum captum et derisum; at request of Louis IX); attrib. Off de gaudiis Marie (AH 24, p? 57)	Words only?	
Bruno of Egisheim (later pope Leo IX), d1054	Rxx of St Gorgonius; of St Hidulf; of St Ottilia; of St Gregory the Great (AH 5, n64); of tr St Gerard (AH 18, no 31); a melody for Gloria in excelsis	*Texts G-J	Bernard, "Les Offices;" Wagner I: 314;315; Gerbert II: 35; Lebeuf, 26; Anonymus Mellicensis ch. 85 [incorrectly cited in Gerbert]
Bryniolphus Algottson bp of Skara, 1278-1317	Off of St Eskillo (AH 26, no1); of St Helen of Sköfde (AH 26, no31)		
Calixtus II, pope, 1119-1124	Off of St James	Codex Calixtinus, c1150-1180	
Calixtus III, pope, 1455-1458	Off of Transfiguration, 1456	Authority only	
Christian of Lilienfeld, d1330	15 offices (AH 41a, no 1-15)	Words only?	Schlager, "Reimofficien," 296
Conantius, bp of Palencia, d. c638	"melodias soni multas noviter edidit"	Ildefonsus, De vir. Ill. *Text A	PL 96, col. 203
Conrad of Megenberg, 1309-1374	Off of St Erhardus		Hankeln, Konrad von Megenberg Lebeuf, 24
Damien aux Païs-Bas, 12s	"...composa des chants admirables en l'honneur de S. Corneille & S. Cyprien."		
Desiderius, ab of Montecassino, 1058-1087	Hymns, Off of St Maur	Peter the Deacon, s 12	Gerbert II: 36
Durandus, ab Troarn, d1088	Various musical compositions	Orderic Vitalis	Gerbert II: 37, citing Ord. Vit.; Lebeuf, 25
Edmund Lacy, bp of Hereford, 1417-1420	Off of St Raphael Archangel	Words ony?	Hughes, BRO 274

Name	Attributed composition	Source of attribution; remarks	Bibliography
Folcardus, abbas Torneiensis (Folcard of Thorney), d1084	"delectabiles ad canendum historias suaviter composuit."	Orderic Vitalis	Gerbert II: 37, citing Ord. Vit. bk. XI, 83
Folquinus, ab of Lobbes, 965-980	Off of St Folquinus (AH 13, no 55)		Hughes LMLO, citing MR8; Wagner I, 314, who cites Gerbert II: 35; Lebeuf, 18. Delaporte; Pothier, 52; Lebeuf, 16
Fulbert of Chartres, c960-1028	Rxx of NatBMV; less reliable: hymns Deus pater piissime, Chorus nove Ierusalem; seq. *Sonent regi*; several offices: [Gilles...Leobinus (AH 18, no 42); Piatus (AH 18, no 40)]	A monk of Bosham, contemp of Wm of Malmesbury, mentions the 3 Rxx of Nat BMV (Delaporte)	
Gerbert of St Wandrille, s11	"dulcisonos cantus Antiphonarum atque Responsoriorum ediderunt."	Orderic Vitalis *Text M	Pothier, 50
Ghislerus of Hildesheim, fl. 1406-23 (ab of St Maurice)	Off of St James the Great (AH 26, no 43)	Words only?	LMLO; Wagner I: 316, citing Blume, "Zur Poesie," 142
Giacomo Gaetani Stefaneschi, card, c1270-1343	Off of St Celestine V (AH 50, no 409)	Words only?	LMLO
Giraldus Cambrensis, 1146-1223	Off of St David, adapted from off of St Thomas	A. Hughes speculates	Hughes, BRO 258
Giselbertus and John, brothers and monks of St Lawrence, Liege, s12	Giselbertus: music for St George; St Regenufla; S Begga; John: Christopher; St Maria Eg., Hist Tobiae; St Steph "heroico pede;" cantica canticorum	Words only?	Gerbert II: 39, citing Pez, *Thesaurus*, bk. III
Goscelin of Canterbury, 1090s	Off of St Mildretha, prob. 1090s; perhaps also older Off of St Augustine	Wm of Malmesbury; words only? *Text O	Hughes, BRO 268; Sharpe, "Words and Music;" Hiley, "Chant Composition."
Goswin of Bossut, s14	Off of St Arnulphus Villariensis (AH 25, no 39), prose off of Maria of Oignies (AH 12, no 323-325: hymns)	Words only?	De Loos, "Chants," 25-28, 37
Gottschalk of Aachen, d1084	Seq, incl. one for *Divisio apostolorum*	Himself (composui)	
Gregory I, pope, 590-604	Gregorian chant	John the Deacon, c 875: "antiphonarius cento"	McGrade

Name	Attributed composition	Source of attribution; remarks	Bibliography
Guillaume Dufay, 1397-1474	Off of Recollectio Festorum BMV; possible Anthony introit (Planchart), Seq.*Naper al-mos rose* (Wright)		Haggh, "The Celebration;" Planchart, "Guillaume;" Wright, "Dufay's;" Strohm, 322
Gurdestin, abb of Lan-dévennec, s9	Off of St Wingualoeo (AH 18, no 100)	Words only?	
Henri Dézier de Latinnes, cantor for Urban VI and Boniface IX	Off of Visitation	Another setting	Strohm, 19, 323
Hericus & Remigius of S Germain, c950	Melodies of Off of St Julian of Le Mans, texts by Guido bp of Langres		Szövérffy I: 463; prob. citing Wagner, I: 314, citing Gerbert II: 35-36, and Lebeuf, 18
Herigerus of Lobbes (Belg), d1007	Off of St Landoaldus; ym BMV *Ave per quam*; 2 ants of Thomas ap (O Thoma Didyme; O Thoma apostole)	'didascalum et musicae artis peritum'	Huglo (NG2); Gerbert II: 36
Hermannus Contractus, 1013-1054	Seq *Grates, bonos* Off of St Afra *Gloriosa et b.* Off of St Wolfgang (or Wilhelm von Hirsau) Songs *E voces, Ter tria, Ter terni?* "cantilenas plurimas de Musica, Cantusque de Sanctis satis auctorabiles edidit."	His pupil Berthold, s11 ¾. *Text F	Oesch, Crocker; Afra office ed Hiley-Berschin; Wolfgang ed. Hiley; Gerbert II: 37: *Anony-mus Mellicensis*, ch. 91
Hildegard of Bingen, 1098-1179	77 pieces, "liturgical" genres	Vita by Gottfried and Dieter	Abundant
Hilduin, ab. of St Denis, d840	Off of St Denis, c835	adapted, as he says in a letter to Louis the Pious, from Gallican version. Words and music?	Robertson, *The Service Books*, 328-30, *passim*.

Name	Attributed composition	Source of attribution; remarks	Bibliography
Hucbald, 840-c930	*Pangat simul*, seq., melody similar to "Frigdola" *Quem vere pia laus*, Gloria A trope (incl. "Regnum tuum") [Rhymed?] Off of St Peter's Chair, *In plateis* 2 hymns for St Thiery for Mont d'Or: (*O quam venerandus; Exultet domino mente serena*) [Off of St Andrew and St Cilinia, attrib. by Guntherus, have not been identified.] Other ascriptions: St Rictrudis (AH 13, no 87); St Eusebia (AH 13, no 49), Maurontus (AH 13, no 77), S Lambertus (AH 26, no 79)	some pieces attrib. by Guntherus of St Amand (d1108), *Translatio S. Cyrici*	Chartier; Schlager, "Reimoffizium"
Ildefonsus of Toledo, d667	Hymns, "deux Messes d'un Chant merveilleux, en l'honneur de S. Cosme & S. Damien."	His successor Julian: "Partem sane tertiam [of his writings] missarum esse voluit, hymnorum, atque sermonum."	PL 96, col. 44a; Lebeuf, 18
Ioannes Caesar-Augustano (Zaragosa), s7	"in ecclesiasticis officiis quaedam eleganter et sono, e oratione composuit"	Ildefonsus, *De viris ill*, s7	PL 96, col. 201
Isembert (Norman abbot), s11	Off of St Ouen, St Nicholas (11c)	Words only?	Wagner I: 315; Pothier, 51
Jacopone da Todi, c1230-1306?	Stabat mater	doubtful?	Fallows et al. (NG2)
Jean du Mont-Cornillon, 1246	Off of Corpus Christi *Animarum cibus*, 1246		De Loos; Boeren, 8-9, 11
Johann Hane, late 15c	? (cantica, *lyram* dulcisonam in hon. BV ymnos etc., MS in bib. Cottoniana)	Words only?	Wagner I: 316, citing Blume, "Zur Poesie," 142. Gerbert II: 39, citing Leyser, 1007.
Johann Hoffmann, bp of Meissen 1427-1451	Off of Inventio pueri Iesu (AH 24, no 2)	Words only?	LMLO; Cited Wagner I: 316, citing Blume, "Zur Poesie," 142
Johannes Benechini de Calamaria (Oeland), d1461	Off of St Birgitta (AH 25, no 56), of St Katharina (of Sweden, AH 26, no 75)	Words only?	LMLO; Schlager, "Reimoffizien," 296

Name	Attributed composition	Source of attribution; remarks	Bibliography
John Horneby, c 1370, Carmelite of Lincoln	Off of Visitation *Eterni/Eliz/Scandit*	Words only?	Schlager, "Reimoffizien," 296
John Peckham, ab of Canterbury 1279-92	Off of Trinity *Sedenti super* (AH 5, no 1)	Derived from Francis office; words only?	Hughes BRO, 279; Wagner, "Zur mittelalterlichen"
Juan Gil de Zamora, c1240-1318	De BMV (AH 17, no 8)	Not same as author of 13c Ars musica?	Schlager, "Reimoffizien," 296, says 15c
Julian of Speyer, d1285?	Off of St Francis, Anthony		Weis, *Julian von Speier*; Strohm, 19; Gerbert II: 35
Lambert, m of St Lawrence, Liège, c1075	Off of St Heribert, others	"officium quoque de S. Heriberto, et de multis aliis Sanctis composuit, et dulci modulatione regulavit."	
Leopold of Steinberg, 1406	Chants for new feast of patrons of Hildesheim cathedral, 1406 (AH 28, no 39)		LMLO; Schlager, "Reimoffizien" 296, citing Wagner I: 316, citing Blume, "Zur Poesie," 142
Letaldus of Micy, c990	Off of St Julian of Le Mans	* Text D	Wagner I, 314, citing Gerbert II: 35f; Lebeuf, 43; Mabillon IV:110
Marquard of Echternach, c936	"...hymnos quoque prosas, et varios in laudem Sanctorum cantus et melodias composuit."		Wagner I, 314, citing Gerbert II: 35
Martialis Auribelli, general of Dominicans, 1453-62, 1465-73	Off of St Vincent Ferrer (AH 5, no 91)	Words only?	Schlager, "Reimoffizien" 296
Nicolaus Hermannsun [Nils Hermanssun], bp of Linköping 1374-91	Off of St Birgitta (AH 25, no 37), of St Anna (AH 25, no 21)	Words only?	Schlager, "Reimoffizien" 296
Notker II of S Gall, d975	Off of St Othmar	Ekkehard, Casus S Galli, c1040	Möller, "Office Compositions;" Berschin, Ochenbein, Möller, "Das Otmaroffizium"
Notker of St Gall, c840-912	Melodies "Frigdola," "Occidentana;" Hymn *Ave beati germinis;* Ant *Media vita*	Ekkehard, c980-c1060 (Seq); SG 381 (hymn); 1613 Metzler[?] (Ant)	Rankin, "Notker and Tuotilo;" von den Steinen

Name	Attributed composition	Source of attribution; remarks	Bibliography
Odilo of Cluny, 961-1049	Off of St Maiolus (AH 18, no 47)	P Damian life? Jotsaldus *Vita*, PL 142?	Wagner I, 314, who cites Gerbert II: 35
Odo, ab of Cluny 926-944	Hymns and chants of St Martin	John's life of Odo, s 13 (PL 133); *Text C (unlikely)	Gerbert II: 34; PL 133, bk. I, col. 48; Lebeuf, 23 Villetard, *Office de Saint Sav.*
Odorannus of Sens, c985-c1046	Off of St Savinianus & St Potentianus (AH 28, no 62a)	Siegbert?	Delaporte, 53; Clerval; Lebeuf, 22
Olbert, ab. of Gembloux, 1012-1048	Off of St Géron, St Waltrude (Waldetrudis) (antiphons)		Gerbert II: 39. Dreves, ed.
Orrigo Scaccabarozzi, 1280	many offices of saints for Milanese liturgy: multa officia Sanctorum "tam in dictamine, quam in cantu complicavit."	His own mss; *Text T	
Peter Abélard, 1079-1142	Hymnal (*O quanta qualia*)	Heloise	Weinrich; Huglo, "Abélard;" Waddell
Peter Damian, c1007-1072	Off of St Silvester; trope and mass of Apollinaris; hymn melodies	Giovanni di Lodi's life of PD, c1080	Lokrantz; Facchini
Peter Olofsson, c1350	Cantus sororum of Bridgettine nuns, c1350	"tradition" ascribes to Master Peter	Servatius
Peter the Venerable, abbot, 1122-156	Off of Transfiguration		Hiley, "The Office"
Peter, canon of St Aubert of Cambrai, c1236	Off of St Elizabeth of Hungary: he "joined neumas to Gerard's ants and Rxx."	A late-13c document from Afflighem *Text S	Haggh, *Two Offices*; Gerbert II: 39
Pierre de Corbeil, d1222	Sens Circumcision office	An assemblage	Villetard
Pierre Duwez, d1508	Off (and Mass?) of the Seven Sorrows	Won competition	Kellman, *The Treasury*, Strohm, 322
Poppo, bp of Metz, c1050-1103	12 rxx of St Martial, the first is *Laeta dies nobis*; 2 hymns of St Valeria, etc.		Gerbert II: 38
Prudentius, 348-after405	Hymns: *Corde natus*; *Salvete flos*	Words only?	
Radulphus of St Trond, c1130	Music for office of St Trudo, text by abbot Theodericus (AH 13, no 96)		
Raimundus [de Vineis] a Capua, Confessor of Cath of Siena, 1330-99	Off of Visitation (AH 24, no 30)	Doc. of 1462; a text (AH 24, p. 98) *Text U	Auda, *L'Office*; De Loos, *Chant*; Gerbert II: 38, citing Trithemius LMLO; Wagner I:316

Name	Attributed composition	Source of attribution; remarks	Bibliography
Rainald bp of Langres, s10?	Off of St Mammes, texts of Walafrid Strabo		Wagner, I: 314; Gerbert II: 36, citing Mabillon saec V; Lebeuf, 19
Ratbod, bp of Utrecht, d917	Off of St Martin; seq *Ave summa praesulum* for the same feast (AH 53, no 182); "de sancti Martini translatione officium composuit. Et varios cantus in honore sanctorum."		Lochner; Szövérffy, *Annalen* I: 463; Gerbert II: 35; Lebeuf, 19; Trithemius, f. 69v
Ratpert of St Gall, d. 890	Hymns, incl. *Ardua spes mundi*	Ekkehard, c980-c1060	Planchart (NG2)
Raynaldus of Colle di Mezzo, ab of Montecassino 1137-1166	Off of St Placidus (AH 28, no 50)	MC MS, s12	Wagner I: 316; Kelly, "Cassinese"
Reginold, bishop of Eichstätt 966-991	an Off of St Nicholas and of Willibald (first bp of Eichstätt)	Anonymous Haserensis, s11	Hofmann-Brandt I: 17; Anonymus Haserensis, ch. 15
Remigius Mediolacensis (Mettlach), c980	Off of Sts Eucharius, Valerius, and Maternus of Trier; of St Bavo; "Litanias et cantilenas" for rogations	at request of abp Egbert; and other chants. *Text E	Haggh, "Sources," 40-41; Wagner I: 314, who cites Gerbert II: 35, Lebeuf, 18. Schalter, "Reimoffizien" p. 296
Richard de Gerberoy, bp of Amiens, 1204-1210	Off of decoll. Joh Bapt (AH 13, no 78)	Words only?	Robertson, 330; PalMus X: 25-26; Huglo, *Tonaires* 91-2, no 2; Lebeuf, 16
Robert II of France (996-1031)	O *Costancia* for St Denis; *Judea et Jerusalem* for first Vsp, Christmas	Once attributed to him	Trowell & Wathey; Hughes, BRO, 278
Robert of Gloucester, canon of Hereford, 1279-1322	Off of St Thomas Cantilupe bp of Hereford (AH 13, no 95)	"perhaps composed"	Hughes, "Fons hortorum," 155-160
Rostagnus OP, 15c?	Off of Presentation (AH 24, no 25)	Words only?	Gerbert II: 33; Lebeuf, 21-22
Siegbert of Gembloux, c1035-1112	Off of St Maclou, of St Guibertus	His own chronicle: *Text K	Gerbert II: 36, citing Mabillon; Rhythmis Adelmanni; Delaporte 52-53.
Sigo of Chartres, 11c	music of responsories of St Florente, texts by Rainaldo scholasticus; 2 hymns of St Florente	Cantor of Chartres	
Stephen of Liège, c850-920	Offices of Trinity, Inv Stephani, St Lambert	Many early attributions. *Text B	Auda; Jonsson; Lebeuf, 19

Name	Attributed composition	Source of attribution; remarks	Bibliography
Theodulph of Orleans, d821	Gloria laus et honor	Words only?	
Thomas Aquinas, d1274	Off of Corpus Christi, est. 1264 "officium festi corporis Christi composuit."	Words only?	Trithemius, f. 105
Thomas of Celano, c1200-c1255	2 seq of St Francis; Dies irae (?)		Vellekoop
Thomas Stubbs, c1320-1383	Off of St Anna (AH 5, no 79)		Hughes, BRO 253
Tuotilo of St Gall, d915	Tropes, incl. Hodie cantandus	Ekkehard, c980-c1060	Rankin 1991; Rankin, Recherches
Udascalc of Augsburg, ab1124-1150	Offices: St Ulrich (AH 5, no 86), St Afra, St Mauritius, St M. Magdalena	Abbots list, cited Hoeynck; *Texts P, Q	Hoeynck
Venantius Fortunatus, c530-c600	Pange lingua, Vexilla Regis, both 569, Salve festa dies	Words only?	
Wandalbert, monk of Prüm, c813-after870	Off of St Chrysantus & St Daria (AH 25, no 73)	Attrib in 15c; words only?	
Warner of Rebais, c1087	Off of St Edmund K&m, c1087	Composed 4 additional antiphons	Thomson, "The Music"
Wulf[s]tan of Winchester, fl 992-6	"aliud opus de tonorum armonia valde utile:" tropes of Ethelwold; Winchester polyphony?	Wm of Malmesbury, d. 1143?	Holschneider; Planchart, The Repertory

is some reason to connect them with the music of the hymns I have not included these authors among the composers. The result may be that I have slighted some very talented musicians... .

There can be various reasons for ascriptions of texts to authors. A famous *auctor* provides *auctoritas* for the text, as with Gregorian and Ambrosian chant. In many such cases, surely, the Pope, bishop, or abbot named as author or composer is the person who caused the piece to exist, and in the sense of being the motivating force, he is in fact the author.

And so, famous pieces get attributed to famous people. *Veni sancte spiritus* is ascribed to Hermannus Contractus, and to Pope Innocent III. *Lauda Syon salvatorem* to Saint Bonaventure and to St Thomas Aquinas. Famous pieces are attributed to kings: Robert of France gets credit sometimes for the responsories of Fulbert of Chartres; Charlemagne (who is yet another author of *Veni sancte spiritus*), Charles the Bald.[4] *Salve regina* is attributed to Hermannus Contractus, Pope Gregory II, Peter, bishop of Compostela, and St Bernard.[5]

There are many reasons, sometimes very good ones, for making an incorrect attribution. Often one is simply misinformed, and misattributions can continue for a very long time. From other times and places we know of very good reasons for attributing music to someone who is not strictly its author. On occasion in the nineteenth century it was the practice to make a gift of a song – to publish a song as the composition of someone one sought to please.[6] In traditional music, a song or a melody is sometimes attributed to a particular person because of the way it is performed – after the manner of David Hiley, or as performed by Giulio Cattin, or in the style of Giacomo Baroffio. Sometimes a lesser artist attaches creations to the reputation of a greater artist, in the hope of ensuring their survival. Some of these procedures may be reflected in the names of composers that survive to us, but it is rare that we can detect them.

If we arrange the list of names in Table 1 chronologically (the list is arranged in that way as Table 2), we see that our earliest

---

⁴ All these kings are named in M. Gerbert, *De cantu et musica sacra a prima ecclesiae aetate usque ad praesens tempus*, St. Blasien, 1774, repr. ed. O. Wessely (Graz: Akademische Druck- und Verlagsanstalt, 1968), Vol. 2: 27, 31.

⁵ Gerbert, *De cantu* 2: 37; for a review of the evidence, see Marie-Noël Colette, "Le *Salve regina* en Aquitaine au XIIe siècle. L'auteur du Salve," in *Cantus Planus. Papers read at the Fourth Meeting, Pécs, Hungary 3-8 September 1990* (Budapest: Hungarian Academy of Sciences Institute for Musicology, 1992), pp. 521-547.

⁶ I am grateful to Petra Gelbart for this suggestion.

XII

Table 2. *Medieval Composers of Liturgical Chant, in Roughly Chronological Order*

Ambrose of Milan, d. 397
Prudentius, 348-after405
Venantius Fortunatus, c530-c600
Gregory I, pope 590-604
Conantius bp of Palencia, d. c638
Ioannes Caesar-Augustano (Zaragosa), s7
Ildefonsus of Toledo, d. 667
Adelmus, English bishop, 8c
Theodulph of Orleans, d. 821
Hilduin ab. of ST Denis, d. 840
Wandalbert, monk of Prüm, c813-after870
Gurdestin abb of Landévennec, s9
Ratpert of St Gall, d. 890
Notker of St Gall, c840-912
Ratbod, bp of Utrecht, d 917
Stephen of Liège, c850-920
Tuotilo of St Gall, d. 915
Hucbald, 840-c930
Marquard of Echternach, c936
Odo ab of Cluny 926-944
Hericus & Remigius of St Germain, c. 950
Rainald bp of Langres, s10?
Folquinus, ab of Lobbes, 965-980
Notker II of St Gall, d 975
Herigerus of Lobbes (Belg), d. 1007
Remigius Mediolacensis (Mettlach), c980
Abbo, ab of Fleury, 945?-1004
Letaldus of Micy, c990
Reginold, bishop of Eichstätt 966-991
Wul[f]stan of Winchester, fl 992-6
Angelramus (Angerlan), s11
Fulbert of Chartres, c960-1028
Adémar de Chabannes, c988-1034
Arnold of St Emmeran
Odilo of Cluny, 961-1049
Odorannus of Sens, c985-c1046
Olbert, ab. Of Gembloux 1012-1048
Berno of Reichenau, s 1047
Bruno of Egisheim (Pope Leo IX, d 1054)
Gerbert of St Wandrille, s11
Ainard, s11
Arnoul of Chartres, s11
Hermannus Contractus, 1013-1054
Isembert (Norman abbot), s11
Lambert, m of St Lawrence, Liège, c1075
Sigo of Chartres, 11c
Desiderius ab of Montecassino 1058-1087
Durandus ab Troarn, d 1088
Folcardus (Folcard of Thorney) d 1084
Hildegard of Bingen, 1098-1179
Peter Damian, c1007-1072
Alfanus, abp of Salerno 1054-1085
Gottschalk of Aachen, d. 1084
Warner of Rebais, c1087

Goscelin of Canterbury, 1090s
Poppo, bp of Metz, c 1050-1103
Siegbert of Gembloux, c. 1035-1112
Calixtus II, pope 1119-1124
Peter Abelard, 1079-1142
Radulphus of St Trond, ca 1130
Adam of St Victor, d1146?
Arnaldus, Belgium, 1141
Bernard of Clairvaux, 1090-1153
Udascalc of Augsburg, abbott 1124-1150
Giselbertus and John, of Liege, s12
Peter the Venerable, abbot 1122-156
Raynaldus ab of Montecassino 1137-1166
Benedict of Peterborough, d. 1193
Richard de Gerberoy, 1204-1210
Giraldus Cambrensis, 1146-1223
Pierre de Corbeil, d 1222
Julian of Speyer, d. 1285?
Peter of Cambrai, c 1236
Jean du Mont-Cornillon, 1246
Arnaut du Pré
Bonaventure, d. 1274
Goswin of Bossut, s14
Thomas of Celano, c1200-c1255
Thomas Aquinas, d. 1274
John Peckham, ab of Canterbury 1279-92
Orrigo Scaccabarozzi, 1280
Jacopone da Todi, c1230-1306?
Bryniolphus Algottson of Skara 1278-1317
Juan Gil de Zamora, c1240-1318
Christian of Lilienfeld, d. 1330
Robert of Gloucester, of Hereford 1279-1322
Giacomo Gaetani Stefaneschi, c1270-1343
Conrad of Megenberg, 1309-1374
Peter Olafsson, c 1350
Birgerus Gregorii, abp Uppsala, d 1383
John Horneby, c 1370, Carmelite of Lincoln
Raimundus [de Vineis] a Capua 1330-1399
Thomas Stubbs, c1320-1383
Nicolaus Hermannus bp of Linköping 1374-91
Adam Easton, d. 1397
Leopold of Steinberg, 1406
Edmund Lacy, bp of Hereford 1417-1420
Ghislerus of Hildesheim, fl. 1406-23
Johann Hoffmann, bp of Meissen 1427-1451
Johannes Benechini (Oeland), d. 1461
Calixtus III, pope 1455-1458
Guillaume Dufay, 1397-1474
Martialis Auribelli 1453-62, 1465-73
Rostagnus OP, 15c?
Arnold Heimericius
Johann Hane, late 15c
Pierre Duwez, d1508

108

"composers" are generally producers of whole bodies of chant: Gregorian, Ambrosian, and probably also the Old Spanish chant, given the seventh-century contributions of John of Zaragosa and Conantius of Palencia; like Gregory and Ambrose, they are high prelates, under whose authority much may well have been accomplished. The other earliest "composers" are poets, like Prudentius and Venantius Fortunatus, and we have no evidence whatever that they composed any of the melodies that accompany their poetry.

There are composers of sequences, of hymns, of tropes, indeed of all those parts of the liturgy where some variability is possible, or even desirable. There are not many masses (although there is a mass of St Apollinaris attributed to Peter Damian).

The chief source of new music – or at least of the names of composers – is the new offices, or *historiae*, that proliferated from the tenth century onward. Whereas new masses were generally assembled from pieces already present in the repertory, the texts of offices, always more variable than masses, could be drawn from the saint's life or composed anew. Many of the authors of offices may well have been their composers, but attributions generally intend only to indicate the source of the texts.

It does not escape attention that, although a great many *historiae* for local saints were created in the later middle ages, there is an outpouring of creative effort in praise of female saints. Karlheinz Schlager, in counting the offices published in *Analecta hymnica*, noted that the saints who have the largest numbers of different offices include Saints Anna (21 offices), Barbara (17), Margaret (16), Ursula (13), and Martha (11).[7] It may be that among those offices there are many whose music was composed by women, but we do not for the moment know their names.

The only woman on the list, in fact, is Hildegarde of Bingen, that remarkable visionary abbess. Her many compositions, most of which are called antiphons and responsories, may or may not be liturgical music, and so by strict definition she should perhaps not be on this list. But given the extent of the music attributed to her, and the stylistic personality that her music displays, it seems obtuse to exclude her.

Almost nobody on the list is a composer. Some of the persons on the list may actually have created – we would say composed – liturgical music that had not existed before, and were remem-

[7] K. Schlager, "Reimoffizien," in K. G. Fellerer, ed., *Geschichte der katholischen Kirchenmusik*, 2 vols. (Kassel: Bärenreiter, 1972-1976), 1: pp. 293-297.

bered, correctly, as having done so. But even in those rare cases, the person named is seldom someone whose business it is to make new music.

What persons in this long list do we believe actually created the music of the liturgical items concerned? We determine this mostly by clear and relatively comtemporaneous attributions which specifically mention the music. Such attributions are relatively rare.

There are some famous names here: Notker, Hildegarde, Hermannus Contractus, Abelard, Guillaume Dufay. Notker may have composed some music, but he is best known, of course, for setting words to existing music.

Hidegarde's music may or may not have been composed by her, and may or may not be intended for liturgical use. Hermannus Contractus, famous for many pieces he did not composer, nevertheless was a musician and composer, as David Hiley's edition of the office of St Wolfgang shows. Abelard was certainly a poet, and perhaps did compose a bit too.

And there are other who evidently did create music.

Hucbald (840-ca. 930) is credited with several pieces by Gunther of St Amand almost two centuries later, even though he certainly did not compose everything attributed to him.

Tuotilo of St Gall (d. 915) seems to be composer as well as poet, painter and sculptor, if we are to believe Ekkehard.

Reginold, bishop of Eichstätt from 966-991, "optimus huius tempus musicus," did indeed compose, says his eleventh-century chronicler (Table 3: Text **E**)

Letaldus of Micy, c. 990, composed the office of St Julian of Le Mans; a text describing how he followed tradition is Text **D** (Table 3).

Wul[f]stan of Winchester (fl. 992-996), composed "aliud opus de tonorum armonia valde utile"; I wonder what this is: tropes for Ethelwold? The famous Winchester polyphony? Whatever it is, it is music.

Adémar of Chabannes does seem to have made all that music for St Martial, and for other offices.

And there is Pope Leo IX, Bruno of Egisheim; we will return to him in a moment.

Ainard, in the 11th century, with Gerbert and Durand, according to Orderic Vitalis, "ad modulandum suaviter potiti sunt; et dulcisonos cantus Antiphonarum atque Responsoriorum ediderunt" (Table 3: Texts **M** and **N**).

Gottschalk of Aachen (d. 1084), himself says that he composed.

[Abbot] Warner of Rebais, at some point before 1087, added four additional antiphons, text and music, to the office of St Edmund.

Goscelin of Canterbury, in the 1090s, created the office of Mildretha, words and music: "Happy the tongue," says Orderic Vitalis, "which has put forth so many melodies for singing" (Table 3: Text **O**).

Siegbert of Gembloux, d. 1112, "mellificavit", in his own words, the offices of Saint Maclou and of Saint Guibertus (founder of Gembloux).

Abbot Udascalc of Augsburg (1124-1150) was an excellent and inspiring composer, to judge from the chronicles (Table 3: Text **Q**).

Abbot Benedict of Peterborough composed text and music for Thomas Becket (Table 3: Text **R**).

Peter of Saint Aubert, Cambrai, about 1236 made the music of the office of Saint Elizabeth to texts by a certain Gerard (Table 3: Text **S**).

Julian of Speyer, (d. 1250) composed the offices of St Francis and St Anthony.

And there are the many offices by the prolific Milanese composer Orrigo Scaccabarozzi.

Pope Leo IX is a special case. Unlikely as it seems, given the frequent and implausible attribution of music to persons in authority, it may be that Bruno of Egisheim, Bishop of Toul and later Pope Leo IX, was actually the author and composer of works attributed to him. The *vita* of Leo, long attributed to a certain Wibert or Guibert, archdeacon of Toul, and more recently attributed to Leo's colleague Cardinal Humbert, specifically mentions Leo's musical abilities, in Table 3: Text **G**. A younger contemporaneous chronicler, Siegbert of Gembloux, compared Leo in his musical abilities to Saint Gregory the Great: "si quis attendat cantus, in honore Sanctorum ab ipso compositos cum primo Gregorio papa merito comparabit" (Table 3: Text **H**). Later chroniclers repeat such praises, varying and increasing the number of offices attributed to Bruno, and assigning their texts sometimes to Cardinal Humbert (Table 3: Texts **I** and **J**). But the music remains Bruno's; Madeleine Bernard's study of the offices that survive with music observes that they all survive only in relatively local manuscripts – from eastern France or western Germany (except of course for the office of St Gregory) and that, while their musical style is not completely consistent, there is nevertheless a style of what she calls developing variation to be found especially among the responsories.

Of all the names on the list, Guillaume Dufay, musician and canon of Cambrai, is almost the only person we would call a composer, though he was not a regular composer of chant, so far as we know. Pierre Duwez was a professional musician in the chapels of Mary of Burgundy, Maximilian, and Philip the Fair, and was Josquin's predecessor as provost of Condé; Duwez won a competition to provide music for the Office and Mass for the feast of the Seven Sorrows of the Virgin for which Petrus de Manso had assembled the text. Such a musical setting exists in a manuscript (Brussels, Bibl. Royale MS 215-216) from the workshop of Petrus Alamire, but we cannot be absolutely certain that this is Duwez's setting. Still, Duwez was not a "composer;" like others who created music, he was skilled in music, and able to create new music when it was needed.

Composing

What words do writers used for the making of a sung liturgical item? It is difficult, even in my own language, to find the right words: if I say a "chant": or a "song," I will necessarily imply the text and the music together, even though they are sometimes created separately. And should I say "make," or "compose," or "create," or "invent?" It depends perhaps on how the piece in question came into being. Some things are "invented," that is, found. Others are "composed," in that they result from the juxtaposition of previously-known elements. The words used in the middle ages are equally varied, and often confusing to anyone trying to determine who made the music.

The word most often used is "**fecit**" ("Fecit inter alios cantus"), as for Udalscalc of Augsburg (Table 3: Text **P**) in the twelfth century.

"**Composuit**" can be used in the sense of placing music with the words, as is also said of Udascalc: "Versibus complexus est easque notis musicis **composuit**" (Table 3: Text **Q**).

"**Complicavit**" is used of Orrigo Scaccabarozzi ("tam in dictamine, quam in cantu **complicavit**," Table 3: Text **T**).

Raymundus of Capua compiled, "**compilavit**," offices of the Visitation and of Saint Catherine of Siena (Table 3: Text **U**).

"**Emiserit**" as used of Goscelin of Canterbury by William of Malmesbury ("Felix lingua, quae tot Sanctis servierit, que tot vocales melodias emiserit," Table 3: Text **O**), seems to be referring to composition rather than only to performance.

Reginold of Eichstätt in making a melisma for a responsory (Table 3: Text **E**) "in fine **notulas apposuit**". Where he got these notes – whether he "found" them elsewhere or made them up himself, is not specified.

"**Neumas apposuit**" is what Peter of Cambrai did to the texts of antiphons and responsories by Gerard (Table 3: Text **S**); surely this is not the adding of melismas to the ends of existing melodies, but adding melodies to existing texts.

Letaldus of Micy (Table 3: Text **D**), did not want to "fashion," **fingere**, barbaric or inexpert music as he "composed" (**in componendo**) the office of St Julian.

Abbot Benedict of Peterborough "engraved" (**insigno**, insignare, not insignio, marked); he engraved the text with song. (Table 3: Text **R**)

Orderic Vitalis writes of Gerbert and Ainard that they brought forth chants (edo, edidi): "dulcisonos cantus Antiphonarum atque Responsoriorum **ediderunt**" (Table 3: Text **M**). The term is used elsewhere also of Constantius of Palencia. (Table 3: Text **A**)

"**Modulare**" is used by Orderic Vitalis of Ainard ("gemina scientia planiter imbutus versificandi et modulandi," Table 3: Text **N**). "**Neumatizavit et composuit**" is what Hermannus of Reichenau did for office-cycles (Text **F**) – perhaps the "composition" is textual?

Siegbert of Gembloux, d. 1112, says of himself, "**mellificavi**" (Table 3: Text **K**), the offices of Saint Maclou and of Saint Guibertus (founder of Gembloux).

"**Effero**," to bear or bring forth: William of Malmesbury says of of Fulbert of Chartres: " … studens musicis modulationibus **extulit**."

"**Stabilire**," to establish: "stabilire curavit," says his successor Richarius in 932 of Stephen of Liège and the Trinity office, making clear that he is taking care about "dulcissima modulatio" (Table 3: Text **B**).

These are words used by chroniclers, who may not be well versed in the language of music. Writers about music, however, use many of the same terms. Guido of Arezzo (Table 3: Text **W**) uses both "**facere**" and "**componere**," the latter word in the sense of placing elements together: "qui cantum faciunt, rationabiliter discretas ac diversas neumas componant."

John of Afflighem uses "componere" in the modern sense of "compose," it seems, when he says "in componendis cantibus" (Table 3: Text **Y**); he also, perhaps in the interest of variety, uses

"modulare" ("prefati sacri cantus officiales in Sancta Ecclesia modulati sunt;" "Primum igitur praeceptum modulandi..." Table 3: Texts **Z, AA**) and "**contexere**," to weave (Table 3: Text **Z**).
Regino of Prüm, like others, differentiates natural from artificial music: "Artificialis musica dicitur quae arte et ingenio humano **excogitata** est et **inventa**..." (Table 3: Text **V**).

Of the names listed here, probably fewer than half are makers of music. Many may not even be the makers of words. But the tendency to assign praise, and names, to the creation of sequences, hymns, and offices, indicates that the liturgical songs were worthy of admiration, and a credit to their composers, whoever they really were. In the papers in this volume I hope that we may come to understand the nature of some of this music, and come to a fuller appreciation of the creative abilities of the medieval composers of liturgical chant.

Table 3. *A selection of medieval texts on composition*

A. Conantius post Maurilanem Ecclesiae Palentinae sedem adeptus est, vir tam pondere mentis quam habitudine speciei gravis, communi eloquio facundus, et gravis, ecclesiasticorum officiorum ordinibus intentus et providus, nam melodias soni multas noviter edidit. Orationum quoque libellum de omnium decenter conscripsit proprietate Psalmorum.

      On Conantius bp of Palencia, d. c638, Ildefonsus, *De viribus illustris*, PL 96, col. 203

B. Venerabilis vir prae[de]cessor noster Stephanus, in honore Sanctae Trinitatis, quaedam responsoria cum antiphonis nocturnalibus, sive matutinalibus necnon vespertinalibus, totumque ad plene officium dulcissimae modulationis stabilire curavit [...]

      Richerus, successor to Stephen of Liege (c850-900), in a document quoted in Anselm's chronicle of the bishops of Liege; (cited Auda, *L'école*, p. 73)

C. Similiter [in addition to three hymns of St Martin] dudoecim antiphonas, ternas per singulas habentes differentias. Quarum verba et vocum consonantias adeo sibi concordant, ut nihil in sensu plus minusve, nihil in symphoniae modulationibus reperiri posse dulcius videatur.

      Iohannes, life of Odo of Cluny (926-944), cited Gerbert 2: 34 note

D. Porro in componendo S. Juliani officio excedere noluit a similitudine veteris cantus, ne barbaram aut inexpertem melodiam fingeret; non enim mihi placet, ait ille, qaorundam <sic> musicorum novitas qui tanta dissimilitudine utuntur, ut veteres sequi omnino dedignentur auctores.

      On Letaldus of Micy, c990, composer of office of Julian of Le Mans, cited Wagner 1: 314n4, citing Annales Benedict. I, 110. (=Mabillon?)

E. [...] in fine [responsorii] notulas apposuit; eisdem notulis versiculos instar sequentiarum subiunxit." He was called "optimus hujus temporis musicus."

      Reginold of Eichstätt in making a responsory trope: Anonymous Haserensis, s11, MGH Scr 7, p. 257l; PL 146, col 1011. Description in Hofmann-Brandt, 1: 17

F. Cantus item historiales plenarios, utpote que musicus peritior non erat, de sancto Georgio, sanctis Gordiano et Epimacho, sancta Afra martyre, sancto Magno confessore, et de sancto Wolfgango episcopo mira suavitate et elegantia euphonicos, praeter alia huiusmodi perplura, neumatizavit et composuit.

      Berthold on Hermannus (contractus) of Reichenau, 1013-1054, MGH Scriptores Annales et chronica aevi Salici 5: 268; PL 143 col 28, cited by Hiley in Hermannus, Contractus, *Historia Sanctae Afrae*, p. xxii.

XII

On Bruno of Egisheim, later Leo IX (d1054):

G. Sapientia diuinarum humanarumque ... maxime artis delectabilis mu-
sice peritia ... nam componens responsoria in ueneratione gloriosi martyris Cyriaci sanctique Hidulfi Treuirorum archiepiscopi, nec non beate
Odile uirginis, atque uenerandi Anglorum apostoli Gregorii doctoris,
diuini laudes seruitii mirificio decore ampliauit.
From the vita of Leo, attrib. to Wibert or Guibert, archdeacon
of Toul s11; or more recently attrib to Cardinal Humbert
(PL 143, cols 465-504, cited in Bernard, "Les offices," p.
90.)

H. Si quis attendat cantus, in honore Sanctorum ab ipso compositos cum
primo Gregorio papa merito comparabit.
Sigebert of Gembloux (1030-1112) compares Leo IX to
Gregory the Great (PL 160; MGH Scriptores 6: 359, cited in
Bernard, "Les offices," p. 101 n18.)

I. Hic in musica subtilissimus fuit, et inter cantus alios quos plurimos
edidit, historiam beatissimi Pape Gregorii satis artificiose composuit.
S12 anonymous life of Leo: *Analecta Bollandiana* 25 (1906)
258-297, the life is on 275-278 (cited in Bernard, "Les offices," p. 91.)

J. Anno quippe Domini 1044, Humbertus abbas Medianimonasterii, uir
clari ingenii, laudesque responsoria dicuntur sanctorum Ciriaci martiris,
Columbani, Odilie uirginis, Gregorii pape, Hidulfi, Deodati episcopo-
rum, rithmice ac metrice componens, Brunoni episcopo supradicto Tul-
lensi tradidit decantandi.
Richer, monk of Senones, in Gesta Senoniensie Ecclesie
1264: MGH Scriptores 23: 280 (cited in Bernard, "Les
offices," p. 91.)

K. Arte musica antiphonas et responsoria de SS. Maclovo [Gerbert has
Macario] et Guiberto mellificavi.
Siegbert of Gembloux, c1070, Liber de scriptoribus eccle-
siasticis, cited Gerbert 2: 33: Cf. PL 160

L. In quibus qui vult, grammaticae artis tramitem, et monochordi sonori
magade inveniet notas.
Peter the Deacon of Montecassino (d. c1140) on abbot Desiderius' (later Pope Victor III) hymns in honor of St. Maur,
cited Gerbert 2: 36

M. Gerbertus Fontanellensis [St-Wandrille] et Ainardus Divensis [St-
Pierre-sur-Dives, dioc Bayeux] et Durandus Troarnensis, quasi tres stel-
lae radiantes in firmamento caeli, sic isti tres archimandritae, multis
modis rutilabant in arce Adonai. Studio divinaeque laudationis in templo
Dei jugiter inhiabant, inter praecipuos cantores scientia musicae artis, ad

116

modulandum suaviter potiti sunt; et dulcisonos cantus Antiphonarum atque Responsoriorum ediderunt.
> Orderic Vitalis (c1075-c1143), bk. 4, 1072, quoted Pothier, "Répons," p. 50

N. . . . gemina scientia planiter imbutus versificandi et modulandi, cantusque suaves edendi peritissimus. Hoc evidenter probari potest in historiis Kiliani Wirtzceburgensis Episcopi et Catharinae Virginis, aliisque plurimis cantibus, quos eleganter idem edidit in Creatoris.
> On Ainard: Orderic Vitalis (c1075-c1143), bk. 4, ch. 24

O. Felix lingua, quae tot Sanctis servierit, que tot vocales melodias emiserit.
> Wm of Malmesbury (d. c1143) on Goscelin of Canterbury; see Sharpe, "Words and music," pp. 94-97

P. Fecit inter alios cantus historiam totam de S. Afra. Similiter et historiam S. Udalrici ep. Aug., quem cantum ad episcopum Constantinensem Udalricum fecit; ita metro dyapente diatessaronque inducit, ac diapason consonantiarum concordi modulatione cum opportunis licentiis et figuris huius artis musicae utitur mirifice, ut in jocunditatem laudesque suaves dei atque viri admirationem tristes quoque mentes quam facile excitari possint. Nec discors verborum sensus a melodiae concentu. Optime enim metrorum genere Udalrici, Afrae autem prosa equidem a metri compendio haud multum distante, vitam pene omnem pariter ligavit ac comprehendit.
> On Udalscalc abbot of St Uldaric and St Afra, Augsburg, 1124-1150, in abbot-list, cited Wagner 1: 315n4-316.

Q. Versibus complexus est easque notis musicis composuit et ad publice decantandas in officiis ecclesiasticis destinavit.
> On Udalscalc abbot of St Uldaric and St Afra, Augsburg, 1124-1150, in abbot-list, cited Wagner 1: 316 n1; Hoeynck, p. 59

R. Unde composuit egregium volumen de passione et miraculis sancti Thome: et hystoriam Studens livor totam fecit: totam dico, quia dictamen cantu excellenter insignavit.
> On Benedict of Peterborough, d. 1193: by chronicler of Peterborough, cited in Hughes, "Chants," 201 n2, citing Hunt, "Notes."

S. Frater Gerardus Monachus sancti Quintini ... composuit etiam antiphonas, et responsoria eleganti dictamine in eiusdem sancte festivitate cantanda. Neumas vero eisdem antiphonis, et responsoriis quidam frater Petrus Canonicus Sancti Autberti Cameracensis apposuit. Idem etiam Petrus Musicae artis peritus dulci modulamine a limato dictamine composuit plurima cantica, quae vulgo condictus vocant.
> Henry of Brussels, in a document of Afflighem date c1270-1280, on Gerard and Peter of Cambrai and Gerard of St Quentin; cited in Haggh, *Two offices*, p. xiv.

XII

T. ... multa officia Sanctorum tam in dictamine, quam in cantu complicavit. On Orrigo Scaccabarozzi, 1280, cited Gerbert 2: 39 from ¿ ɪ Milan cathedral MS

U. Iste magister [Raimundus a Capua] sepultus est in Nuremberga. Et ipse compilavit historiam de visitacione matris Dei et legendam sanctae Katharinae de Senis cuius fuit confessor.
AH 24, no 98 states that an unnumbered manuscript of 1462 in the Dominican house in Vienna has this notice; Wagner 1: 316.

Some musical theorists on composition

Musica and *Scolica enchiriadis,* s9ex, essentially discuss chants as existing, observed, phenomena. Well-made chants have certain qualities, but there is no though of altering them or making new ones. Most of the examples, but not all, are not from the liturgy.

Regino of Prüm, d915
V. Artificialis musica dicitur quae arte et ingenio humano excogitata est et inventa [...]
cited Bruyne 1: 313, from G., I, 233a-236b, PL 132, c 491.

Guido (995-1050), *Micrologus* ch 17, is on composing grateful melodic lines. It is not clear whether he is speaking of liturgical song, but he cites a liturgical song (Int. *Ad te levavi*).

W. ... ita et qui cantum faciunt, rationabiliter discretas ac diversas neumas componant. (Guido, ed. Smits, p. 172 *Neuma* means a phrase or less).

X. ... ut in tristibus rebus graves sint neumae, in tranquillis iocundae, in prosperis exultantes et reliqua. (Guido, ed. Smits, p. 174; this is really for singers).

Johannes Afflighemensis/Cotto: John: has a section on composition, based largely on word-tone relationships and on modal qualities. His chapters 18, 19, and 20 are about composition. Ch 20 is about composing with vowels, in the manner first suggested by Guido, and is not really about composition of practical liturgical chant. As with Guido, his examples are from liturgical chants, but it is not clear whether his compositional recommendations are for liturgical chant.

Y. ... in componendis cantibus bene cantus musicus ita sibi providere debet, ut eo modo quam decentissime utatur, quo eos maxime delectari videt quibus cantum suum placere desiderat. (Guido, ed. Smits, pp. 109-110).

118

Z. Verum quia non solum prefati sacri cantus officiales in Sancta Ecclesia modulati sunt, sed et alii quidam non longe ante nostra tempora cantuum compositores extitere, quod nos quoque cantum vetet contexere non video. Nam etsi novae modulationes nunc in Ecclesia non sunt necessariae, possumus tamen in rythmis et lugubribus poetarum versibus decantandis ingenia nostra exercere. (Guido, ed. Smits, p. 116)

AA. Primum igitur praeceptum modulandi subnectimus, ut secundum sensum verborum cantus varietur. (Guido, ed. Smits, p. 117)

BB. ... ut quod verba sonant cantus exprimere videatur. (Guido, ed. Smits, p. 117)

Hieronymus de Moravia O. P., *Tractatus de musica* after 1272

CC. ... in unoquoque modo et numero ad placitum componentis, secundum videlicet quod exigit harmonica pulchritude. (Hieronymus, ed. Cserba, p. 176)

"Cujusdam Carthusiensis monachi Tractatus de musica plana"

DD. [On modal order in offices:] Nec videtur reprobandum cum hoc fiat propter tedium removendum. Esset enim tediosum multum diversos cantus eiusdem materie sub eodem tono frequenter iterare. Secus tamen foret in cantilenis vel motetis que potius componi debent sub tonis eis competentibus quoad materiam
"Cujusdam Carthusiensis monachi Tractatus de musica plana", CS II, 445.

119

Bibliography

AH = Guido Maria Dreves and Clemens Blume, eds. *Analecta Hymnica Medii Aevi*, 55 vols. (Leipzig: 1886-1922)

Auda, Antoine, *L'école musicale liégeoise au Xe siècle; Étienne de Liége* (Brussels: Maurice Lamertin, 1923)

Auda, Antoine, *L'Office de Saint Trudon. L'École liégeoise au XIIe siècle* (Paris: 1911)

Bernard, Madeleine, "Les Offices versifiés attribués a Léon IX (1002-1054)," *Études Grégoriennes* 19 (1980), pp. 89-164

Berschin, Walter, and David Hiley, eds., *Die Offizien des Mittelalters: Dichtung und Musik*, Regensburger Studien zur Musikgeschichte 1 (Tutzing: H. Schneider, 1999)

Berschin, Walter, *Biographie und Epochenstil im Lateinischen Mittelalter*, 4 vols. in 6 (Stuttgart: A. Hiersemann, 1986-2004)

Berschin, Walter, Peter Ochsenbein und Hartmut Möller, "Das älteste Gallusoffizium," in *Lateinishche Kultur im X. Jahrhundert. Mittellateinisches Jahrbuch* 24/25 (1989/1990)

Berschin, Walter, Peter Ochsenbein und Hartmut Möller, "Das Otmaroffizium," in Berschin and Hiley, *Die Offizien*, pp. 25-57

Björkvall, Gunilla und Andreas Haug, "Text und Musik im Trinitätsoffizium Stephans von Lüttich," in Berschin and Hiley, *Die Offizien,* pp. 1-24

Blume, Clemens, "Zur Poesie des kirchlichen Stundengebetes," *Stimmen aus Maria Laach* 55 (1898), pp. 132-145

Boeren, Petrus Cornelis, *Catalogus van de liturgische handschriften van de Koninklijke Bibliotheek* ('s-Gravenhage: Koninklijke Bibliotheek, 1988)

Bruyne, Edgar de, *Études d'estétique médiévale*, 2 vols. (Bruges: de Tempel, 1946)

Chartier, Yves, *L'oeuvre musicale d'Hucbald de Saint-Amand* (Saint-Laurent, Québec: Ballarmin, 1995)

Clerval, Alexandre, *Les écoles de Chartres au moyen âge: du Xve au XVIe siècle* (Paris, 1895, repr. Frankfurt: Minerva, 1965)

Crocker, Richard L., "Hermann's Major Sixth," *Journal of the American Musicological Society* 25 (1972), pp. 19-37

CS = Coussemaker, Edmond de, *Scriptorum de musica medii aevi Novam seriem ...* 4 vols. (Paris: Durand, 1864-76, repr. Hildesheim: Olms, 1963)

XII

Delaporte Yves, "Fulbert de Chartres et l'école chartraine de chant liturgique au XIe siècle," *Etudes grégoriennes* 2 (1957), pp. 51-81

Dobszay, László, "Zur Stilistik der Melodien des Emmeram-Offiziums," in Berschin and Hiley, *Die Offizien,* pp. 87-108

Dreves, Guido Maria, ed. *Orrigo Scaccabarozzi's, Erzpriesters von Mailand, Liber officiorum, nach einer Handschrift der Kapitels-Bibliothek von Mailand* (Leipzig: O. R. Reisland, 1893)

Emerson, John A., "Two Newly Identified Offices for Saints Valeria and Austroclinianus by Adémar de Chabannes (MS Paris, Bibl. Nat., Latin 909, fols 79-85v)," *Speculum* 40 (1965), pp. 31-46

Facchini, Ugo, *San Pier Damiani, l'eucologia e le preghiere: contributo alla storia dell'eucologia medievale: studio critico e liturgico-teologico* (Rome: CLV, 2000)

Falconer, Keith, "Zur Offizium des hl. Medardus," in Berschin and Hiley, *Die Offizien,* pp. 69-85

Fassler, Margot, *Gothic Song. Victorine Sequences and Augustinian Reform in twelfth-century Paris* (Cambridge: Cambridge University Press, 1993)

Fassler, Margot, "Who was Adam of St Victor? The Evidence of the Sequence Manuscripts," *Journal of the American Musicological Society* 37 (1984), pp. 233-269

Gerbert, Martin, *De cantu et musica sacra a prima ecclesiae aetate usque ad praesens tempus,* St. Blasien, 1774, repr. ed. Othmar Wessely (Graz: Akademische Druck- und Verlagsanstalt, 1968)

Grier, James, "*Ecce sanctum quem Deus elegit Marcialem apostolum:* Adémar de Chabannes and the Tropes for the Feast of Saint Martial," *Beyond the Moon: Festschrift Luther Dittmer,* eds. B. Gillingham and P. Merkley (Ottawa: Institute of Mediaeval Music, 1990), pp. 28-74

Grier, James, "Roger de Chabannes (d. 1025), Cantor of St Martial, Limoges," *Early Music History* 14 (1995), pp. 53-119

Guidonis Aretini *Micrologus,* ed. Joseph Smits van Waesberghe ([Rome]: American Institute of Musicology, 1955)

Haggh, Barbara, "The Celebration of the 'Recollectio Festorum Beatae Mariae Virginis', 1457-1987," *Studia Musicologica Academiae Scientiarum Hungaricae* 30 (1988), pp. 361-373

Haggh, Barbara, "Sources for plainchant and ritual from Ghent and London: a survey and comparison," *Handelingen der Maatschappij voor Geschiedenis en Oudheidkunde te Gent,* Nieuwe reeks, deel 1 (1996), pp. 23-72

Haggh, Barbara, *Two Offices for St Elizabeth of Hungary: Gaudeat Hungaria and Letare Germania* (Ottawa: Institute of Mediaeval Music, 1995)

Hankeln, Roman, "Die Antiphonen des Dionysius-Offiziums in Clm 14872 (St. Emmeram, XVI. Jh.)," in Berschin and Hiley, *Die Offizien,* pp. 109-128

Hankeln, Roman, *Konrad von Megenberg (1309-1374). Historia Sancti Erhardi* (Ottawa: Institute of Mediaeval Music, 2000)

Hieronymus de Moravia O. P., Tractatus de musica, ed. Simon M. Cserba (Regensburg: Pustet, 1935)

XII

Hiley, David, "Chant composition at Canterbury after the Norman Conquest," in Bernhard Hangartner and Urs Fischer, *Max Lütolf zum 60. Geburtstag. Festschrift* (Basel: Wiese Verlag, 1994), pp. 31-46

Hiley, David, "Das Wolfgang-Offizium des Hermannus Contractus," in Berschin and Hiley, *Die Offizien*, pp. 129-142

Hiley, David, "The Office of the Transfiguration by Peter the Venerable, Abbot of Cluny (1122-1156) in the manuscript Paris, Bibliothèque nationale de France, fonds latin 17716," in *Chant and its Peripheries. Essays in Honour of Terence Bailey*, eds. Bryan Gillingham and Paul Merkley, Musicological Studies; vol. 72 = Wissenschaftliche Abhandlungen Bd. 72 (Ottawa: Institute of Mediaeval Music, 1998), pp. 224-40

Hiley, David, *Historia Sancti Emmerammi Arnoldi Vohburgensis: circa 1030* (Ottawa: Institute of Mediaeval Music, 1996)

Hiley, David, *Hermannus Contractus (1013-1054). Historia sancti Wolfgang episcopi ratisbonensis* (Ottawa: Institute of Mediaeval Music, 2002)

Hiley, David and Walter Berschin, *Hermannus Contractus (1013-1054). Historia sanctae Afrae martyris Augustensis* (Ottawa: Institute of Mediaeval Music, 2004)

Hoeynck, F. A., *Geschichte der Kirchlichen Liturgie des Bisthums Augsburg: mit Beilagen*. Monumenta liturgiae Augustana (Augsburg: Litterar. Institut von M. Huttler [Michael Seitz], 1889)

Hofmann-Brandt, Helma, *Die Tropen zu den Responsorien des Officiums*, 2 vols., Inaugural-Dissertation, Erlangen, 1971

Holschneider, Andreas, *Die Organa von Winchester. Studien zum ältesten Repertoire polyphoner Musik* (Hildesheim: G. Olms, [1968])

Hughes, Andrew, "Chants in the Rhymed Office of St Thomas of Canterbury," *Early Music* 16 (1988), pp.185-201

Hughes, Andrew, "Fons hortorum. The Office of the Presentation: origins and authorship," in Berschin and Hiley, *Die Offizien*, pp. 153-177

Hughes, BRO = Andrew Hughes, "British Rhymed Offices. A catalogue and Commentary," in Susan Rankin and David Hiley, eds., *Music in the Medieval English Liturgy, Plainsong & Mediaeval Music Society Centennial Essays* (Oxford: Clarendon, 1993), pp. 239-284

Huglo, Michel, "Abélard poète et musicien," *Cahiers de civilization médiévale* 22 (1979), pp. 349-361

Huglo, Michel. *Les tonaires: inventaire, analyse, comparaison* (Paris: Société française de musicologie, 1971)

Hunt, Richard, "Notes on the *distinctions monasticae et morales*," *Liber Floridus: Mittellateinische Studien Peul Lehmann zum 65. Geburtstag*, ed. Bernard Bishoff and Suso Brechter (St Ottilien: Eos Verlag der Erzabtei, 1950), pp. 255-262

Iohannes Afflighemensis, *De musica cum tonario*, ed. J. Smits van Waesberghe (Rome: American Institute of Musicology, 1950)

Jonsson, Ritva, *Historia. Études sur la genèse des offices versifiés*. Studia Latina Stockholmiensia 15 (Stockholm: Almquist & Wiksell, 1968)

Kellman, Herbert, ed., *The Treasury of Petrus Alamire: Music and Art in Flemish Court Manuscripts, 1500-1535* (Ghent: Ludion; [Chicago, Ill.]: Distributed by The University of Chicago Press, 1999)

MEDIEVAL COMPOSERS OF LITURGICAL CHANT

Kelly, Thomas Forrest, "The Cassinese Metrical Office of Saint Placidus," forthcoming

Lebeuf, Jean, *Traité historique et pratique sur le chant ecclesiastique. Avec le directoire qui en contient les principes & les règles, suivant l'usage présent du diocèse de Paris, & autres. Précedé d'une nouvelle methode, pour l'enseigner, & l'apprendre facilement* (Paris: C. J. B. Herissant, 1741)

Leyser, Polykarp, *Historia poetarum et poematum medii aevi* (Halle, 1721; repr. Bologna: Forni, 1969)

LMLO = Andrew Hughes, *Late Medieval Liturgical Offices : Resources for Electronic Research: Texts* (Toronto: Pontifical Institute of Mediaeval Studies, 1994)

Lochner, Fabian, "Un Évêque musicien au Xe siècle: Radbod d'Utrecht," *Tijdschrift van de Vereniging voor Nederlandse Muziekgeschiedenis* 38 (1988), pp. 3-25

Lokrantz, Margareta, *L'opera poetica di S. Pier Damiani* (Stockholm: Almqvist & Wiksell, 1964)

Loos, Ike de, Index of "Composers and Text Writers": *Chant Behind the Dikes*: http://utopia.ision.nl/users/ikedl/chant/ike/index.htm

Loos, Ike de, "Saints in Brabant: a survey of local Proper chants," *Revue Belge de Musicologie / Belgisch Tijdschrift voor Muziekwetenschap* 55 (2001), pp. 9-39

Mabillon, Jean, *Annales ordinis sancti Benedicti occidentalium monachorum patriarchae* (Paris: Charles Robustel, 1703)

McGrade, Michael, "Gottschalk of Aachen, The Investiture Controversy, and Music for the Feast of the Divisio apostolorum," *Journal of the American Musicological Society* 49 (1996), pp. 351-408

Michel, Alain, *In hymnis et canticis. Culture et beauté dans l'hymnique chrétienne latine* (Louvain: Publications universitaires; Paris: Vander-Oyez, 1976)

Migliavacca, Luciano, "Elementi di autenticità degli inni ambrosiani," *Rivista Internazionale di Musica Sacra* 9 (1988), pp. 155-175

Möller, Hartmut, "Office Compositions from St. Gall: Saints Gallus and Otmar," in Margot E. Fassler and Rebecca A. Baltzer, eds., *The Divine Office in the Latin Middle Age* (Oxford: Oxford University Press, 2000), pp. 237-256

NG2 = Stanley Sadie, ed.*The New Grove Dictionary of Music of Musicians*, 2d ed. (London: Macmillan, 2001)

Oesch, Hans, *Berno und Hermann von Reichenau als Musiktheoretiker* (Berne: P. Haupt, 1961)

PalMus = *Paléographie musicale: les principaux manuscrits de chant grégorien, ambrosien, mozarabe, gallican, publiés en facsimilés phototypiques par les moines de Solesmes*

Pez, Bernhard, ed. *Anonymus Mellicensis saeculo XII de scriptoribus ecclesiasticis* (Augsburg, 1716)

Pez, Bernhard, *Thesaurus anecdotorum novissimus*, 6 vols. (Augsburg, 1721-9)

PL = Jacques-Paul Migne, *Patrologiae cursus completus. Series latina*, 221 vols. (Paris, 1878-1890)

XII

Planchart, Alejandro Enrique, "Guillaume Du Fay's Benefices and his Relationship to the Court of Burgundy," *Early Music History* 8 (1988), pp. 117-171

Planchart, Alejandro Enrique, *The Repertory of Tropes at Winchester*, 2 vols. (Princeton: Princeton University Press, 1977)

Pothier, Joseph, "Répons 'Virgo flagellatur' de l'office de Sainte Catherine," *Revue du chant grégorien* 5 (1897), pp. 49-54

Rankin, Susan, "From Tuotilo to the First Manuscripts: The Shaping of a Trope Repertory at Saint Gall," in Wulf Arlt and Gunilla Björkvall, eds., *Recherches nouvelles sur les tropes liturgiques*, Studia Latina Stockholmiensia 36, pp. 395-413

Rankin, Susan, "Notker and Tuotilo: Schöpferische Gestalter in einer neuen Zeit," *Schweizer Jahrbuch für Musikwissenschaft* n.s. 11 (1991), pp. 17-42

Robertson, Anne Walters, *The Service-Books of the Royal Abbey of Saint-Denis* (Oxford: Oxford University Press, 1991)

Schlager, Karlheinz, "Reimoffizien," in Karl Gustav Fellerer, ed., *Geschichte der katholischen Kirchenmusik*, 2 vols. (Kassel: Bärenreiter, 1972-1976), 1: pp. 293-297

Servatius, Viveca, *Cantus sororum: musik- und liturgiegeschichtliche Studien zu den Antiphonen des birgittinischen Eigenrepertoires* (Uppsala, Stockholm: distributor, Almqvist & Wiksell International, 1990)

Sharpe, Richard, "Words and music by Goscelin of Canterbury," *Early Music* 19 (1991), pp. 94-97

Steinen, Wolfram von den, *Notker der Dichter und seine geistige Welt* (Bern: A. Francke, 1948)

Steiner, Ruth, "Gruppen von Antiphonen zur Matutin des Afra-Offiziums," in Berschin and Hiley, *Die Offizien,* pp. 59-67

Strohm, Reinhard, *The Rise of European Music 1380-1500* (Cambridge: Cambridge University Press, 1993)

Szendrei, Janka, "In basilica sancti Emmerami," in Berschin and Hiley, *Die Offizien,* pp. 143-152

Szövérffy, Josef, *Annalen der lateinischen Hymnendichtung, ein Handbuch,* 2 vols. (Berlin: E. Schmidt [1964-65])

Thomson, Rodney M., "The Music for the Office of St Edmund King and Martyr," *Music & Letters* 65 (1984), pp. 189-193

Trithemius, Johannes, *De scriptoribus ecclesiasticis* (Paris: B. Pembolt, 1512)

Trowell, Brian and Andrew Wathey, "John Benet's 'Lux fulget ex Anglia - O pater pietatis - Salve Thoma,'" in M. Jancey, ed., *St Thomas Catilupe, Bishop of Hereford: Essays in his Honor* (Hereford: 1982), pp.159-80

Valère, André, *Bibliotheca Belgica. De Belgis vita scriptisq. claris. Praemissa topographica Belgii totius seu Germaniae inferioris descriptione* (Louvain: I. Zegers, 1643)

Vellekoop, Kees, *Dies Ire Dies Illa; Studien zur Frühgeschichte einer Sequenz* (Bilthoven: Creyghton, 1978)

Villetard, Henri, *Office de Pierre de Corbeil (Office de la circoncision) improprement appelé "Office des fous"* (Paris: A. Picard, 1907)

124

Villetard, Henri, *Office de Saint Savinien et de Saint Potentien, premiers évêques de Sens* (Paris: Picard, 1956)

Waddell, Chrysogonus, "Peter Abelard a Creator of Liturgical Texts," in Rudolf Thomas, ed., *Petrus Abaelardus: Person, Werk, Wirkung* (Trier: Paulinus-Verlag, 1980), pp. 267-286

Wagner, Peter, *Einführung in die gregorianischen Melodien*, 3 vols., 4^{th,} 3d, & 2d ed. (repr. Hildesheim: Olms, 1962)

Wagner, Peter, "Zur mittelalterlichen Offiziumskomposition," *Kirchenmusikalisches Jahrbuch* 21 (1908), pp. 13-32

Weakland, Rembert, "The Compositions of Hucbald," *The Musical Quarterly* 42 (1956), pp. 66-84

Weinfurter, Stefan, *Die Geschichte der Eichstätter Bischöfe des Anonymus Haserensis. Edition-Übersetzung-Kommentar* (Regensburg: F. Pustet, 1987)

Weinrich, Lorenz, "Peter Abaelard as Musician," *The Musical Quarterly* 55 (1969), pp. 295-312

Weis, Johannes Evangelista, *Julian von Speier, [d.] 1285 : Forschungen zur Franziskus- und Antoniuskritik, zur Geschichte der Reimoffizien und des Chorals* (Munich: J. J. Lentner, 1900)

Wright, Craig, "Dufays *Nuper rosarum flores*, King Solomon's Temple, and the Veneration of the Virgin," *Journal of the American Musicological Society*, 47 (1994), pp. 395-441.

XIII

EARLY POLYPHONY AT MONTECASSINO *

Manuscript 111 in the Archivio della Badia of Montecassino contains a marginal essay at polyphony of the late eleventh century that is, to my knowledge, the only surviving medieval evidence of practical attention to polyphonic practice at the abbey.

Montecassino 111 is not a music-book. It is a liturgical homiliary of 422 pages consisting of three parts: pages 1-396 are from the first half of the eleventh century; pages 397-409, written in the late eleventh century, contain homilies for the Nativity of the Virgin; pp. 409-422, added still later (twelfth century, palimpsest on older pages) contains various additional lives of saints.[1]

The polyphony that concerns us occurs in the bottom margin of p. 409: on the recto, that is, of what was for a time the last page of the book. After the last homily two scribes, also of the late eleventh century, each added a hymn in honor of the Virgin ascribed to St. Peter Damian. *O genitrix eterna virgo*[2] has its first verse notated in ink now very faint. The second hymn, notated throughout in Beneventan neumes

* I should like to express my thanks to the National Endowment for the Humanities and to the American Council of Learned Societies for their support of this research.

1 On the manuscript see MAURO INGUANEZ, *Codicum casinensium manuscriptorum catalogus*, 3 vols., Montecassino 1915-1941, I, pp. 163-171; see also the bibliography in ELIAS AVERY LOEW, *The Beneventan Script. A History of the South Italian Minuscule*, second edition prepared and enlarged by Virginia Brown, 2 vols., Roma, Edizioni di Storia e Letteratura 1980 (« Sussidi eruditi », 33-34), II, p. 68.

2 The manuscript has *O genetris eterni*; see ULYSSE CHEVALIER, *Repertorium hymnologicum* (= *RH*), 6 vols., Louvain and Brussels 1892-1920, no. 13024; text edited in MARGARETA LOKRANTS, *L'opera poetica di s. Pier Damiani*, Stockholm, Almqvist & Wiksell 1964 (« Studia Latina Stockholmensia », 12), pp. 76-80; and in GUIDO MARIA DREVES, *Analecta hymnica medii aevi* (= *AH*), XI, Leipzig, Fues 1891, repr. New York and London 1961, p. 57; see also *AH* XLVIII, *ibid.*, 1905, repr. 1961, pp. 52-53, which gives a longer text. Montecassino 111 sets fourteen of the twenty-six verses.

of the Cassinese type, is *Quis est hic qui pulsat*,[3] which continues on
p. 410; it is perhaps the scribe of this second hymn who transcribed the
melody of *O genitrix* in the bottom margin of p. 409, and who above
it tried his hand at polyphonic composition (see Plate 1a-b).
The scribe has written a polyphonic essay whose two voices are
distinguished by using black and red ink. The writing is careful, showing
no hesitation or correction, and the neumes are accurately heightened
although there is no reference-line to guide them. The music generally
proceeds note against note, neume against neume (a two-note neume
in one voice matched by a two-note neume in the other, etc.), although
the red voice twice has a *podatus-plus-clivis* where the scribe might
have written a *scandicus flexus*. There are three places where the numbers
of notes do not correspond: the scribe has apparently omitted to repeat
the *punctum* that follows the first *virga* of the red voice; and two
cadential points are marked in the red voice with a sign usually used
for a two-note liquescence where the black voice has a single *punctum*
(somewhat like the *oriscus* used at cadences in the organal voices of the
Winchester troper).
It needs only a glance to recognize that the black voice is « the
melody » while the red voice is its counterpoint. The presence of the
« franculus » cadence (so often found in sequences) twice in the black
voice, and the comparative disjunctness of the red voice, make this clear.
I have not been able so far, however, to recognize in the black voice
any passage from a sequence known elsewhere (the notation is certainly
not the syllabic notation of sequences), nor is its melody drawn from
either of the nearby hymns.
Except for an opening passage in parallel fourths, the counterpoint
moves in contrary motion to the black voice, sounding perfect consonances (unison, fourth, fifth, octave, twelfth) with the exception of a few
intervals of a sixth to be considered presently.[4] The result is a certain

---

[3] *RH* no. 16713; text ed. in DREVES, *AH* XLVIII, 76. On the doubtful ascription to
Peter Damian see M. LOKRANTZ, *op. cit.*, p. 188, and G. M. DREVES, *loc. cit.*

[4] Of early theoretical works the counterpoint follows most nearly the precepts of the
organum treatise from Laon *Ad organum faciendum* and is highly reminiscent of its
examples, particularly the often-cited Kyrie-verse *Cunctipotens genitor Deus*. The treatise,
found in the early twelfth-century Milan, Biblioteca ambrosiana, ms. M. 17 sup., ff. 56v-61v
(see *RISM* B IV¹: *Manuscripts of Polyphonic Music. 11th-Early 14th Century*, ed. Gilbert
Reaney, München-Duisburg, Henle 1966, pp. 792-793), is edited (with errors) in EDMOND
DE COUSSEMAKER, *Histoire de l'harmonie au moyen âge*, Paris 1852, repr. Hildesheim,
Olms 1966, pp. 225-243, and partially in FRIEDER ZAMINER, *Der vatikanische Organum-
traktat (Ottob. lat. 3025)*, Tutzing, Schneider 1959, pp. 111-114.

ungainliness in the red voice when compared with contemporaneous monophony.

Montecassino, Archivio della Badia, Ms. 111, p. 409, transcription.

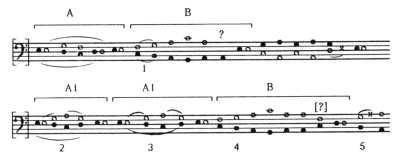

Repeated figures in the black voice call forth reiterated counterpoints; see the passages marked 'A1 ' and ' B ' (but note the apparent omission of a note in the counterpoint for the first appearance of ' B '). But while passage ' A ' has the same melody in the black voice as does ' A1 ', the counterpoint is different. Perhaps the scribe was unsatisfied with his first solution: the only parallel motion in fourths occurs between the second and third notes, and the parallel unisons that follow may be less than stylishly elegant. The second solution (A1) is better, and it is retained a second time.

The presence of several intervals of a sixth (numbered 1-5) in poly-phony clearly oriented to perfect consonances is curious until one con-siders alternatives. Contrary motion to perfect consonance seems to be the overriding desideratum; strict observance of this in passage ' B ' (avoiding the sixths labeled 1 and 4) would produce a melody rising at least to G, separating the counterpoint by two octaves from its melody and requiring a two-octave range for the red voice (not to mention a leap of an augmented fourth at the pitch suggested here). In order to avoid the sixths in passage ' A1 ' (labeled 2 and 3) the counterpoint would read E-A-C-A-E (or E-G-C-G-E): perhaps the many leaps of a fourth are considered the greater evil.

But what about the last sixth, number 5? Why not simply have the counterpoint here sound the fifth, rising through the sixth to the final octave? The answer is related to the pitch of the piece as a whole. If the scribe had a specific interval-content in mind (and I think he did) he did not reveal it with a clef. But in fact there is only one satisfactory solution. If the piece ended on C it would contain five harmonic augmented fourths; if on D, four. With a final of F the « franculus » cadence reads E-F-F (stylistically unlikely) and the augmented fourth in the last three notes of the black voice, with the diminished fifth in the counterpoint, make for a very unsatisfactory finish. A final of G produces two diminished fifths in the counterpoint. Final B produces extremely unlikely outlines in both voices.

Two possibilites remain, and each produces music with no awkward intervals, harmonic or melodic. Finals of A and E are both satisfactory. But the final A seems to me the likely solution, for it alone explains the sixth just before the final cadence: the use of a sixth here avoids the more natural fifth, which is not available in this position because the penultimate note is B and the fifth is diminished.

This little sketch is the only evidence of polyphonic activity in South Italy in this period. The earliest polyphony from South Italy known until now is the fourteenth-century *Benedicamus* trope *Ad honorem marie virginis* (in Gothic script and square notation) discovered by Agostino Ziino in the margin (f. 8*r*) of Benevento, Biblioteca capitolare, ms. 37.[5] The Vatican manuscript Borg. lat 211, a ritual written at Montecassino between 1094 and 1105, has been cited as having polyphonic additions on f. 15*r-v*; but these thirteenth-century non-Beneventan neumes were added after the manuscript's transfer to Velletri, and in any case they are not polyphonic.[6]

We do not know on what theoretical basis our scribe made his compositional decisions; the only surviving theoretical reference to polyphony at Montecassino, though contemporaneous with our example, is from a different stylistic sphere. Montecassino possesses an important eleventh-century manuscript of music theory: Montecassino 318[7] in-

---

[5] AGOSTINO ZIINO, *Polifonia « primitiva » nella Biblioteca capitolare di Benevento*, « Analecta musicologica », XV, 1975, pp. 1-14, plus plate.

[6] Reaney (*RISM* B IV¹ cit., p. 794) and Bannister (ENRICO [HENRY] MARRIOTT BANNISTER, *Monumenti vaticani di paleografia musicale latina*, I, Leipzig, Harassowitz 1913, pp. 116-117, No. 336) thought these neumes were polyphonic because of the repetition of text on the page. In fact, the three appearances of the word *ordo* in red were designed as rubrics to signal the start of new sections in the original ritual. They remain visible on the erased page and thus might appear to be the simultaneous text of a polyphonic piece when they are mistaken for the text of the neumes added to the erased page much later. On the manuscript see E. A. LOEW, *The Beneventan Script* cit., I, p. 72 and II, p. 163.

[7] See M. INGUANEZ, *Codicum casinensium* cit., II, pp. 151-155; *RISM* B III²: *The Theory of Music from the Carolingian Era up to 1400*, ed. Pieter Fischer, München-Duisburg, Henle 1968, pp. 64-69. See also ADRIEN DE LA FAGE, *Essais de diphtherographie musicale*, Paris, Legouix 1864, repr. Amsterdam, Knuf 1964, pp. 392-408.

4

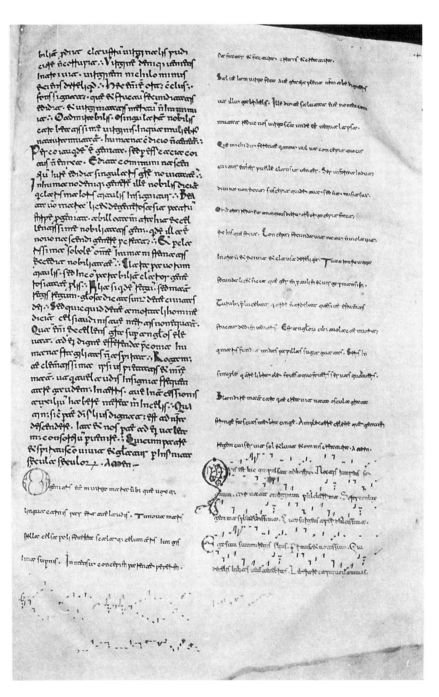

Plate 1a. - Montecassino, Archivio della Badia, Ms. 111, p. 409.

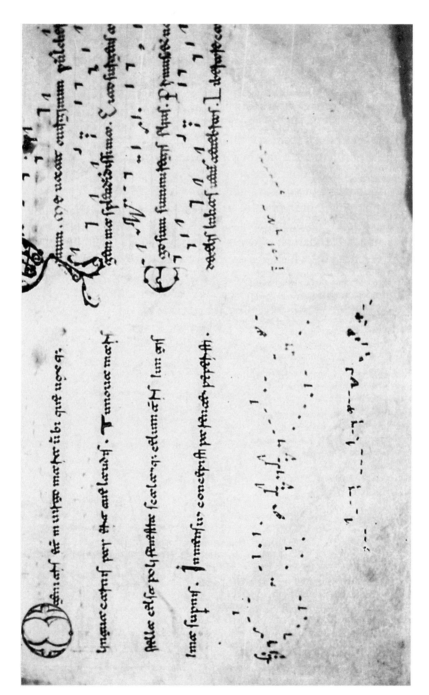

cludes, among many other things, a copy of Guido's *Micrologus*, including its section on organum.[8] Guido's recommendations, however, are not those followed by our scribe.[9] He must have had access to ideas and sources which we can no longer trace. This is no surprise when we consider that our scribe writes during the period of the great abbot Desiderius (abbot 1058-1087), under whom Montecassino gathered artists, scholars, and books from far and wide.[10] Montecassino 318 may be the accidental survivor of a much wider interest in musical practice of which our little polyphonic fragment perhaps gives another hint.

This workmanlike piece of counterpoint does not prove the existence of a flourishing polyphonic practice at Montecassino, but it does reflect the far-ranging interests of its monks at the time of the abbey's greatest flourishing under Desiderius; and perhaps it is a further witness of the unwritten practice to which Nino Pirrotta has so often called our attention.

---

[8] The *Micrologus* is edited in GUIDONIS ARETINI *Micrologus*, edidit Joseph Smits van Waesberghe, [Roma], American Institute of Musicology 1955 («Corpus scriptorum de musica», 4); the chapters on polyphony occupy pp. 196-227.

[9] See note 3 above.

[10] For an introduction to artistic activity at Montecassino under Desiderius see HERBERT BLOCH, *Monte Cassino in the Middle Ages*, 3 vols., Roma, Edizioni di Storia e Letteratura 1986, I, pp. 40-110; on literary activity see ID., *Monte Cassino's Teachers and Library in the High Middle Ages*, in *La scuola nell'Occidente latino dell'alto Medioevo* («Settimane di studio del centro italiano di studi sull'alto Medioevo», XIX), vol. II, Spoleto, presso la sede del Centro 1972, pp. 563-605.

5

INDEX OF INCIPITS

Compiled by Christina Huemer

INDEX OF MANUSCRIPTS

Compiled by Christina Huemer

Manuscripts are listed by city, depository, and shelf/catalog number; the original provenance will be found in the Index of Names and Places.

INDEX OF NAMES AND PLACES

Compiled by Christina Huemer